Deconstructing Whiteness, Empire and Mission

Deconstructing Whiteness, Empire and Mission

Edited by

Anthony G. Reddie
and
Carol Troupe

scm press

© The editors and contributors 2023

Published in 2023 by SCM Press
Editorial office
3rd Floor, Invicta House,
108–114 Golden Lane,
London EC1Y 0TG, UK
www.scmpress.co.uk

SCM Press is an imprint of Hymns Ancient & Modern Ltd
(a registered charity)

Hymns Ancient & Modern

Hymns Ancient & Modern® is a registered trademark of
Hymns Ancient & Modern Ltd
13A Hellesdon Park Road, Norwich,
Norfolk NR6 5DR, UK

All rights reserved. No part of this publication may be reproduced,
stored in a retrieval system, or transmitted,
in any form or by any means, electronic, mechanical,
photocopying or otherwise, without the prior permission of
the publisher, SCM Press.

The editors and contributors have asserted their right under the Copyright, Designs
and Patents Act 1988 to be identified as the Authors of this Work

All scripture quotations, unless otherwise marked, are from the Revised Standard
Version of the Bible, copyright 1946, 1952 and 1971 by the Division of Christian
Education of the National Council of the Churches of Christ in the USA.
Used by permission. All rights reserved.

Scripture quotations marked (NRSVUE) are taken from the New Revised Standard
Version Updated Edition. Copyright © 2021 National Council of Churches of Christ
in the United States of America. Used by permission. All rights reserved worldwide.

Scripture quotations marked (ESV) are from The ESV® Bible (The Holy Bible,
English Standard Version®), copyright © 2001 by Crossway, a publishing ministry
of Good News Publishers. Used by permission. All rights reserved.

Scriptures and additional materials marked (GNB) are from the Good News Bible ©
1994 published by the Bible Societies/HarperCollins Publishers Ltd UK, Good News
Bible© American Bible Society 1966, 1971, 1976, 1992. Used with permission.

British Library Cataloguing in Publication data

A catalogue record for this book is available
from the British Library

ISBN 978-0-334-05593-8

Typeset by Regent Typesetting
Printed and bound in Great Britain by
CPI Group (UK) Ltd

Contents

Acknowledgements   ix
Contributors   xi

Introduction   1

Part One: Decolonizing Theological Education

1. Beyond Theological Self-Possession   13
   Mike Higton

2. Deconstructing Whiteness in the UK Christian Theological Academy   27
   David L. Clough

3. Re-Distributing Theological Knowledge in Theological Education as an Act of Distributive Justice in Contemporary Christian Mission   39
   Eve Parker

4. Dealing with the Two Deadly Ds: Deconstructing Whiteness and Decolonizing the Curriculum of Theological Education   52
   Anthony G. Reddie

Part Two: Perspectives on History

5. Octavius Hadfield: Nineteenth-century Goodie or Twenty-first-century Baddie? Learnings from the Complexities of Mission and Empire   75
   James Butler and Cathy Ross

6 Stolen Myths: Pālangi, Fairness, Native Theologies 91
  Jione Havea

7 Postcolonialism and Re-stor(y)ing the Ecumenical
  Movement 102
  Peniel Rajkumar

8 A Happy Ecumenical Legacy for the London Missionary
  Society? Exposing the Coloniality Between Churches
  Engaged in Mission 120
  Victoria Turner

9 Speaking to the Past: A Black Laywoman's Theological
  Appraisal of the LMS Archives 136
  Carol Troupe

10 Mission and Whiteness: Archival Lessons from LMS
   in British Guiana (Guyana) 151
   Michael N. Jagessar

Part Three: Personal Reflections

11 Coming Full Circle: Christianity, Empire, Whiteness,
   the Global Majority and the Struggles of Migrants and
   Refugees in the UK 173
   Paul Weller

12 'I Know Where You're Coming From': Exploring
   Intercultural Assumptions 193
   Jill Marsh

13 See, Judge, Act: Wrestling with the Effects of Colonialism
   as an English Priest in Wales 208
   Kevin Ellis

Part Four: Exploration of Whiteness

14 Unbecoming: Reflections on the Work of a White
    Theologian   225
    Rachel Starr

15 'Turning Whiteness Purple': Reflections on Decentring
    Whiteness in its Christian Colonial Missionary Mode   245
    Peter Cruchley

16 'Come we go chant down Babylon': How Black Liberation
    Theology Subverts White Privilege and Dismantles the
    Economics of Empire to Save the Planet   265
    Kevin Snyman

17 'Holding the space': Troubling 'the facilitating obsession
    of whiteness' in Contemporary Social Justice-focused
    Models of Mission   281
    Al Barrett and Ruth Harley

Index of Names and Subjects   305

Acknowledgements

Our first thanks must go to all of our contributors. The invitation to write for this book was sent out towards the end of a very challenging couple of years for many of us. We are immensely grateful that, despite this backdrop and the continuing demands and difficulties of work and life, so many of them were both willing and able to make their contribution to this project.

Thanks also go to Council for World Mission for funding Carol's work, and to former CWM colleagues Peter Cruchley and Michael Jagessar for supporting our contributions to the Legacies of Slavery project, and also to Regent's Park College, University of Oxford, for their support.

Finally, to friends and family for their ongoing encouragement, and to the Creator, who comforts, sustains and inspires.

Carol Troupe
Editor

Contributors

Al Barrett is a Church of England priest and has been Rector of Hodge Hill Church in east Birmingham since 2010, where he has been engaged in a long-term journey of 'growing loving community' alongside his neighbours. He is author of *Interrupting the Church's Flow: A Radically Receptive Political Theology in the Urban Margins* (SCM Press, 2020) and co-author (with Ruth Harley) of *Being Interrupted: Re-imagining the Church's Mission from the Outside, In* (SCM Press, 2020). In 2022 he co-edited (with Jill Marsh) a special themed issue of *Practical Theology* on 'Critical White Theology: Dismantling Whiteness?' He is engaged in ongoing research, writing and teaching in practical and political theology, particularly through the lenses of race, class, gender and ecology.

James Butler is MA Lecturer at Church Mission Society, Oxford, and postdoctoral researcher at the University of Roehampton, London. He has been involved in mission both in the UK and in Uruguay. His research interests are centred on mission and practical theology and recently he has been researching grassroots experience of learning and discipleship and exploring the theology of lay pioneering.

David Clough is a White British theologian, Chair of Theology and Applied Sciences at the University of Aberdeen, President of the Society for the Study of Theology, and a past President of the Society for the Study of Christian Ethics. His recent research is on the place of animals in Christian theology and ethics, with a particular focus on the ethics of animal agriculture. He is a Methodist local preacher and has represented the Methodist Church on national ecumenical working groups on the ethics of warfare and climate change.

Peter Cruchley works in the World Council of Churches as the Director of the Commission for World Mission and Evangelism. He is a mission theologian from the UK but has worked in the international mission agency context for some years, pressing especially for engagement in legacies of slavery and reparation. He has published in the areas of Whiteness, coloniality and mission, mission and postmodernity and mission ecumenism and justice.

Kevin Ellis is an English-born priest in the Church in Wales. He is the Vicar of Bro Madryn on the Llyn Peninsula. Kevin has a PhD in New Testament Studies and is working for another PhD, looking at how to use the Bible in Wales.

Ruth Harley is a priest in the Church of England, and Curate of Watling Valley Ecumenical Partnership in Milton Keynes in the Diocese of Oxford. She is the co-author (with Al Barrett) of *Being Interrupted: Reimagining the Church's Mission from the Outside, In* (SCM Press, 2020). Her academic interests include feminist ecclesiology, women's experience of vocation, the use and abuse of power within the church, and theological approaches to safeguarding. She is the Chair of the Mission Enabling Group for On Fire Mission.

Jione Havea is co-parent for a polycultural daughter, native pastor (Methodist Church in Tonga), migrant to Naarm (renamed Melbourne by British colonizers, on the cluster of islands now known as Australia) and research fellow with Trinity Methodist Theological College (Aotearoa New Zealand) and with Australian Centre for Christianity and Culture (Charles Sturt University, Australia). An activist-in-training, on the ground and in the classroom, Jione is easily irritated by bullies and suckers.

Mike Higton is an Anglican theologian specializing in doctrine, teaching at Durham University. He is part of the leadership for the Common Awards scheme, which provides academic validation for much of the Church of England's ordination training. He is the author of a number of works, including *The Life of Christian Doctrine*, *A Theology of Higher Education* and *Difficult Gospel: The Theology of Rowan Williams*, and he serves on the Church of England's Racial Justice Commission.

Michael N. Jagessar, a former Mission Secretary of Council for World Mission, researches and writes across theological disciplines drawing on a range of Caribbean resources. Michael, who hails from Guyana, locates himself as a Caribbean diasporan traveller. While located in the UK, he writes, thinks and engages from where he *dwells* – that is, Guyana and the Caribbean. More on Michael's writings can be found at https://caribleaper.co.uk/publications/.

CONTRIBUTORS

Jill Marsh is a Methodist minister who has lived and worked in Birmingham, London, Sheffield, Rotherham and Leicester. Both of her grandads were coal miners in Annesley, Nottinghamshire, and all her Methodist grandparents passed on to her a strong belief that every person is precious to God. Jill has previously worked as a Mission Enabler and sees active commitment to anti-racism as integral to both discipleship and mission. Her doctoral work focused on the intercultural relationships between members of local congregations. Jill is currently the Inclusive Church Implementation Officer for the Methodist Church in Britain, helping the Methodist Church to implement the Strategy for Justice, Dignity and Solidarity.

Eve Parker is Lecturer in Modern Christian Theology at the University of Manchester. Her recent publications include *Trust in Theological Education: Deconstructing 'Trustworthiness' for a Pedagogy of Liberation* (SCM Press, 2022) and *Theologising with the Sacred 'Prostitutes' of South India: Towards an Indecent Dalit Theology* (Leiden: Brill, 2021).

Peniel Rajkumar is Global Theologian for United Society Partners in the Gospel (USPG) and a faculty member of Ripon College Cuddesdon. He previously served as Programme Executive for Interreligious Dialogue and Cooperation at the World Council of Churches, Geneva. He is the author of many books, including *Dalit Theology and Dalit Liberation* (Ashgate/Routledge, 2010), *Mission at and from the Margins* (edited, Regnum, 2014) and *Faith(s) Seeking Justice: Dialogue and Liberation* (edited, WCC Publications, 2021).

Anthony G. Reddie is the Director of the Oxford Centre for Religion and Culture in Regent's Park College, University of Oxford. He is also an Extraordinary Professor of Theological Ethics and a Research Fellow with the University of South Africa. He is the first Black person to get an 'A' rating in Theology and Religious Studies in the South African National Research Foundation. This designation means that he is a leading international researcher. He is a prolific author of books, articles and chapters in edited books. He is the editor of *Black Theology: An International Journal* and is a recipient of the Archbishop of Canterbury's 2020 Lambeth, Lanfranc Award for Education and Scholarship, given for 'exceptional and sustained contribution to Black Theology in Britain and Beyond'.

Cathy Ross is Head of Pioneer Leadership Training at Church Mission Society and Lecturer in Mission at Regent's Park College, University of Oxford. She comes from Aotearoa New Zealand. She has previously worked in Rwanda, Congo and Uganda with New Zealand Church Missionary Society (NZCMS). Her research interests are in the areas of mission, world Christianity, contextual and feminist theologies and hospitality. She enjoys co-researching and co-writing and has published widely on mission.

Kevin Snyman was ordained in the Uniting Presbyterian Church of Southern Africa, and currently manages the global justice programme of the United Reformed Church. Raised in apartheid South Africa, Kevin is keenly aware of how easily people are shaped and fooled by the assumptions and demands of domination systems. He works to expose those assumptions in the theologies and economics of empire in order to subvert the racist assumptions, wealth and power of the 1 per cent. Kevin is married to Nadene, enjoys film-making, motorcycling and going to the gym.

Rachel Starr is Director of Studies at the Queen's Foundation for Ecumenical Theological Education in Birmingham. She completed her doctorate in Buenos Aires, Argentina, researching the impact of theologies of marriage on domestic violence. Publications include *Reimagining Theologies of Marriage in Contexts of Domestic Violence* (Routledge, 2018) and, with David Holgate, *SCM Studyguide: Biblical Hermeneutics*, 2nd edition (SCM Press, 2019).

Carol Troupe is a Research Associate on Council for World Mission's Legacies of Slavery project. She is also the Reviews Editor for *Black Theology: An International Journal* and holds an MPhil in Education from the University of Birmingham.

Victoria Turner is a PhD candidate in World Christianity at the University of Edinburgh. Her thesis explores how missional theology from the non-Western world influenced mission practice in Britain, directed abroad and at home to the working classes. Victoria's PhD was funded by Council for World Mission and she is a tutor at the University of Stirling and associate tutor at Westminster College, Cambridge Theological Federation. Victoria has published an edited book, book chapters and articles about ecumenism, practical theology, political theology, youth studies and Scottish church history. She currently works part-time with Sabeel-Kairos as the Advocacy Officer (under-35s).

CONTRIBUTORS

Paul Weller is Non-Stipendiary Research Fellow in Religion and Society at Regent's Park College, University of Oxford. Over four decades, as a Baptist Christian who originally worked for Christian churches, and more recently as an academic working in what the German scholar Udo Tworushka calls 'Practical Religionswissenschaft', he has been variously involved in wider activist engagements around peace, racial justice and interreligious relations. His chapter includes a poem by his deceased (2010) wife, Margret Preisler-Weller, a Catholic Christian who worked in the former West German Ökumenische Centrale of the Arbeitsgemeinschaft Christlicher Kirchen, followed by the Youth Unit of the then British Council of Churches.

Introduction

The roots of this book lie in the remote conference hosted by the Oxford Centre for Religion and Culture (OCRC), in partnership with two of our contributors, the Revd Drs Al Barrett and Jill Marsh.[1] My two colleagues, an Anglican, Church of England priest and a Methodist minister respectively, both White and very much seeing themselves as critical White allies, approached me to discuss the possibilities of the OCRC[2] hosting a conference under its auspices.

After further discussions and planning, supported by one of my then doctoral students, Saiyyidah Zaidi, we organized a one-day remote event, which over 300 people attended. I shall say a little more about the conference shortly because the 'back story', so to speak, to the event underpins the necessity for this book and the excellent chapters contained within it.

For the moment, however, it is imperative that we go back in history, to events over a quarter of a century ago, in Birmingham. I remember attending one of the first meetings of the National Black Theology Forum, which was, in its nascent developments, meeting at the Centre for Black and White Christian Partnership in Selly Oak, under its then chair, Dr Emmanuel Lartey. In this meeting, one of the other participants asked why there needed to be a Black Theology Forum and why wasn't there a White Theology Forum? Various responses were proposed as to why there was not a corresponding meeting for White people. One obvious response was that there were lots of White Theology forums in existence across the city and, of course, the country.

Most academic departments of theology were, in effect, White forums. Most of what was taught was White and European in origin. At the time, there were few Black theologians in the UK in academic posts aside from Emmanuel Lartey, George Mulrain and Robert Beckford, all three working at the University of Birmingham, Kingsmead College (part of the Selly Oak colleges), and the then Queen's College, respectively. Of the three, only Beckford had a post that explicitly named him as a 'Black theologian'.

While the consensus of the meeting was that there was no explicable reason for arguing for White theological forums, nonetheless the elephant that remained unacknowledged in the room was the obvious fact that *something* had to be done about Whiteness itself. So long as 'Whiteness' remained, this invisible norm that determined truth, power, normality and acceptability, rendering all those 'non-White' as either second best or of no significance at all, the cause of justice and equity would remain stunted and stalled.

What Blackness has done before Whiteness even tried

Over the years, as my work as a Black liberation theologian in the UK has grown, I have habitually asked the question of my White colleagues about the challenge of engaging with Whiteness. The plural movement that is 'Black Theology in Britain' has sought to do what Whiteness, until very recently, has never done; that is, to recognize the need to interrogate notions of identity, history and what constitutes a sense of belonging. Black identities have always been diverse and complex. They defy any simplistic ways of categorizing people. The term 'Black' has to be understood within the context of the UK and the tradition of identity politics that emerged in the 1970s. So the term 'Black' does not simply denote one's epidermis but is rather also a political statement relating to one's sense of politicized marginalization within the contested space that is the UK. In other words, being 'Black' is not just about those who are of 'African descent' living in the UK. It also relates to other non-White groups who suffer and experience racism.

Using the term 'Black' is to identify oneself as being on the alternative side of the fence in terms of what constitutes notions of being considered acceptable and belonging when juxtaposed with the dominant Eurocentric discourses that dominate the normal ways in which we see and understand what it means to be *authentically British*.[3] This tradition of political mobilization around the once maligned and socially constructed term 'Black' has its roots in the political left and the rise of coalition politics in the 1970s.[4] While Black theology in Britain has been dominated by Black people of African and Caribbean descent, Asian scholars of the ilk of Inderjit Bhogal,[5] Mukti Barton[6] and Michael Jagessar[7] have made an impressive and much-needed contribution to the development and refining of this theological discipline. In using the term 'Black theology', we mean a radical rethinking of how we conceive of God and Jesus in light of the ongoing suffering and oppression of Black people in a world run and governed by white people. Black theology identifies God revealed in Jesus as committed to liberation and freeing Black people from racism and oppression.

One of the central claims of Black theology in seeking to reaffirm the significance of Blackness as the lens through which divine revelation is effected has been the necessity to counter 'colour-blind' claims of 'all of us being the same'. As I have written elsewhere,[8] the rationale for sameness is not in itself wrong or problematic, but when seen through the lens of the kind of Whiteness that propagated empire and colonialism, often resisting the claims of difference that would have allowed indigenous peoples to hold on to their customs and cultures, the lure of sameness can become a means of effecting control and domination over others.

Black theology has always sought to rehabilitate the notion of Black as a problematic identifier. Often, the appeal to a colour-blind doctrine of Christian anthropology is predicated on the notion that we are all one in the Spirit and that the Spirit of God has no colour.

Dismantling Whiteness

Back to the question of Whiteness. Black theologians have long been requesting those racialized as 'White' to take responsibility for dealing with the socio-political, economic and cultural realities arising from the normalization of Whiteness. It was with surprise and a great deal of curiosity that I responded to an enquiry from Al Barrett and Jill Marsh to assist them in organizing a conference that would explore the development of critical White theology; that is, the type of theological activity and gathering many of the Black people in that early Black Theology Forum had once envisaged.

The conference was a necessary and important undertaking but was also a fraught one. In the lead-up to the conference I received a great deal of racist abuse from trolls on Twitter in addition to a number of angry letters from Regent's Park College alumni. I remember one such encounter, where the White author of an email commenced by stating that whatever I was going to say about organizing a conference seeking to 'dismantle Whiteness', I was resolutely wrong! I soon learnt that responding to such anger and vitriol was a pointless effort because my antagonists, by virtue of simply being White, all knew more than me. As far as they were concerned, I was wrong and they were right as a result of them being White and me being Black. Interestingly and ironically, neither of my two White colleagues and partners in this undertaking received any racist abuse.

The importance of dismantling Whiteness was never more firmly exemplified than when considering the reactionary and racist abuse thrown at me for having the temerity to organize (with two White colleagues) a conference seeking to rethink history, theology and Christian practice in a more critical and less myopic fashion. Significant portions of that conference have since been published in a special issue of *Practical Theology*.[9]

Following on from this landmark conference and the publication of this special guest-edited issue of *Practical Theology*, my co-editor, Carol Troupe, and I were busily engaged in research exploring a process of demythologizing empire and critically reassessing the legacies of slavery and colonialism. At a time when considerable intellectual effort is being made to mollify and even justify the ethics of colonialism and empire,[10] Carol and I have been clear that our task, as the descendants of enslaved peoples, is to speak back to these justifying processes of White hegemony.

The genesis for this book arose from the joint work we have been undertaking for Council for World Mission's (CWM) Legacies of Slavery project.[11] Working with our then CWM colleagues, Peter Cruchley and Michael Jagessar, it was agreed that an important research output arising from our work should be a major academic text exploring the relationship between whiteness, empire and mission. The aim would be to invite leading academics, practitioners and activists, predominantly White people in Britain, to explore the contested dynamics of empire and mission and the central role that White privilege, entitlement and power played in shaping the history and the world in which we live. Several of the chapters in this book are from authors whose work has been shaped directly or indirectly from this project funded and supported by CWM.

A central part of the book is the necessity to critique the alleged superiority of White people or the notion that 'Whiteness' should predominate. In using the term 'Whiteness' I am referring to the lens through which we see the world and how social and economic relations are organized for the benefit of White people. In many respects, the relationship between the British empire, colonialism and Christianity remains the unacknowledged elephant in the room. Empire and colonialism became the basis on which notions of White supremacy were based. The intellectual underpinning of White supremacy, the notion that White people are superior to peoples who are not White, was based on a corruption of Christianity, in which Whiteness was conflated with the Christian faith. The conflation of Whiteness with Christianity led to a clear binary between notions of White people being the progenitors of salvation and civilization and Black people being the base recipients of the gracious largesse of the former.[12]

The continued paucity of theological texts written by White British theologians that address the legacy of slavery, colonialism and racism in the British psyche remains troubling. The reason why most White British theologians and White Christians have not engaged with issues of Whiteness is largely a result of the normative invisibility of Whiteness. In other words, for most White people, they do not see or think about Whiteness. The truth is, Whiteness does not need rescuing from centuries of negative stereotyping and the notion that White people are backward and inferior.[13] Whatever the hardships are that face poor, marginalized White people (which I do not dispute, I hasten to add), these do not include a historic set of symbolic associations surrounding the unacceptability of being White in and of itself.

So Whiteness operates on the basis of stealth, holding a pivotal place for that which is considered normal and as it should be. It becomes central to all that is believed to be ideal, better than, and deemed the epitome of supposed civilization and acceptability.

The sad fact is that most White people take this so much for granted that it rarely occurs to many of them that we live in a world in which Whiteness is so embedded as the norm – namely, that how the world is organized, and what we see as normal or acceptable, is often predicated on Whiteness. This can be likened to a fish swimming in the sea. The fish is normalized to its existence so that all it knows is that the sea represents its total existence.

White supremacy has been the basis on which the world has been organized for the last 500 years. The reason why we do not have a 'White Lives Matter' movement is because there has never been any serious impediment to assert otherwise. This is not to say that poor White people or White women have not suffered or been oppressed, but none of this was a result of the fact that they were simply 'White'. Such has been the opposite for Black people over the past 500 years, beginning with slavery and then colonialism; our lives have been a constant battle to assert that we matter as much as White people do, be they poor, or women, advantaged or disadvantaged economically, culturally or politically.

The construction of this book

This book is divided into four parts.

Part One explores how the norms of Whiteness have become enshrined within British academia. The four chapters in this part outline the particular problems found in academic Christian theology and the various ways in which this can be redressed.

Chapter 1 is written by a white English scholar, Mike Higton, the former President of the Society for the Study of Theology (SST). His chapter explores how the particular form of mastery and control that emanates from the phenomenon of Whiteness has impacted how academic theology, particularly systematic or dogmatic theology, has been produced and reproduced over many decades.

Chapter 2 is written by Mike Higton's successor as President of the SST, David Clough, another White English systematic theologian and ethicist. Clough's chapter can be seen as a companion piece to that of his predecessor. For while Higton writes from a more subjective, insider perspective, Clough's chapter draws on wider empirical work to demonstrate the systemic myopia of Christian theology, especially that housed within academic departments in British universities.

Chapter 3 is written by Eve Parker, a White British woman academic. Her chapter charts the colonial ethic of control and the internalizing of the norms of Whiteness as they have been enshrined in British Christian missionary work and its relationship to theological education. She reminds us that much that claims to be 'neutral' in current mission history scholarship is anything but, often reifying tropes of White supremacy even while asserting a benign and non-contentious stance.

The final chapter in Part One – Chapter 4 – is written by Anthony Reddie, a Black British-born man of Caribbean roots. His chapter offers a self-confessed liberationist and postcolonial polemic against the hitherto biased and tendentious way in which British academic theological life has been expressed over the past three centuries or so. The chapter is a radical riposte to contemporary, reactionary modes of theological engagement that continue to argue that the status quo should remain normative and without any substantive change or amelioration.

Part Two of the book, the longest part, explores the historical antecedents that have shaped the current epoch of Black Lives Matter, Rhodes Must Fall and the present call for the decolonization of theological curricula. When the invitation to contributors was sent out, my co-editor and I had in mind an eclectic set of players representing a variety of streams of intellectual thought. An important arena was those working with historical materials.

The first chapter in Part Two – Chapter 5 – is by James Butler and Cathy Ross, a White British and a White New Zealander, respectively. Butler and Ross represent the more traditionalist end of mission studies in the UK. Their chapter is a nuanced reappraisal of missionary activity in New Zealand in the nineteenth century, exploring a seemingly heroic figure whose legacy eschews the binary of 'goodie' and 'baddie'. The inclusion of this chapter refutes any notion that our book is simply a crude example of postmodern 'woke' revisionism.

Chapter 6 is by a Tongan scholar, Jione Havea, whose work explores the damaging legacy of missionary work on the Pacific islands, of which his homeland is one. In his forensic linguistic analysis of the language of colonization and gospel transmission, Havea demonstrates the epistemological 'slippage' that occurs when one attempts to override so-called 'native' customs, with new idioms that were never intended in these differing 'missional' contexts. This chapter tackles the lie that missionary activity was mostly beneficial and benign to those on whom it was imposed.

Chapter 7 is from an Indian scholar, Peniel Rajkumar. His chapter retells the story of the ecumenical movement but from a postcolonial perspective. In this work, his retelling of what is, for some, a familiar narrative but from an alternative focus – the perspective of the global majority – represents a crucial alternative perspective for truth telling that is the central modus operandi of this book.

Chapter 8 is written by Victoria Turner, a young White Welsh doctoral candidate (at the time of writing) and the youngest contributor to this book. Her work also explores the ecumenical movement but this time through the lens of CWM and the transition from a more traditional top-Western-led body to a supposedly more egalitarian, global body of reciprocity and partnership. She demonstrates that the good intentions and fine rhetoric are not always as they seem.

Chapter 9 is written by Carol Troupe, a British-born Black woman of Caribbean roots. Her chapter, like Turner's that precedes it, focuses on CWM; but in this case the focus is on one of its progenitor organizations, the London Missionary Society (LMS), and how the archives reveal a problematic underlying intent when it comes to their theology and the resulting practice of Christian mission among peoples of African descent. As with Chapter 8, Carol shows us in her chapter that all is not as it seems when perusing the details of Christian mission history.

The final chapter in Part Two – Chapter 10 – is written by Michael Jagessar, an Indo-Caribbean man from Guyana. Jagessar's chapter delves into Guyanese history, once again through the lens of the LMS and the Demerara rebellion of enslaved peoples in 1823. In this rebellion, a White LMS missionary, John Smith, was implicated and subsequently died while awaiting the final sentence of death. Jagessar's postcolonial re-reading of the archives reveals problematic tropes underpinning this narrative that is often invoked as a means of justifying missionary activity as essentially radical and pro-enslaved peoples, essentially anti-hegemonic in nature.

Part Three contains three chapters, in which the writers are reflecting more personally on their own experience and their concomitant Whiteness as they undertake their respective work as scholars, activists and ministers.

Chapter 11 is written by Paul Weller, a White British academic of Baptist roots. Weller's chapter reflects on his life-long journey as an anti-racist activist and academic. Using poetry and subjective reflections on his life and that of significant others, Weller explores the ways in which his own consciousness has been changed over the years as it pertains to his Whiteness, against a backdrop of the changing socio-political climate, especially post-Brexit.

Chapter 12 is from Jill Marsh, a White Methodist minister whose roots lie in the East Midlands. Her chapter takes a critical look at her Christian formation within the Methodist Church, delineating the broader theo-social character of Methodist charisms and values in terms of real-life examples from her family and in one of the churches she has served as a Methodist minister. Like Weller in Chapter 11, Marsh poses the question as to why some White people can see beyond the problematics of 'race' and others cannot.

The final chapter in Part Three – Chapter 13 – is by Kevin Ellis, a White English-born Anglican priest serving in Wales. Ellis's chapter charts his own growing conscientization as he seeks to become a contextual theologian and priest in Wales, largely through the medium of the spoken idiom – particularly his attempts to learn the Welsh language. His critically honest reflections on the embedded nature of his own Whiteness and Englishness open up a plethora of concerns around the intersectionality between Whiteness, colonialism and nationality, in terms of the relationship between Wales and England.

The final part of the book, Part Four, consists of four chapters all explicitly exploring the phenomenon of Whiteness but in more socio-political and historical terms than the chapters in Part Three.

The first chapter – Chapter 14 – is by Rachel Starr, a White English woman. Starr's chapter juxtaposes reflections on a landmark piece she wrote in 2001 (one of the first such Christian theological pieces to explore the significance of Whiteness) alongside her more contemporary thoughts on what she has learnt and understood as essential truths in the intervening period. Her chapter is a timely reminder that cultures, language and ideas are not static, and one cannot assume that a piece of learning at one particular juncture in life will become the ready-made answer or response for all time.

Chapter 15 is written by Peter Cruchley, a White British United Reformed Church minister, missiologist and activist. Like Reddie, Turner, Troupe and Jagessar, Cruchley's chapter uses CWM's Legacies of Slavery project and the LMS archives as its backdrop to explore the phenomenon of Whiteness in historical and biblical terms. He reflects on pivotal 'White' figures in the gospel narrative surrounding Jesus' crucifixion and links these to key figures in the self-serving narrative of the LMS to justify itself when seen through the prism of White privilege.

INTRODUCTION

The penultimate chapter, Chapter 16, is by Kevin Snyman, a White South African URC minister and activist. Snyman's chapter charts the ways in which debt has inveigled itself into the machinations of empire and created the template on which global capitalism has corrupted human relationships and led to a top-down world of greed and capital accumulation for a minority and poverty and marginalization for the majority.

The final chapter in the book, Chapter 17, is written by Al Barrett and Ruth Harley. Barrett and Harley are both White, British Anglican priests in the Church of England. Their chapter is a critical exploration of the surreptitious dangers of facilitation for White progressive, social justice-orientated practitioners like themselves. Using Willie James Jennings's dissection of Whiteness as their point of departure, Barrett and Harley caution us against the presumptions bound up in patrician forms of 'do-gooding' that are often predicated on very similar assumptions to the actions and activities of some missionaries and ardent colonialists in previous eras.

I commend to you the work of these diligent and committed writers in helping to bring to fruition this landmark text, the first of its kind in British theological and ecclesial life. I hope you enjoy the book.

Anthony G. Reddie – Lead Editor

Notes

1 The conference was entitled 'Dismantling Whiteness' and was held on Saturday 17 April 2021. Details on the conference, including a recording of the keynote speeches, can be found at the following link: https://www.youtube.com/watch?v=LV5icLHjknQ.

2 The OCRC was founded in 1994 by the then Principal of Regent's Park College, the Revd Professor Paul Fiddes. Since its inception there have been three Directors; I am the third incumbent in this post. Details on the Centre can be found at the following link: https://www.rpc.ox.ac.uk/research-life/oxford-centre-christianity-culture/.

3 See Michael N. Jagessar and Anthony G. Reddie (eds), 2007, *Postcolonial Black British Theology*, Peterborough: Epworth, pp. xiii–xiv.

4 See Harry Goulbourne, 2003, 'Collective Action and Black Politics' in Doreen McCalla (ed.), *Black Success: Essays in Racial And Ethnic Studies*, Birmingham: DMee Vision Learning, pp. 9–38.

5 See Inderjit S. Bhogal, 2000, 'Citizenship' in Anthony G. Reddie (ed.), *Legacy: Anthology in Memory of Jillian Brown*, Peterborough: The Methodist Publishing House, pp. 137–41; and Inderjit S. Bhogal, 2001, *On The Hoof: Theology in Transit*, Sheffield: Penistone Publications.

6 Mukti Barton, 2005, *Rejection, Resistance and Resurrection: Speaking out on Racism in the Church*, London: Darton, Longman & Todd.

7 Among his many books, see especially Michael N. Jagessar, 1998, *Full Life for All: The Work and Theology of Philip A. Potter*, Geneva: WCC Publications; and 2015, *Ethnicity: The Inclusive Church Resource*, London: Darton, Longman & Todd.

8 See Anthony G. Reddie, 2019, *Theologising Brexit: A Liberationist and Postcolonial Critique*, London: Routledge, pp. 13–37.

9 See 'Practical Theology: Critical White Theology: Dismantling Whiteness?', a special issue of *Practical Theology*, 15(1 and 2) (2022), guest-edited by Al Barrett and Jill Marsh.

10 It has not gone unnoticed that, as myself and colleague Carol Troupe are in the process of creating anti-imperial and critically challenging intellectual resources resisting the logics of colonialism, there are other Oxford academics seeking to do the exact opposite. See the following links for details: https://www.mcdonaldcentre.org.uk/sites/default/files/content/publications/report_2020-21_15_june_2021.pdf.

11 For more details on CWM's Legacies of Slavery project, see the following link: The Onesimus Project at https://www.cwmission.org/programmes/the-onesimus-project/ (accessed 23.03.2023).

12 For excellent explication of the dialectical binary between saved versus unsaved, civilized versus heathen, see Kelly Brown Douglas, 2005, *What's Faith Got to Do with It? Black Bodies/Christian Souls*, Maryknoll, NY: Orbis Books, pp. ix–xix.

13 See Robert Beckford, 2004, *God and the Gangs*, London: Darton, Longman & Todd, pp. 72–81.

PART ONE

Decolonizing Theological Education

I

Beyond Theological Self-Possession

MIKE HIGTON

In his remarkable book *After Whiteness: An Education in Belonging*, Willie James Jennings diagnoses the 'Whiteness' that bleaches Western theological education.[1] He explains that the term refers neither to skin colour nor to ethnic origin but to a set of 'cognitive and affective structures', 'a way of being in the world and seeing the world'. His book is a call beyond that way of being and seeing.

Western theological education is, he argues, haunted by the figure of a 'white self-sufficient man, his self-sufficiency defined by possession, control, and mastery'.[2] This figure, 'lodged deeply in our educational imaginations',[3] seduces us into 'its habitation and its meaning making'.[4] It lures us into desiring 'control of knowledge first, and of one's self second, and if possible of one's world'.[5] It is 'the quintessential image of an educated person, an image deeply embedded in the psyche of Western education and theological education'.[6]

I am a White, middle-class male academic whose entire academic career has been spent teaching theology in research-intensive universities in the UK (Cambridge, Exeter and Durham). I *know* this White, self-sufficient, self-mastering man. I recognize his ways of seeing and feeling. His desire for possession, control and mastery is a desire that I acknowledge in myself – and to read Jennings's unmasking of him was to be tipped repeatedly into uncomfortable self-recognition.

For Jennings, however, this figure bears a particular face: that of the 'racial paterfamilias'.[7] Theological education arranged around this image, he says, takes the form of a 'pedagogy of the plantation', and:

> even places and settings and people involved in theological education far removed from the history of the slaveholding United States are implicated in this scene ... inhabiting a building formed with this same enslaving design: an ecclesial reality inside a white patriarchal domesticity, shaped by an overwhelmingly white masculinist presence that always aims to build a national and global future that we should all inhabit.[8]

And yet the White, self-sufficient man whose image haunts my own academic imagination does not openly wear the face of a plantation owner. When I read Jennings's depiction of 'a southern gentleman, each word carrying a plantation cadence', I could not say, as he does, that 'I knew exactly who he was' or that 'I had felt his presence before'.[9] Dressed in those clothes, his is not itself an image that has wormed itself deeply into my mind, and it is not the image by which the structure of White, self-sufficient seeing and feeling has gained its imaginative hold on me. In fact, if I focus too directly upon the image of a plantation owner, I find it all too easy to think that his is an image that haunts minds other than my own.

Nevertheless, the same cognitive and affective structures that Jennings describes have certainly taken root in my imagination. It is only the face that they wear that is different.

The self-possessed man

If I try to diagnose the patterns of my own imagination, sifting through the various pictures that have a hold on me, I find one figure that has particular power. I do not quite know what to call him. I could, perhaps, call him a 'gentleman', though that is a word with too many valences to be very useful. Seeking greater precision, I could – with awareness that there are painful ironies here that require unpacking – call him an 'honourable man', or a 'decent man'. For now, I will simply call him the 'self-possessed man'.

Think of David Niven's airman, Peter Carter, at the start of Powell and Pressburger's 1946 film *A Matter of Life and Death*.[10] His Lancaster is going down in flames, and he, left without a parachute, is speaking to June (Kim Hunter), a radio operator on the ground, while he readies himself for death. His situation could hardly be worse, but he unquestionably retains his hold upon himself.

We first hear Peter responding to June's request for his position. He tells her his position is 'nil', then repeats it. Instead of finishing the conversation at that point, he gives June lots of other information: details about his 'violently interrupted' education; his age – 27; his religion – Church of England; politics – 'conservative by nature … Labour by experience'. But then he starts asking June to tell him about herself, compliments her on her voice, and for having the 'guts' that he says she must have to be an on-the-ground radio operator in these terrible circumstances. Peter does not give way to fear and expresses the hope that he has not frightened June by telling her of his decision to jump rather than 'fry'. He certainly shows feeling, but he is not mastered by it; he has long practice at keeping it in check.

Finally, he leaves June with one request: would she be so kind as to send his mother a telegram, telling her that he loved her right up to the end, and always had loved her, even though he may not always have shown her this enough in words.

Even as his plane goes down, he remains a man borne up by his education. He quotes Raleigh and Marvell, mentions Plato, Aristotle and Jesus, comforted by the beauty held in his well-stocked mind. He also retains his sense of humour, joking about the possibility of coming back as a ghost. June wants to find a solution for him, but he will have none of it. He wants to do it his way. Even at this moment of extremity, he is master of all he surveys.

Years of watching black and white films on television on weekend afternoons, and of reading English detective and spy stories and classic novels, have left me with many such self-possessed men in my imagination, from Mr Knightley to George Smiley via Lord Peter Wimsey.[11] And among the hundreds of children's books that I snorted like an addict when young were innumerable stories of boys 'learning to wear these shoes'. This is, for instance, the role that John Walker is learning to inhabit in *Swallows and Amazons*. It is what Eustace most definitely is not, but then starts to become, in *The Voyage of the Dawn Treader*.

Whatever I may now make of these images at the level of conscious evaluation, and whatever flaws these characters turn out to have in the books, plays and films that tell their stories, I know that the image they each reflect – the image of the self-possessed man – has a subterranean hold on me. At some level, I do still want to be Mr Knightley, or Wimsey, or Carter, or Smiley, or John Walker – or even Eustace Clarence Scrubb, once Aslan has got his claws into him. Despite myself, I find that I desire their stoicism, their diffidence, their self-deprecating humour, their confident knowledge of their duty, their nobility in self-sacrifice, their enduring self-sufficiency. That desire has refused to die, however much I now know about the world that made these men, and that they helped to make.

The self-possessed man stands at the centre of concentric circles of possession. He possesses himself, his feelings, his knowledge, his vocation, his estate and ultimately his empire. Under the cloak of his nobility, the self-possessed man is a man made for colonial rule, even if the colonial context that called him forth and that funds his existence is left far outside the frame of the picture.

One does not have to tilt the frame far, however, to bring that imperial background into view. Consider, for instance, Kipling's famous poem,

'If'. I have never been much of a fan, but all the self-possessed men who inhabit my imagination embody the ideal that Kipling sets out, or aspire to something like it. They keep their heads while all about them are losing theirs, trust themselves when all men doubt them, and dream – but don't make dreams their master. They meet with triumph and disaster and treat those two impostors the same – and all men count with them, but none too much.[12] And yet this Kipling version of the image provides a link in the short, clanking chain that runs from Peter Carter straight back to Jennings's 'racial paterfamilias'. The man described in Kipling's poem is precisely a colonial master. He is the bearer of what another of Kipling's poems calls the 'White man's burden' – which is in part the burden of keeping oneself under tight check even when dealing with hot-headed colonials.[13] This man's self-possession is the footing that will enable him to carry the weight of paternalistic rule over the childlike peoples of the empire.

The self-possessed scholar

The self-possessed man can appear in academic dress too. The most mesmerizing version I can remember was Nigel Hawthorne's portrayal of C. S. Lewis in the 1989 stage production of *Shadowlands* – a very different inhabiting of this role from either Joss Ackland or Anthony Hopkins in the television and film versions, respectively.[14] When Hawthorne strode on to the stage at the start of the play and began lecturing the audience, his confidence – his presence – was utterly captivating. He spoke as one who knew. He eschewed jargon and bluster, not needing them to shore up a position already secure. He was there to lead his audience, step by plausible step, to conclusions of which he was already the avuncular master. His hold over his audience was anchored by his hold upon his argument, and by his apparent hold upon himself.

The academic world that I inhabit is haunted by such images of self-possession. *I* am haunted by them. I am haunted by the idea of individual brilliance – of the academic as sage, who sees further than others, and more penetratingly. I am haunted by the aspiration to mastery, to possessing a map of the terrain and having such familiarity with it that one may place any new thing upon it with little apparent effort. I am haunted by the kind of academic production that hides the effort involved, so that all that is on display has an already achieved clarity, in which nothing seems laboured.

This image is largely that of an individual scholar. He may have an audience captivated by his insight. He may be surrounded by students who could be mistaken for disciples. He may engage with colleagues – other brilliant eccentrics who together form something like an idealized Oxbridge Senior Common Room. But the heart of the self-possessed scholar's work is conducted in isolation, his disciplined mind against his subject-matter – and his breakthroughs are his own, properly bearing his name.

It is often an image of a scholar distracted and dishevelled. He is likely to fail or be forgetful when it comes to the tasks of ordinary life – such trivial matters as turning up on time, clothing and feeding himself, managing domestic tasks and local relationships, and keeping order where he lives.[15] His mind is on higher, grander things, and his achievement as an academic is proportional both to this abstraction and to the distraction from the mundane that accompanies it. And there are almost certainly, hidden in the background, women who manage these practicalities for him. There is, in this academic imaginary, something slightly suspicious about the academic with a tidy desk, a scholar accomplished at ordinary life.

It is easy to push this image towards caricature. But something like it props up the cognitive and affective structures of the academic world that I inhabit. He lends support, for instance, to various overlapping and contradictory hierarchies of academic value. There is the hierarchy in which the best work approaches the status of mathematics, its orderly and explicit arguments leaving no reasonable room for doubt. There is the hierarchy in which the best work is supremely lucid, free of jargon and technicality – and yet with a verbal precision capable of dividing the world at its joints. There is the hierarchy in which the best work wears immense learning lightly, dazzling in its range of reference without ever getting lost in minutiae.

New entrants to the world haunted by this self-possessed scholar are taught to aspire to a certain kind of authorial voice. They are taught to desire a voice of their own, distinctive and recognizable – a style for which their surname might eventually yield an adjective. But it will not be a voice *from* somewhere, nor a voice with an embodied life beyond the page and the podium. It will be a voice suited for laying out the map, not a voice that can be located on it. When, eventually, PhD theses are written that focus on such scholars, it will be possible for them to treat their subject as a series of publications and archived texts and recordings. Some context may be necessary to explain the course that this series takes, but it will largely be the context provided by other texts. Little about the voice that the self-possessed scholar has achieved will invite deeper engagement with the life they lived, the communities of which they were a part, the contexts in which they were embroiled, or the material and social conditions that enabled their work. They will have taken their place in the pantheon of White, self-sufficient men, defined by what they have possessed, controlled and mastered. The academic work of the self-possessed scholar is orientated towards this apotheosis.

The self-possessed doctrinal theologian

I am most deeply familiar with specifically theological versions of this scholarly self-possession, and especially with the version that haunts my own sub-discipline: doctrinal theology. To describe the self-possessed doctrinal theologian is, once again, to describe a caricature, rather than to do justice to the embodied complexity of any particular theologian. But it is to describe a caricature that squats somewhere in my own imagination, and perhaps the imagination of others, whispering spells that influence our work.

The self-possessed doctrinal theologian would be one who has pushed through the thickets of Christian practice and ecclesiastical politics to achieve a loftier vantage point, gained by means of engagement with Christianity's articulate tradition. He is one for whom Christianity is above all a conversation of texts, and especially of those texts that display something like the abstraction and distraction from the mundane that the theologian desires for himself. The theologian's task, taken to be the task of the textual tradition with which he engages, is to lay out the conceptual canopy that overarches the drama of ordinary Christian faith. It is to discover what we must say about God, what we must say about the whole drama of salvation, in order to make orderly sense of all the particular things that we say and do here and now. Its lofty vantage point is necessary to this overarching task.

The self-possessed doctrinal theologian arranges a hierarchy of sub-disciplines, with his own at the top. Pastoral or practical theology is still too embroiled in the mess of Christian living to be intellectually satisfying. It is resistant to order and clarity, and for clearer air one needs to push higher, towards philosophical and doctrinal theology. And as one ascends that path one's voice is purified; it loses its accent. Eventually, one achieves a voice that speaks from nowhere in particular – a voice fitted to speaking the unsullied truth about God and the world. Compared to the purity of that air, the atmosphere of actually existing Christian communities is often stifling.

The journey towards such self-possession is driven by a recognizable pattern of desire. Those who take this path normally do so by way of encounter with the articulate tradition – a textual archive left by

Christianity's pantheon of self-possessed men. They encountered in the works of this articulate tradition an intoxicating new world of intellectual possibility. They discover the possibility of mapping Christian faith, and of knowing where each element fits upon that map. They discover the power of definition and distinction to bring order and clarity. They discover, and follow, the lure of intellectual mastery.

As I have written elsewhere:

> The typical product of this process is a particular kind of knowing subject. Stereotypically, it is in our own era the White, male, middle-class theologian, who now knows better than the church what the church should believe. He is the champion of the articulate whole from which the fragmentary ordinary has declined. He has lost sight of the ways in which the articulations in which he trades are themselves, and always have been, no more than fragments of the life of the church; he mistakes them for the real substance of the church's faith. He reads the inarticulate present in the unforgiving light of the articulate past, and takes ordinary Christian practice to be the inconsistent application of intellectual principles inadequately grasped, not the skilful deployment of a repertoire of practical habits. He might even suppose that, as a doctrinal theologian, and by means of his articulacy, he knows God more fully and more clearly than do others.[16]

The words that I have just quoted, and all the words of this sub-section, do of course describe a cartoon version of the doctrinal theologian. I am, however, uncomfortably aware that, even in this cartoonish form, they depict an attitude that I recognize in myself. They name a kind of mastery that I still furtively desire. They name attitudes against which I find I need to guard, and into which I still fall whenever my guard slips. Whether or not this works as a description of anyone else, I myself am haunted by this figure of the self-possessed doctrinal theologian.

The Society for the Study of Theology (SST)

To give this portrait a little more specificity, let me describe one of the contexts in which I was inducted into this pattern of desire: the annual conference of the UK's Society for the Study of Theology (SST). The SST has been running these conferences since 1952, for people with a graduate-level scholarly interest in Christian theology. I first attended in 1994, as a PhD student. In those days, if memory serves, the conference attracted about 120 people, mostly from the UK but with a few international colleagues, especially from the Netherlands. We met that year in Westminster College, Oxford, to hear papers from Stanley Hauerwas, Janet Soskice, Christoph Schwöbel, Luco van den Brom and Richard Burridge.

Like many people attending their first academic conference, I was nervous. I had at that point been studying academic theology for only three years. I had veered into it from maths late in my undergraduate career, and was very aware of how little experience I had. Over the first few years of attending, however, I began to feel at home. I gave a short paper in a small group session in 1995, and it wasn't a disaster. I practised asking questions in plenary sessions, my heart drumming in my throat. I learnt (slowly) to navigate the receptions and the refreshment breaks, trying not to rely entirely upon chatting to the few people I already knew, and trying not to be marooned on the outskirts of a huddle that I did not know how to enter. I found that I loved long – often hilarious – conversations in the SST bar at the end of each day, sometimes in a circle gathered around one of the Society's prominent figures – maybe David Ford, John Webster or Colin Gunton. The SST conference became an event that I looked forward to and relished. In 2001, I became the Society's treasurer; in 2003 I took over as secretary and until 2007 took the leading role in making the practical arrangements for each year's conference.

The SST helped me orientate myself to the academic world into which I had wandered. The abstract and daunting task of finding my place in my chosen field became the quite concrete task of finding my place in the SST – learning the different approaches and expectations that people brought to it, and learning the ways in which they interacted. I can remember walking towards the opening reception at a conference in 2011, hearing the buzz of voices ahead of me, remembering the fear with which I had first approached the conference, and thinking, 'These are my people!' These days, I approach the SST conference each year with a sense of homecoming. I belong, and I know that I belong.

It took me a shamefully long time to see that the welcome I had experienced was not universal. I did not recognize how much that sense of welcome, and my growing experience of being at home, was contingent upon my having discovered there a lot of people 'like me'. I may have felt like an impostor when I first walked through the doors, but I didn't have to hunt around to see other White men, to find people speaking with an accent like mine, to find conversations that displayed a similar middle-class background.

Neither did I recognize how much my experience of welcome was contingent upon my having been habituated to valuing certain kinds of theology – and how much the SST was instrumental in deepening my attachment to those very habits of valuation. I approached the SST as someone already in the process of being formed in the image of the self-possessed doctrinal theologian I have described above – a development for which I had been primed by a much longer formation in more general self-possession. I was learning to value certain kinds of work, and deprecate others. At the SST conferences, I would hear papers and other contributions that displayed in varying degrees the forms of rigour that I was learning to desire; I would participate in conversations where I could experiment in making judgements that expressed these values; I would make contributions of my own, and receive affirmation (and sometimes criticism) that reinforced my commitment to these values.

I am still straightforwardly thankful for much of this formation. The SST has often (not always) been good at inviting speakers from multiple theological subdisciplines, and from disciplines beyond theology, and taking them seriously. It has often (not always) been a space for respectful and thoughtful conversation. It has often (not always) been a space in which disagreements are handled well. Until quite recently, however, it has also been an engine for perpetuating a hierarchy in which practical, political and contextual theologies were secondary to doctrinal and philosophical theology, and in which some of those who pursued such approaches were made to feel that they belonged elsewhere. It has been a space in which attention to context was a secondary matter, often dispensable – and in which those who majored on the paying of such attention were made to feel that their work was of secondary importance. It has been a space in which reference to a limited canon of White, European theologians has been a recognizable calling card – an indication that one can be taken seriously.

The SST has, of course, never been uniform. There have always been disagreements and tussles, differing visions of rigour and excellence jostling against one another. There have been different levels of appetite for interdisciplinary engagement, different styles of presentation, different visions of what it means for the field of theology to flourish. It has, nevertheless, been a space often marked by the hierarchies I have mentioned, and it has been a space marked by persistent forms of marginalization and effective exclusion. It has, in other words, been an academic engine engaged in the reproduction of theological self-possession.

Change

There is also, however – and thankfully – a different story to tell about the SST. There has been a growing acknowledgement of the forms of marginalization and exclusion that mar the Society's life, and an increasing effort to overcome them. The most visible of these stories in recent years relates to 'race'. The SST has, until very recently, been overwhelmingly a White gathering. Back in the 1990s and early 2000s, I simply didn't notice this – and, to the extent that it was pointed out, thought it simply a reflection of our field. It never occurred to me that the SST was less diverse than the field of theology as a whole, nor that theology as a whole was less diverse than many other related disciplines. It certainly never occurred to me that the SST was one of the means by which my field's lack of racial diversity was maintained. And yet the hierarchies of academic value that the SST reproduced certainly had a racist effect. The deprecation of attention to context, for instance, was a factor in our exclusion of voices from the discipline of Black theology – and in the Society's ability to marginalize those voices when we did hear them.

There had been conversations about this situation in the Society at various points, but it was not until Robert Beckford presented a stark challenge to the Society in 2014 that it finally rose to the top of the agenda. A subgroup of the Society's committee focused on Theology and Race was formed in 2016 and reported in 2017, following conversation with a range of UK Minority Ethnic/Global Majority Heritage (UKME/GMH) scholars. Since then, the Society has pursued the agenda set out in the report in a number of ways.[17]

One strand of that work has involved building in accountability to the Society's structures. In 2018, an Advisory Group was formed, to meet with the SST committee each year and track progress on the commitments made in the report, and in 2020 two 'BAME representative' roles were added to the standard elected membership of the committee. Another strand of work has focused on building relationships. Members of the committee – whether or not they are themselves UKME/GMH – have been encouraged to attend events around the country focused on Black and other diverse theologies, so that the committee's deliberations can be informed by the work going on in those spaces, and in order to make connections with some of the people involved. Another strand has focused on making attendance more affordable for UKME/GMH theologians, with the creation of a targeted bursary scheme. Still another has focused on the Society using its voice, in a series of public statements, to support UKME/GMH scholars facing a variety of challenges.

All of this work seems to have had an impact. There is more to do to secure the changes of the past few years, but I am writing these words shortly after returning from the 2022 conference, where the diversity of attendees, those presenting papers and plenary speakers was very much greater than in 2014 – and my conversations with several UKME/GMH scholars during and after the conference suggest that they are beginning to find the SST to be a space in which they belong. At the end of the conference, for instance, Anthony Reddie tweeted, 'I loved being at the SST 2022 annual conference. Weird suddenly feeling like an insider having been outsider for so long.'[18]

Below the surface, however, I am very aware that these changes are accompanied by a still unfinished renegotiation of the visions of rigour and excellence that shape the SST's life – the visions of what it means to be a theologian that are assumed and passed on. I am aware, for instance, of people raising questions about whether the Society is now less serious about doctrinal theology, or about whether we are in danger of losing one of the few institutional homes in the UK for the kind of work for which the Society used to be known. And it is in this arena – the arena of disciplinary identity, of academic visions and desires – that the prickliest arguments about the changes in the Society are playing out.

Beyond self-possession

These conversations within the SST and within my discipline more broadly are no simple contest between, say, progressive and reactionary voices. There are elements that take such oppositional form, but in my experience the conversations are more complex and open-ended, shaped by many different currents of thought and practice.

To view it optimistically, I think that my colleagues and I are engaged in an as-yet unfinished work of reimagination and experimentation. That work has been going on for decades, powered by the work of feminist, liberation, contextual, practical and Black theologians among many others – but it is still in process. And I would say that I don't yet know all that my discipline needs to become 'after Whiteness', or what we might be able to become together once those of us haunted by the desire to be self-possessed men have experienced exorcism.

I recognize two foci for many of our attempts to reimagine and experiment. In processes that are by no means new but that are now taking place with a new inflection in relation to race, we are learning, I think, to desire *abstraction without distraction*, and *solitude without isolation*.

To practise doctrinal theology without yielding to the desire for self-possession does not mean the rejection of abstraction, but its grounding.

That is, it involves learning to desire abstraction only as a move within a longer movement, one limited form of service within a richer task. To abstract as doctrinal theologians abstract is to lay one's hand to a set of powerful tools – but that action is always performed in some particular place. My location influences the abstractions that attract me, and my sense of the work that they need to do. The abstractions that I choose and employ in turn shape the impact that I have in the contexts within which I work. Abstraction is always abstraction from somewhere, and on the way to somewhere. However useful – even necessary – it may be, abstraction is always and only a detour.

I am captivated by the possibilities of the doctrinal tradition: the concepts of systematic theology and the thoughts that they make possible. I do not think this captivation itself is a mark of my desire for self-possession. The excellence that I hope to desire, however, is abstraction without distraction – abstraction that does not forget that it is a detour, an exercise undertaken in a place and for a place. The excellence I hope to desire is a form of abstraction audibly aware of its contextual entailments. I see a great deal of enticing work in this area today: work that is serious about the conceptual distinctions and connections that are the stock in trade of the articulate doctrinal tradition, *and* serious about the politics of this conceptual work (using the word 'politics' in its broadest sense). I don't think I yet inhabit a world in which that double seriousness has become unremarkably habitual, a shape into which scholars are typically formed by the cultures and institutions into which their academic careers take them – but I do think that such a world is coming into being.

The other focus I see for the ongoing work of reimagination and experimentation has to do with solitude. It is no new thought to say that learning is inherently social. I have written before that 'The *form* that Christian learning takes ... is inherently that of an ongoing corporate life':

> The fulfilment of learning towards which the Spirit's work leads is, therefore, not the static individual possession of perfect understanding, but an ongoing circulation in the body in which each is attending to every other, challenging every other, learning from every other, and displaying in her own particular way, in her own particular location, what he or she goes on learning.[19]

The thought is a commonplace. Imagining a discipline thoroughly shaped by it in its practices and patterns of formation is, however, quite another matter.

Just as with abstraction, I do not think that solitude itself is the problem. For all that I love gatherings like the SST ones, I recognize that I desire solitude as a necessary beat in the rhythm of theological work. As with abstraction, however, it is important to see solitude as detour rather than as goal. As I write these words, I am alone in my study. This solitude still feels to me to be where I do my most serious thinking. But it should be a pause in the midst of a longer journey. It is enabled by the relationships and contexts that surround me, and the work that I do here properly returns to those contexts – its value consisting in its fruitfulness upon return. Solitude cannot itself be the goal.

I recognize, however, that I am still captivated by the idea that the work done in solitude – paradigmatically, the writing of a book – is itself the goal of academic work. I know, for instance, the desire to write at least one good book before I die, as if that book might itself be the proper end product of an academic life. I have been involved in and have benefited from all sorts of experiments in collaborative work, and heard about many others, but in my imagination and desire I know that those experiments remain secondary to the work I do in solitude. I don't yet know what it would mean to inhabit an academic world, and to pursue an academic life, in which I desired the ongoing conversation more deeply than the solitary achievement that sometimes enables and resources it. The whole machinery of my education, the whole shape of my academic career, the whole cognitive and affective structure that I inhabit, seems to militate against such a transformation of desire. And yet I suspect that I will not shake free from the image of the self-possessed man until I have shaken free from this desire.

I recognize, then, that I inhabit an academic world formed in the image of the self- possessed man – a man fitted for colonial mastery. I recognize that the patterns of imagination and desire that structure this world are deep-rooted and pervasive. I recognize, too, that we are in the midst of a long revolution in which the power of the self-possessed man is being challenged. But I recognize that the revolution is unfinished – and that I don't yet know how much will need to change if we are to pursue anything like Jennings's vision of an 'education in belonging'. Formed as I am in the image of the self-possessed man, I can't yet imagine all that may come after Whiteness.

Notes

1 Willie James Jennings, 2020, *After Whiteness: An Education in Belonging*, Grand Rapids, MI: Eerdmans.
2 Jennings, *After Whiteness*, p. 6.
3 Jennings, *After Whiteness*, p. 82.
4 Jennings, *After Whiteness*, p. 9.
5 Jennings, *After Whiteness*, p. 29.
6 Jennings, *After Whiteness*, p. 32.
7 Jennings, *After Whiteness*, p. 87.
8 Jennings, *After Whiteness*, p. 82.
9 Jennings, *After Whiteness*, p. 47.
10 Michael Powell and Emeric Pressburger (dir.), 1946, *A Matter of Life and Death*, London: The Archers; originally released in the USA as *Stairway to Heaven*.
11 From, respectively, Jane Austen's *Emma*, John le Carré's spy novels and Dorothy L. Sayers's detective fiction.
12 Rudyard Kipling, 1910, 'If –' in *Rewards and Fairies*, London: Macmillan, pp. 175–6; See also http://www.kiplingsociety.co.uk/poem/poems_if.htm.
13 Rudyard Kipling, 'The White Man's Burden', *McClure's Magazine*, 12, no. 4 (February 1899), pp. 290–1, and *The Times*, 4 February 1899, p. 14, http://www.kiplingsociety.co.uk/poem/poems_burden.htm.
14 William Nicholson, 1989, *Shadowlands*, dir. Norman Stone, Queen's Theatre, London.
15 For this phrase, see Ursula K. Le Guin, 1989, 'Brin Mawr Commencement Address' in *Dancing at the Edge of the World: Thoughts on Words, Women, Place*, New York: Grove, p. 154.
16 Mike Higton, 2020, *The Life of Christian Doctrine*, London: Bloomsbury, pp. 98–9.
17 I can claim no credit for this. At the time of writing, I have just stepped down as the Society's president, but most of what I am about to describe took place when I played no role in leading the Society.
18 Anthony G. Reddie (@AnthonyGReddie), *Twitter*, 31 March 2022, https://twitter.com/AnthonyGReddie/status/1509642827143262208 (accessed 7.03.2023).
19 Mike Higton, 2012, *A Theology of Higher Education*, Oxford: Oxford University Press, p. 160.

2

Deconstructing Whiteness in the UK Christian Theological Academy

DAVID L. CLOUGH

Academic Christian theology in the UK is disproportionately White in relation to the ethnicity of academic staff and students in comparison with the UK population as a whole and the UK Christian population. There is good evidence that this negatively impacts members of the UK Minority Ethnic (UKME) and Global Majority Heritage (GMH) population in relation to recruitment of students into Christian theology courses, attainment within those courses, progression to taught postgraduate and research degrees, employment in academic posts, and the academic promotions process. Some of the causes of these negative impacts are societal, some specific to the academy, some specific to the humanities and some specific to Christian theology. Those with responsibility for shaping the discipline need urgently to attend to the causes of these negative impacts and work to mitigate them for five key reasons.

First, access to academic Christian theology is an issue of justice and the discipline has both legal and moral obligations to combat the ways in which it operates to discriminate against members of non-White racial groups. Second, the Whiteness of the discipline impedes the attainment of excellence in research and teaching because of the resulting narrowness of its vision. Third, the lack of sufficient racial diversity in UK Christian theology results in disproportionately poor experiences for UKME and GMH students and staff. Fourth, the negative impacts experienced by those not racialized as White repeats historical injustices in which Christian theology was used to legitimize discriminatory practice, giving Christian theologians particular and additional grounds to take reparative action. Fifth, the Christian theological academy is self-replicating in many respects, so a failure to address the issue will result in the problems continuing for decades to come.

In this chapter, I survey evidence that UK academic Christian theology operates to the disadvantage of members of the UKME and GMH population, resulting in a relative privilege for those racialized as White. I then consider the various causes of the problem, before turning to consider priorities for action. I write as a White male straight cis-gendered person who benefited from education at Cambridge, Oxford and Yale Universities and now holds a senior academic post in the UK Christian theological academy. It is likely that these biographical details are part of the reason that my recognition of this problem is so belated in comparison with peers racialized in other ways. I have been heavily dependent on learning from them and scholars of colour in other disciplines. My education in a comprehensive school and my nonconformist Methodist background, on the other hand, may have been an asset in recognizing what it means to be a relative outsider in certain Christian theological contexts. It is helpful for White academics to recognize their positionality in approaching this issue because it highlights three reasons they may fail to engage it. First, because of their lack of first-hand experience of racial discrimination they are much less likely than non-White peers to recognize discriminatory practice or consider it serious. Second, once they have recognized the issue, the need to acknowledge their lack of competence in comparison with scholars with first-hand experience of racial discrimination is a temptation to prefer thinking and writing about topics where it is easier to make claims of expertise. Third, once one recognizes that the status quo has operated and continues to operate to one's own relative advantage, there are self-interested reasons not to pursue effective change. White scholars nonetheless have a responsibility to overcome these reasons for non-engagement because they are likely to have been privileged unfairly in relation to potential or actual UKME and GMH peers, because this operation of White privilege means they are disproportionately likely to be in positions of responsibility, and with the greatest opportunity to address the issue, and because the future of their discipline depends upon it.

It is crucial at the outset to head off one argument for downplaying the importance of racial disparities in the UK Christian theological academy or the importance of addressing them. This is the obvious truth that there are other characteristics according to which students and staff are unfairly treated within the theological academy. Ten years ago, Mathew Guest, Sonya Sharma and Robert Song published the report *Gender and Career Progression in Theology and Religious Studies*; this highlighted the gender imbalance and experiences of gender discrimination in UK Theology and Religious Studies (TRS) departments, and the past decade has certainly not eliminated the problem.[1] No discipline-specific research has been conducted into other forms of discrimination, but wider studies within UK Higher Education strongly suggest that people with disabilities and LGBTQI people are likely to experience discrimination and obstacles to full participation in academic theology.² The impact of class and socio-economic status on participation in academic Christian theology has not been investigated either, but it seems likely that Christian theology has a particular problem with enabling access to the discipline to those from working-class and poorer backgrounds. Work is required urgently to understand better and address each of these issues. The existence of these multiple and overlapping characteristics, which result in adverse impacts for the participation of particular groups of students and staff in academic Christian theology, mean that we should not address issues of 'race' to the exclusion of other concerns or without attending to the ways racial injustice relates to other forms of discrimination. The fact that people are treated badly within the UK Christian theological academy for reasons apart from their 'race' is not, however, a reason to fail to recognize and address the issue of racial discrimination in UK academic Christian theology.

By 'Whiteness', in this chapter, I mean primarily a system of privilege that advantages those racialized as White and disadvantages those racialized in other ways. Steve Garner's *Whiteness* is a good academic introduction to the topic in a UK context; Robin Diangelo's *White Fragility* provides a more practically orientated approach in the context of the USA.³ Both authors emphasize the importance of recognizing that being racialized as White has implications for how people are treated and their view of the world. They also stress that Whiteness should be understood as a system of privilege, rather than focusing on racism as something only morally bad people do.

My focus in this chapter is on Christian theology in the UK academy. 'Theology' is used as a disciplinary self-description by academics working in religious traditions other than Christianity, so I use 'Christian' as a qualifier of theology in this chapter. At the same time, it is important to recognize that 'theology' is used to mean 'Christian theology' in virtually all UK academic positions, societies, departments and subject areas, programmes, courses and modules that refer to 'theology'. The term 'Theology and Religious Studies' is widely used to group Christian theology with other disciplines, and I have followed that usage when discussing the broad subject area.

What's the problem?

There are different ways to specify the problem of how Whiteness functions in UK academic Christian theology. I will consider aspects of the problem in two categories: those aspects that affect other disciplines and those that are specific to Christian theology. In the UK academy, Christian theology is usually grouped organizationally with other disciplinary approaches to studying religions, non-religious worldviews, and religious texts, as well as theology within other religious traditions. As I will indicate shortly, there is limited data specific to theology and religious studies as a whole, let alone Christian theology as distinct from these other subject areas. I suggest that it makes sense nonetheless to consider aspects of the problem that are specific to Christian theology because Christian theology stands in a particular relationship to 'race' and Whiteness.

A valuable reference point in considering the aspects of the problem that UK academic Christian theology shares with other disciplines is the 2018 report by the Royal Historical Society (RHS), 'Race, Ethnicity and Equality in History: A Report and Resource for Change'.[4] Much of the data presented in the report are not disaggregated below the category of Historical and Philosophical Studies (HPS), which includes Theology and Religious Studies. Staff and student numbers in History outweigh other subject areas in this grouping, but the statistics are the best currently available and likely to be broadly indicative of the situation in theology and religious studies.

The RHS report notes that, despite the transformation of understanding resulting from research into Black history and histories of 'race', imperialism and colonialization, the racial profile of students and staff in UK History departments remains overwhelmingly White; Black and Minority Ethnic (BME) students and staff have disproportionately negative experiences; attainment of BME students lags behind their peers; and school and university curricula fail to incorporate fully the new diverse histories that academics are producing.[5] The report notes that in 2018, in UK undergraduate cohorts, the proportion of BME students in HPS was only 11 per cent, the lowest proportion of any subject area. This was much lower than the proportion of BME students in the overall UK undergraduate population (23.9 per cent).[6] At postgraduate taught level, the proportion of BME students in HPS drops further to 9.3 per cent, compared with 22 per cent in the overall postgraduate population. The RHS report notes that academic staff in UK History departments are even less diverse than these student cohorts, with 93.7 per cent White and 6.3 per cent BME, compared to 85 per cent White and 15 per cent BME among all UK academic staff. Within this 6.3 per cent BME figure, only 0.5 per cent are Black.[7] Discipline-specific data are available from the Higher Education Statistics Agency but have not been collated or reported in relation to TRS disciplines, though the disciplinary association TRS-UK is undertaking work to address this lack. There is no reason to think that the proportion of BME staff in UK TRS departments and subject areas is higher than the proportion in History.

The RHS report also includes findings from a survey attracting 737 responses from academic staff and postgraduate students in UK history departments. It found that 18.8 per cent of respondents had witnessed discrimination against, or abuse of, a BME colleague. Some 9.5 per cent of respondents had directly experienced discrimination or abuse in relation to 'race' or ethnicity, but this rose to 29.8 per cent among BME respondents.[8] The survey also identified the perception among some respondents that school and university curricula are too narrow and fail to engage history beyond the UK and Europe, histories of empire, and 'race' and ethnicity, despite 58 per cent of respondents reporting attempts to widen the curriculum in relation to 'race' and ethnicity.[9] Similar research is needed among those working in TRS in the UK, but there is no reason to believe that the incidence of racial discrimination and abuse is lower than in History, nor that TRS curricula have been diversified more effectively.

The 2019 Universities UK report 'Black, Asian and Minority Ethnic Student Attainment at UK Universities' documents the attainment gap between the proportion of BME students attaining first-class and upper-second-class degrees compared with their White peers. It finds an overall attainment gap between White and BME students of 13 per cent. After controlling for prior attainment, gender and age, the Office for Students identifies an unexplained difference of 17 per cent in the performance of White and Black students, and of 10 per cent between White and Asian students.[10] The report notes the importance of avoiding a 'deficit model' interpretation of this attainment gap that makes the ungrounded assumption that BME students lack skills, knowledge or experience.[11]

The RHS and Universities UK reports highlight several issues concerning how Whiteness operates within UK universities that are likely to be shared by academic Christian theology together with other disciplines: the disproportionate Whiteness of students and academic staff; the discrimination and abuse experienced by BME students and staff; the lack of sufficient diversity in school and university curricula; and the attainment gap between White and BME students. In addition to these issues applicable to other disciplines, academic Christian theology also needs to attend to discipline-specific aspects of how Whiteness functions to disadvantage UKME and GMH students and staff.

The first issue to address is relevant demographic data to assess participation in UK academic Christian theology. The 2011 UK census reported that 86 per cent of the UK population identified their 'race' as White, 7.5 per cent Asian, 3.3 per cent Black, and 2.2 per cent Mixed 'race'.[12] This puts the UK combined UKME population as 14 per cent of the total.

For the subject area of TRS, as for the HPS subject area more generally, there seems no good reason that the university student and staff population should not be representative of the UK population as a whole. This means the 14 per cent UKME population is an appropriate comparator to evaluate the declining proportion of UKME students in HPS from 11 per cent at undergraduate level to 9 per cent at postgraduate taught level, and the 6 per cent proportion of UKME staff in History. As noted above, comparable research on 'race' and ethnicity of academic staff has not yet been done for the TRS subject area and is urgently needed. Anyone with knowledge of the field, however, will be aware that UKME people are significantly underrepresented in comparison with the 14 per cent proportion of UKME individuals in the UK population. To assess the situation of UK Christian theology in particular would require still more analysis, but until we have this it is clear that there is underrepresentation of Black scholars in UK academic posts in Christian theology.

Alongside the demographics of particular relevance to UK academic theology, there are other ways in which Christian theology has particular connections to Whiteness. One key issue is the way that Christian theology was historically an important component in the construction of Whiteness, and remains a significant reference point for how Whiteness functions in the UK. In the USA, the connection between Christian theology and Whiteness has been most fully explored in the works of James Cone. His first book, *Black Theology and Black Power*, condemned the White church for its involvement in slavery and racism and for its contribution to the doctrine of White supremacy.[13] His second book, *A Black Theology of Liberation* (1970), identified American White theology as 'a theology of the white oppressor, giving religious sanction to the genocide of Amerindians and the enslavement of Africans'.[14] After completing doctoral work on the theology of Karl Barth, Cone criticized European and North American Barthians 'who used him to justify doing nothing about the struggle for justice'.[15] His 1998 essay 'White Theology Revisited' calls out the 'appalling silence of white theologians on racism'. Cone observes that 'progressive white theologians, with few exceptions, write and teach as if they do not need to address the radical contradiction that racism creates for Christianity.' He identifies the problem with the professional practice of White theologians: 'white theologians in the seminaries, university departments of religion and divinity schools, and professional societies refused to acknowledge white supremacy as a theological problem and continued their business as usual, as if the lived experience of blacks was theologically vacuous.'[16] In a 2015 article, Cone called the silence of White theologians in the face of White supremacy 'Theology's Great Sin'.[17]

The connections between Christianity and Whiteness in a British context have both similarities with, and differences from, Cone's North American context. Kenneth Leech's *Struggle in Babylon*, published in 1988, argued that Christianity provided the theological basis for the ideology of racial superiority, and the association of Christianity with Whiteness has had devastating effects all over the world. Leech drew attention to the connections between injustices based on 'race' and class, and criticized the Church of England as the British institution that is most unequal, allied to privilege, culture-bound, rooted in the private education system and most alien to working-class people.[18] In his 2005 work, *Changing Society and the Churches: Race*, Leech noted that all British mainstream churches failed to engage with migrants from the Caribbean on the basis of equality, which led many to set up Black-led churches.[19] Robert Beckford's *Dread and Pentecostal* made the case that Christianity in the UK works to support White supremacy.[20] In one of his more recent books, *Theologising Brexit: A Liberationist and Postcolonial Critique*, Anthony Reddie argues that Christianity helped to shape White supremacist notions of entitlement and superiority alongside a toxic form of Black self-negation.[21] There are strong connections in the UK between nationalism; the nation state; the monarchy and aristocracy; social class; the Church of England as established church; and the role of Christianity more broadly in understandings of the life of the nation. Christianity and Christian theology in the UK are therefore intricately connected with institutional structures that have established and maintained White privilege. Understanding the operation of Whiteness in UK theology must include attention to these linkages.

Christian theology is not unique as an academic discipline that has been used to defend White supremacy. Other disciplines have been marshalled to the cause of legitimizing racism, including History and English among the humanities, and Anthropology and Biology among the social and natural sciences. Arguably, however, these other academic disciplines have been less significant in the formation and maintenance of racist ideologies because they are not linked to communities of religious practice and, in particular, the established religion of the British nation state. There is also the question of the scandalous gap between the heights of professed belief and the realities of belief and practice. Christian preachers proclaim a gospel message where the powerful are brought down from their thrones, the lowly lifted up, captives released and the oppressed freed, while Christianity and Christian theologians operate in a way that erects, maintains and fails to question racist power structures within and beyond the church. Any adequate engagement with Whiteness in the UK theological academy must recognize the particular ways in which

Christian theology and White supremacy bear upon one another in a UK context.

An understanding of the problem of how Whiteness operates in the UK theological academy must incorporate both aspects of the problem that theology has in common with other cognate disciplines, such as History, and those that are particular to the discipline of Christian theology. Taken together, even in advance of necessary further research, they indicate that academic Christian theology in the UK has a serious problem to address in the way it operates to disadvantage members of the UKME and GMH population as students and academic staff at all stages. They also indicate that some of the entanglements between Christian theology in the UK and White privilege have both long historical roots and relate to current educational and ecclesial institutional structures. Recognizing these entanglements is an important step in identifying appropriate actions to address the problem.

What can those in the UK Christian theological academy do about it?

The task of challenging the ways in which White privilege operates in the UK Christian theological academy to disadvantage UKME and GMH students and staff is demanding for two key reasons. First, the problem is complex, with a wide range of causal factors that are difficult to change, as discussed in the previous section. Second, the group of those currently in senior positions in UK academic theology best placed to make changes to address the issue is disproportionately White – as well as unrepresentative in relation to other characteristics such as gender, social class and disability – so least likely to be well placed to recognize and be motivated to address the problem. The current system has operated to advantage this group, so its default preference is likely to be for business as usual. My own positionality as a member of this group impedes my ability to see the problem clearly, but also gives me a good understanding of the context in need of change. Effective progress in relation to any of the strategies discussed below is likely to depend on a combination of convincing these and other academics in the UK Christian theological academy of the ethical imperative to take action despite apparent contrary interests, increasing external pressure in relation to the unacceptability of the status quo, and identifying ways in which acting to challenge the operation of Whiteness within the discipline of Christian theology can be recognized as beneficial to everyone working in it.

I suggest four key priorities for action in relation to the problems I have set out. First, there is a need to discuss the connections between Christian theology, Whiteness and 'race' more generally in the theological academy. Until recently, most White UK theologians had never encountered discussions of 'race' in a theological context in their own education, at academic conferences, nor in wider professional contexts, so had not considered the implications of the issue for their practice. It remains the case that many Christian theologians believe that this is an issue for those with specialist interests, rather than a structural issue requiring attention from everyone in the field. There are some belated but promising signs of change in relation to the increasing prominence of the issue in UK theological discussions and the work of academic societies. There are also cases where academic spaces within UK Christian theology have been used for initiatives that seem aimed at resisting or reversing the work of engaging theology with anti-racist and decolonial perspectives, such as Nigel Biggar's 'Ethics and Empire' project at Oxford University (2017–22) or James Orr's hosting of Jordan Peterson at Cambridge University in 2021. The sustained culture change required within the UK theological academy to counter the ways in which UKME and GMH scholars are disadvantaged is only likely to be realized when recognition of the need for urgent action is the clear shared view of a substantial majority of those working in the field. This consensus will only be established and sustained through continued discussion of the issue within university departments and subject areas and at UK academic theology conferences, so that the change is driven by shared values rather than seen as the external imposition of particular policy norms.

Second, there is a need for more research. Measuring action in relation to increasing the representation of UKME and GMH students and staff in UK Christian academic theology and ensuring their progression depends on establishing and monitoring those statistics. The data are publicly available but research comparable to the 2018 RHS report, discussed above, has not been done. TRS-UK has indicated interest in undertaking this research but progress has been slow. Those with interest in the dimensions of the problem relating specifically to Christian theology will have to give thought to the implications of any TRS-wide analysis for theology in particular. Ongoing research with a broader focus is also necessary to uncover and narrate the linkages between Whiteness and Christian theology, the Church of England and other British churches, UK political structures, and the history of educational institutions where theology is done, continuing and taking forward pioneering contributions by Kenneth Leech, Robert Beckford, Anthony Reddie, David Haslam, John Wilkinson and others. One way of avoiding making this work dependent merely on the available time of researchers motivated to undertake it is collaborative work on applications for funding to resource the time required for it.

A third key priority for action is in relation to recruitment processes for academic posts in Christian theology. The fact that academic staff in UK Christian theology are disproportionately White has a range of powerful impacts on who sees themselves as welcome in theological spaces; who considers a professional future in the academic discipline; the ability of staff to recognize and address issues of equality and diversity in the workings of the discipline; the kind of topics that are selected for theological research; and the way curricula and courses are designed and delivered. Strong efforts need to be made towards the goal that those holding academic posts in the UK Christian theological academy are representative of racial and ethnic demographics in relation to some balance between the UK Christian population and the global Christian population. To attain this, continued attention must be given to racial bias in academic recruitment processes. The RHS report has a range of constructive advice for those leading appointment panels: ensuring that staff and students involved know university policy and the law in relation to equality and inclusion; improving equality and diversity training for participants in recruitment processes, going beyond institution-wide workshops if necessary; ensuring staff reading and writing references are aware of literature concerning how this process is often biased against marginalized people; and being proactive about recruitment of UKME/GMH staff.[22] Consideration should also be given to the operation of White-dominated informal professional networks within UK academic theology. These are often powerful influences on which potential candidates receive good mentoring advice on how to make themselves 'shortlistable'; who is encouraged to apply for appropriate posts; who gets the most useful feedback on draft application materials and interview preparation; who has the best referees; and who gets appointed to academic posts. The best remedial action here is likely to be proactive work to make these informal networks accessible to junior scholars of colour, together with consideration about formalizing new mentoring programmes. It is notable that some theological education institutions, such as the Queen's Foundation in Birmingham, have done much better in relation to recruiting UKME and GMH academic staff, and others should learn from their good practice.

A final key priority for action is to re-evaluate the content of theological research and teaching with a view to their role in continuing cycles of privileging White, colonial and Eurocentric theological perspectives. Attention to this aspect of the issue often provokes fears that sacred canons or long traditions of academic formation are under threat. But the reception and transmission of theology in the academy has always been a critical task through which the tradition passed on is interrogated rigorously with regard both to its coherence and its relationship with pressing new questions arising from attending to the context of new times and places. Reassessing the task, content and methods of Christian theology in the UK in relation to the issue of 'race' and Whiteness is therefore a continuation, rather than an interruption, of the task of participating in the tradition of Christian theology. Evaluating what in the theological tradition needs reconsideration and rethinking in the light of these critical questions is an essential part of the responsibility of Christian theologians in the UK in the first part of the twenty-first century, just as engaging with other pressing contextual questions was the lot of Bede, Anselm and Mother Julian in their day. Reviews in relation to the Inclusive Curriculum Framework pioneered at Kingston University and similar initiatives elsewhere are already enabling academics in some departments and subject areas to review programmes, courses and modules in Christian theology in relation to questions of how far they encourage the full participation of diverse student cohorts. More work is required in this area, but similar questions need to be asked much more widely: in calls for papers for academic conferences, in proposals for PhD projects, in academic peer review publication processes, and so on, to encourage research activity to be similarly informed by critical rigour in relation to this key contextual issue.

As a holder of a senior academic post in the UK Christian theological academy, I recognize my responsibility to be active in relation to these four priority actions relating to the challenge of deconstructing Whiteness in the discipline and my accountability for doing so. Others have seen the problem sooner and acted more quickly, and I am grateful to them. Up to this point, most of those calling attention to the Whiteness of academic theology in the UK have been Black scholars. These pioneering contributions must be recognized and celebrated, but it is now past the time for the burden of acknowledging and addressing the problem to be more widely shared. White UK theologians in particular need to be active and visible in addressing the wide range of actions required, recognizing that this important work should take place alongside other remedial action in relation to gender, social class, disability, gender identity, sexuality and other characteristics. The motivation to take this action should be based on a recognition of academic responsibility in relation to the just working of institutions; a commitment to the necessary conditions for establishing a flourishing theological discourse that is rigorous, critically aware, diverse and inclusive; and an acknowledgement of the fact that only in this way will the academic study of Christian theology in the UK have a future, or deserve to.

Notes

1 M. Guest, S. Sharma and R. Song, 2013, *Gender and Career Progression in Theology and Religious Studies*, Durham: Durham University.

2 M. Hector, 2020, *Arriving at Thriving: Learning from Disabled Students to Ensure Access for All*, London: Policy Connect; and T. Sundberg, P. Boyce and R. Ryan-Flood, 2021, *Challenging LGBT+ Exclusion in UK Higher Education*, London: UCU.

3 S. Garner, 2007, *Whiteness: An Introduction*, London: Routledge; and R. Diangelo, 2019, *White Fragility: Why It's So Hard for White People to Talk About Racism*, London: Penguin Books.

4 H. Atkinson et al., 2018, *Race, Ethnicity and Equality in History: A Report and Resource for Change*, London: Royal Historical Society.

5 Atkinson et al., *Race, Ethnicity and Equality*, p. 7.

6 Atkinson et al., *Race, Ethnicity and Equality*, pp. 36–8.

7 Atkinson et al., *Race, Ethnicity and Equality*, p. 41.

8 Atkinson et al., *Race, Ethnicity and Equality*, p. 50.

9 Atkinson et al., *Race, Ethnicity and Equality*, pp. 63–4.

10 Universities UK, 2019, *Black, Asian and Minority Ethnic Student Attainment at UK Universities: #closingthegap*, London: Universities UK, pp. 11–15.

11 Universities UK, *Black, Asian*, p. 16.

12 UK Government, 2018, 'Population of England and Wales', *Gov.uk*, https://www.ethnicity-facts-figures.service.gov.uk/uk-population-by-ethnicity/national-and-regional-populations/population-of-england-and-wales/latest#by-ethnicity (accessed 19.05.2022).

13 J. H. Cone, 1997, *Black Theology and Black Power*, Maryknoll, NY: Orbis Books, p. 72.

14 J. H. Cone, 2010, *A Black Theology of Liberation*, Maryknoll, NY: Orbis Books, p. 4.

15 J. H. Cone, 1985, *My Soul Looks Back*, Maryknoll, NY: Orbis Books, p. 45. I explore Cone's critique of Barthian theologians in more detail in D. L. Clough, forthcoming, 'Using Barth to Justify Doing Nothing: James Cone's Unanswered Challenge to the Whiteness of Barth Studies, Fifty Years on' in P. D. Jones and K. Dugan (eds), *Karl Barth and Liberation Theology*.

16 J. H. Cone, 1999, *Risks of Faith: The Emergence of a Black Theology of Liberation, 1968–1998*, Boston, MA: Beacon Press, pp. 130, 134.

17 J. H. Cone, 'Theology's Great Sin: Silence in the Face of White Supremacy', *Black Theology: An International Journal*, 2 (2004), pp. 139–52.

18 K. Leech, 1988, *Struggle in Babylon: Racism in the Cities and Churches of Britain*, London: Sheldon Press, pp. 167, 171, 179.

19 K. Leech, 2005, *Changing Society and the Churches: Race*, London: SPCK, p. 103.

20 R. Beckford, 2000, *Dread and Pentecostal: A Political Theology for the Black Church in Britain*, London: SPCK.

21 Anthony G. Reddie, 2019, *Theologising Brexit: A Liberationist and Postcolonial Critique*, London & New York: Taylor & Francis, p. 25.

22 Atkinson, *Race, Ethnicity and Equality*, pp. 78–81.

3

Re-Distributing Theological Knowledge in Theological Education as an Act of Distributive Justice in Contemporary Christian Mission

EVE PARKER

The natural character of the people may also be considered as unfavourable. They are credulous to a high degree in what refers to their own system; generally fickle, imbecile, and easily affected by what strikes the sense. Public exhibitions always work powerfully on their minds. Idolatrous processions, with all the other gaudy shows connected with temple worship, prove exceedingly imposing, independently of the superstition which operates. Scripture truth, therefore, simply promulgated and unaccompanied by exterior show and parade, finds in the habitual constitution of their minds no preparation for its reception.[1]

The Christian missions of the British empire often professed a claim to moral authority over and against the religious and cultural beliefs and practices of the so-called 'heathens' and 'aboriginals'; they did so because they believed 'it was their divinely ordained Christian duty to look after the well-being of the aboriginals'.[2] Yet in the process the theological knowledge, wisdom and insights of the indigenous communities in the colonized lands were often disregarded and degraded. This was made visible in the colonial missionary ethnography of the nineteenth and early twentieth centuries, where dichotomous notions of personhood were professed through missionary writings. This was a time when people were described in terms of being Christian/heathen, civilized/uncivilized, during a period where, as Dasgupta remarks, 'ethnology emerged as the most "scientific" framework for the study of the linguistic, physical, and cultural characteristics of so-called dark-skinned, non-European, uncivilized peoples.'[3] The colonial missionaries played a crucial role in reporting on the particular locations in which they served, and often depicted the colonialized as 'savages' in the process. As the anthropologist John Cinnamon comments, they often fabricated '"a synthetic savagery drawn from a standardized myth" where such accounts relied on tropes of racial inferiority, demasculinization, and "infantilization"'.[4] Eurocentric Christian notions of morality and decency influenced the lens through which the missionaries witnessed and reported on the colonialized practices and belief systems. The missionary role became integral not only in the transmission of the Christian Gospels, but also in the propagation of European civilization, science and epistemology. The missionaries also became 'expert witnesses' in the social scientific study of ethnography, where 'the everyday lives' of the colonialized peoples became of increasing interest to European ethnologists and anthropologists – who themselves were often guilty of reconstructing the cultural traditions, beliefs and practices through the lens of European epistemology.[5]

Yet despite the integral role of the missionaries across the British empire in 'studying' colonialized communities, anthropologists at the time, more often than not, failed to acknowledge the extent to which they relied on missionary cooperation in their studies and writings. However, the Christian missionaries of the British empire often also played the role of social scientist. This is apparent not only in the missionary reports and writings of the time, but also in the work of the International Institute of African Languages and Cultures of the early twentieth century for example, where the role of the missionary and social sciences are explicitly addressed, noting that missionaries at the time were encouraged to be trained as anthropologists.[6] At the heart of such studies was the desire for greater knowledge for the sake of power and control – under the premise that the West had a moral and religious duty to 'civilize' and 'save' the people of the empire. Where, as Dirks remarks, the 'colonial state' operated as an 'ethnographic state', where there was a desire 'to collect information for the purposes of governance', this involved colonial knowledge production where the colonialized were products to be consumed by the 'imposition of new, imported epistemic regimes of Western/European knowledge systems'.[7] Victorian anthropology and ethnographic research enabled a 'production of knowledge' that *othered* the colonialized, by depicting the people as 'primitive', 'exotic others' and the 'information supplied by ethnographers indeed helped colonial empires find ways to exert political domination and economic exploitation'.[8]

What is apparent is how faith and European social science are interrelated during this period, and the subject of ethnographic research was the colonialized peoples, who seemingly remained voiceless and choiceless in the process. The epistemology of the colonialized was rendered as unworthy, uncivilized, and incomprehensible based upon Western notions of rationality. This was an act of 'epistemic injustice',[9] where the so-called progress of the Enlightenment went 'hand in hand with the progress of Christianity',[10] and the colonialized peoples were dehumanized in the process while the epistemology of the colonialized was rendered worthless 'heathenism'. Racism, patriarchy and Eurocentric rationality heavily influenced such notions of progress and social scientific studies. Such ideologies have no doubt led to continued racism, and socio-political and economic marginalization today – as well as the continued suppression of epistemologies from the majority world. This includes the failure to give theologies from the majority world equal worth in the curricula of theological education today, particularly in the West. This has been made possible through continued 'white ignorance': as Miranda Fricker notes, white ignorance:

> ... is a racialized form of ideological thinking. It names a certain kind of collective interested or motivated cognitive bias in what social interpretations and/or evidence for such interpretations a racially dominant group attends to and integrates into the rest of their beliefs and deliberations ... it involves some self-serving epistemic fault on the part of whites – a conscious or unconscious resistance to accepting or learning about the sources of their social advantage, for instance.[11]

Such ignorance is visible not only in the missionary narratives throughout the colonial period, but also in the continued domination of White epistemology in theological education today. This is where Black and majority world theologies are often missing from curricula, where staff bodies are dominated by the White middle classes, and where theologies that stem from the privileged White, male elites are deemed as trustworthy knowledge, in comparison to the 'contextual theologies' that stem from the bodies of the marginalized. In light of such epistemic injustice, the question I want to pose is how theological education can enable the redistribution of epistemic justice. I will argue that distributive justice requires a decolonization of theological education and the praxis of Christian missiology. The premise of my argument is that epistemic injustice in Christian theology and missiology is a question of distributive justice for the global church. Such justice requires decolonizing Christian theology in order to search intentionally for alternatives to dominant discourses of Eurocentric Christianity that have silenced the theologies and truth claims of those in the majority world. This requires what Walter Mignolo has referred to as 'epistemic disobedience' – meaning 'de-linking from the magic of the Western idea of modernity and ideals of humanity'.[12]

In response, I will focus on the need for redistributing knowledge as a process of 'epistemic disobedience', arguing that the global church should privilege the voices of indigenous and subaltern theologies as a means of redistributive justice. I will concentrate on the idea of epistemic injustice as an example of distributive unfairness with particular focus on dominant discourses of Christian theology, and then look to the role of theological education in enabling for the redistribution of theological knowledge as a form of missiological justice. In doing so, I will give attention to discriminatory epistemic injustice in Christian theology and praxis made apparent in historical Christian missions, which denied the truth claims of the colonialized. I will then give focus to redistributing theological knowledge by giving voice to the indigenous theologies of the subaltern as a means of distributive epistemic justice. Such redistribution of knowledge is vital as a means of reparations for the sins of colonialism and the continued White ignorance that dominates in spaces of learning and curricula in the West.

Colonial 'knowledge' in Christian mission

In 1914, Archdeacon McMahon, a missionary serving in Madagascar, reported on his ethnographic findings alongside the work of the missions in various regions of Madagascar; under one subheading, entitled 'People and Ethnography', he writes:

> The BETSILEO is the next tribe of importance, numbering over half a million; they live on the central plateau to the south of the Hova. They have frizzy hair and are darker than the Hova. There is a good deal of the negroid strain in them. They are much more robust than the Hova, especially the women; they are patient and docile, but much addicted to drink and very superstitious. Next to the Hova the Betsileo have made more progress in religion and education than any other tribe.[13]

The same missionary goes on in his report to describe another 'tribe' as being 'not particularly intelligent'.[14] The missionary is guilty of epistemic injustice; in labelling the indigenous people as 'unintelligent', 'docile' and 'superstitious', he denies the indigenous people of 'their capacity as a knower or as an epistemic subject'. Such beliefs were not only held by missionaries though; the infamous British philosopher John Locke, for example, made the argument that the heads of the indigenous were filled with 'love and hunting', maintaining that 'they had "vulgar conceptions of the divine", which rendered their religions nothing more than superstition or atheism.'[15] Such dehumanizing beliefs were also professed by the likes of the British philosopher John Stuart Mill who, when writing on the liberties of man, suggested that the indigenous and colonized did not qualify as deserving of liberty or justice, 'observing that because Indigenous peoples lacked the capacity to think for themselves, the government could rightfully subject them to "civilization" programs'.[16] At the core of such beliefs proclaimed by philosophers held in the highest esteem in the curricula of the European schools of thought is White ignorance – that is, ignorance embedded in a racist ideology of White supremacy; this ignorance enables epistemic injustice against indigenous communities, as such peoples are denied of their rights as 'knowers'.

McMahon's missionary account also exposes the racism of Eurocentric ethnography and epistemology; his description of 'the negroid strain' racially ranks the Betsileo people through a White, European lens, where the darker the skin, the further removed they become from the 'ideal' European White male. Such accounts fed into anthropological studies of the nineteenth and twentieth centuries, and impacted the lives of the indigenous people by culturally 'othering' communities of people into allegedly 'primitive characters'. As Rebecca Tsosie remarks, 'the philosophical constructions were justified by reference to nineteenth-century science, which held that Europeans were at the apex of civilization, while Africans were at the lowest rung … The field anthropologists of the day were working with evolutionary theory and social hierarchies.'[17]

In describing the religion of the Malagasy people, McMahon writes:

> This want of respect for God's Name shows how little the heathen native thinks of God. Other things, witchcraft especially, have usurped His place; while it is probable that this bare acknowledgment of God is responsible for many of the shortcomings of the Malagasy Christians.[18]

> The native is more or less a fatalist to begin with, and believes that everything good or bad is from God, like the Jews of old; so divination and destiny find fertile ground and will take a long time to root out.[19]

In the ethnographic writings of the missionary, a form of a qualitative scientific research[20] used as a source of knowledge in the British empire and study of anthropology, the colonialized people were 'racially ranked'; the 'colonial wound' is apparent in the description of a people who are supposedly 'underdeveloped economically and mentally' and theologically.[21]

To understand epistemic injustice in contemporary theological education and mission, it is important to see the historical roots of such injustice, and here in the missionary writings are the historical wrongs of racism, antisemitism and ideological claims of superiority that profess a White supremacist ideology. Unlike other disciplines where epistemic injustice is also apparent, God is 'used' in theology as a weapon in the claim of epistemic superiority, where the oppression of the indigenous communities becomes 'divinely justified'. By presenting the indigenous people as 'uncivilized' the missionaries were free to deny them of their rights as 'knowers'; as Tsosie remarks, 'native peoples were considered too "savage" to merit legal rights or to engage in a reasoned discourse about the nature of their rights.'[22] The religious beliefs of the communities were mocked as 'superstitious', 'witchcrafts', and when communities did convert to Christianity, even then the Christianity lived out was not considered 'proper' or 'pure' Christianity from the perspective of the Europeans.

The ethnographic writings of the missionaries also distorted the theological and religious practices of the indigenous communities. Take, for example, a description by Shirley Dickins, when writing on the missionary George Grenfill's expeditions in Cameroon. She describes the religious practices at the death of a loved one, stating: 'little delay was allowed between the death and burial, and the custom was to take the personal belongings of the dead man, break them, and stack them under a rough shelter opposite his house. There seemed to be no reason for this action, and it was performed merely because it was "fashionable" so to do.'[23] Dickins degrades the religious practices of the indigenous communities as 'fashionable' and, in doing so, she dismisses the epistemology of the people and lessens the worth and authenticity of their faith understanding. The colonial demand to 'leave behind' aspects of indigenous epistemology is rooted in the colonial desire to impose notions of Western rationality. As imperial power consisted of political, material, religious and ideological suppression of the colonialized, Christian mission was intertwined with such power dynamics through the growth of empire and colonial rule. Theologies that stem from the bodies of the marginalized continued to be disregarded with the same rhetoric, either through the denial of allowing the space in curricula for theologies that display the hybridity of Christian religious belonging in the majority world, or by denying the authenticity of such Christianity. This is also a form of what Fricker has referred to as 'hermeneutical injustice', 'that is experienced by individuals or groups (usually minorities) who do not possess the shared social resources or linguistic tools to make sense of their particular experiences'.[24] This has had a lasting impact on theological curricula, where theologies from the majority world are not represented. The implications of this can lead to people, particularly those who exist outside of the realm of the White, middle-class male, attempting to theologize and make sense of the world with resources that undermine their own experiences and ways of knowing. In speaking on the importance of an Africanized philosophy curriculum, Edwin Etieyibo makes this point, stating:

> For if the perspectives of African or an African tradition contribute something rich to our understanding of the world, then undermining or excluding them starves both Africans and others or the world at large of some important perspectives that are necessary in navigating our world ... that is, because the tradition has something valuable to add to the body of knowledge or meaning-making, it is well worth it for us or beneficial for world philosophy if our philosophy curriculum does not exclude it.[25]

Historically, Christian missions have also been guilty of 'testimonial injustice'; this, as Miranda Fricker has commented, 'occurs when prejudice causes a hearer to give a deflated level of credibility to a speaker's word'.[26] This is made apparent in the silencing of the voices, experiences and epistemology of the colonialized peoples. As stated, the missionaries and colonialists were also guilty of 'hermeneutical injustice'; this is when there exists a 'gap in collective interpretive resources' that disadvantages people based upon their social experiences and geopolitical location. In other words, as a result of structural prejudice a person is not trusted or believed, usually as a consequence of their gender or ethnicity. Consequently, indigenous peoples lost their right to interpret their own history, religions and culture, 'they were also subjected to the impositions of alien ways of understanding.' This has resulted in centuries of continued marginalization of indigenous knowledge, made most apparent in academic and church institutions, where the voices of the colonized continued to be pigeon-holed, reduced to contextual theologies or silenced altogether. Indigenous people were reduced to objects of conversion and civilization, and consequently Black, Asian, mujerista, feminist, womanist and other such critical theologies continue to 'suffer from participatory prejudice and informational prejudice' as part of a lasting legacy of social scientific and theological epistemic injustice.[27]

Redistributing knowledge in theological education

Edward Said declared that 'the subaltern can speak, as the history of liberation movements in the twentieth century eloquently attests.'[28] The problem is, however, that the 'subaltern' continue to be silenced in the spaces that have throughout history rendered the knowledge of the 'subaltern' to be of less worth. It is therefore vital to focus on the need to redistribute knowledge as a means of epistemic justice, because 'knowledge is no less important than material resources in enabling individuals to lead flourishing lives and exercise their rights effectively.'[29] If contemporary theological education is to be trusted and truly formative, it must take seriously the need to decolonize the curriculum as a means of distributive justice; this means addressing the reality of epistemic injustice, and the academies' role within such injustice, as well as the need to challenge the social production of knowledge. This requires a 'decolonial thinking' in theological education, in order to unveil and expose 'epistemic silences of Western epistemology and affirming the epistemic rights of the racially devalued'.[30] This is not a simple task, as it involves exposing a network of norms, practices, policies and institutions[31] that have systemically shamed and silenced epistemology from the majority world. The redistribution of knowledge would be a means by which White ignorance can be addressed; however, as Paulo Freire has remarked, 'it would be naive to expect oppressor elites to denounce the myth which absolutizes the ignorance of the people.'[32] The issue is that epistemic injustice can operate as a seemingly invisible injustice, as epistemic inequality has been normalized, in that Western knowledge systems that dominate are built upon a notion of rationality 'seen as principled, fair, and neutral. In comparison, Indigenous knowledge systems are often seen as deficient because they are perceived as faith-based "religious systems" and/or as the more primitive forms of cultural knowledge associated with "tribal" groups.'[33] Distributive justice in relation to epistemic injustice, particularly in the context of Christian theology and mission, therefore involves the sharing of indigenous knowledge as a means of testimonial justice – so that the theologies and experiences of those who have been marginalized by dominant discourses of Eurocentric epistemology become speaking subjects in theological education, church and society.

The continued 'injustice in the distribution of the epistemic good of knowledge' also applies to the experiences of those in the majority world, where there exists unequal access to education and resources. This has been made even more apparent during the COVID-19 pandemic where the digital divide has become even more apparent.[34] Noting the role of technology in distributive justice, particularly in light of epistemic injustice, is of great significance in contemporary society. However, as a result of structural inequalities, 'low-income households, people of colour, older people', as well as indigenous communities, people in the global south and rural communities in particular, are on the wrong side of the digital divide. Furthermore, many people around the world continue not to have access to the Internet. This is of great significance to distributive justice, given that the Internet is a main source for information and knowledge sharing; it also means that there is increasing epistemic injustice affecting communities that have throughout history experienced marginalization. Contemporary Christian mission that seeks to take the side of the oppressed must be 'prepared to rethink technology from the ground up, rather than naively recirculate the forms of technology given to us'.[35] In doing so, theology and digital science enter into a dialogue where the silenced epistemologies of the indigenous communities and other marginalized people are privileged as a means of distributive justice, as a means of sharing different ways of expressing scientific and theological knowledge. Addressing such realities as the digital divide in the work of decolonizing theological education is vital as it is not possible to redistribute knowledge without addressing the unequal access to resources, technologies and knowledge sharing, noting that the structural inequalities with regard to digital technologies perpetuate social and economic disparities in society. The digital divide, according to Mossberger and colleagues, consists of multiple divisions including 'an access divide, a skills divide, an economic opportunity divide, and a democratic divide',[36] and I would like to add to this – an epistemic divide. Based upon the fact that if already marginalized groups of people are missing from online spaces, so too is their 'knowledge' that is in itself an act of digital dehumanization.[37]

If we are to take seriously the implications of centuries of racist epistemic injustice within Christian missiology, theology and ethnography, we must consciously work for epistemic justice and make use of all resources available for the dissemination of knowledge today. The British philosopher John Rawls, in his argument for distributive justice, outlined that 'inequalities in the distribution of primary goods, such as knowledge, can be acceptable, but only if such inequalities are to the advantage of the least well off, such as the information have-nots'.[38] This is particularly relevant when we come to addressing access to theological resources, inclusive of journal access and online networks – as such networks, including networks of scholars, have the potential to create global communities of solidarity and resistance, where collectively theologians who seek to give voice to the marginalized can share tools for decolonizing curricula. This will require the redistribution of knowledge in learning resources, publications, online spaces and curricula; however, given that such spaces were often created by and dominated by the most well off, such distributive justice will not be a simple task. It is also a matter of asking whose knowledge is visible and what are the theological consequences of the lacuna of silenced epistemologies in such spaces of resource sharing.

In efforts to redistribute theological knowledge in theological education, it will also be necessary to give a great deal of focus to decolonizing the curriculum and encouraging critical pedagogies that allow for the space to challenge the churches' colonial history. There is therefore a need to be more subversive in higher education, in order to privilege the voices of silenced epistemologies and spaces of learning, including curricula and pedagogy, where the epistemologies of the indigenous and subaltern are centred – not sidelined as some sort of 'tourist attraction' theology, for the curious Western scholar to sneer at through the same lens that diminished the embodied theologies and epistemologies of the colonialized. If theological education is to address the sins of colonialism through distributive justice, there is also a need to repent for the silencing of the languages of the indigenous communities, by encouraging spaces for theological sharing in all languages. Theologies from the majority world must not only be acknowledged but also redistributed through a process of decolonization, to learn and relearn from the perspective of marginalized communities: to share the uncomfortable aspects of our histories, and collectively resist the systems that continue to silence the global oppressed. Decolonizing theological education as an act of distributive justice therefore involves an epistemological shift in our understanding of the discipline of Christian theology in order to challenge normative ways of knowing that have silenced epistemologies from the majority world. Central to such decolonial efforts is solidarity; as Boaventura de Sousa Santos outlines, 'solidarity is the knowing obtained in the ever-unfinished process of one becoming capable of reciprocity through the construction and recognition of intersubjectivity. The emphasis on solidarity converts community into the privileged sphere of emancipatory knowledge.'[39] Such solidarity goes beyond the transformation of curricula; it involves addressing the cultures of academic spaces of learning, including pedagogies that have consciously and subconsciously created a hierarchy of knowledge production that is fundamentally unjust and operates to the detriment of Black and ethnic minority voices and bodies.

Conclusion

The injustice of the colonialization of the mind is one of the gravest injustices that has been committed against the majority world. Colonialism under the British empire dehumanized entire populations and enabled an 'epistemicide' – in other words, the killing and annihilation of systems of knowledge.[40] The mission histories of the British empire expose the racism and White ignorance at the heart of such systemic acts, where colonial conquests, including Christian missions, ideologically sought to colonize both the minds and bodies of entire populations. The same ideologies continue to dominate in theological education today, where certain voices and ways of knowing are both consciously and subconsciously missing from curricula and not acknowledged as being of equal worth in Christian thought. This presents us with a world in which the power and privilege of colonialism and empire continue to define accepted ways of knowing. Yet by making use of all resources of learning available, including curricula, online learning platforms, networks and pedagogies, it is possible to work towards distributive justice. The redistribution of knowledge in theological education through a process of decolonization is required as an act of repentance for the epistemic injustice of the colonial mission era. In agreement with de Sousa Santos, 'global social injustice is therefore intimately linked to global cognitive injustice. The struggle for global social justice will, therefore, be a struggle for cognitive justice as well.'[41] Such struggle involves learning from multiple ways of knowing, and affirming knowledge that has been oppressed and marginalized in theological education, as a means of justice.

Notes

1 This quote is from a Church Mission Society (CMS) missionary writing in Ceylon, India, under the subheading 'On the obstacles to the propagation of Christianity in India'. The words capture the systemic shaming of the colonial missions that degraded the minds, bodies and religions of the indigenous communities. See 1833, *Statement of the Ceylon Mission of the Church Missionary Society for the Year M.DCCCXXXII eds. Rev J. Bailey*, Ceylon: Church Mission Press, p. 35.

2 Sangeeta Dasgupta, '"Heathen Aboriginals", "Christian Tribes", and "Animistic Races": Missionary Narratives on the Oraons of Chhotanagpur in Colonial India', *Modern Asian Studies*, 50(2) (2016), pp. 444–5.

3 Dasgupta, 'Heathen Aboriginals', p. 445.

4 John M. Cinnamon, 'Missionary Expertise, Social Science, and the Uses of Ethnographic Knowledge in Colonial Gabon', *History in Africa*, 33 (2006), pp. 413–32, 418.

5 Cinnamon, 'Missionary Expertise', p. 427.

6 Edwin Smith, a twentieth-century missionary and anthropologist in Africa, for example, noted, 'the need for an application of scientific method to a solution of the questions arising generally from the contact of Western civilisation with African culture'.

7 See Dasgupta, 'Heathen Aboriginals', pp. 437–78.

8 Nasir Uddin, 'Decolonising Ethnography in the Field: An Anthropological Account', *International Journal of Social Research Methodology*, 14(6) (2011), pp. 455–67, 459.

9 Epistemic injustice includes, but is not limited to, books, online databases and journals, where dissemination of existing knowledge is unequally distributed. The distribution of knowledge, in agreement with Irzik and Kurtulmus, refers to 'the production of knowledge, its dissemination, and ensuring that people have the capability to assimilate what is disseminated by providing them with the necessary educational background and intellectual skills'. See Gürol Irzik and Faik Kurtulmus, 'Distributive Epistemic Justice in Science', *The British Journal for the Philosophy of Science* (2021), p. 3.

10 E. O. McMahon, 1914, *Christian Missions in Madagascar*, Westminster: The Society for the Propagation of the Gospel in Foreign Parts, p. 75.

11 Miranda Fricker, 2016, 'Epistemic Injustice and the Preservation of Ignorance' in Rik Peels and Martijn Blaauw (eds), *The Epistemic Dimensions of Ignorance*, Cambridge: Cambridge University Press, pp. 144–59, 152.

12 Walter D. Mignolo, 'Epistemic Disobedience, Independent Thought and Decolonial Freedom', *Theory, Culture & Society*, 26(7–8) (2009), pp. 159–81, 161.

13 McMahon, *Christian Missions in Madagascar*, p. 24.

14 McMahon, *Christian Missions in Madagascar*, p. 27.

15 See Kathy Squadrito, 'Locke and the Dispossession of the American Indian', *American Indian Culture and Research Journal*, 20(4) (1996), pp. 145–81.

16 Rebecca Tsosie, 2017, 'Indigenous Peoples, Anthropology, and the Legacy of Epistemic Injustice' in Ian James Kidd, José Medina and Gaile Pohlhaus (eds), *The Routledge Handbook of Epistemic Injustice*, New York: Routledge, p. 358.

17 Tsosie, 'Indigenous Peoples', p. 358.

18 McMahon, *Christian Missions*, pp. 46–8.

19 McMahon, *Christian Missions*, p. 57.

20 Social scientists at the time relied on the support of missionaries in their research efforts yet also criticized them in the process; Herskovits, for example, 'praises missionaries for bringing literacy to Africans but criticises them for undermining their cultural values'. The lack of awareness of the social scientists displays the arrogance of Western epistemology in failing to recognize how European literacy also undermined the indigenous cultural values. See Sjaak van der Geest and Jon P. Kirby, 'The Absence of the Missionary in African Ethnography, 1930–65', *African Studies Review*, 35(3) (1992), pp. 59–103, 65.

21 See Mignolo, 'Epistemic Disobedience', p. 161.

22 Tsosie, 'Indigenous Peoples', p. 357.

23 Shirley J. Dickins, 1910, *Grenfell of the Congo: Pioneer Missionary and Explorer*, London: Sunday School Union, p. 26.

24 Edwin Etieyibo, 2018, *Decolonisation, Africanisation and the Philosophy Curriculum*, New York: Routledge, p. 46.

25 Etieyibo, *Decolonisation*, p. 46.

26 Miranda Fricker, 2007, *Epistemic Injustice: Power and the Ethics of Knowing*, Oxford: Oxford University Press, p. 1.

27 Tsosie, 'Indigenous Peoples', pp. 358–9.

28 Edward W. Said, 2003, *Orientalism* (25th anniversary edition), New York: Random House, p. 335.

29 Irzik and Kurtulmus, 'Distributive Epistemic Justice', p. 4.

30 See Mignolo, 'Epistemic Disobedience', p. 162.

31 See Cathrine Holst, 'Global Gender Justice: Distributive Justice or Participatory Parity?', ARENA Working Paper 3 (2019), p. 3.

32 Paulo Freire, 1970, *Pedagogy of the Oppressed*, London: Heinemann, p. 134.
33 Tsosie, 'Indigenous Peoples', p. 360.
34 D. Coady, 'Two Concepts of Epistemic Injustice', *Episteme*, 7(2) (2010), pp. 101–13, 112.
35 Kavita Philip, quoted in 'Centering Knowledge from the Margins: Our Embodied Practices of Epistemic Resistance and Revolution', *International Feminist Journal of Politics*, 22(1) (2020), pp. 6–25.
36 K. Mossberger, C. J. Tolbert and M. Stansbury, 2003, *Virtual Inequality: Beyond the Digital Divide*, Washington DC: Georgetown University Press, p. 2.
37 Cythnia K. Sanders and Edward Scanlon, 'The Divide is a Human Rights Issue: Advancing Social Inclusion Through Social Work Advocacy', *Journal of Human Rights and Social Work*, 6 (2021), pp. 130–43, 131.
38 See Don Fallis, 'Social Epistemology and the Digital Divide', *Conferences in Research and Practice in Information Technology*, 37 (2004), p. 82.
39 Boaventura de Sousa Santos, 2017, *Decolonsising the University: The Challenge of Deep Cognitive Justice*, London: Cambridge Scholars Publishing, p. 61.
40 See Beth Patin, 'Interrupting Epistemicide: A Practical Framework for Naming, Identifying, and Ending Epistemic Injustice in the Information Professions', *Special Issue: Paradigm Shift in the Field of Information*, 72(10) (2021), pp. 1306–18.
41 Boaventura de Sousa Santos, 'Beyond Abyssal Thinking: From Global Lines to Ecologies of Knowledge', *Eurozine*, 33 (2007), pp. 45–89, 63.

4

Dealing with the Two Deadly Ds: Deconstructing Whiteness and Decolonizing the Curriculum of Theological Education

ANTHONY G. REDDIE

Deconstructing Whiteness

My point of departure in this chapter is the deeply embedded nature of empire and surreptitious Whiteness that foreshadows the existence of Christianity across its 2,000-year history.[1] One needs to acknowledge the necessity of recognizing issues of power in the construction of epistemology. For three-quarters of her life, the church was the primary institution that helped to define truth and the rationale for what it meant to be human. Central to this framing of epistemology has been the power of Whiteness.[2]

Willie James Jennings's *After Whiteness: An Education in Belonging* is an important text that explores how this phenomenon has informed Christianity and the development of Christian theology. The church, as the primary institution that helped to define truth and the rationale for what it meant to be human, was central to this framing of epistemology. At the centre of this framing was – and remains – the power of Whiteness.[3] This, allied to the belief in the 'Divine Right of Kings',[4] creates a synergy between the church and political power that reinforces the epistemological weight of ecclesial authority. Theological education and ministerial training[5] are shaped in and by this framework. Willie James Jennings's long-awaited sequel to his highly significant *The Christian Imagination: Theology and the Origins of Race*[6] seeks to explore the ways in which Whiteness has become the template on which theological education and broader Western education have been dominated by this phenomenon.

In *After Whiteness*, Jennings critiques the phenomenon of Whiteness, arguing that the conflation of European mastery, White male, colonial power and the internalization of notions of White superiority become the means by which epistemology is developed.[7] Jennings illustrates how Whiteness became conjoined with patriarchy and colonialism to unleash an ethic of mastery, self-sufficiency and control as the defining elements for what constitutes notions of development and progress. Jennings's work, which is aimed primarily at theological education, distils the means by which the production of knowledge and pedagogical insights on the craft of ministry have been informed by coloniality and Whiteness. Jennings is clear that this analysis is not about White people per se. Rather, it is the epistemological underpinning of a set of theo-cultural constructs, systems and practices that govern how theology and education operate in the West and which inform our ways of being and our praxis.[8]

In charting the epistemological framing of this work, Jennings outlines the intentionality of this text as that which is seeking to reform and reconceptualize the very nature of theological education. In outlining what is at stake he writes: 'The argument for cultural sovereignty in theological education grows out of collapsing the struggle against whiteness into a struggle for personhood. This is understandable, given the ways whiteness has historically destroyed a reality of people for so many groups.'[9]

One of the many great insights I take from this work is the extent to which a cult of mastery, self-sufficiency and top-down notions of patrician control, all executed under the aegis of Whiteness, has stymied the emotional and intellectual agency of people racialized as White as much as it has traduced those racialized as the 'other'.

The whole of Jennings's book, in many respects, is summed up in chapter 1, which is titled 'Fragments'. Like the remainder of the book, the author uses poetry, narrative vignettes and theological reflection in order to outline the problems in how a neo-colonial ethic of Whiteness has impacted the task of forming men and women into the mind of Christ through the medium of theological education. *After Whiteness* deploys an eclectic set of optics by which our gaze on to the mechanics of theological education is laid bare. What comes into clear view is the way in which the phenomenological framing of Whiteness has become the template on which all our axiomatic assumptions on what constitutes theological normality are predicated. This ethic of neo-colonial mastery, which represents the foundational creation of Whiteness, finds expression in a variety of modes, be they Christian formation, pedagogy, the intellectual expertise of one's subject, content of curricula purity or the ethic of patronage around candidature for ministry.

The power of Whiteness finds expression in a great deal of Western intellectual discourse,[10] where there is often little or no attempt to locate the various positionalities of the writer and how their subjectivity might influence the nature of their reflections. In Christian theology many attempts have been made to studiously avoid engaging with embodied difference, especially if that difference is reflected in White bodies. When I was an undergraduate student in Church History at the University of Birmingham in the mid- to late 1980s, we spent a great deal of time looking at the writings of great luminaries such as Martin Luther, John Calvin, among others. At no point were they ever racialized – that is, ever described as 'White authors' or 'White thinkers'. These individuals were simply 'authors' or 'thinkers'. Their ideas were generic and, most importantly, they had universal implications for all peoples.

In my long history within theological education, the underlying theme that has informed the teaching and learning of Christian theology and ministry has been one of Whiteness. It has always been the proverbial elephant in the room, but rarely seen or acknowledged, no matter how loudly it trumpeted its presence and no matter the amount of waste matter it produced. If we look at the subterranean constructs of British theological education, there is no attempt to locate the ethnic and cultural positionality of the authors, as if there is no relationship between the formative identity of the creator of knowledge and the construction of that knowledge. As I have indicated in a previous book, this form of generic universalism is where theological ideas are developed with little in the way of contextual specificity and reflexivity identified in the work.[11]

After Whiteness stands as a paradigmatic text within the context of theological discourse for the ways in which it seeks to bring academic theology into conversation with the wider arena of 'Critical White Studies'. The latter tradition, operating largely through the aegis of sociology and cultural studies, history and anthropology, has begun the task of naming and unmasking the privileged construct that is 'Whiteness'. Whiteness operates as an overarching construct, which assumes a central place in all epistemological and cultural forms of production, thereby relegating other positions or perspectives as 'other'. While this work is more commonplace in Cultural Studies and Sociology, it remains in its infancy within academic theology and theological education.

The substantive challenge of engaging with Whiteness is the necessity to seek to provide an imaginative account of exposing the shadowy hinterland of the phenomenological agency that is Whiteness. Central to this process is 'Decentring Whiteness'. Decentring is a process of changing the point of focus for the articulation of experience and the production of knowledge. In this new epistemological enterprise, the initial point of departure is no longer the centre, but a subversive and systematic shift to the margins.[12]

Given the centrality of Whiteness in academic theological articulation, one cannot underestimate the significance and importance of wrestling with this phenomenon as it pertains to theological education in the UK. There has been a long historical relationship between the church, theological education and Whiteness. Part of the power of Whiteness as it pertains to epistemology in general, and Christian theology in particular, is what I have termed previously 'generic universalism',[13] which only seeks to mask the presumption that the authors of major intellectual work are actually White and not some ghostly apparition that has no embodied reality in itself.[14] My critique of Whiteness is as a macro epistemological framework for privilege and superiority, sometimes even triumphant supremacy. This first conversation is principally about the development of ideas and discursive practices as opposed to the subjectivities and positionalities of White people per se. I am not arguing that every White person is imbued with either power or privilege – particularly of the economic kind in terms of the latter. But what I am interested in and trying to assert in this exploratory chapter are the ways in which Whiteness operates as a tacit, concealed form of normative framing for what we have come to know as truth, especially that which contains a universal posture to its ideological claims for itself.

Decolonizing the curriculum

One of the difficulties in seeking to decolonize the theological curriculum lies in the ways in which generic universalism is built into how we see and assess philosophical ideas. Christian theology, often called 'The Queen of the Sciences' has been in operation for nearly 2,000 years now, and in that time it has imbibed the invisible constructs of Whiteness to the point where attempts to deconstruct its historic edifice would lead to the complete demise of the whole enterprise. Of course, there will be many who will argue that the complete demise of the abstract, theological enterprise of the West that has given us collusion with slavery, colonialism and White supremacy is no bad thing. I have some sympathy with this view, but given that I am a practical theologian, whose work is often focused on issues of pragmatism and assessing what is possible, I am of the opinion that the academic and ecclesial establishment will not be voting for the necessary deconstructionist overhaul of theological education any time soon.

Decolonizing the curriculum in its broadest sense is the deconstruction of the normative frameworks of the established canon of Western intellectual work, in order to remove the contamination and desecration of knowledge and truth that has been impacted by White supremacy, which in turn arose from the phenomena of empire and colonialism. The best analogy for decolonizing the curriculum comes from the brilliant utterances of the Revd Dr Jeremiah Wright Jr, the emeritus pastor-scholar of Trinity United Church of Christ in Chicago. Wright gives the analogy of someone baking a cake and forgetting to put any sugar into the initial mix. Upon putting the completed baked cake on a tray and cutting the first piece, the baker of this cake realizes their mistake in not adding any sugar. In order to rectify their mistake, they begin to smear honey, icing sugar and an assortment of other sweeteners on top of the cake in order to make the cake more edible. As Wright notes, this form of cosmetic correction does nothing to change the substance of the cake. Plus, the additional sweeteners on the top of the cake can soon be brushed off if and when the moment arises, when others think that these cosmetic, last-minute, token additions have outstayed their usefulness. What is really needed, asserts Wright, is for the cake to be dismantled, thrown away and started all over again. This time, with an increased intentionality that the correct ingredients are put into the mix before the cake is put in the oven.[15]

Wright uses this analogy as a means to critique the various amendments added to the basic US Constitution, arguing that these later additions are like putting sweeteners on to the top of a cake that was baked without a crucial ingredient in the mix. These later additions do not change the basic constitution of the cake itself. Wright's point is that the US Constitution was not created with justice in mind for people of colour, be they enslaved African Americans or First Nation, or Native Americans. Adding sweeteners to the top of the cake no more makes the cake itself edible than adding various amendments to a constitution that was never created with them in mind gives justice to minority ethnic groups in the nation.

Dismantling the cake and starting again is the only true recourse for those seeking to bring about a wholesale and comprehensive justice for minority ethnic people in the USA. Similarly, when borrowing Wright's metaphor for the task of decolonizing the curriculum, one can see that the only serious recourse for academic theology and theological education is that of dismantling an inedible confectionery that never had Black or Global Majority Heritage (GMH) people in mind when it was being created. It was created to serve the needs of White Europeans.

Given the investment of White people and White-run institutions in building and defending this edifice, I do not expect anyone is in any hurry to dismantle it any time soon. Therefore, my more pragmatic and stealthy proposal is to get a syringe and to inject the necessary sweeteners into the cake from various positions. This is the middle way between its complete deconstruction and the cosmetic attempts to diversify the curriculum in terms of adding new, optional, 'contextual' courses that can soon be removed, much like clearing the sweeteners off the top of a sugarless cake. That is, normality can soon be maintained once the fad of attempting to appear 'woke' has worn off.

My proposal for decolonizing the curriculum is the metaphorical attempt to inject Black and postcolonial perspectives into a White-dominated edifice in which the blandishments of Whiteness have held centre stage for so long.

Recognizing the problem in the first place

One of the earliest ways in which the productive power of Whiteness that dominates educational curricula first impacted on my consciousness emerged when looking at the world of literature. Long before I began my work in theological education, I was a callow youth undertaking my studies in A-level English at Tong Comprehensive school on the outskirts of Bradford, West Yorkshire. I had chosen to undertake a course in English literature, but on commencing the course I was struck at once by the universal 'Whiteness' of all the literature on view within the syllabus. A few months into the course, I discovered the writing of Chinua Achebe. His landmark novel *Things Fall Apart*[16] was described as a brilliant African novel. Achebe writes about the social and cultural world of which he is a part. It is one of the first great postcolonial novels. It was soon made clear to me that Achebe was *only* an African writer. His work was important, for it shed light upon a particular community and cultural reality in postmodern, post-independence Africa. But I was intrigued that Achebe's work was limited in this way, as a result of the precise milieu in which he was located and the particularity of his reflections upon that specific context. And yet the same limitations and parameters were not placed upon Jane Austen and her work, which I had to endure for the two years of that course.

Why was the precise, particular social and cultural milieu of Austen worthy of universal application and celebration? The world in which she is located, and which serves as the basis for her work, is no more universal and transcendent of context than that of Achebe. Austen's world is universal because it is located within the wider framework of Whiteness. Austen's Whiteness makes her universal. So if Austen is universal and her work speaks of an enduring truth about the human condition that transcends context or particularity, then equally so does the work of, say, Karl Barth, but not James Cone. Why is it that a White man in theology or a White woman in literature can be read as having universal application or what I am calling generic universalism? Irrespective of context or socio-political and cultural positionality, the power of generic universalism becomes the means by which orthodoxy is imposed on a world in which theological heterogeneity has always been in evidence. We see this in the apposite words of the great Robert E. Hood in *Must God Remain Greek?*, and by 'Greek', Hood really means 'White'. A generic universal text does not need to name its particularity. Rather, it simply assumes a normative position for its unspoken Whiteness, by resorting to generic patterns of abstract philosophizing, as it addresses context-less concerns that affect all people.

The invisibility of Whiteness in the positionality and abstract ways in which knowledge is constructed can be juxtaposed with the invisibility of Blackness, even when the proponent of one's study is thought to be Black. This was the case when I studied St Augustine as an undergraduate. In my studies in Church History, I do not recall one moment when studying St Augustine when we discussed his ethnicity and cultural point of departure. In more recent times, more conservative church historians have argued that incorporating racialized terms like Black to a pre-modern human subject is unhelpful, as Augustine himself would not have thought of himself as Black. That is indeed true. The purpose of posing the question about his ethnicity is less to do with the historicity of this 'fact' as it is to do with why so many White historians are so resolute in their desire not to broach this. Why do we so often read his words out of context as if his social and cultural milieu had little or no impact on his intellectual ideas?

Nothing about Augustine's context was ever discussed. But when studying Martin Luther, one of the great religious reformers, we had to know his context. One professor even proudly opined that one could not understand the radicalism of Luther's work *without understanding his context*. Why? Was context important in the latter case but not in the former? I believe this is the case because we cannot argue with Augustine's genius, and believing that Africa is a 'dark continent', in which people are barbaric and uncivilized, must mean that his genius has nothing at all to do with the ethnic and cultural world from which he came. He must be 'atypical'; knowledge is embodied but Whiteness removes itself and operates as an invisible norm. Knowledge construction by White people of European descent is superior, generic and universal. It is built on notions of mastery and control. Augustine and many of the early church 'Fathers' of the Patristic period were most likely people whose ethnic origin would see them deemed to be 'people of colour' in our postmodern context, and yet they are taught as people without any embodiment, *as if they were White*.[17]

Decentring Whiteness

Decentring is a process of changing the point of focus for the articulation of experience and the production of knowledge. In this new epistemological enterprise, the initial point of departure is no longer the centre, but is instead a subversive and systematic shift to the margins.[18]

Reflecting on my subjective agency, I have reflected on the ways in which a predominantly White society like the UK has a penchant for stigmatizing Black males like myself. Black people in general – and Black men in particular – are often perceived and treated as immoral degenerates. We are troublemakers and undesirables, but some of us, of course, *can* be acceptable. If we have the right accent, can mimic the cultural mores of polite White bourgeois society, then we too can be invited to a seat at the table of theological education. Much like my African American peers, people like Willie James Jennings and I have become assimilated insiders, having been granted admission to the inner edifice of neo-colonized Whiteness. Some of us are now deemed sufficiently 'civilized' in order to gain access to the respectable world of bourgeois learning within the carefully calibrated White world of self-sufficient, pseudo intellectual mastery that is theological education. Decentring is to pose potentially 'dangerous' questions – and perhaps, less dramatically, difficult ones – around who gets to frame the rules of belonging, around which Whiteness has enveloped itself, creating and then framing the nature of being.

To what extent Black theological educators can seek an alternative substantive form of subjective identity and existential agency to provide oppositional archetypes that can challenge the normative hinterland of hierarchical, top-down forms of White, male, neo-colonial modes of intellectual learning remains a moot point. It is now over 50 years since the great Paulo Freire reminded us of corruptions of the 'Banking Model' of education that continues to be the norm in most educational settings across the world.[19] Freire's groundbreaking work in devising appropriate pedagogies for teaching marginalized and oppressed peoples is legendary.[20] Freire developed a philosophy of education that challenged poor and oppressed people to reflect upon their individual and corporate experiences and begin to ask critical questions about the nature of their existence. The radical nature of this critical approach to the task of teaching and learning brought Freire to the attention of the military government in Brazil in 1964. He was subsequently imprisoned and then exiled. In exile, he began to refine further his educational philosophy and method.

In *Pedagogy of the Oppressed*, Freire laid the foundations for a seismic shift in the whole conception of how poor, oppressed and marginalized people might be educated. In the realms of critical pedagogy and theological education, Freire's ideas are credited with being an invaluable source for Gustavo Gutiérrez's groundbreaking *A Theology of Liberation*, and the basis for a committed and ideologically driven theology of and for the poor. Freire's later work with the World Council of Churches throughout the 1970s and 1980s as an international consultant led to his work becoming hugely significant in many parts of the world, especially among poor and oppressed peoples in the global south.

The importance of Paulo Freire cannot be overstated. In developing a rigorous and critical approach to the task of educating those who are poor and oppressed, Freire created an essential template by which religious educators and practical theologians might reconceptualize their task. One of Freire's central concepts was that of 'conscientization'. This is a process whereby poor and oppressed people become politically aware of the circumstances in which they live and the ways in which their humanity is infringed upon and blighted by the often dehumanizing contexts that surround them.[21] Allen J. Moore, commenting on this aspect of Freire's work, says:

> Conscientization in Freire's work is apparently both an individual experience and a shared experience of a people who are acting together in history. A way of life is not determined from thinking about the world but is formed from the shared praxis. In this critical approach to the world, basic attitudes, values, and beliefs are formed and a people are humanized or liberated. Conscientization, therefore, leads to a life lived with consciousness of history, a life lived that denounces and transforms this history in order to form a new way of life for those who are oppressed.[22]

Freire's approach to education has opened up new vistas for religious educators, along with pastoral and practical theologians. His work contains a profound humanizing spirit that draws extensively upon his Roman Catholic upbringing and catechesis. For one who would not consider himself a theologian or a religious educator, Freire's work has always been marked by a firm, implicit theistic content. This became increasingly visible as his writings matured and he advanced in years. John Elias, in his assessment of Freire as a religious educator, states:

> The religious element in Freire's social philosophy has become increasingly more explicit in later writings and speeches. He sees the Christian Gospel as proclaiming the radical re-ordering of society in which men [*sic*] are oppressed ... Christians who involve themselves in revolution-

ary action against oppression involve themselves in a new Passover, a new Easter.[23]

Freire's concern for the radical and revolutionary intent of education as the basis for socio-political change forms the underlying epistemological framework for my pedagogical approach to teaching and engaging in Practical theology.

Having read and re-read Jennings's *After Whiteness* one is forced to wonder about the extent to which the insights of Freire, and the critical challenge presented by *Pedagogy of the Oppressed*, have been largely bypassed by the rigid conforming to post-Enlightenment notions of patrician control of disciplines, curricula and notions of untrammelled intellectual expertise of the teacher. The Banking Model of education is alive and well and rumours of its demise have been greatly exaggerated. In many respects, the epitome of this symbiotic relationship can be found in the existence of Common Awards.

British theological education and the implications for Common Awards

Common Awards arose out of the concerns of the House of Bishops and Ministry Division of the Church of England to provide a centralized curriculum for theological education and ministerial training. It was agreed that the academic oversight of the curriculum would be held at Durham University.[24] Common Awards is the normative framework for Anglican ministerial training and many of its ecumenical partners who work with the Church of England in theological partnerships.

I want to reflect for a few moments on the epistemological significance of this for Common Awards in light of Willie James Jennings's *After Whiteness*. Given the centralizing of the curriculum both in its location within a historic university like Durham – and also in terms of the framework that is underpinned by episcopal power and acceptance – one has to wonder to what extent the curriculum itself is one that is replete with the very kinds of bourgeois respectability one finds replete in all forms of neo-colonial theological enterprises.

One of the central claims of *After Whiteness* is that the epistemological power of the phenomenological basis of Whiteness lies in its centralizing, imperialistic control of theological curricula. To what extent can theological education be decolonized when, as social science scholars have reminded us, most social institutions remain captive to a phenomenon identified as a 'Hierarchy of Credibility'. This refers to a ranking of epistemological power in which people's accounts of truth are attested to according to their place in social and ecclesial hierarchies.[25] Part of the additional problems elicited by theological education in the UK is that the very construction of Christian epistemology reifies the embedded constructs of Whiteness that have controlled Christian theology for a millennium. Discernment and training are often overlaid by metaphysics – what some scholars called pneumatological pedagogy, where the Spirit guides human activity and knowing in order to reveal the truth of God's desires.[26] And yet, as Jennings demonstrates, the hermeneutical processes that govern how we deconstruct the privileging of knowledge and bodies within Western institutions are anything but a neutral affair.[27] The ways in which institutions have reified the tropes of White, hetero-normative patriarchy are embedded so deeply that it should come as no surprise that most of those engaged in the enterprise of Christian theology do not see it.

Consider this insight from Jennings on the functional life of most theological institutions and the role of gatekeepers in policing the parameters of acceptability and acceptance in the institution:

> Here the white gatekeeper moves inside psychic space haunting interpretations of work and professional life and interrupting genuine self-affirmation. I have known too many scholars who have fallen into an abyss of critique or concealment against critique, moving through the academy in constant shadowboxing, throwing punches at anyone and everyone, bobbing and weaving, bracing for the impact of words that will surely sting.[28]

What I take from this comment are the ways in which theologians and students, engaged within the construct of Christian formation, are always invariably on their guard, seeking to defend themselves from the brickbats of others, as we all jostle for acceptance and visibility within institutional life that is built on an ethic of patronage.

The hierarchical framing of power that is replete within the 'Hierarchy of Credibility' is one that is informed by human power, which we believe is verified by God. Because the ethic underlying theological education and ministerial training is shaped by the wider epistemological frameworks of patronage, via a hierarchy of credibility, this means that those wishing to be inducted into the existing norms (that is, joining the club) must convince others of their fitness to do so.[29] As *After Whiteness* demonstrates, the coloniality of Whiteness that finds expression in the outworking of patronage, in which patriarchy, hierarchical epistemology, and the coloniality of Whiteness, coupled with concomitant notions of mastery and self-sufficiency, are conjoined to dictate who is accepted and is acceptable and who is not. Applying Jennings to the bourgeois processes of discernment and the selection of ministerial candidates in the UK system of theological education is to remind ourselves of the absolute respectability politics that drench the whole enterprise within a preferential option for middle-class White people. In this regard, our processes are the antithesis of the radicalism espoused in the iconic scholarship of the late great Marcella Althaus-Reid and her work in *Indecent Theology*.[30] UK theological education, operating largely under the aegis of the patronage of the Church of England as it is constituted within the framework of 'Common Awards', is in many respects the antithesis of Althaus-Reid's notion of the 'indecent'. It is an exercise in neo-colonial rubrics of bourgeois acceptability politics.

While we have a criterion that is often predicated on the tripartite norms of 'Being', 'Knowing' and 'Doing', with historical, spiritual and theological markers for determining what these are, the emphasis is often on replication of existing norms, by means of continuity and conformity. It is why the church has struggled to embrace changes in the demographics of those wanting to 'join the club', whether such ministerial students or those in the process of theological formation are Black or Asian, LGBTQI, working class or women. Given the aforementioned, it is no surprise that Black and other minority ethnic peoples, and those defined as transgressive figures, are often not chosen. Patronage ensures that 'problematic' types are rejected, or accepted predicated on the expectation that they will conform.[31]

The essential question is whether Common Awards is the very type of constructed artifice that cannot help but reify the tropes of neo-colonialism and the means by which subliminal Whiteness is often built into the very edifice of the corporate whole.[32] Given the aforementioned, Common Awards has the problem of trying to effect transformative models of teaching and learning within an ethic of colonial, top-down control. Some religious educators have always argued that theological curricula are more concerned with Christian 'instruction' than with 'education', given the existing norms to which learners or students are expected to adhere.[33] How can Common Awards support a decolonized and anti-oppressive curriculum given the wider historic epistemological framework to which it is beholden?

Yes, I accept that there are modules that reflect the existential positionality of those formative experiences or ancestries that emerge from the global south, but it could be argued that they are nothing more substantive than the 'epistemological margins' when compared to the generic universalism of the 'normative standard'. Yes, *some people* can study World Christianity or 'Theologies from the Majority World', but the 'generic universalism' of such disciplines as 'Doctrine', 'Biblical Studies' or 'Church History' reflects the compulsory subjects that are often predicated on a form of White, Eurocentric hegemony.[34] I still remember visiting a well-known university where a senior member of staff, an established biblical scholar, was forced to admit that he had never heard of the recently deceased African American biblical scholar Cain Hope Felder, nor his younger counterpart, the equally brilliant Randall Bailey. Of course, he had heard of N. T. Wright and James Dunn, and of course their work had to be taught, but clearly not that of Felder[35] or Bailey,[36] or Brian Blount,[37] Mitzi Smith,[38] Will Gafney,[39] Musa Dube[40] or Annie Tinsley[41] and others. Most crucially, his lack of knowledge of *any* Black biblical scholars was no impediment to a highly successful academic career. The same could be said of many White systematic theologians and ethicists for that matter.

Reflecting on my own recent research and considerations, I want to offer three important moves by which the curriculum of theological education and ministerial training might be decolonized.

Practical solutions

Affirming reflexivity

Given the ways in which Whiteness is embedded within the epistemological norms of Common Awards and indeed in wider academic theology, I believe it is imperative that all existing courses and the people who teach them be informed by an acute sense of reflexivity. What are the norms that are taken for granted? In what ways is the normative power of Whiteness influencing the discourse for how the subject is being taught? What are the ways in which 'contextual' ideas and religio-cultural particularities are being read as generic universals?

Decentring Whiteness

How do we recognize the power dynamics between the 'standard' normative perspectives and those that are considered marginal and optional? What gets to be seen as standard and in what ways is that simply reifying the tropes of colonialism and that of embedded Whiteness? How do we assert the significance of the particular as a way of understanding the universal, rather than the converse, which tends to be the means by which curriculum development is undertaken?[42]

In my 2017 co-edited book *Journeying to Justice*, a group of Baptist scholars, activists and I sought to retell the story of a 200-year relationship between the British Baptist Union and the Jamaica Baptist Union.⁴³ In the official narrative, the history of the Jamaican work starts with White missionaries from England, such as John Rowe from the Bristol Academy (now Bristol Baptist College), who travels from England to Jamaica in order to start the official work in 1814. However, the Baptist work in Jamaica does not start with John Rowe. It actually starts with George Liele and Moses Baker, enslaved Africans, who in the 1880s started the Baptist work on the island, but fused Christianity with African epistemologies and indigenous African practices that many modern Jamaican Baptists still find uncomfortable. This is especially the case in light of what Toussaint L'Ouverture and others had done in using *Vodun* – voodoo in popular parlance – as their means of creating a philosophy and identity with which to overthrow their White French colonial masters and create the first Black republic in the West in 1804.⁴⁴

Decolonizing theological education is the recognition that the construction of recognized doctrines of Christianity has been influenced by, and overlaid with, White Eurocentric norms that have reified White bodies and denigrated Black ones. In the context of the development of Caribbean Christianity, for example (part of my own heritage), it means the rehabilitation of Black, African-derived religious sensibilities that have been demonized and pathologized for centuries by White Mission Christianity.

Robert E. Hood's groundbreaking text *Must God Remain Greek?*⁴⁵ and Dianne Stewart's *Three Eyes for the Journey*⁴⁶ are important constructive theological sources for rethinking contemporary Christian theology, given that the burgeoning growth of the Christian faith now lies in the global south, especially on the African continent and in Latin America. In these books, both Hood and Stewart offer a more expansive appraisal of the relationship between dogmatic truths and their religio-cultural antecedents, which speak to Black-embodied resistance to White hegemonic epistemological norms. Their work reminds us that 'syncretism' – a pejorative term often thrown at African-derived religions – is a facet of all religious traditions: namely, the borrowing from other cultures and modes of thinking and religious mythologies. In the case of these African-derived religions, it is the existence of Mission Christianity and its nexus with West and Central African religions (Candomblé in Brazil, Santeria in Cuba, Myalism in Jamaica, Vodun in Cuba, Shango in Trinidad).⁴⁷ Each of these traditions sought to disrupt European notions of purity and absolute fidelity to one code – which are themselves often expressions of empire.

Dianne Stewart's *Three Eyes for the Journey* focuses on Jamaica in particular, and the way in which there has been a Christianization of Caribbean theology and the religiosity of ordinary poor working-class people. Engaging in these forms of constructive theological work is a reminder of the importance of contestation that is often a feature of the development of differing models of theological reflection. This is not about replacing existing sources but supplementing them and reflecting on the implications and the intellectual issues at play in such contestations.

In a similar vein, Noel Erskine's *Plantation Church*[48] offers an additional theological focus on the development of Caribbean theology, in which the historical development of the contextual theologizing of former enslaved Africans is offered as an alternative vista to the normative theologizing of Karl Barth. This work does not seek to replace the substantive importance of Barth, but it does pose the question as to why Caribbean peoples have often trusted the theological ideas of a White man who never set foot on their shores nor understood their existential realities as enslaved peoples and whose followers often dismissed them – usually the very type of White reformed Christian represented by Barth himself.

In the purest sense, decolonizing the curriculum entails the complete deconstruction of our received notions of epistemology and how we conceive of intellectual truth. The truth is, however, that the embedded norms of Whiteness and their concomitant forms of privilege that are expressive of existing forms of knowledge construction are not going to entertain such deconstructionist curricula any time soon.[49] A more ameliorated form of decolonizing the curriculum is not asserting the complete removal of existing theological norms in how we conceive constructive or systematic theology. Rather, I am asking that we seek to juxtapose alternative and contested forms of theological construction, not in a zero-sum form of reductionism, but instead in order to raise the question as to why some forms of epistemology are considered more notable than others.

This form of decolonizing the curriculum is an explicit acknowledgement of the contextuality of theological construction and articulation. That is to say, all knowledge is partial and contingent. It affirms the value of knowledge from the margins. This provides other ways of seeing and knowing.

Finding new voices for the norm

As an addendum to the previous point, we need to find alternative interlocutors who can speak to and inform substantive epistemological points that often undergird the curriculum. In one of my earliest staff meetings, while still working as a visiting member of staff, I remember a Black female student being penalized for writing an essay about the doctrine of Christ, which had the temerity to use only Black women sources; these sources were Black women whose work understood the subject perfectly well, but who were not the 'usual suspects' for teaching what was a standard, normative position that is evocative of Whiteness. But why can't Kelly Brown Douglas's *The Black Christ* be the source text for teaching Christology? Why can't Michael Joseph Brown's *The Lord's Prayer Through North African Eyes*[50] be a source text for teaching patristics? Why can't Mercy Amba Oduyoye's *Beads and Strands*[51] be used as a source text for teaching theological anthropology?

The most substantive point one can make regarding all of the aforementioned is that of intentionality. Namely, how much commitment is there to decolonizing the curriculum? What is the intentionality for seeking to challenge the power relations in terms of the episteme that connotes the underlying constructs of the curriculum of Common Awards or that of wider academic theology within what are still rarefied ivory towers like Oxford and Cambridge?

Given the strictures for candidating, selection and then formation for ordained ministry, one has to acknowledge the bourgeois notions of respectability politics that pervade theological education and ministerial training. How can we challenge the middle-class hegemony of a formational process that is still predicated on a top-down patrician model of socialization that rewards the middle-class sensibilities of those who are being trained to lead and control others? How can we deconstruct a curriculum that is created to serve ecclesial institutions that remain committed to forms of patronage and patrician control and top-down notions of episcopal largesse as the price for being welcomed to the metaphorical club that is ordained ministry?

The extent to which this form of pedagogical and epistemological transformative change is possible will have everything to do with how desperate the church is in feeling the need to change. History shows us that change only takes place when environmental factors necessitate it. In an epoch of falling attendance in churches within the White historic denominations, closing churches and a shortage of clergy, perhaps things are desperate enough now for us to realize that this might be time for substantive change. Maybe the necessity to decolonize the curriculum has arrived. Is now the time to debunk the normative power of the 'epistemological centre'?

Places like Oxford and Cambridge universities have nothing to fear from decolonizing the curriculum. By bringing the margins to the centre, we are complexifying the world and knowledge and acknowledging the messiness and contestation that is life. It is training young minds to think critically and to engage with a wide range of sources, ideas and perspectives. It's not ideological distortion. Ideological distortion already exists. Much of our current, largely Eurocentric, White-dominated knowledge construction and teaching that is offered as monolingual truth is already that. Decolonization of the curriculum is opening things up, reappraising existing truths, offering contestation and challenge from the margins, and moving away from rigid certainties around what constitutes the canon of knowledge in any field – but especially in terms of Christian theology and religious studies. The future starts now and the present moment seems an apposite one for seeking and instilling substantive change to the curriculum of academic theology and theological education.

Notes

1 Although Robert Hood's work as a historian of religion does not name 'Whiteness' as a religio-cultural framing for Christianity, he nonetheless identifies Greek epistemological thought as the subterranean shaper of New Testament and early Christian literature, which remains White in complexion. See Robert E. Hood, 1990, *Must God Remain Greek? Afro-Cultures and God-Talk*, Minneapolis, MN: Fortress Press.

2 See Willie James Jennings, 2010, *The Christian Imagination: Theology and the Origins of Race*, New Haven, CT: Yale University Press, pp. 1–10.

3 See Jennings, *The Christian Imagination*, pp. 1–10.

4 This term refers to a doctrine that argues kings derive their authority directly from God and not from their subjects. This form of direct, vertical authority represents the conjoining of political and ecclesial power. For further details on the epistemological implications of this, see Thomas H. Groome, 1998, *Sharing Faith: A Comprehensive Approach to Religious Education and Pastoral Ministry*, Eugene, OR: Wipf & Stock, pp. 12–36.

5 In using the term 'theological education', I am speaking to the process of teaching and learning for persons undertaking a mode of formation in which they are inducted into the charisms of the church in order that they may take on leadership roles – most usually, public, authorized forms of ordained ministry. This mode of theological inquiry and learning is often adjacent to – but not the same as – more professional or objective forms of theology undertaken in public research universities. For a detailed articulation of theological education, see Dietrich Werner, Namsoon Kang, David Esterline and Joshva Raja (eds), 2010, *Handbook of Theological Education in World Christianity: Theological Perspectives – Regional Surveys – Ecumenical Trends*, Oxford: Regnum.

6 See Jennings, *The Christian Imagination*.

7 See Willie James Jennings, 2020, *After Whiteness: An Education in Belonging*, Grand Rapids, MI: Eerdmans.

8 Jennings, *After Whiteness*, pp. 23–156.

9 Jennings, *After Whiteness*, p. 10.

10 I am aware of the fact that I am making a huge generalization here, which, I will readily admit, is a great weakness in this discourse. The generalization, however, arises from the fact that even with more nuanced methodological approaches like 'contextual theology' or 'feminist studies', it remains comparatively rare to see the, often White, authors be specific about their embodied subjectivity and how that has shaped their subsequent discourse. In some respects, the generalization is perhaps a kind of conceit, used as a means of 'overstating' the case in order to make the argument in the first instance.

11 See Anthony G. Reddie, 2003, *Nobodies to Somebodies: A Practical Theology for Education and Liberation*, Peterborough: Epworth Press, pp. 68–70, 142–6.

12 See R. S. Sugirtharajah (ed.), 1995, *Voices From The Margins*, London: SPCK and R. S. Sugirtharajah, 2002, *Postcolonial Criticism and Biblical Interpretation*, Oxford: Oxford University Press. See also Leela Gandi, 1998, *Postcolonial Theory*, Edinburgh: Edinburgh University Press.

13 By this I mean how White authors write and speak in an alleged universal language and whose work then has universal applicability.

14 See Reddie, *Nobodies to Somebodies*, pp. 68–70 and pp. 142–6.

15 For the full version of this anecdote, see the following video. Wright commences the analogy around minute 27. Urban Health Institute, 'Reverend Dr. Jeremiah Wright Transforming Urban Communities: Building Equity and Equality', YouTube, 16 February 2013, https://www.youtube.com/watch?v=62qdwaC2b6g (accessed 7.03.2023).

16 Chinua Achebe, 1992, *Things Fall Apart*, London: David Campbell.

17 Many of these issues are addressed in Michael Joseph Brown, 2004, *The Lord's Prayer Through North African Eyes: A Window into Early Christianity*, New York: T&T Clark International.

18 See Sugirtharajah, *Voices* and Sugirtharajah, *Postcolonial Criticism*. See also Gandi, *Postcolonial Theory*.

19 See Paulo Freire, 1996, *Pedagogy of the Oppressed*, London: Penguin Books.

20 See Freire, *Pedagogy of the Oppressed* and also 1990 (1973), *Education for Critical Consciousness*, New York: Continuum and 1999, *A Pedagogy of Hope: Reliving Pedagogy of the Oppressed*, New York: Continuum.

21 Freire, *Education*, pp. 18–20.

22 Allen J. Moore, 1989, 'A Social Theory of Religious Education' in Allen J. Moore (ed.), *Religious Education as Social Transformation*, Birmingham, AL: Religious Education Press, p. 27.

23 John L. Elias, 'Paulo Freire: Religious Educator', *Religious Education*, 71(4) (January–February, 1976), pp. 40–56.

24 See Durham University Common Awards website: Durham University, 2012, 'News: Durham University to be Church of England's Sole Validation Partner for Ministerial Training', *Durham University*, 20 June, https://www.dur.ac.uk/news/newsitem/?itemno=14864 (accessed 7.03.2023).

25 See Herbert P. Altrichter, Peter Posch and Bridget Somekh, 1993, *Teachers Investigating their Work*, London: Routledge.

26 See Cheryl Bridges Johns, 2010, *Pentecostal Formation*, Eugene, OR: Wipf & Stock.
27 Jennings, *After Whiteness*, pp. 84–94.
28 Jennings, *After Whiteness*, p. 118.
29 See Nicola Slee, 2020, *Fragments for Fractured Times*, London: SCM Press.
30 See Marcella Althaus-Reid, 2000, *Indecent Theology*, Oxford: Routledge.
31 See R. S. Sugirtharajah, 2004, *Postcolonial Reconfigurations*, London: SCM Press.
32 See Jennings, *After Whiteness*, pp. 47–76.
33 James Michael Lee, 1971, *The Shape of Religious Instruction*, Birmingham, AL: Religious Education Press.
34 See Kevin Considine, 'To Resist the Gravity of Whiteness: Communicating Racialized Suffering and Creating Paschal Community through an Analogia Vulneris', *Black Theology: An International Journal*, 15(2) (2017), pp. 136–55.
35 See Cain Hope Felder, 1990, *Troubling Biblical Waters*, Maryknoll, NY: Orbis Books and Cain Hope Felder (ed.), 1991, *Stony the Road We Trod*, Minneapolis, MN: Fortress Press.
36 See Randall C. Bailey (ed.), 2002, *Yet With A Steady Beat*, Atlanta, GA: Society for the Study of Biblical Literature.
37 See Brian K. Blount, 2005, *Can I Get A Witness? Reading Revelation Through African American Culture*, Louisville, KY: Westminster John Knox Press.
38 See Mitzi Smith (ed.), 2015, *I Found God in Me*, Eugene, OR: Cascade Books.
39 See Wilda C. Gafney, 2017, *Womanist Midrash*, Louisville, KY: Westminster John Knox Press.
40 See Musa W. Dube, 2000, *Postcolonial Feminist Interpretation of the Bible*, St Louis, MO: Chalice Press.
41 See Annie Tinsley, 2012, *A Postcolonial African American Rereading of Colossians*, New York: Palgrave Macmillan.
42 Within the context of the Church of England's role as the dominant consumer of theological education within the body politic of the UK, a number of Anglican, Black liberation theologians have critiqued the endemic racism within the Church of England. See David Isiorho, 2019, *Mission, Anguish and Defiance*, Eugene, OR: Wipf & Stock and A. D. A France-Williams, 2020, *Ghost Ship*, London: SCM Press.
43 See Anthony G. Reddie, with Gale Richards and Wale Hudson Roberts, 2017, *Journeying to Justice: Contributions to the Baptist Tradition Across the Black Atlantic*, Milton Keynes: Paternoster Press.
44 For further details on the religio-political significance of the Haitian Revolution, see Celucien Joseph, 2013, *From Toussaint to Price-Mars: Rhetoric, Race, and Religion in Haitian Thought*, New York: CreateSpace Independent Publishing Platform.
45 Hood, *Must God Remain Greek?*
46 Dianne M. Stewart, 2005, *Three Eyes for the Journey: African Dimensions of the Jamaican Religious Experience*, New York: Oxford University Press.
47 For a more recent contextual theological appraisal of this work, see Carlton Turner, 2020, *Overcoming Self-negation: The Church and Junkanoo in Contemporary Bahamian Society*, Eugene, OR: Pickwick Publications.
48 See Noel Leo Erskine, 2014, *Plantation Church: How African American Religion Was Born in Caribbean Slavery*, New York: Oxford University Press.

49 An example of this can be seen in the hyperbolic response to the moderate and relatively pain-free suggestions of curricula change suggested by the Church of England anti-racism report *From Lament to Action*. Various conservative Anglican commentators have lambasted it as selling out to the dubious blandishments of 'Critical Race Theory' when this concept is not mentioned in the report and the suggested recommendations (as opposed to top-down stipulations) are not requiring a wholesale deconstruction of the theological curriculum. Therefore, *From Lament to Action* is not an example of decolonizing the curriculum. For an example of such an 'unreasoned' response, see the following link: Ian Paul, 2021, 'From Lament to Action. How Should the Church Respond to Race?', *Psephizo*, 30 April, https://www.psephizo.com/tag/from-lament-to-action/ (accessed 7.03.2023).

50 See Brown, *The Lord's Prayer*.

51 See Mercy Amba Oduyoye, 2013, *Beads and Strands: Reflections of an African Woman on Christianity in Africa*, Maryknoll, NY: Orbis Books.

PART TWO

Perspectives on History

5

Octavius Hadfield: Nineteenth-century Goodie or Twenty-first-century Baddie? Learnings from the Complexities of Mission and Empire

JAMES BUTLER AND CATHY ROSS

Introduction

We begin this chapter acknowledging where we write from. We write from within empire. As Dorothee Sölle has said, we are doing our theology while still living in Egypt.[1] While we may not like this label, we have to acknowledge that we are White, living in a prosperous nation, and continue to benefit from empire. As we turn to discuss Octavius Hadfield, we acknowledge that we have a lot more in common with Hadfield than with the Māori. As much as we want to critique and learn, there is something in us that wants to name Hadfield as the goodie, as the one who was compromised by empire but tried to do his best, to be faithful to God and to be a good friend of the Māori. We too have experienced this tension in cross-cultural mission: Cathy in Rwanda, Congo and Uganda; James in Uruguay and other Latin American countries. We know we have not done everything right. We have struggled with our privilege and position, have felt the pressure to evangelize to show ourselves worthy of the support we received, and sought to be good friends and allies to those we worked with. We want to be known as the 'goodies'. But can we step back enough to ask deeper questions? Perhaps in reading Hadfield we can get beyond asking whether he was mostly a goodie or whether he was compromised by empire, and instead ask deeper questions that can disclose our own complicity with the empires of our time. Our tendency to relate more easily to Hadfield than the Māori clearly shapes this chapter. It would undoubtedly look very different from the perspective of the colonized, those not living in Egypt.

Octavius Hadfield was a Church Missionary Society (CMS) missionary in Aotearoa New Zealand from 1839 until he became Bishop of Wellington in 1870 and later primate. He died in 1904 at the age of 91. He was born on the Isle of Wight, studied at Pembroke College in Oxford but never completed his studies due to ill health. He had always wanted to be a missionary and was accepted by CMS in 1837. He went to Australia, where he was ordained a deacon. As he did not have a university degree he could not be ordained a priest, but this changed when Bishop Broughton of Sydney was asked to visit Aotearoa New Zealand in 1839. He became the first priest to be ordained in that country. He spent nearly all of his missionary service in Waikanae and Otaki, 40 miles north of Wellington. His geographical area of responsibility was huge and stretched to include roughly the bottom third of the North Island. The incident that we are considering occurred 20 years into his missionary service and concerned the unjust sale of Māori land to settlers in Taranaki, on the west coast of the North Island. Hadfield was fluent in Māori and was considered to be, by Māori, missionaries and the government alike, an expert in Māori land ownership. He had also prevented a major Māori attack on Wellington. He was considered a peacemaker, friend of the Māori, and respected by some in the colonial government. By others he was called 'a traitor' and the most hated man in New Zealand for his advocacy for, and defence of, local Māori.[2] In this chapter we will consider the following issues: land and Māori responses, justice, theological anthropology, the colonial logic of mission, and what we have learned.

Land/Māori responses

Unusual among missionaries of the time, Hadfield was extremely well informed on Māori understandings of land. He had spent 18 years studying native titles to land and wrote a paper on this subject for Governor Sir George Grey. He was so incensed by the injustice of the sale of this particular tract of land in Taranaki that he wrote a series of pamphlets to the Secretary of State for the Colonies, the first of which was titled 'One of England's Little Wars' and where he excoriated in the strongest terms the 'flagrant act of injustice by the Governor', the ignorance of the land commissioners and the attack ('little war') on the local Māori.[3]

Hadfield had learned that indigenous attitudes to land, and ownership of it, are very different from English understandings. However, in the nineteenth century, many missionaries challenged the understanding shared by indigenous peoples about their sense of identity, their sense of well-being and relationship with the land, creation and the place.

Those early Europeans came to new places which they defined on their own terms. They designated in categories familiar to them, they divided ancient groupings, they created borders with straight lines, they developed racial categories. They challenged and destroyed the deeply held beliefs and practices of indigenous peoples. The African American theologian Willie James Jennings explains that the early missionaries brought a very different understanding of how to be in the world:

> This crucial educational hope was to disabuse Native peoples of any idea that lands and animals, landscapes and seasons carried any communicative or animate destiny, and therefore any ethical or moral direction in how to live in the world. Instead they offered peoples a relationship with the world that was basically one dimensional – we interpret and manipulate the world as we see fit, taking from it what we need, and caring for it within the logics of making it more productive for us.[4]

For indigenous peoples the place is in them – they are the place, the land, the creation. I know this as someone from Aotearoa New Zealand, where the Māori define themselves according to their place, their mountain, their river or sea and their tribe. In the Māori language, the word for land and placenta, *whenua*, is the same. Māori are the land. The land is them. Just as in the Genesis creation account, indigenous myths of origin are closely linked to the land and these are a source of identity and orientation to the world. Enrolled member of the Citizen Potawatomi Nation and professor of botany, Robin Wall Kimmerer, explains this indigenous worldview: 'For all of us, becoming indigenous to a place means living as if your children's future mattered, to take care of the land as if our lives, both material and spiritual, depended on it.'[5] The Tongan biblical scholar Jione Havea explains how the land is gendered both male and female for island peoples in the South Pacific: 'As mother, the land is the primary carer of us ... As father, the land connects us to those who have passed, to one another, to those who are to come, and to the circles of life around us.'[6] He asserts that the colonial project has feminized the land to license its taking and exploitation.

Jennings takes this further by claiming that colonialism has resourced and produced a theology of extraction supported by 'three crucial agents necessary for that earth shattering work – the merchant, the missionary and the soldier'.[7] This is clearly demonstrated in Hadfield's explanation of the unjust sale of land in his letter to the then General Secretary of CMS, Henry Venn:

> The Government has taken hostile proceedings against a chief Wiremu Kingi, and his tribe, because they have resisted the survey of land which belongs to them, but which an individual native, Teira, has sold to the Government Land Agent ... To my utter astonishment a few weeks ago I learnt that the Governor had taken troops to Taranaki; had issued a proclamation authorising martial law; and had marched troops onto the disputed land, and on the withdrawal of the natives, who were residing in pas (villages) quite indefensible, had destroyed these.[8]

In this instance Hadfield is the missionary who defends the indigenous worldview and advocates on their behalf both to CMS and to the British government in his series of pamphlets to the Secretary of State for the Colonies. The merchant is the government land agent acquiring land for the settlers and the soldiers are sent by the British government forcibly to subdue the Māori and begin what Hadfield calls 'one of England's little wars'.

Wiremu Kingi is a Christian and a friend of Hadfield. He resolutely opposes the sale of their land to the settlers and writes movingly to the Governor:

> *I will not agree to our bedroom being sold ... for this bed belongs to the whole of us;* and do you not be in haste to give the money. Do you hearken to my word. If you give the money secretly, you will get no land for it. You may insist but I will never agree to it ... All I have to say to you, O Governor, is, that none of this land will be given to you, never, never, not till I die.[9]

This Māori understanding of land contrasts with a European worldview that has so often reduced the land to an inert or utilitarian resource for our own use. This is indeed an extraction worldview whereas many indigenous cultures practise more of a gift mentality. The Māori theologian Jay Matenga writes that the Māori worldview is of a sharing and gift economy but that when industrialization was imposed, it was 'out of sync with our souls and like most indigenous people around the world, it proved a fast track to poverty'.[10]

He reminds us of their spiritual and emotional connection to material reality just as Jesus had a relationship with the created order where we see that the winds and the waves obeyed him. He claims that 'private ownership is not typical in indigenous ways of knowing. But it is endemic to Western thinkers.'[11] In the extract above from Kingi's letter to the Governor, we see his personal and familial attachment to the land – it is their bedroom. He is not interested in money because you do not sell the family bedroom as it belongs to everyone and no one person has any right, or desire, to sell it. Hadfield understood and appreciated this relationship with the land, and he had assured the Māori that the British government 'never would unjustly seize their lands'.[12] In this instance, he realized that he had misled them and was therefore ashamed to meet with them.

Kingi also declares: 'that piece of land belongs to us, it belongs to the orphan, it belongs to the widow.'[13] Again we see here a deeply communal understanding of ownership as well as one that prioritizes those on the margins and those at risk.

This has striking resonances with a biblical understanding of the land and how it can serve the poor and the widow, such as in the Old Testament story of Ruth. As we have seen, for Māori, their lives and their identity depended fundamentally on their land, so they were not going to give up their land easily nor were they prepared to engage in violence. They were certainly not willing to accept the investigation initiated by the government on behalf of the Governor, as Hadfield explained in his pamphlet, 'whose business is to purchase land, and who by the very nature of his office, is disqualified in the estimation of the natives, impartially to investigate claims to land'.[14] However, colonial logic was quickly adopted and soldiers were sent on a warship to deal with the situation. Jennings claims that this triad of merchant, missionary and soldier 'reordered our sense of land, animal, plant, earth and each other through forming life into abiding enclosure'.[15] This then led to new understandings of boundaries, identity and existence which were then internalized.

The production of lines to separate spaces that were in fact not separate took on a new economic determination as the privatization of land and places sliced through the forms of identity, both spatial and human. Yet the line outside the body was also the line within the body as people were habituated to see the line that was not in fact there and internalized the line as a boundary of existence.[16]

In this context in Taranaki, the lines were literally being drawn by surveyors marking out the land between their pegs. This was privatizing land, creating enclosures and taking away more than just land. This was the literal slicing of identity – in space, body and time. Local Māori responded to these invasive actions in a creative and subversive way. The women and children not only removed the surveyors' measuring pegs, but they also hugged them so that they could not do any surveying. This demonstrates their commitment to peaceful protest in contrast to the British response of sending troops and gunships. We also see here a fascinating gendered response and a clever use of bodies to thwart the surveyors. The Governor then declared martial law and when the local

Māori refused to give up their land a party of surveyors fired the first shots, followed by field guns and naval rocket tubes pouring a barrage of shells at them. And so began the first wave of the Land Wars. Hadfield expressed his opinion to the Secretary of State for the Colonies, in the strongest language possible, 'the Governor's attack on William King [Kingi] was, not only impolitic, but under the present circumstances of the colony, an act of folly closely bordering on insanity.'[17]

While Hadfield wrote a lengthy pamphlet to the colonial powers, local Māori took both a personal and communal approach. We have quoted excerpts above of Kingi's own letter to the Governor outlining his refusal to sell the land. Some 500 chiefs also wrote a petition to the Queen imploring her to act justly:

> This unjust conduct on the part of the Governor has filled us all with grief and consternation. We are quite sure that your Majesty has not sanctioned the principle that land is to be forcibly taken away from your Majesty's subjects, many of them widows and orphans. For these reasons we Your Majesty's faithful and loyal subjects address your Majesty and pray that this Governor may be recalled, that this island may not be involved in war, and that Your Majesty will send another Governor who may know how to govern in accordance with the law and your Majesty's instructions, and that we and the white inhabitants may dwell together in peace and love to Your Majesty. And we will ever pray that your Majesty's sovereignty may prosper.[18]

It is notable that they appeal to the Queen, believing her to be the highest authority, and that again they refer to the widows and orphans, appealing to a sense of justice on behalf of the marginalized. They are clear that they want the current Governor removed because of his unjust actions, which resulted in a war. Twice they refer to prayer. The Māori approach is clearly communal and invokes Scripture by their reference to widows and orphans. Their worldview seems to have been shaped by a Christian frame of reference alongside their own indigenous cultural values.

Hadfield had an unparalleled understanding of Māori customs and culture with respect to land ownership for a settler, and he had an important role in communicating and translating that to the settler population. It is heartening and encouraging to see his close friendship with Kingi and his support for him. However, this was all framed within a peculiarly British understanding of justice.

Justice

As we have already seen, Hadfield immediately recognized and spoke out about the injustice of the British possession of the land. His pamphlets, on which we are reflecting here, are an attempt to highlight this injustice and they appeal to the British government. Hadfield's public condemning of the government reveals a bold and deep commitment to his Māori friends. His tone is direct and demonstrates his anger at the injustice, as this extract demonstrates:

> WHEN a flagrant act of injustice has been committed by the Governor of a British colony in the name of Her Majesty the Queen, it is not easy to determine on what course to pursue. If, indeed, an Englishman were the sufferer, either the Courts of law or the public press would afford a sufficient guarantee that the injustice would be remedied. But when an aboriginal chief is affected by such an act of injustice, neither of these avail him: he may be two hundred miles distant from any Judge of the Supreme Court; and he fails to enlist the sympathy of the public press. Feeling deeply convinced that such an act of injustice has been committed by Colonel Browne, the Governor of this colony, in his recent forcible expulsion of William King from land inherited by him from a long line of ancestors, I venture to address your Grace, as Her Majesty's Secretary of State for the Colonies, and to call your attention to the facts of the case.[19]

As well as demonstrating his anger at injustice, this extract also draws our attention to the ways in which Hadfield views justice. Implicit in his writing is a belief that the British government is committed to justice, and that a disclosure of the facts of the case would be enough to reverse this unjust decision. However, his confidence might seem misplaced. Perhaps an Englishman with the same kind of education and background as Hadfield might be able to expect justice, but it would not take much searching to find a litany of people who had suffered injustice because of the British government within Britain itself.[20] It appears that for Hadfield one of the key problems facing Kingi and the displaced Māori is their distance from the court and the difficulty they would have in enlisting public sympathy through the press.

This appeal to the British government can be reframed in a less hopeful light by turning again to Jennings and his reflections on James's execution and Peter's imprisonment in Acts 12. He states: 'The prison always announces worldly power and reveals those intoxicated with the lust for violence.'[21] He does not mean the violence of the inmate, but the violence of the system, of the state and those in power. The prison is part of the tools of statecraft and empire, and the kind of justice offered by the prison is the justice of King Herod, not of Jesus. It is designed to silence opposition and to bring pleasure to the political and religious leaders. He continues: 'Christians, like no one else, should understand how easy it is to return to prison, not because of human failing but because of failed systems that are calibrated against the powerless, the weak, and the poor and work best against insurgent voices pressing for systemic change.'[22] Through Jennings's reading of Acts 12, Hadfield's hope for justice can be interpreted as misplaced because the state's priority is maintaining power, not justice. It draws attention to the fact that throughout the entire pamphlet Hadfield does not seem to doubt that the route to justice is through the courts, and he does not appear to ask the question of what a biblical conception of justice might bring.

As Audre Lorde has reminded us, the master's tools will not dismantle the master's house,[23] and here the tools of British justice will not reverse the injustice of the British empire. Returning to Jennings and his reflections on prison, it is interesting to note that the church's response in Acts 12 is not to seek justice from the state, but to turn to prayer, as did the 500 Māori chiefs in their petition to the Queen.[24] We can see resonances with the confidence a White person would have in calling the police as compared to a Black person.[25] The Māori are much more aware of the structures of power and injustice, and while Kingi seeks to appeal Monarch to Monarch, they know that the justice they seek is not given by the courts of the empire, but by God.

Of course, there may be another way of reading this. We are assuming that the pamphlet expresses Hadfield's feelings and understanding, but this may not be true. In community organizing, Saul Alinsky's fourth rule is 'Make the enemy live up to their own book of rules'.[26] The 'have nots' make the 'haves' live up to their own rules. Hadfield's is a public letter and therefore written with an audience in mind. A more generous reading of Hadfield would suggest he is trying to reveal the acts of the British empire for what they are; not the noble generosity of a common wealth, but the smash and grab of a criminal. It is one of a series of ways to shame one's opponent into acting justly, to show them the gulf between what they claim and how they act. His letter could then be read as an act of contextualization, and of public shaming. In some ways it is effective, the governor is removed, but the injustice at the heart of the problem, the illegal taking of land, remains unremedied.

Ultimately, justice was not done. The British empire did not act justly. Not only that, but – as in many former places of the empire – the acts of the unjust are celebrated and remembered by having streets named after them, whereas those mistreated are forgotten. In many ways Hadfield can be seen to be on the 'right' side of history, but it is not clear whether these experiences around seeking justice and the lack of justice for the Māori caused him to question underlying assumptions about British justice.

Theological anthropology

As we turn to reflect on Hadfield's theological anthropology, another extract from his pamphlet is helpful; this extract shows both his deep love and respect for the Māori, and at the same time an understanding of indigenous people that is jarring when read in the twenty-first century:

> Nothing but the deepest conviction of the present critical state of this colony, and Colonel Browne's utter incapacity to rescue it from disaster and ruin, has induced me to address your Grace. It is still possible that the presence of some superior man might restore the confidence that is lost. A little delay may occasion a war of races. No doubt Great Britain has men and money wherewith to carry on against the native race a war of extermination. But is this to be the issue of the endeavours to establish Christianity and civilization among one of the most intelligent and tractable of races. Are we in the middle of the nineteenth century to confess to the whole civilized world that our Christianity and our civilization have given us no advantage over these people but that of a more scientific use of material force? Is the pride of Englishmen to exclude from their breasts all sympathy for a race but recently emerging from barbarism, because it has qualities too nearly resembling their own – because it repudiates degradation, and refuses to be submissively trampled under foot? Is the sound of war once heard to deafen their ears to the cry of justice.[27]

In this extract it is difficult to unpick the seemingly paradoxical nature of Hadfield's theological anthropology. On the one hand, Hadfield values his relationships with the Māori and sees the way that diversity enriches the community. But in the next sentence he seems able to name them as a formerly barbaric race. To do this he seems to draw on a type of British exceptionalism. He sees the British as a pinnacle of civilization to which the Māori should aspire. He appeals to this pride, naming it as a reputation to be maintained by not descending into war, but to be 'civilized'.

John Hull explores how the use of the Christian faith as the ideology of the British empire changed and distorted theology and the Christian faith. Studying the sermons of chaplains to the trading companies and the writings of other theologians in the sixteenth century, as the British Empire began to expand across the world, he identifies this distortion. One particularly stark theme is the turn to the Old Testament, where he notes how 'the political classes were attracted more to the ideals of the Hebrew kingdom than to those of the suffering Messiah.'[28] The justification became 'when a Christian nation conquers a non-Christian nation, it is really Christ who is the conqueror'[29] and led to a sense of 'superiority of the faith of the English'[30] over other colonizing nations. According to Hull, these developments and the expansion of the British empire led to an 'emphatic contrast between Christianity and the dark savagery of the non-Christian world'. As this stark contrast plays out in North America, Hull notes: 'The argument is simple. God has given the earth to human beings, but the native peoples of North America are not human; they are mere beasts. Having dehumanized them, any objection to their colonization is void, and the way is cleared for Christian Britain to follow the example of Joshua.'[31] The requirements of power and possession shape biblical interpretation, Christian doctrine and the practice of faith rather than being challenged by them.

This tying together of civilizing the savage and the Christian faith is clearly visible in Hadfield's account. The underlying anthropology inherited from the requirements of empire shapes Hadfield's worldview. In a sermon on the Māori mission, he points to their 'degrading superstitions', their cannibalism, the maintenance of a particularly brutal form of slavery and infanticide, noting, 'Human life was not valued very highly.'[32] He then tells stories of how violent Māori become peaceful, civilized Christians. This narrative maintains and reinforces the binary described by Hull. It feels particularly striking from the twenty-first-century standpoint that he could use brutal slavery as evidence of their barbaric state, with no reference to the equally horrific Atlantic slave trade exploited by the British not many years before he was writing. Interestingly, in an article about the chief, Aperahama, Te Ruru, he describes how 'No careful observer could fail to notice' the courage, self-reliance and independence of the Māori.[33] He praises them for not being 'a revengeful people' and yet maintains the language of 'savages'.[34] This close attention allows him to call into question some of the assumptions about indigenous people in the particular setting of the Māori, but it does not cause him to question his own language and inherited assumptions about indigenous people generally. He accounts for it within the logic of the anthropology he has inherited; as 'one of the most intelligent and tractable of races',[35] allowing him to place them on a continuum closer to the civilized end – an exception to the rule rather than a debunking of the whole theory.

So what would have happened if his deep friendship and appreciation of the Māori had not just caused him to look more positively on this particular indigenous people, but also to begin to question the colonial logic of how he was encouraged to look at them in the first place? Would it have been possible for his friendship with many Māori to actually cause him to ask questions about the colonial logic under which his missionary endeavour took place?

Colonial logic of mission

All of the above shows how Hadfield continued to operate in a logic of empire. This was a logic of land ownership, of private property, of courts and judges. Significantly, it was a logic that tied Christian faith with British culture. This logic caused him to see aberrations rather than a broken system. In the argument over land, he saw the problem as being corrupt individuals rather than a systemic problem. There is an implication that the Māori need to be fully incorporated into empire rather than empire itself needing to be challenged. For example, in 'One of England's Little Wars' he briefly refers to the Kīngitanga, the Māori King Movement, where a number of tribes came together to try and elect a king to oppose British rule. Hadfield praises Kingi's refusal to participate and to stand for the Crown as one of the key reasons the uprising failed. He appeals to Kingi's loyalty to the British empire as one of the reasons why this injustice should be righted.

Having shown that in many ways Hadfield continued to operate according to a logic of empire, rather than argue for him being a 'goodie' or 'baddie', this more complex account can be a means to interrogate the logics of empire within contemporary mission. As we identified at the beginning, this chapter is written within empire and we must avoid the temptation to suggest that the answer is simply to step outside of the logic of our own system. Luke Bretherton, in his careful study of capitalism, points out the naivety and the inherent anthropology in an assumption that some act of revolution or some alternative ideology will somehow restore order. He notes the need to 'resist rendering contingent social, political, or economic orders immutable and determinative of what it means to be human'.[36] He argues that capitalism needs to be unveiled as neither natural nor inevitable, but that the answer is not revolution. This assumption, that it is possible to be outside the system and untainted by it, fails to account for sin and domination and it makes the same mistake of seeing a temporal programme as being able to bring what only Jesus' return can. He suggests that what is required theologically is both sober and radical; a hope for change that seeks to convert and reconfigure both from within and without: 'Redirecting its discursive and structural apparatus to different, God-given ends. This entails both recollection and rupture, being salt and light, conservative and radical, continuity and change, prophetic critique of what is and was as well as messianic hope for what will be but is beyond human control or determination.'[37]

Jennings says something similar in his reflections on the book of Acts about being between empire and diaspora: 'Faith is always caught between diaspora and empire. It is always caught between those on the one side focused on survival and fixated on securing a future for their people and on the other side those intoxicated with the power and possibilities of empire and of building a world ordered by its financial, social, and political logics that claim to be the best possible way to bring stability and lasting peace.'[38]

What does it mean for Hadfield to be an advocate, friend and participant and to live in between empire and diaspora? Some would like to convince us that revolution can overthrow empire, as if some utopia exists this side of the eschaton. Some would like to convince us that we have to be a separate people, a city on a hill, separate from the machinations of empire. And yet Hadfield attempted a middle road. Hadfield knew the complications, and he attempted to take this middle road within the logic of the empire of which he was a part. We cannot draw a simple line between empire and revolution; instead, there is a need to embrace the complexity. But even in saying all this, it is clear from our critique above that while there is much to learn from how Hadfield got this right, there is also much to learn from how Hadfield got this wrong: his blind spots, assumptions and unwillingness to question the logic within which he lived.

Learnings

We began our chapter with a question about whether Hadfield was a 'goodie' or a 'baddie'. We hope, as you reach this point in the chapter, it is clear that such labelling is too simplistic and generally unhelpful. And yet so often the temptation is to do just that, to find a way of either justifying some as good or writing them off as bad. But in raising questions about Hadfield our intention is not a simplistic judgement of history; instead, it allows the lens to be turned on us in the twenty-first century. As we have shown, Hadfield stood up to the British empire in a number of ways, engaged in good practices of cross-cultural mission and developed deep friendships with Māori, and yet he also had blind spots to the ways in which empire shaped his worldview and practice. As the historian Tony Ballantyne has so deftly explored in *Entanglements of Empire: Missionaries, Māori, and the Question of the Body*, relationship with empire and with Māori is complex, layered and rarely straightforward.[39] We are embedded in empire and we are not. The aim is not to discredit Hadfield, nor to hold him up as a model, but to see him as someone like us, who has a complex relationship with his political and social context. How can we learn, from both Hadfield's strengths and his blind spots, about our own entanglements with empire?

While we may not feel we are part of blatant colonialist expansion, we are still entangled within the logic of our day. We have already highlighted capitalism and the complex relationship that Christians and churches have with its particular construction of what it means to be human. We could add to that list money, race, gender, sexuality, being differently abled, neurodiversity and climate change. We have suggested that Hadfield's encounter with difference through his friendship with the Māori raised awareness of the injustice, but that there was much more to be opened up. Similarly, we have suggested that a closer reading of Scripture with the Māori might have caused Hadfield to question some of these underlying assumptions that come through his writing.

If revolution is not the answer, how might we open ourselves up to difference and to Scripture in such a way to, in the words of Walter Wink, unmask the powers?[40] In what ways are we complicit with unjust systems that dehumanize us and others? What is the implicit anthropology in capitalism and why is it that society seems unable to confront climate change? Similarly, we might question the patterns of investment by churches. We recently heard of Christian organizations being encouraged to 'sweat their assets', but with little theological reflection on what that might mean. But there is also a deeper critique to be made: churches investing in the latest technology, multi-million-pound refurbishments, failing to pay a living wage to their cleaners, or importing the logic of capitalism around perpetual growth into their theology of the kingdom.[41]

We may feel like we are living faithfully, but there are plenty of voices encouraging us to listen more carefully and to reflect more deeply. UK Minority Ethnic (UKME) Christians are telling us that our structures and patterns of ministry remain racist; we need to listen carefully. People living in areas that will be wiped out as sea levels rise as a result of climate change are telling us this is urgent.[42] Differently abled friends tell us they are tired of being marginalized and overlooked. In many parts of our world and in our own society, women still experience a glass ceiling and feel unsafe not only on the streets but also in their own homes.

We are just as entangled in the empires of today as Hadfield was in his. If there is no option to step out of it, how can we be 'sober and radical', and be part of realigning it from the inside and out? Perhaps it starts by listening, and listening well. It may require painful exchanges as we slowly learn how we continue to emulate empire. It may require learning other languages (both actually and metaphorically) and having friends, as Hadfield did, in these various communities. We cannot step out of empire, but we can be exposed to its brutal reality, learn to live differently within it, and seek its conversion from both the inside and the outside.

Notes

1 Dorothee Sölle, 'Resistance: Toward a First World Theology', *Christianity and Crisis*, 39(12) (23 July 1979), pp. 178–82.

2 June Starke, 'Octavius Hadfield', *Historical Journal, [Otaki Historical Society]*, 3 (1980), p. 11.

3 Octavius Hadfield, 1860, *One of England's Little Wars: A Letter to the Right Hon. the Duke of New Castle, Secretary of State for the Colonies*, London: Williams & Norgate, p. 3.

4 Willie James Jennings, 2018, 'Can White People Be Saved? Reflections on the Relationship of Missions and Whiteness' in Love Sechrest, Johnny Ramirez-Johnson and Amos Yong (eds), *Can "White" People Be Saved? Triangulating Race, Theology, and Mission*, Downers Grove, IL: IVP Academic, p. 33.

5 Robin Wall Kimmerer, 2013, *Braiding Sweetgrass: Indigenous Wisdom, Scientific Knowledge and the Teachings of Plants*, Minneapolis, MN: Milkweed, p. 9.

6 Jione Havea, 2021, *Losing Ground: Reading Ruth in the Pacific*, London: SCM Press, p. 6.

7 Willie James Jennings, 'Reframing the World: Toward an Actual Christian Doctrine of Creation', *International Journal of Systematic Theology*, 21(4) (October 2019), p. 197.

8 Hadfield Papers, NZ Church Collection, 'Letter from Octavius Hadfield to Rev H Venn, Otaki, Wellington, New Zealand', 31 March 1860.

9 Wiremu Kingi to the Governor, in Octavius Hadfield, 1861, 'The Second Year of One of England's Little Wars', London and Edinburgh: Williams & Norgate, Appendix E, p. 51. Italics in the original.

10 Jay Matenga, 2021, 'Indigenous Relationship Ecologies: Space, Spirituality and Sharing', p. 4, https://jaymatenga.com/pdfs/MatengaJ_IndigenousEcologies.pdf (accessed 8.03.2023).

11 Matenga, 'Indigenous Relationship Ecologies', p. 4.

12 Hadfield, *One of England's Little Wars*, p. 4.

13 Ann Parsonson, 1990, 'Te Rangitāke, Wiremu Kīngi', *Dictionary of New Zealand Biography*, Auckland: Auckland University Press; *Te Ara – the Encyclopedia of New Zealand*, https://teara.govt.nz/en/biographies/1t70/te-rangitake-wiremu-kingi (accessed 8.03.2023).

14 Hadfield, *One of England's Little Wars*, p. 18.

15 Jennings, 'Reframing the World', p. 398.
16 Jennings, 'Reframing the World', p. 399.
17 Hadfield, *One of England's Little Wars*, p. 20.
18 Hadfield Papers, NZ Church Collection, 'To our Beloved Sovereign the Queen', Otaki, 30 March 1860.
19 Hadfield, *One of England's Little Wars*, p. 3.
20 For example, the Highland Clearances were taking place during this time in Scotland, and land enclosure in England was taking land from common use into private ownership. Hayes's and McIntosh's accounts of these events demonstrate that this is not a problem of distance from justice, but a habitual practice of the British empire. Alastair McIntosh, 2004, *Soil and Soul: People versus Corporate Power*, London: Aurum Press; Nick Hayes, 2020, *The Book of Trespass: Crossing the Lines That Divide Us*, London: Bloomsbury Publishing. The complicated relationship between the poor and the justice system in the nineteenth century is explored here: Douglas Hay, 'Crime and Justice in Eighteenth- and Nineteenth-century England', *Crime and Justice*, 2 (1980), pp. 45–84.
21 Willie James Jennings, 2017, *Acts*, Louisville, KY: Westminster John Knox Press, p. 125.
22 Jennings, *Acts*, p. 126.
23 Audre Lorde, 2017, *The Master's Tools Will Never Dismantle the Master's House*, London: Penguin Classics.
24 Hadfield Papers, NZ Church Collection, 'To our Beloved Sovereign the Queen', Otaki, 30 March 1860.
25 For example, the Cabinet Office report from 2017 says Black men are three times more likely to be stopped and searched by the police than White men, and it identifies this as a significant reduction since 2008–09. Cabinet Office, 'Race Disparity Audit: Summary Findings from the Ethnicity Facts and Figures Website', *Gov.uk*, October 2017, https://www.gov.uk/government/publications/race-disparity-audit (accessed 8.03.2023).
26 Saul David Alinsky, 1989, *Rules for Radicals: A Practical Primer for Realistic Radicals*, London: Vintage Books.
27 Hadfield, *One of England's Little Wars*, pp. 24–5.
28 John M. Hull, 2014, *Towards the Prophetic Church: A Study of Christian Mission*, London: SCM Press, p. 89.
29 Hull, *Towards the Prophetic Church*, p. 95.
30 Hull, *Towards the Prophetic Church*, p. 97.
31 Hull, *Towards the Prophetic Church*, p. 103.
32 Octavius Hadfield, 1902, *Maoris of By-gone Days*, London: J. B. Shears & Sons, p. 27.
33 Hadfield, *Maoris of By-gone Days*, p. 12.
34 Hadfield, *Maoris of By-gone Days*, p. 12.
35 Hadfield, *One of England's Little Wars*, p. 24.
36 Luke Bretherton, 2019, *Christ and the Common Life: Political Theology and the Case for Democracy*, Grand Rapids, MI: Eerdmans, p. 352.
37 Bretherton, *Christ and the Common Life*, p. 353.
38 Jennings, *Acts*, p. 6.
39 Tony Ballantyne, 2015, *Entanglements of Empire: Missionaries, Maori, and the Question of the Body*, Auckland: Auckland University Press.

40 Walter Wink, 1993, *Unmasking the Powers: The Invisible Forces that Determine Human Existence*, Minneapolis, MN: Fortress Press, available at https://public.ebookcentral.proquest.com/choice/publicfullrecord.aspx?p=5423712 (accessed 8.03.2023).

41 Andrew Root sees this in the desire for relevance, suggesting that the church is allowing Silicon Valley to set the time. Andrew Root, 2021, *The Congregation in a Secular Age: Keeping Sacred Time against the Speed of Modern Life*, Grand Rapids, MI: Baker Academic.

42 Havea, *Losing Ground*, pp. 68–9.

6

Stolen Myths: Pālangi, Fairness, Native Theologies

JIONE HAVEA

Myths inform and shape theologies. And, in return, theologies preserve myths. I make these generalizing assertions not in order to unmoor theologies from the harbours of truth(-claims), but to call attention to the intertwining, and inter-feeding, between myths (read: narratives) and theologies (read: schemes that narrativize and historicize).[1] Myths are nourishing and captivating, and theologies feed on the plots and powers of myths. This is not to say that theologies innocently consume myths. Theologies are not innocent, nor detached. On the other hand, theologies are inspired, driven, intentional, biased, and a host of other descriptions that reveal the political natures of theologies. On that note, one may also claim that theologies pre-serve myths.

In general, myths and theologies are bound by space and time, and they do not easily translate or transport. When translated or transported, across languages or cultures, those myths and theologies alter. The myths of Whiteness, for instance, work differently against Black and Brown people in formally colonized lands (for example, across Africa and India) as compared to the ways that those same myths subjugate descendants of Black and Brown people taken (as slaves and cheap labourers) into White colonial societies (for example, the British empire). Furthermore, the same myths function differently against descendants of enslaved Black and Brown people who were raised in plantations to serve White empires in the so-called new world (for example, in the Caribbean islands). It is unfair to the different Black and Brown subjects to take the myths of Whiteness as if they are the same across lands and seas, and across time. Yes – there are diverse myths of Whiteness. And yes – despite being in different versions – the myths of Whiteness unite to pre-serve the subjugation of Black, Brown and minoritized people. However, the myths (and rhetoric) of Whiteness do not operate in all corners of the world. No myth or theology is timeless and universal, and so to assume that the myths of Whiteness ever had universal dominance is to give them too much credit.

In my home context of Pasifika (for Oceania, Pacific Islands),[2] the terms 'White' and 'Whiteness' are not even labels that we use when we speak of colonizers and colonization, of the colonial past or of the ongoing festering of coloniality. In my humble opinion, White and Whiteness are 'White labels' constructed by and for White-dominated societies.

In Pasifika, each of our native languages has a term for the European colonizers and their cultures, and the term in my native tongue is *pālangi* (alt. *pālagi*; compare to Māori *pākehā*). 'Pālangi' is the term that our ancestors gave to the European invaders, for a specific reason, as i explain below. But soon after the pālangi (as traders, colonialists, missionaries, etc.) came uninvited, the term that identified them changed its connotations and i attribute this change to the Christian mission, which in Pasifika is also a pālangi project.

In our context, the colonizing of native minds included taking over and appropriating (read: theologizing) native terms and languages (read: myths), by and in the interests of the pālangi. In this connection, and in the wider context of Pasifika, the inter-feeding of myths (stolen from the natives) and theologies (done by pālangi) is clear. In between these inter-feedings are the tentacles of racism.

Caveat emptor: This reflection pre-serves native interests. I am not participating in this project in order to please the pālangi, as if i am a noble savage. Rather, i participate in order to widen the space in the pālangi world for native theologies. I participate in order to call attention to and to keep the space available for native theologies rather than to be a gatekeeper of them. There are many versions of native theologies, waiting for pālangi gatekeepers to lift their bans.

Pālangi

In Tongan oral traditions, the term 'pālangi' (which is also used in other Pasifika languages) was assigned to the Europeans because they came in big ships with tall masts that reached up and touched (*pā*) the sky (*langi*). The designation had to do with the vessels, rather than being about the voyagers or their cargo. Our people had canoes and boats, but the European ships were bigger and taller. In the beginning, size mattered.

A second explanation, which locates the pālangi in a privileged position, is also in circulation: in touching the sky, the European ships were said to have brought people, matters and manners of/from the sky. This second explanation is privileged in Christian circles, where sky is easily confused with heaven and divinity. In this connection, bearing in mind that the pālangi brought Christianity to Pasifika, the pālangi people and their ways are seen as heavenly and godly.

It is, however, revealing that there is no Tongan term for heaven (as space, or value).[3] We have a term for sky (*langi*), and 'heaven' is transliterated as *hēvani*. One way to make sense of this lack in the Tongan language is to think of heaven as a pālangi concept and space, which has been introduced (in the second explanation) to overtake the Tongan space of *langi*. As such, i take the second explanation to be a later pālangi projection, by and in the interests of the pālangi.

In the Tongan worldview, life is lived at the interweaving and inter-feeding of four spheres: land (*fonua*), sea (*tahi, moana*), sky (*langi*), and underworld (*lolofonua, Pulotu*). What is experienced in one sphere is related to something that has happened, is happening or about to happen, in the other three spheres. For instance, the rain that the clouds announce is expected to fall when the tide returns to the deep and the breeze quiets down, unless the big fire beneath the sea and the island awakes to push the clouds away. (In pālangi terms, this is Epistemology 101.) In this kind of worldview, which Tongans share with other Pasifika communities, there is a place for *langi* as sky (with energy and fleeting gifts) but not *langi* as heaven (abode of divinities). The heavenizing of *langi* is part of the pālangi agenda, and it stands under the protection of the Christian mission.

The colonizers came from Europe, the pālangi world, and they colonized the (is)lands and carried away the resources of our sea of islands. That they also colonized the sea, the sky and the underworld has become clearer in the age of climate change. Even more drastic is the fact that they also colonized our minds and hearts, faiths and hopes by – to start with – appropriating (read: stealing, theologizing) our languages and worldviews (read: myths).

In the worldwide history of colonization, Pasifika was the last to be 'discovered'. Our smaller islands did not experience the wrath of colonization like the more populated and wealthier continents of Africa, America and Asia. But our larger islands are rich with the resources of the land (e.g. hardwood), sea (e.g. tuna) and underworld (e.g. minerals), with the wide sky being subdivided for the stationing and docking of pālangi satellites and globalizing (neo-colonial) networks. The key motivations behind these acts of colonization are wealth and capital, which are deposited into the pālangi 'commonwealth' – wealth that is common not because it is shared, but because it has been taken from common people.

In light of the foregoing, i add a third understanding of the term 'pālangi', on account of the term *pā* also referring to something that busts or explodes. A balloon or tyre that busts, and a firecracker or bomb that explodes, are described as having *pā*. In this third understanding, *pā-langi* refers to the busting or exploding of the sky. In this connection, the pālangi people and ways are appropriately named – they bust (*pā*) the sky (*langi*), which in the Pasifika worldview intertwines with land, sea and underworld. Their busting of the sky is evident in the troubles of the land, the sea and the underworld.

This third understanding is not traditional, but (figuratively speaking) a modern slap on the wrists of both the pālangi and the Christian natives for stealing (appropriating) a native term (pālangi) and myth. My aim here is not to return to the first (original) understanding, which some of my diehard nativist colleagues prefer, but to participate in narrativizing (read: theologizing) one of our native terms. While the second understanding was narrativized by the pālangi and preserved by the native Christians, the third understanding pushes back at the pālangi as well as invites other natives to (re)narrativize the pālangi (pun intended: pālangi as term, and pālangi as people and culture).[4]

(un)Fairness

For Pasifika, in my humble opinion, the English term 'fairness' (in the place of the Tongan terms *matalelei* and *failelei*) is a more appropriate label for what is experienced in other contexts as 'Whiteness'. Strictly speaking,[5] 'fairness' does not represent the dynamics of *matalelei* ('look well') and *failelei* ('do well'), but it provides a site-of-intersection for discussing those two native values (or utopias) together, among the native terms and myths that the pālangi have stolen.

Put directly: *matalelei* ('look well') and *failelei* ('do well') are valued by Pasifika natives, for native reasons (as i explain below), but when the pālangi arrived they presented themselves as the models for *matalelei* and their ways as the blueprint for *failelei*. The upshot was that the pālangi (people and culture) became the standards for 'fairness' (*matalelei* and *failelei*). Put differently: the pālangi saw that fairness is a delight to the eyes (of the natives) and good as a source of nourishment and knowledge (see Gen. 3.6) – so they stole our 'myths of fairness'.

In this part of my reflection, i will muse over two of the understandings of fairness – fairness in terms of complexion and appearance (*matalelei*, on the outside), and fairness as even-handed judgement and guidance (*failelei*, which comes from the inside). The fusion of the two understandings increases the appeal of the myths of fairness; the confusion, and the overtaking (stealing) of, the native valuation of fairness with the pālangi assumption of superiority give the pālangi the licence to claim rule and have dominion over the natives and our myths.

Matalelei

First, fairness in terms of complexion. A fair complexion is favoured across Pasifika, and this is the key reason why natives stay in the shade or use umbrellas on sunny days. We naturally tan, so we stay out of the sun in order to avoid getting 'less fair' (read: darker). This behaviour and attitude is not unique to Pasifika; our neighbours in Asia – where cosmetic products that are expected to make one's complexion fairer are big business – share the same fixations.

There are less-fair natives in each of the island groups and across Pasifika, but the natives with fairer complexions are seen to be 'classier' than their darker relatives. The old native explanation (read: myth) for this attitude and the resulting behaviour carry classist subtexts: the people who work under the sun are burnt, hence they are less-fair; on the other hand, the favoured and 'posh' people (*pele* and *hou'eiki* in Tongan) are protected, and part of their protection involves other people labouring under the sun for and on their behalf.[6] The favoured and posh people are fairer in complexion because they are served and protected, in and by their families and communities. In this regard, the first understanding of the native myths of fairness was about the willingness of families and villagers to protect and privilege someone(s) that they favour.

Then the pālangi arrived, with their complexion looking fairer than the poshest of the natives, and the natives lost our myths of fairness to the white skins. The native myths were appropriated by the (theologizing) invaders and fairness thus became about colour rather than care (favour) and protection (privilege) and more about supremacism than the dedication of families and communities. The myths of fairness (complexion) have thus been appropriated (stolen) to engender supremacism, by and for the pālangi.

Failelei

Second, fairness in terms of judgement. Following upon the explanations above, the favoured and protected native people were respected in – and thus they were mentored to guide and lead – their families and communities. They avoided the burn of the sun, but they had to carry the responsibility of connecting-to-memory (with the past) and the practical-know-how (for the present) of their families and communities (both of which are extended).

One of the Tongan terms that describes their function is *taula*, which has three basic meanings – 'anchor', 'healer', 'priest'. In the old days, the favoured and protected (fair-skin) people were the *taula* of their families and communities – they *anchor* their families and communities in both the traditions and in their present context, they (as healers) guide their families and communities to *well-being*, and they (as priests) *inspire and instruct* healthy options for their families and communities as they move into the future. The *taula* were fair in complexion and fair in their judgement and counsel; they were fair both on the outside and the inside.

When the pālangi arrived, with their Christian religion and theologies, the respect for the *taula* was taken over (read: stolen) by the Christian *misinale* ('missionary') and *faifekau* ('minister', 'pastor'). The work and mission of the *misinale* and *faifekau* were directed upwards, towards the heavenly world, and they projected themselves as the carriers of light and truth – both of which were preached as coming from above. The native *taula*, on the other hand, were relegated to the realm of darkness and death, not to be trusted or consulted. So, in Tongan, the *misinale* and *faifekau* were *taula-'eiki* ('noble taula') while the native taula became the *taula-tevolo* ('demonic taula'). The myths of fairness were appropriated (stolen) by the pālangi to justify why natives should need them and their teachings.

Re-theologize

Among the unnamed scars of the colonial project in Tonga, and Pasifika in general, are the appropriation of native tongues and sites of belonging.[7] That the pālangi forced themselves on us is obvious, but what has not been named is that the pālangi also manipulated our languages and myths. Put directly: they stole our myths (terms, narratives), and the foregoing reflection exposes that as unfair behaviour – i see similar behaviour in the construction of theologies – as well as asserts the right to re-theologize our myths.[8] Since pālangi missionaries appropriated 'fairness' to reference 'light' (read: right, moral, ethical, Christian), i invite the re-theologizing of 'darkness' (the missionary code for natives and native ways). I suggest two procedures in this re-theologizing move:

First, we re-theologize darkness by naming and affirming the wisdom (read: light) in dark native bodies and native minds. Natives were savages in the eyes of the pālangi who invaded our shores, but those dark natives had wisdom that benefited the pālangi; however, the pālangi did not give the natives due credit. For instance, the British explorer Captain James Cook (1728–79) is credited with 'discovering' Aotearoa New Zealand in 1769 but the official records do not name nor credit Tupaia of Raiatea – the native who read the stars, the winds and the currents, and helped navigate the HMS *Endeavour* across from Maohi Nui (known nowadays as French Polynesia) to Aotearoa.

Upon the arrival of HMS *Endeavour* to the so-called Bay of Poverty,[9] the native Māori were drawn to Tupaia and accepted his negotiation for the lives of the pālangi. Tupaia was not as fair in complexion as the white-skinned James Cook, but Tupaia was mentored in the wisdom of the native *taula* (*tohunga* for Maohi and Māori) at Taputapuātea marae, in Raiatea. His negotiation with the Māori – Tupaia knew the language that made sense to, and the oratory skills that convinced, the Māori – saved Cook and his White company. Naming and affirming Tupaia, and other natives like him, are part of the re-theologizing tasks, because these show that the natives were people of the light. In the days of James Cook, Tupaia was not the only wise and articulate native. There must have been many native lights!

The foregoing re-theologizing (re-storying and re-valuing) does not suggest that i unreservedly celebrate Tupaia. What i named above is Tupaia's contribution to the White colonial project. What if Tupaia had run the HMS *Endeavour* aground on some reef on the way to Aotearoa? He would have thereby wrecked one of the flagships of the British empire and delayed the White colonial and missionary projects.

At the underside of the re-theologizing above are the obvious connections between Tupaia's Maohi people and the Māori people of Aotearoa. In the encounter at Poverty Bay, the Māori saw Tupaia as one of them – he looked and sounded like them. Such connections support the assertion in our myths that the ancestors of the Maohi and the ancestors of the Māori were navigators who shared the same heritage, and they spread across Moana-nui-a-Kiwa (now known as the Pacific Ocean) in a series of migrations. And lest the other natives are overlooked, the ancestors of natives from the sea of islands between Maohi Nui and Aotearoa shared in that heritage and participated in the same series of migrations. On the way, Rarotonga, Samoa, Tonga and the other groups were settled, and Aotearoa was the final destination. The shared heritage of our ancestors included teachings by and about native deities, who inspired and directed our ancestors in their migrations. Our ancestors were God-fearers and theological navigators, even though they did not worship the pālangi God or know the pālangi theologies.

The re-theologizing exercise that i invite here involves naming the wisdom in native bodies and native minds, and affirming the divine influences

– by native deities – in native wisdom. Native wisdom is theological, and paying due respect to it requires re-theologizing both the native and the pālangi theologies.

Second, we re-theologize by naming and affirming the 'light' (good, acceptable) in what the myths of the pālangi call 'darkness'. In this second procedure, building upon the first, we problematize the minds of the pālangi. I attended to the pālangi myth that natives were savages above; here, i turn to the Bible – a foundational scripture for pālangi theologies – and its views on darkness.

In the first biblical myth of creation, darkness is named as the covering over the face of the deep (Gen. 1.1–2). There is no value judgement placed upon the darkness or the deep, other than that the deep was in a different state compared to 'the earth [which] was complete chaos' (NRSVUE). Darkness is presented in the same breath as a wind from God, which 'swept over the face of the waters' (Gen. 1.2). In the first two verses of this foundational myth, darkness and wind were coverings over bodies that were presented as unproblematic.[10]

God then called for light, and light *was*. God saw that the light was good, 'and God separated the light from the darkness' (Gen. 1.4b). This raises a simple question: from where did light *become*? This biblical myth suggests two answers: (i) light was in the deep, and it be/came through (that is, from under) the darkness; (ii) light was in the darkness that covered the deep, and it be/came out (up, forth) from that darkness. In both answers, light was connected to darkness. In my native mind, light was intertwined with darkness.[11]

In God's eyes, light was good. But God did not see nor announce darkness as 'not good' (or bad). In this re-theologizing reading, light and darkness are co-dependent. One *is* because of, and in relation to, the other. There is no suggestion in this initial myth that one was better than the other. The initial biblical worldview therefore contradicts the view of pālangi missionaries that darkness (code for the natives, savages) was 'not good', and even wicked.

To be fair, there are biblical bases for the missionaries' de-meaning of darkness. In the New Testament, Jesus hammered the missionary nail when he spoke of himself as 'the light of the world. Whoever follows me [Jesus] will not walk in darkness, but will have the light of life' (John 8.12 ESV). Jesus spoke against darkness, for it does not lead to life. There are discriminating texts in the Old Testament as well, as in these wisdom texts: 'Then I saw that there is more gain in wisdom than in folly, as there is more gain in light than in darkness' (Eccles. 2.13 ESV; Jer. 13.16) and 'The way of the wicked is like deep darkness; they do not know over what they stumble' (Prov. 4.19 ESV; Isa. 9.2, 42.16). Darkness is the way of fools, a lost cause.

The missionaries were biblically informed, but they did not notice the biblical texts – few in number – that affirm darkness. For instance, darkness is where God was in a key event at Sinai: 'Then the people stood at a distance, while Moses drew near to the thick darkness where God was' (Exod. 20.21 NRSVUE). This affirming text provides a space for the re-theologizing move that i invite in this reflection, while at the same time being mindful of Isaiah's distress (Isa. 5.20 NRSVUE):

Woe to those who call evil good and good evil,
who put darkness for light and light for darkness,
who put bitter for sweet and sweet for bitter!

Isaiah's distress may rightly be raised against my re-theologizing procedures. One may thus condemn me for putting 'darkness for light and light for darkness'. Guilty as charged.

But light and darkness in whose eyes?
Who decides what is light, and what is darkness?

I humbly ask that the same condemnation be placed on the pālangi: they too 'put darkness for light and light for darkness'. My re-theologizing procedures find light in the darkness that is *in the eyes of the pālangi*, and darkness *in the pālangi version of light* (fairness).

Native theologies

Little things, too, matter. Exodus 20.21 and Isaiah 5.20 are both examples of little things that matter. Over the path of this reflection, native terms (qua little things) matter because there are meaningful and meaning-giving myths in and behind them. And because they matter, the re-narrativizing and re-theologizing of native terms and myths are critical tasks for doers of native theologies.

Re-narrativizing is what the pālangi did to the term 'pālangi' (they gave it a second understanding), and also what i did in response (i gave it a third understanding). And re-theologizing is what i called for in response to the unfairness of the pālangi, focusing on the pālangi myths of light and darkness.

The two tasks of re-narrativizing and re-theologizing are not to be confused with the kind of theologies that pālangi expect natives to do: contextual(izing) theologies. They expect us to contextualize by making theological concepts or biblical texts meaningful in and for our local/

native contexts. One way we do this is to provide a local reality (for example, Minjung, Dalit, Buffalo, Kāinga, Moana, Poverty, Women, Queer, Blind, Deaf etc.) as a vessel for the theological teachings or biblical texts. The concepts or texts become meaningful for the natives and locals, and in response the natives and locals are expected to be grateful and celebrate. But are contextual(izing) theologies free of the colonial project; in other words, are they not licensed and baptized forms of stealing our myths?

I avoided directly addressing racism, one of the toxic expressions of Whiteness, because it has different manifestations in my context. One of those manifestations is the expectation that natives will not see, nor question, that we participate in our own colonization (at least of our minds and hearts) in the theologies that we do and produce. To produce theologies as the pālangi expect us to do – both in the traditional and the contextual modes – is to participate in a racial(ized) and racializing enterprise. Pālangi theology and doing theology to satisfy the pālangi are racial(ized) and racializing pursuits – they preserve Whiteness and racism.

Theology is one of the tools of the pālangi master. Using this tool to construct native theologies – theologies that break the bans of traditional and contextual methods – is one of the tasks that can help shed the racial(ized) and racializing 'preserves' of theology. I offer this reflection as a marker for that space, and as a sample to stimulate and simulate what can happen in that space, with the interests of dark native lights.

Notes

1 I use the labels purposefully: 'myths' (like 'legends') is one of the labels given to the 'narratives' of native Pasifika people, while 'theologies' are associated with the narratives by Europeans – and there is a common assumption that their theologies are true and universal. When our people do theologies, those tend to be qualified – contextual theologies, indigenous theologies, native theologies and so on – as compared to the authorized (true, pure, unqualified) theologies by the Europeans. This reflection calls these default views into question.

2 Pasifika was the last to be 'discovered' by the pālangi, and the smaller island groups (including Tonga) may have appeared too small to be of value to the land-grabbers. Some of the small islands were rich in minerals, such as Banaba and Nauru, and they were overturned and mined for the profit of the pālangi. Some of the larger island groups, like Solomon and Papua, are rich in resources and were hot properties for the pālangi. Papua is a painful case for the resource-rich western half – for West Papua is still under occupation by Indonesia. The other foreign empires occupying Pasifika islands are the USA (Tutuila), France (Maohi Nui, Kanaky) and Chile (Rapanui).

3 The Tongan mythological space that serves the functions of the Christian heaven (for example, home of the *atua*, 'deities') is *Pulotu*. There are several points

of entry to Pulotu, and they are through water bodies (the most popular entry is *at the place where the sun sets*). Pulotu in Tongan mythologies is below, rather than above in the sky.

4 I presented this (re)narrativizing move in another place as reStorying: 'Going Native: reStorying Theology and Hermeneutics', *Modern Believing*, 62(4) (2021), pp. 349–57.

5 Meanings are cultured, and they transcend the limits of language. In this context, 'fairness' does not translate *matalelei* or *failelei* but 'fairness' *works* because of the subject matter and the cultured meanings that i wish to convey. At play here is the politics of translation.

6 The labourers are sun-burnt but that does not mean that they belong to a lower class or status. Here, 'class' is not determined by one's economic strength or one's place in the mode of production. Rather, class is understood in terms of one's responsibility for the upkeeping of families and communities. Obviously, families and communities depend on the sun-burnt labourers.

7 i present these scars in contrast to the obvious and festering wounds due to White supremacism in White-dominated societies, and cultural 'Whitewashing' inspired by White policies in the new world.

8 Compare this invitation to re-theologize with my earlier call for repatriation: 'Repatriation of Native Minds' in Jione Havea (ed.), 2020, *Mission and Context*, Lanham, MD: Lexington Books/Fortress Academic, pp. 1–13.

9 It was named 'Bay of Poverty' because the White British experienced the Māori there as hostile, compared to the welcoming Māori at the 'Bay of Plenty' farther north.

10 In the native worldview, on the other hand, the deep and the waters are full of energies that can trouble, as well as uplift, life on earth.

11 In my native mind also, separating light from darkness would not have been an easy process as the biblical text implies.

7

Postcolonialism and Re-stor(y)ing the Ecumenical Movement[1]

PENIEL RAJKUMAR

Even as I put my finishing touches to this chapter, the eleventh assembly of the World Council of Churches (WCC), the broadest and most inclusive expression of the modern ecumenical movement, will take place in Karlsruhe, Germany. The WCC assembly will focus on the theme 'Christ's Love Moves the World to Unity and Reconciliation'. Unity and reconciliation can no longer be understood only in intra-Christian terms. Recent developments both in Europe and around the globe, especially following the Black Lives Matter movement, as well as the various calls for reparations for legacies of slavery, have reminded us that the unity and reconciliation that matter today are inextricably linked to historical legacies that have shaped the unjust present reality of deadly inequalities and violent discriminations.

Our growing political consciousness today no longer includes only challenging the great evils of slavery and colonialism. It has now extended its reach to address what Philomena Essed calls 'everyday racism', as in the case of the two young persons in Fort de France, Martinique, who toppled a statue of the widely celebrated French Republican abolitionist Victor Schoelcher on the accusation that Schoelcher facilitated and justified post-slavery colonization, leading to the present day, which is still organized by 'race' and inhabited by the colonial past.[2] This subversive act has been understood as an attempt to tear down the 'veil of the politics of deadly respectability and assimilation' that shapes White saviourism and the 'false promises of equality in a world structured by racism, inequalities and injustices'.[3] In such a context, the return of a WCC assembly to Europe inevitably also entails a 're-turn' to questions of colonialism, 'race', power and privilege.

In this chapter I will reflect on ecumenism from postcolonial perspective(s). As Claudia Jahnel has pointed out, postcolonial theories announce a departure from the West as the world's centre of gravity and from

Eurocentric hegemonic claims of superiority. They unmask the West's universalist claims as particularisms, whether the belief in the universality of Western values, knowledge culture and science, or the 'neoliberal universalism of the unhindered, free flow of capital'.[4] In what follows, I will examine postcolonialism both as *a tool to analyse* many of the injustices that need to be addressed by the ecumenical movement today, and as a *tool to transform* some of the historical and global injustices that we face today. This is because these two concerns are at the heart of the various ways in which postcolonialism is defined and understood, to which we now turn.

What is postcolonialism?

Robert J. C. Young argues that postcolonialism involves:

> ... first of all, the argument that the global South, the Tri continental countries, that is the nations of the three non-Western continents (Africa, Asia, Latin America, while not forgetting Oceania), for the most part remains in a situation of subordination to Europe and North America, typically in a position of economic inequality. Postcolonialism names a politics and philosophy of activism that contest that disparity, and so continues in a new way the anti-colonial struggles of the past. It asserts not just the right of African, Asian, and Latin American peoples to access resources and material well-being, but also recognises the dynamic power of their cultures, cultures that are now intervening in and transforming the societies of the West.[5]

It is important to recognize the dual dimension in Young's definition of postcolonialism, namely:

- the ongoing subordination of the global south, and
- the political and philosophical activism that seeks to redress and transform this situation of domination.

Others have also understood postcolonialism as a way of thinking of and reading history against the grain. Borrowing from Christopher Duraisingh's understanding of postcolonialism as 'a new mode of imagining, a new cultural logic posited over against the eurocentric monologic and the colonial manner of thinking and visioning reality',[6] Michael Jagessar and Anthony Reddie understand postcolonialism not as 'the demise of colonialism as "post" since it embodies both "after" and "beyond" but more about a critical stance, oppositional tactic or subversive reading strategy'.⁷ This view, that the prefix 'post' of post-colonialism refers 'not so much to a particular historical period, but to the ideologies and practises of resistance by the native people against their foreign rulers', is also emphasized by others – including Wai Ching Angela Wong.[8]

It may also be useful to understand postcolonialism alongside the concept of decoloniality, which involves uncoupling and delinking one's thinking from 'the rhetoric of modernity and the logic of coloniality' and recovering and rearticulating 'the knowledge of subalternized groups which emerge from alternative forms of justice and ways of living'.[9] What links both forms of thinking is the understanding that historical processes of dispossession and colonialism are fundamental to the shaping of the world and the shaping of the possibilities of knowing the world.[10] This fundamental belief is what is emphasized by Gurminder K. Bhambra when he writes: 'The very creation of what we understand the global to be ... are created in the context of dispossession and appropriation.'[11]

Therefore, when we speak of postcolonialism what is generally implied is a set of practices and ideas that both recognize, as well as seek to reverse, the presence, pervasiveness and persistence of colonialism (both in the past and the present) as not just a political reality but also an epistemological one. It is therefore intrinsically concerned with the transformation of one's mindset and values, which is the precise reason why postcolonial thinking 'disturbs the order of the world' and 'threatens privilege and power'.[12]

Christianity and colonialism: The unholy alliance of the missionary, military and the merchant

One way of understanding the relationship between Christianity and colonialism may be through the lens of what the Sri Lankan theologian Aloysius Pieris calls the unholy alliance of the missionary, the military and the merchant.[13] This has also been understood slightly differently by others as the nexus between Christianity, civilization and commerce – all of which are, in varying degrees of complexity, related to the colonial project of conquest.

One can understand the presence and influence of European Christian missionaries in many parts of the world during the modern period as broadly necessitated by one or more of the following reasons:

- a pastoral concern to extend spiritual care to their own European people in these parts, without interference or outreach to locals;

- a missionary zeal to reach out to the locals in these contexts, building upon the 'inroads' that have already been established, and creating new structures for the spread of Christian faith (for example, Bible translation) and Christian service (mainly Western-style education and modern healthcare, which some also understood as a means for the spread of Christian faith);
- an imperial mindset that employed Christianity to justify colonial conquest and exploitation.

While the first meant in most cases chaplaincies, the second led to the presence of European missionaries whose primary mission was to spread the Christian faith rather than to support European trade or imperial forces. A few examples that I can cite from my own Indian context are missionaries like William Carey, the first Baptist missionary also known as the father of the Serampore Mission,[14] and Bartholomäus Ziegenbalg, the German Pietist missionary sent to India by the Danish King Frederick IV of Denmark (1682–1719).[15] William Carey's missiological pamphlet *An Enquiry into the Obligations of Christians, to use Means for the Conversion of the Heathens*, published in 1792, gives an indication of his missional orientation.[16] However, it is important to recognize that these missionaries also built upon existing European presence and influence in India. Interestingly, both of them were linked to the Danish–Norwegian connections in Serampore and Tranquebar,[17] a connection that is often effaced in history by the other better-known European links with India – the Portuguese, Dutch, French and British.[18] Therefore, on the basis of the Indian experience, it can be argued that the 'progress' of Christianity beyond Europe in the modern period cannot easily be separated from commerce or colonialism, both of which can be loosely considered to be facets of the empire. However, this does not mean that all European missionaries were directly involved in either commerce or conquest, even though they exploited the contacts and routes established by commerce or conquest for their missionary activities.

The third reason represented a malevolent face of Christianity where European powers used Christianity as a tool for colonization using the idea of 'civilizing mission'. Margaret Kohn and Kavita Reddy point out that it was the Spanish conquistadores and not the British in the nineteenth century who invented the idea of 'civilizing mission' and 'legitimized military conquest as a way to facilitate the conversion and salvation of indigenous peoples'.[19] Arguing that the Spanish colonists 'explicitly justified their activities in the Americas in terms of a religious mission to bring Christianity to the native peoples', they wrote that:

The Crusades provided the initial impetus for developing a legal doctrine that rationalized the conquest and possession of infidel lands. Whereas the Crusades were initially framed as defensive wars to reclaim Christian lands that had been conquered by non-Christians, the resulting theoretical innovations played an important role in subsequent attempts to justify the conquest of the Americas. The core claim was that the 'Petrine mandate' to care for the souls of Christ's human flock required Papal jurisdiction over temporal as well as spiritual matters, and this control extended to non-believers as well as believers.[20]

Gradually, Christian missionary activity was enlisted as a spiritual alibi by other European regimes, and accorded moral justification for European colonialism 'transforming imperial projects into moral allegories'.[21] Jamie S. Scott makes an important statement when he points out that: 'by the middle of the nineteenth century, under the double aegis of "the Bible and the flag", governments, merchants, explorers, and other adventurers were exploiting the aura of ethical responsibility lent by religion to every effort to carry British civilisation to a benighted world.'[22]

Such missionary activity was foregrounded in a superior understanding of Europe's culture and religion – a superiority that emerged and was sustained by wilful and culpable ignorance of the cultural and religious richness of other countries. Mark Chapman, in his introduction to Anglicanism, mentions the London cleric Samuel Purchas's injunction to use the European achievements of printing and the god-given opportunity of navigation to spread 'the message of an "almost wholly and onely European" Jesus Christ "who hath long since given a Bill of Divorce to ingratefull Asia where hee was borne, and Africa the place of his flight and refuge"'.[23] This is just one example of the European Christian zeal to see 'that in the Sun-set and Evening of the World, the Sunne of righteousness might arise out of the West to illuminate the East'.[24]

It would be a mistake to understand this feeling of superiority as benign. It was the very root of a supremacy that used Christianity to provide justification for the colonization and conquest of other countries by European powers.[25] In many cases this was also an implicit supremacy, without the overt crudeness of demonization of the colonized 'other'. This was because political and moral philosophers of the time struggled with the incompatibility of natural law and notions of justice with colonial practices. In the end, the notion of 'civilizing mission', 'which suggested that a temporary period of political dependence or tutelage was necessary in order for "uncivilized" societies to advance to the point where they were capable of sustaining liberal institutions and self-government', was used to accord legitimacy to colonialism and imperialism – ironically by those very people who defended principles of equality and the intrinsic worth of every human.²⁶ However, in this focus on the malevolent dimensions of the empire one needs also to ensure that 'the "business as usual" dimensions of imperialism cannot simply be whitewashed'.²⁷ This prompts us to ask: how, then, can we deal with the taint of colonialism?

Dealing with colonialism beyond colonialism

Shashi Tharoor writes:

> As we embark on the twenty-first century, it seems ironically clear that tomorrow's anarchy might still be due, in no small part, to yesterday's colonial attempts at order ... But in looking to understand the forces that have made us and nearly unmade us, and in hoping to recognise possible future sources of conflict in the new millennium, we have to realise that sometimes the best crystal ball is a rear-view mirror.²⁸

One can argue that colonialism is a thing of the past with nothing much to do with us today. However, despite the departure of colonial powers in many countries, it is important to remember that 'for those who follow world affairs', it 'would not be entirely wise to consign colonialism to the proverbial dustbin of history'.²⁹ It is important to remember this as the ecumenical movement becomes more intensively engaged in questions of justice, peace-building, reparations and reconciliation. I see a few important areas in public life in which one continues to experience the effects and after-effects of colonialism that may be of interest to the ecumenical movement today.

A global (dis)order built upon 'careless anthropology' and 'motivated sociology'

The impact of colonialism is so enduring on the current world order that there is a stinging truth to the comment that 'the memory of European imperialism remains a live political factor everywhere from Casablanca to Jakarta, and whether one is talking nuclear power with Tehran or the future of the renminbi with the Chinese, contemporary diplomacy will fail if it does not take this into account.'³⁰ One can identify several 'residual problems' that are the 'result of untidy departures' by colonial powers in Western Sahara, Cyprus, Palestine, Ethiopia and Eritrea, Syria and Iraq as well as 'the chronic hostility between India and Pakistan'.³¹

While reflecting upon these 'messy legacies of European colonialism', one should also pay attention to the indirect effect of colonialism. It may be worth quoting Tharoor in full here:

> ... the intellectual history of colonialism is littered with many a wilful cause of more recent conflict. One is, quite simply, careless anthropology: the Belgian classification of Hutus and Tutsis in Rwanda and Burundi, which solidified a distinction that had not existed before, continues to haunt the region of the African Great Lakes. A related problem is that of motivated sociology: how much bloodshed do we owe, for instance, to the British invention of 'martial races' in India, which skewed recruitment into the armed forces and saddled some communities with the onerous burden of militarism?[32]

To the above-mentioned issues one can also add the continuing problems posed by the geographical boundaries drawn during the colonial rule. This is very clear in contexts like Iraq and Myanmar as well as Africa, 'colonial constructions' that have forced disparate ethnic communities together 'by the arbitrariness of a colonial mapmaker's pen'. This has led to the mangling of long-standing identities and 'older ethnic and clan loyalties' which gradually led to the 'manufacture of unconvincing political myths, as artificial as the countries they mythologize, which all too often cannot command genuine patriotic allegiance from the citizenry they aim to unite', and have led to internecine ethnic conflicts.[33]

Europe beyond Europe: The power of ideas

To treat Europe as just the sum of its politics, geography, religion and economic impact would be a gross limitation. One also needs to engage critically with the notion of Europe as a system of ideas that has shaped thinking and continues to shape the world. In other words, the Europe that we need to be thinking of is the 'invisible Europe' that has managed to hide and multiply itself in various thought and knowledge systems, and has managed to perpetuate itself as the universal and the normative in our thinking.

The postcolonial scholar Dipesh Chakrabarty, in his important work *Provincializing Europe*, lifts up how much of modern political thought is caught up in a 'first in Europe and then elsewhere' frame of thinking, and writes of the need to deprovincialize and decentre this 'imaginary figure' of Europe 'that remains deeply embedded in clichéd and shorthand forms in some everyday habits of thought'.[34] According to Chakrabarty, the domination of Europe in the social sciences departments is such that 'the so-called European intellectual tradition is the only one alive in the social science departments of most, if not all, modern universities.'[35] While acknowledging that 'an entity called "the European intellectual tradition" stretching back to the ancient Greeks is a fabrication of relatively recent European history', Chakrabarty makes the point that 'fabrication or not, this is the genealogy of thought in which social scientists find themselves inserted.'[36] Such has become the pervasive epistemological influence of the European intellectual traditions that it has rendered other intellectual traditions that were 'once unbroken and alive' as 'now only matters of historical research', treating them 'as truly dead, as history'.[37] Chakrabarty goes on to add that in contrast to this, 'past European thinkers and their categories are never quite dead for us in the same way. South Asian(ist) social scientists would argue passionately with a Marx or a Weber without feeling any need to historicize them or to place them in their European intellectual contexts.'[38] The epistemic power of colonialism has not just (re)ordered the world, but has also shaped our means and possibilities for analysing and understanding this world. This makes postcolonial and decolonial approaches to Christian history and mission all the more important for the ecumenical movement. So how can postcolonialism and decolonial perspectives help the ecumenical movement?

Postcolonialism and the ecumenical movement

The prophetic potential of postcolonialism lies in its refusal 'to acknowledge the superiority of western cultures ... Its radical idea is to demand equality and the well-being of all human beings who dwell in our planet, that there should no longer be any wretched of the earth.'[39] It is good therefore to not just understand postcolonialism as an abstract theory but as a critical commitment to the transformation of the current world (dis)order brought about by colonialism. In this lies the potential of postcolonialism as an interpretive tool for developing a transformative ecumenical vision for the twenty-first century in the context of the eleventh assembly of the WCC.

The few ways in which postcolonialism can help ecumenism today are as follows:

Identifying and engaging the empire in our midst

One of the most important tasks of postcolonialism today is calling attention to the empire in our midst. Michael Hardt and Antonio Negri remind us that the empire in our times is 'a decentred and deterritorialized apparatus of rule'.[40] It enables us to understand the empire today as 'massive concentrations of power which permeate all aspects of life' and which 'seeks to extend its control as far as possible, beyond the commonly recognized geographical, political and economic spheres, to include the intellectual, emotional, psychological, spiritual, cultural, and religious arenas'.[41]

With its intersectional focus one of the important contributions of postcolonialism to the European context can be helping it to understand the growing populist nationalisms in the context of the empire. The Indian Pulitzer Prize-winning author and activist Arundhati Roy brings out the relationship between empire and nationalism very clearly. She writes:

> Nationalism has long been part of the corporate global project. The freer global capital becomes, the harder national borders become. Colonialism needed to move large populations of people – slaves and indentured labor – to work in mines and on plantations. Now the new dispensation needs to keep people in place and move the money – so the new formula is free capital, caged labor. How else are you going to drive down wages and increase profit margins? Profit is the only constant. And it has worked to a point. But now capitalism's wars for resources and strategic power (otherwise known as 'just wars') have destroyed whole countries and created huge populations of war refugees who are breaching borders. The specter of an endless flow of unwanted immigrants with the wrong skin color or the wrong religion is now being used to rally fascists and ethno-nationalists across the world. That candle is burning at both ends and down the middle, too. It cannot all be laid at the door of resource-plundering or strategic thinking. Eventually it develops a momentum and a logic of its own.[42]

This intersection between religion, capitalism and politics is going to be one of the biggest challenges for Christian churches, not just in Europe but beyond. Sathianathan Clarke talks about a 'Knotted Interreligious Age'. What he says about this world is worth taking note of:

> Globalization and religious fundamentalism are somewhat coupled. The aggressive ethos of markets combine with violent religious sources to wrest control of the shrinking world. The flattening of the world

therefore has not led to much flattery for religion. There is a dangerous growth of 'muscular religion', which is turning out to be the expansion of hurtful and harmful expressions of religious faithfulness across the world.[43]

A postcolonial analysis that locates populist nationalisms in the matrix of the empire opens up possibilities for responding to violent nationalisms in ways that are rooted in justice, inclusivity and the affirmation of dignity.

ReStorying our mission histories

Postcolonialism and decolonialism offer many 'trans-formative' possibilities for ecumenism and mission which can help us move beyond the way our missional, theological and ecumenical mindsets are formed. In this I find the concept of reStorying proposed by the Tongan theologian Jione Havea useful.

Havea proposes that one way of dealing with colonial histories is through the process of reStorying, which includes the elements of *retelling*, *reimagining* and *repurposing*. This reStorying process would involve '*retelling* the colonial and missionary stories in ways that privilege the interests of native people'.[44] Through such retelling, both indigenous and non-indigenous people could 'also learn to *reimagine* the so-called contact between Europeans and Natives' in ways that celebrate 'the wisdom and courage of the natives … and the dependence of European explorers and missionaries' on those they termed 'pagans' and 'savages'.[45] Writing in a context in which he is addressing questions around the 'glamourization' as well as the 'repatriation' of native remains and artefacts, which are 'boxed, shelved and closeted abroad', Havea says that through such *retelling* and *reimagining*, all these remains of indigenous people can be *repurposed* 'not as dead items for exhibitionists to study, but dead bodies that *talk* on behalf of living Natives back in Pasifika and in other parts of the new world', thereby repurposing 'the so-called mission field (to be converted and saved), as schooling (is)lands that have teachers and wisdom'.[46] The larger point he makes is how one should learn to embrace the art, remains, and relics of indigenous peoples – that are often 'exoticized', objectified and domesticated – as living and sacred wisdom that can challenge and transform.

At the heart of Havea's process of reStorying is an invitation to privilege the interests of all those whom colonialisms marginalized and exploited, to celebrate their agency in mission, and to learn from their experience – all of which are connected to the question, 'Whose interests are served?' in the whole process and whose interests are protected. I see this proposal as having immense potential for transforming mindsets of implicit colonialism. It challenges us to think how acts of *retelling*, *reimagining* and *repurposing* can transform our perspectives of ecumenism. This reStorying holds particular potential for the way in which we understand our histories – missional, ecumenical and Christian. Very often our histories are told from perspectives that reinforce the same centre–periphery dynamics that characterize and characterized colonialism and Eurocentrism. This has particularly been the case with mission histories, which have often valorized the benevolent European missionaries as those who brought education and healthcare to indigenous peoples without due appreciation of the role of these people in this story.

But we need also to understand that 'the exchange of the gospel often escaped the meticulous planning' of missionaries and 'the calculating appropriations by local communities'. Rather, mission in its 'concrete expressions ... exhibited transformative directions that were hardly imagined by the missionaries'.[47] The credit for this lies with the local missionaries, whose stories are often effaced in mission histories. One example that illustrates the local 'colonized' peoples as agents and not actors of mission comes from the South Indian context, where European missionaries are often celebrated for their work among the Dalit (former 'untouchable') communities. The usual narrative is that the missionaries brought Christianity, education and healthcare to these communities, which led to their upliftment. However, if we pay attention to grassroots stories of the mission (hi)stories from the perspective of these marginalized communities, a very different history emerges. Most of the missionaries who came to South Indian contexts had limited understanding of the caste structures in South India. Therefore, subverting the caste system, or 'liberating' the Dalits from the caste system, was not part of their mission agenda at all. Their ministry of education largely targeted the upper-caste Indians, and most of them were able to reconcile the Christian gospel with caste in a way that perpetuated caste discrimination.

In such a context, it was the Dalits themselves who 'converted' the missionaries to the liberative dimensions of the Christian gospel and enlightened them about the heinous nature of the caste system and goaded them to come to Dalit settlements and minister there. This led to the building of churches in the segregated Dalit settlements (*cheri*, 'colony', *peta*), and also access to education and employment outside their traditional defiling occupations. It was the Dalits who re-baptized the missionaries to the liberative riches of the Christian gospel in a way that resonated with the life and ministry of Jesus Christ. They were the missionaries to the European missionaries – who 'rediscovered' the

Christian gospel in a way that was hidden to the European missionaries. As I and a few colleagues pointed out in a study project on 'Mission At and From the Margins' that we undertook for the centenary celebrations of the Edinburgh 1910 conference in 2010 (and which later shaped the 'Mission from the Margins' section of the WCC's mission text *Together Towards Life*): 'It was the Dalit communities which humanised missions and gave them a humane face. They were the primary agenda-setters in "converting mission" into concern for the marginalized.'[48]

Another way in which the agency of colonized communities is erased also emerges in the narratives around the history of the modern ecumenical movement that relate to its beginnings in the Edinburgh 1910 conference – which was primarily a mission conference. The unfortunate repercussion of this understanding is that it effaces the earlier and more effective impulses towards ecumenism that were already initiated in Asia. Reflecting on the Eurocentricity in which this narrative is embedded, the Indian historian T. V. Philip writes:

> Western historians cite as evidence for that argument the great missionary conferences in mission fields and in the West led to the great world missionary conference in 1910 at Edinburgh, which is considered to be the beginning of the modern ecumenical movement. It must be noted that the missionary conferences in mission fields were concerned with cooperation in mission for the sake of evangelistic efficiency, but not with unity as such. The real impetus for Christian unity came from Asian Christians who under the inspiration of the national movement took the initiative for Christian unity and for the building up of indigenous churches. In fact, it was the protest of the Asian Christians against western denominationalism and missionary paternalism which led to church unity discussions in some of the missionary conferences. The Asians not only initiated ecumenical ventures in Asia, but also contributed, through the missionary movement, to ecumenical developments in the West.[49]

It was two Asians at the conference who made strident calls for ecumenism.[50] They were V. S. Azariah from India and Cheng Jingyi from China, the youngest delegate, who urged all participants to 'go, with our Divine Master, up on the top of the Mount of Olives' to 'obtain a wider, broader, and larger view of the needs of the church and the world'.[51] Their respective contributions in their own contexts in shaping Christian unity as the overcoming of division testify to their spiritual will to translate convictions into actions. Though these expressions of ecclesial unity pre-dated other modern attempts at Christian unity, we need to ponder why they were never considered as worthy prototypes.

Related to this is also the question of what is considered 'real ecumenism' today. Has our ecumenical quest for unity become embedded in a Eurocentric foundation, based on texts, conferences and pacts? Are other living examples of ecumenism not considered the ecumenical norm and embraced with the recognition they deserve? This leads to the issue of the European gaze, which retains a Eurocentric core as the norm for ecumenism, and in the name of diversity still orientalizes the ecumenical 'others' when it comes to Christian theology as well as Christian history.

European gaze: The neo-orientalism of our times

The Eurocentrism that I mentioned earlier in relation to the social sciences is also something that can be extended to Christian theologies and ecumenism itself. Today the perception of Western theological tradition 'as *the* overarching "benchmark" against which other (less elaborated) theologies are compared and found wanting is primarily a consequence of colonial modernity'.[52] It is here that postcolonialism and postcolonial theologies might help. Postcolonial theologies apply the term postcolonialism 'largely in the sense of anti-imperialism, the battle against the legacy of Eurocentric theologies which imposes its universal claims over Christians of non-Western cultures and histories'.[53] As an 'intellectual tool' employed critically by diaspora theologians in the West, 'postcolonialism has served a discursive function of reclaiming the voice of the minorities on the margin over against the dominant power of the centre in the identity politics of the West.'[54]

Bringing the postcolonial lens to Christian theology can also help challenge the ways in which the current Eurocentric privilege within Christian theologies is sustained and perpetrated, often in the name of valuing difference itself. Today global theologies inhabit a strange context of 'anthropological culturalism' where, while wanting to 'acknowledge the diversity and particularities of all cultures and recognise others on an equal footing … such recognition is still operative within a cultural assumption that western culture is the most advanced and that white people need to tolerate those who are different from them'.[55] Out of such a context has emerged an impulse to contextualize all theologies and celebrate them in a provincialized way. However, the normativity that is accorded to Eurocentric methods and modes of theologies is so ingrained in the theological academy that the only way of engaging with 'other' theologies is through a neo-orientalism that romanticized them while not allowing the methods and motivations of these theologies to critique and challenge European ways of doing theology. The normative status that is accorded to European theologies remains intact and established. This European gaze within the theological academy that 'others' certain theologies and makes them 'reactive' theologies needs to be challenged. The same challenge can be extended to ecumenical theology itself, which has defined the ecumenical quest for unity using a European rule book and has imbued it with such a Eurocentric foundation that living examples of ecumenism – like that of the united and uniting churches in South Asia, which are based on an appreciation of the fluidity of ecclesial identity and the inventiveness and tentativeness of following the leading of the Spirit (the Church of South India has been called the second Pentecost) – are not considered the 'ecumenical norm' and embraced with the recognition they deserve.

In such a context, doing ecumenical theology from a postcolonial context today means being critically perceptive as to how the embrace of difference can be transposed to an ideological framework that still perpetuates and preserves the status quo. The important issue for us to engage with is one that Kwok Pui Lan raises in the wider context of religious difference, but can also be used in the context of intra-Christian differences – which entails examining how 'Christianity constructs difference in various historical epochs, taking into consideration the contestation of meaning, the shaping of the imagination, and the changing power relations', paying particular attention to how understandings of difference are 'constituted and produced in concrete situations, often with significant power differentials'.[56] In other words, we need to question whether the Christian appreciation of difference is still embedded in a matrix of power, which has usurped the language of difference only to tolerate 'other' theologies and not necessarily to decentre Europe and the West from the epistemic core of Christian theology and ecumenism itself.

Revisiting 'Mission from the Margins'

ReStorying as a postcolonial lens also offers space for the ecumenical movement to revisit the missiological paradigm of 'Mission from the Margins'. Despite its seeming suitability as a relevant missiological approach, this paradigm of Mission from the Margins has also been deeply contested, not least for employing the language of centre and margins that many consider ambiguous. Some detest and desist from understanding our systems and structures in terms of centre and margins. The common question that is raised is 'Who determines or defines who constitutes the centre or who constitutes the margins?' In a complexly interconnected world characterized by the intersection of 'race', class, caste, gender, ethnicity, language and religion, each with its own power quotient, there can be no easy delineation of margins and centre in flattened-out and binary terms. Marginalization is always relative and needs to be understood in its concrete contextual embeddedness. Therefore, when we are talking about the language of margins it is not implied in a homogenous sense but in a relative one. The term 'margins' can refer to all those put in an 'outsider' status and whose value, voice and vision are sidelined and undermined by the rigid yet ubiquitous gridlines of our structure of hierarchy, ideology and, I should add, epistemology because the gridlines are very much part of our thinking systems.

An important function of the language of centre and margins is its capacity to recognize the way privilege and 'un-privilege' are structured systemically. The language of centre and margins helps one to name oppression and discrimination in their myriad forms. It helps the powerful and privileged to acknowledge their implicit complicity in dominance. We know of real-life situations where structures of power and privilege are made to revolve systemically and systematically around the interests of some at the expense of others. Therefore, in one sense the language of centre and margins is actually 'speaking truth to power', calling attention to relative privileges that we often overlook, and ensuring that power is exercised in ways that subvert structures that permit domination and oppression overtly or covertly.

A postcolonial praxis of reStorying that is rooted in an affirmation of the agency of the margins and a willingness to learn lessons from history can help address the different layers in which the empire is present in our midst. It can not only embolden us to address the current colonial (dis)order, but also speak to the reality of the 'non-White empire', where nations like China – by using other nations 'as a stepping stone' – are 'employing the codes of colonial logic embedded in the operating system', and 'building their emerging economies ... based on the brutal exploitation of their own poor, whose bodies are sacrificed on the altar of progress'.[57] Such a praxis of reStorying not only helps us to 'joyfully engage in the ways of the Holy Spirit, who empowers people from the margins with agency, in the search for justice and dignity',[58] but can also lead us to a discipleship rooted in transformative faith rooted in hope and love, which can manifest itself as the assurance of things hoped for and the conviction of things unseen (Heb. 11.1) in the context of the future of the ecumenical movement.

Notes

1 This chapter relies heavily on an earlier article by the author entitled, 'Retelling, Reimagining, and Repurposing: Europe in a Postcolonial Perspective', *Ecumenical Review*, 74(2) (April 2022), pp. 179–96.

2 Françoise Vergès, 2020, 'The White Saviour or Racism without Race', *Rosa Luxemburg Stiftung, Brussels Office*, 6 October, https://www.rosalux.eu/en/article/1800.the-white-saviour-or-racism-without-race.html (accessed 8.03.2023).

3 Vergès, 'The White Saviour'.

4 Claudia Jahnel, '"The Universal Word Speaks only in Dialect": Postcolonial Impulses for an Ecumenism of Sensual Unity and an Aesthetic Ecumenical Theology', *Ecumenical Review*, 73(4) (2021), pp. 495–508, 495.

5 Robert J. C. Young, 2020, *Postcolonialism: A Very Short Introduction*, 3rd edition, Oxford: Oxford University Press, p. 6.

6 Christopher Duraisingh, 2001, 'Towards a Postcolonial Revisioning of the Church's Faith, Witness and Communion' in Ian T. Douglas and Kwok Pui Lan (eds), *Beyond Colonial Anglicanism*, New York: Church Publishing, pp. 337–67, 337, cited in Michael N. Jagessar and Anthony G. Reddie (eds), 2007, 'Introduction' in *Postcolonial Black British Theology: New Textures and Themes*, Peterborough: Epworth Press, p. xvii.

7 Jagessar and Reddie, 'Introduction', p. xvii.

8 Wai Ching Angela Wong, 2015, 'Postcolonialism and Hong Kong Christianity' in Peniel Rajkumar (ed.), *Asian Theology on the Way: Christianity, Culture, and Context*, Minneapolis, MN: Augsburg Fortress, pp. 56–64, 56.

9 Kwok Pui Lan, 2021, *Postcolonial Politics and Theology: Unravelling Empire for a Global World*, Louisville, KY: Westminster John Knox Press, p. 30.

10 Gurminder K. Bhambra, 2014, *Connected Sociologies*, London: Bloomsbury Academic Press, p. 145, cited in Pui Lan, *Postcolonial Politics and Theology*, p. 30.

11 Bhambra, *Connected Sociologies*, p. 30.

12 Young, *Postcolonialism*, p. 11.

13 Aloysius Pieris, 1988, 'Asia's Non-semitic Religions and the Mission of Local Churches' in *An Asian Theology of Liberation*, Quezon City: Claretian, p. 50.

14 'Carey, William (1761–1834): English Baptist Bible translator, pastor, and father of the Serampore mission', *BU School of Theology*, https://www.bu.edu/missiology/missionary-biography/c-d/carey-william-1761-1834/ (accessed 8.03.2023).

15 Gerald H. Anderson, 'Ziegenbalg, Bartholomäus (1682–1719): Pioneer German Missionary in South India', *BU School of Theology*, https://www.bu.edu/missiology/missionary-biography/w-x-y-z/ziegenbalg-bartholomaus-1682-1719/ (accessed 8.03.2023).

16 William Carey, 1792, *An Enquiry into the Obligations of Christians, to use Means for the Conversion of the Heathens. In Which the Religious State of the Different Nations of the World, the Success of Former Undertakings, and the Practicability of Further Undertakings, Are Considered*, Leicester: Ann Ireland.

17 For more on this, see this fascinating research project by Esther Fihl undertaken at the University of Copenhagen, 'Danish Colonialism in India: The Encounter with Indian Commercial and Agrarian Traditions', https://ckk.tors.ku.dk/english/individual-projects/danish_colonialism_in_india/ (accessed 4.11.2022). See also Esther Fihl and Caroline Lillelund, 2015, 'Danish Era (1620–1845)', *National*

Museum of Denmark, https://en.natmus.dk/historical-knowledge/historical-knowledge-the-world/asia/india/tranquebar/danish-era-1620-1845/ (accessed 8.03.2023).

18 Charukesi Ramadurai, 2016, 'India's Scandinavian Secret', *BBC News*, 30 September, https://www.bbc.com/travel/article/20160929-indias-scandinavian-secret (accessed 8.03.2023).

19 Margaret Kohn and Kavita Reddy, 2017, 'Colonialism' in Edward N. Zalta (ed.), *The Stanford Encyclopaedia of Philosophy* (Fall 2017 edition), https://plato.stanford.edu/entries/colonialism/ (accessed 4.11.2022).

20 Kohn and Reddy, 'Colonialism'.

21 For more on this, see Anna Johnston, 2003, 'The British Empire, Colonialism, and Missionary Activity' in *Missionary Writing and Empire, 1800–1860*, Cambridge Studies in Nineteenth-Century Literature and Culture, Cambridge: Cambridge University Press, pp. 13–37. Published online by Cambridge University Press, 10 December 2009, https://www.cambridge.org/core/books/abs/missionary-writing-and-empire-18001860/british-empire-colonialism-and-missionary-activity/82E91D7828CEB48FD7237D0CE1B30438 (accessed 8.03.2023).

22 Jamie S. Scott, 1996, 'Introduction' in Jamie S. Scott, *And the Birds Began to Sing: Religion and Literature in Post-colonial Cultures*, Amsterdam, Atlanta, GA: Rodopi, p. xvii. Also cited in Johnston, 'The British Empire'.

23 Mark Chapman, 2006, *Anglicanism: A Very Short Introduction*, Oxford: Oxford University Press, p. 6.

24 Chapman, *Anglicanism*, p. 6.

25 Archie C. C. Lee, 2008, 'Cross-textual Hermeneutics and Identity in Multi Scriptural Asia' in Sebastian C. H. Kim, *Christian Theology in Asia*, Cambridge: Cambridge University Press, pp. 179–204, 186, 187.

26 Even people like Franciscus de Victoria who, alongside Bartolomé de Las Casas, was one of the staunchest critics of the demonization of the Indians in the Americas by Spanish colonists, faltered in this bias: 'Victoria's understanding of the Law of Nations led him to defend the practice of Spanish colonialism, even though he emphasized that warfare should be limited to the measures required to attain the legitimate objectives of peaceful trade and missionary work. Within Victoria's critique of the legality and morality of Spanish colonialism was a rationalization for conquest, albeit a restrictive one.' Kohn and Reddy, 'Colonialism'.

27 Duncan Dormor, 'Guest Editorial: The Case for Postcolonial Theology', *Modern Believing*, 62(4) (Autumn 2021), pp. 327–37, 329.

28 Shashi Tharoor, 2016, *Inglorious Empire: What the British Did to India*, New Delhi: Penguin Books, p. 249.

29 Tharoor, *Inglorious Empire*, p. 236.

30 Mark Mazower, 'From the Ruins of Empire', *Financial Times* (27 July 2012), quoted in Tharoor, *Inglorious Empire*, p. 236.

31 Tharoor, *Inglorious Empire*, pp. 245, 246.

32 Tharoor, *Inglorious Empire*, p. 247.

33 Tharoor, *Inglorious Empire*, p. 248.

34 Dipesh Chakrabarty, 2007, *Provincializing Europe: Postcolonial Thought and Historical Difference – New Edition*, Princeton, NJ: Princeton University Press, p. 4, http://assets.press.princeton.edu/chapters/i8507.pdf (accessed 8.03.2023).

35 Chakrabarty, *Provincializing Europe*, p. 5.

36 Chakrabarty, *Provincializing Europe*, p. 5.

37 Chakrabarty, *Provincializing Europe*, p. 6.

38 Chakrabarty, *Provincializing Europe*, p. 6.

39 Young, *Postcolonialism*, p. 11.

40 Michael Hardt and Antonio Negri, 2000, *Empire*, Cambridge, MA: Harvard University Press, p. x.

41 Jeorg Reiger, 2007, 'Christian Theology and Empires' in Kwok Pui Lan, Don H. Compier and Jeorg Reiger (eds), *Empire and the Christian Tradition: New Readings of Classical Theologians*, Minneapolis, MN: Fortress Press, pp. 1–13, 3.

42 Avni Sejpal, 'How to Think About Empire', interview with Arundhati Roy, *Boston Review*, January 2019, https://www.bostonreview.net/articles/arundhati-roy-thinking-about-empire/ (accessed 8.03.2023).

43 Sathianathan Clarke, '"Mission-shaped Church" in a Knotted Interreligious Age', *Current Dialogue*, 59, December 2017, pp. 12–20, 13.

44 Jione Havea, 'Going Native: reStorying Theology and Hermeneutics', *Modern Believing*, 62(4) (2021), pp. 350–7, 353.

45 Havea, 'Going Native', p. 352.

46 Havea, 'Going Native', p. 352.

47 2015, 'Introduction' in Mark Chapman, Sathianathan Clarke and Martyn Percy (eds), *The Oxford Handbook of Anglican Studies*, Oxford: Oxford University Press, pp. 1–18, p. 6.

48 2011, 'Parallel Sessions – Theme 1: Foundations for Mission' in Kirsteen Kim and Andrew Anderson (eds), *Edinburgh 2010: Mission Today and Tomorrow*, Oxford: Regnum Books, p. 123. For more on this project, see Peniel Rajkumar et al. (eds), 2014, *Mission At and From the Margins: Patterns, Protagonists and Perspectives*, Regnum Edinburgh Centenary Series, vol. 19, Oxford: Regnum Books, https://www.ocms.ac.uk/wp-content/uploads/2021/01/Mission_at_the_Margins-final-WM.pdf (accessed 8.03.2023).

49 T. V. Philip, 1994, *Ecumenism in India*, New Delhi: ISPCK.

50 Dana L. Robert, 2011, 'Keynote Address: Mission in Long Perspective' in Kirsteen and Anderson, *Edinburgh 2010*, pp. 55–68, 57.

51 Robert, 'Keynote Address', pp. 57, 58.

52 Dormor, 'Guest Editorial', p. 333; emphasis original.

53 Wong, 'Postcolonialism and Hong Kong Christianity', p. 56.

54 Wong, 'Postcolonialism and Hong Kong Christianity', p. 56.

55 Kwok Pui Lan, 2005, *Postcolonial Imagination and Feminist Theology*, London: SCM Press, pp. 198, 199. Kwok is referring here to the work of Rey Chow, 2002, *The Protestant Ethnic and the Spirit of Capitalism*, New York: Columbia University Press.

56 Pui Lan, *Postcolonial Imagination and Feminist Theology*, p. 205.

57 Kehinde Andrews, 2021, *The New Age of Empire: How Racism and Colonialism Still Rule the World*, London: Allen Lane, p. 162.

58 World Council of Churches, 2018, 'Arusha Call to Discipleship', *World Council of Churches*, https://www.oikoumene.org/resources/documents/the-arusha-call-to-discipleship (accessed 8.03.2023).

8

A Happy Ecumenical Legacy for the London Missionary Society? Exposing the Coloniality Between Churches Engaged in Mission

VICTORIA TURNER

This chapter questions the proud ecumenical legacy of the London Missionary Society (LMS). It uncovers the complicated journey of the LMS's inter-church relations and explains the processes that led to the formation of the Congregational Council for World Mission (CCWM) and the eventual 1977 Council for World Mission (CWM). I outline how these three missionary models each employed different understandings and expressions of ecumenism. A theological analysis of the ecumenical journey of this missionary society exposes how the blanket acceptance of an ecumenical legacy whitewashes the colonial and racist assumptions held towards people and churches in the non-Western world and argues that exposing the difficult journey will better enable us to embrace change in the future.

The interdenominational practice of the London Missionary Society: Mission to the non-Western world

Desmond Van der Water, General Secretary of CWM from 2002 to 2011, in a 2008 article published in the *International Review of Mission*, stated that: 'One of the enduring legacies that LMS bequeathed to CWM was the organisation's ecumenical character.'[1] Similarly, Kirsty Murray, who completed her PhD on the early mission to Tahiti in 2002, reflected that the 'ecumenical roots' of the LMS differentiated it from its counterparts.[2] The eminent theologian John de Gruchy, a Congregationalist from South Africa, in an introduction to his edited volume exploring the LMS in South Africa, writes: 'the second reason for remembering the LMS legacy is an ecumenical one.'[3] Even the eminent historian of Christian missions and empire, Andrew Porter, claims: 'Founders of the London Missionary Society (act. 1795), were a group who came together with the interdenominational, essentially ecumenical vision of uniting within and outside Britain as many supporters as possible of Christian missions.'[4] What each of these scholars mean by 'ecumenical' is unclarified.

Usually, the Fundamental Principle of the LMS is pointed to as showing the society's ecumenical foundations. Alexander Waugh, a minister of the Secession Church at this time, drafted the Fundamental Principle that laid out the aims of the Missionary Society in 1795:[5]

> As the union of Christians in various denominations in carrying on this great work is a most desirable object, so, to prevent, if possible, any cause of future dissension, it is declared of being the fundamental principle of The Missionary Society that its design is not to send Presbyterianism, Independency, Episcopacy, or any other form of church or government ... but the glorious gospel of the blessed God to the heathen; and that it shall be left (as it ought to be left) to the minds of the persons whom God may call into the fellowship of his Son from among them to assume for themselves such a form of church government as to them shall appear most agreeable to the word of God.[6]

At this time, the London Missionary Society was not the name of this body. It was called simply the Missionary Society before 1818, to convey its status as a mission society for both evangelical Anglican and nonconformist denominations, both in the UK and from Europe. The Netherlands and Germany sent a good number of missionaries through the LMS. It was celebrated by the directors in a 1795 publication that recorded the sermons that inaugurated the society that 'such a multitude of ministers and private Christians have so affectionately united to form the Missionary Society'.[7]

The LMS was made up mostly of Congregationalists, Independents, Calvinistic Methodists and Presbyterians who united in this common cause. It attracted a few evangelical Anglicans, and even fewer Wesleyans and Baptists. It is important for our purposes to emphasize that this group was not, or could not be, ecclesiastically formulated through official church structures (for this idea of central ecclesial authority did not exist for Congregationalists), but instead was an association of diverse individuals, the majority being members of Congregational churches.

This non-ecclesiastical component is relevant for discounting the ecclesial definition of ecumenism from the LMS. The creation of the pan-denominational Missionary Society did not influence denominations to unite. The LMS owes its creation to the Evangelical Revival, the beginning of which is usually traced to Wales, with the evangelistic conversions of the schoolteacher Howell Harris, and shortly after Daniel Rowland, in the spring of 1735.[8] The Revival is characterized by its evangelistic animation and missional ardour that impacted both home and overseas. The Wesleyan and Calvinistic influences produced a 'catholic spirit' in the beginning of the Evangelical Revival, where a common aim transcended denominational divisions.[9] This period has been seen as the forerunner to the modern-day ecumenical movement but is more accurately described as a period of pan-evangelicalism. The main thrust of the Revival was to see a recommitment by all Christians to preaching Christ alone. An article published in 1802 in the *Christian Observer* explained that the aims of the evangelically minded antisectarians was 'not being so much to proselyte them to their own communion, as to re-animate them, by exciting attention to the vital truths of Christianity'.[10] Concern was not focused on breaking down ecclesiastical systems but attention was paid to influential travelling preachers, the cross-denominational Sunday School movement and home social justice endeavours, including Bible distribution projects, in order to ignite the piety of the average layperson.[11] The ultimate ambition of this movement was to reawaken the piety of believers, and not uniform this piety into one denomination. Even the overtly denominationally linked voluntary missionary societies kept their distance from the affairs of their ecclesiastical bodies.[12] William Carey, the architect of the Baptist Missionary Society established in 1792, promoted the 'capitalist model of the trading company', where ordinary Christians bought shares in the mission.[13]

If ecumenism is understood as people from different backgrounds coming together to discuss their similarities and differences, we could question the distinctiveness of each of the men involved in the founding of the LMS. Kenneth Hylson-Smith comments that as the movement moved away from the established church, small groups began to form, and the personal conversion emphasis led to the followers developing a strong sense of identity and belonging.[14] Hubs such as Trefeca College in South Wales brought students from a variety of Protestant denominations, alongside evangelical Anglicans, and although their denominational allegiances usually remained, they created their own connexion of evangelical preachers.[15] This college was financed by Lady Selina Huntingdon, who came from and married into aristocratic lines and used her influence to further the work of John Wesley and George Whitefield. John Eyre, one of the pioneers of the LMS, trained under Howell Harris at Trefeca College. He was brought up in a liberal Calvinistic tradition but chose to be ordained in the Church of England. Eyre edited the *Evangelical Magazine* and published in it a review of Melville Horne's *Letters on Missions: Addressed to the Protestant Ministers of the British Churches* in November 1794.[16] The reviewer was Thomas Haweis, personal chaplain to Lady Huntingdon. In the spring of 1794, Eyre called a meeting in the Dr Williams's Library, London, which included a Calvinistic Methodist, a Congregationalist and Presbyterians.[17] Eyre later became the treasurer of the LMS. This example acts as a glimpse into the evangelical network that connected the men involved with the LMS. The LMS did not create a new ecumenical body or even a new space for interdenominational dialogue. Rather, it was an organic extension of the home-concerned Protestant–Anglican evangelical network that already existed.

An increasing Congregational identity and practice on the ground

The increasing success of denominational mission societies and the emergence of other societies led the Missionary Society in 1818 to change its name to the London Missionary Society. This was not necessarily by choice from the directors, who benefited from the Missionary Society having the freedom to visit multiple denominations to ask for funding. The original name of the society could be confused with the denominationally tied voluntary society of a particular church, so that, for example, Baptist Christians could be convinced to give to the Missionary Society instead of giving to the Baptist Missionary Society.[18] With a more constricted name the society began to adopt a more Congregational identity. This more stable identity was also assisted by the formation of the Congregational Union in May 1831. At the Society's anniversary in 1806 a group of Independents created the first Congregational Union, but this dissolved after only three years. The LMS, according to Roger Martin, acted as a 'surrogate union' for the Congregational churches.[19]

The increasing Congregational identity at home, according to LMS historians, did not necessarily affect relations on the ground. Cecil Northcott commented in 1945 that 'Although the LMS has been the sole pioneer in many great areas, it has never attempted to establish "territorial churches" with a central authority, as an episcopal society would do.'[20] Northcott was pointing towards the practice of LMS-planted churches to centralize the authority of the individual churches. This practice is central to Congregational forms of church government where the local church meeting is the highest authority and, considering the majority of LMS missionaries were from a Congregational background, it made sense that this familiar way of running churches for the missionaries was passed on to their new congregations.[21] In practice, the level of freedom attributed to the new congregations was limited as strong-minded missionaries took centre stage and enthusiastically shared resources and teachings.[22] Therefore, this particular form of Congregational ecclesiology was inherited by local churches.

Bernard Thorogood, the General Secretary of the CCWM from 1971, held that the relaxed attitude towards Congregational church government, given by the LMS to the new churches, allowed them to explore ecumenical unions with other churches, as displayed in China, India, Zambia, Madagascar, Papua New Guinea and Jamaica, and with churches of different ecclesiological orientations in north and south India.[23] Brian Stanley, conversely, argues that ecumenism arose organically in the field by the logic of mission. Stanley comments that the missionary would often behave like a bishop, meaning Independent styles of churches became more Episcopal/Presbyterian in nature, whereas traditional Episcopal structures did not relate to church government effectively overseas and became more voluntary.[24]

Perhaps, however, there is some truth in the interdenominational nature of the sending Missionary Society seeping into their planted churches. The figure who shouted the loudest at the Edinburgh 1910 World Missionary Conference for the churches to unite in the mission field was Beijing-born Cheng Jingyi, an LMS convert and 1896 graduate of the Anglo-Chinese Institute of the LMS and newly ordained pastor of the independent Mi-shih Hutung Church in the East City of Beijing at the time of the 1910 conference.[25] At only 28 years old, easily the youngest delegate of the conference, his brave plea for 'a united Christian Church without any denominational distinctions' in China attracted an even greater volume of contemporary contempt than Azariah's former plea for egalitarian friendship.[26] The aim was for the missionaries at this conference to work well together in the field rather than influence the church structures at home or abroad. Cheng Jingyi especially caught the attention of John R. Mott and was selected to be the only Chinese delegate on the 35-person Continuation Committee. He then became joint secretary for the Chinese committee in 1913, which eventually led to the formation of the National Christian Council of China in 1922; he was nominated the first moderator and later general secretary for the Church of Christ in China, a union of 16 nonconformist denominational missions. Although the LMS history has glimpsed at the achievements of Cheng Jingyi, in general it has tended to concentrate on the achievements of the White missionaries who influenced ecumenical unions.[27] The voice of the 'native' Christian has often been superseded.[28] Martin commented that 'No doubt the founders assumed rather naively that once in the mission field, surrounded by a great multitude of heathens, such diversities of polity and church government would seem irrelevant and insignificant.'[29] The evidence points towards denominational divisions being a continuing problem for missionaries rather than indigenous Christians, considering only the youngest, and one of the geographically marginalized members of Edinburgh 1910, had the passion to fight against denominational competition. Rather than missionaries pushing indigenous churches towards uniting, it is just as likely that as newer Christians sought to enculturate Christianity, they saw the divisions as outside of what they deemed important.

The paternal ecumenism of the Congregational Council for World Mission: Mission for the non-Western world

The centrality of British missionaries in the LMS, which overshadowed indigenous church leaders, also influenced the children's work. The glorification of missionaries was promoted at home through LMS resources for children, especially relating to the John Williams missionary ships and later in 1936 through the organization of Pilots, now a United Reformed Church (URC) organization. The heroic visualizations of missions and uncivilized versions of non-Western people had to be unlearned by these young people as society became more egalitarian and the role of young people changed in the organization.[30] The romantic missionary narrative was primarily employed to inspire and educate children about the work of the mission and ultimately to raise funds that at one time made up 20 per cent of the LMS's income.[31] Historically, the agenda or perspectives of young people did not influence the internal workings of the LMS, despite the indispensability of their fundraising. The amalgamation of the girls/boys auxiliaries into the Livingstone Fellowship after the Second World War increased the voices of the young in the LMS and produced many influential missionaries and church leaders.[32] In 1958 the young people in the Livingstone Fellowship and the Congregational Fellowship of Youth decided their aims were aligned, and so they made the decision to unite. These young people were a precursor to the 1966 creation of the CCWM, where the Congregational churches altered their structures and consequently had a closer relationship with the Missionary Society.

The end of the Second World War, decolonialization, and majority world churches wanting their independent identity, and thus creating their own ecumenical unions, led the LMS to reconsider its approach to mission as fewer missionary candidates were presenting themselves.[33]

Equally significant was the theology forming in ecumenical circles, which stated that mission was the work and responsibility of the whole church rather than voluntary societies; this led to the LMS seeking closer relationships with its associated 'sending' Congregational unions, beginning with the Congregational Union of Scotland in 1952.[34] In 1961 two important Commissions from the Congregational Union of England and Wales (CUEW) were approved, one asking for the churches to enter into a covenanted relationship with each other, while the other was in the form of a letter, dated 24 April, to be sent to the LMS asking for it to restructure in the form of a 'churchly body'.[35] The proposal from the CUEW, to reformulate the LMS as one missionary body incorporating mission at home and overseas, was assessed with caution by LMS directors. They were wary that the CUEW might overshadow the smaller Congregational unions. The move, however, was supported by 90 per cent of the serving LMS missionaries in 1962, showing how the feeling on overseas ground aligned with the movement of the churches at home.[36] The LMS-associated non-Western churches were not asked.

Another significant influence was the integration of the International Missionary Council (IMC) into the WCC as the Commission for World Mission and Evangelism (CWME) at the November–December 1961 WCC Assembly in New Delhi.[37] This may go some way in explaining the overwhelming support from missionaries. A report from the joint committee of the LMS, the Congregational Commonwealth Missionary Society, and the associated national Congregational unions was formally brought to the 1966 May CUEW Assembly, alongside a constitution to move towards a covenanted church body, the Congregational Church of England and Wales, and both were passed.[38] The model of voluntary auxiliaries, committees, and a 300-member board was changed to a Mission Council that worked through the seven associated Congregational unions. The new model that replaced the LMS and the Congregational Commonwealth Missionary Society was named the Congregational Council for World Mission in July 1966.[39] Andrew Prasad regards this shift towards a church-led organization as a 'half-way reform to CWM', which enabled the churches of the global south to also voice for their inclusion.[40]

Instead of individuals directing the mission of the missionary society as with the voluntary body, with the CCWM the Congregational churches were in direct relationship with one another. Even though the CCWM undoubtedly adopted a Congregational nature, missionaries from other denominations were invited to serve with the CCWM, and the Fundamental Principle carried through the reform. The decisions about the direction of the CCWM lay with British, Irish, South African, Australian and New Zealand Congregational unions, who were named 'Constituent

Churches'. Majority world churches were those in the Pacific (Samoa, Tuvalu, Nauru, Papua New Guinea and the Solomon Islands), East Asia (Malaysia, Hong Kong, Korea, Myanmar, Singapore and Taiwan), South Asia (India and Bangladesh), Africa (Malawi, Madagascar, Zambia and South Africa), and the Caribbean (Guyana, Jamaica and the Cayman Islands), and these churches were named 'Associate Churches'. The method of conversation had improved for the majority world churches associated with the CCWM. They could now speak to the Western churches that were directing their mission rather than the individuals who sat on the missionary society voluntary board, but they were still powerless. It was a relationship that saw them as 'less than' and continued the connotations of majority world churches needing to 'mature' or 'grow' before being allowed to make their own decisions. Their purpose was to be missioned to by the global north churches and to accept what was judged best in their context by the aliens in their land.

Another example of how the Associate Churches were overlooked is the change in name from the Congregational Council of World Mission to the Council for World Mission after the creation of the URC in 1972. The URC brought together the CUEW and the Presbyterian Church of England[41] and consequently brought into the union the (English) Presbyterian Board of Missions (1847). The Board of the CCWM and the staff decided to remove Congregational from the name to create the Council for World Mission. The creation of the URC was not the first time a Presbyterian denomination had entered the missionary society partnership. In 1908 the Congregational and Presbyterian churches united to form the South India United Church, the 1927 Church of Christ in China which brought together a number of Reformed and Presbyterian churches; the 1947 Church of South India; and the 1970 Church of North India, which also brought Episcopal ecclesiology into their unions. Rather than being seen as an exciting new venture into ecumenical life, these overseas unions were even seen as problems.[42] Perhaps the question of why majority world churches are less engaged with the Faith and Order agenda that the WCC is grappling with today can find an answer here. Unions only seem to be significant when they happen in the Western – and fundamentally British – context.

The journey towards real partnership: Mission with the non-Western world

The 1963 Mexico City Conference of the WCC's Commission on World Mission and Evangelism called for mission to be a partnership between the six continents. Other missionary bodies were calling for similar changes. The Conference of Missionary Societies in Great Britain and Ireland was described by Thorogood as the 'annual self-flagellation of missionary societies held at Swanwick in June' in the first of his 'meditations'; these were a collection of five theological documents that he wrote to explain his thinking about the place of CCWM during this time of rapid missiological change.[43] Divergent views were also expressed in the annual CCWM conference in the Hayes Conference Centre, Swanwick, a legacy inherited from the LMS, originally set up as an information-sharing event from missionaries on furlough and as a recruitment drive. One response from a missionary, Elsie Jacquet, to the 1970 conference expressed:

> I feel I must tell you how bewildered, distressed and worried I am both for myself and I know some other members of the Conference ... CCWM was criticized and ridiculed in a most negative way and I have come home wondering whether I have wasted my life completely ... I think the 'Radicals', as they called themselves, were given more than enough key time without time nor opportunity for the other side [the Conservatives] to be heard.[44]

The CCWM conference attracted both dedicated missionary supporters and a good number of interested young people. These younger members were probably influenced by the Student Christian Movement, who had already disbanded their missionary arm, SVMU, in 1952 and were emphasizing mission as being cross-cultural and political in nature.[45] Robert Steel, Professor of Geography at the University of Liverpool, was also to provide feedback and commented that the sometimes 'disturbing' conversations may have shaken older members but that it is not a bad thing if it 'provokes us into further enquiry'.[46]

Thorogood believed that the general negativity towards missionary societies was not necessarily applicable to CCWM. In a response to the World Council of Churches Divisions of World Mission and Evangelism and Interchurch Aid (now CWME), then headed up by Alan Brash and Philip Potter, the document 'On the Ecumenical Sharing of Personnel' called for an international exchange of personnel, stemming from resolutions from the 1968 Uppsala Assembly. Thorogood wrote:

We [CCWM] feel that the practical thrust of the WCC paper is not something we would wish to encourage, and that the theological thinking behind it is not very adequate ... the role of the Church in mission cannot be readily circumvented or replaced.[47]

Thorogood simply did not 'accept the paternalistic pattern which seems to be the writer's views on missionary bodies' and therefore, as an organization, they could not take seriously the urgency of the report for restructure.[48] Thorogood lamented the 'striking' lack of confidence in the UK, in her churches and in her missionary calling; and the 'doubt as to the standing of the white missionary anywhere in the coloured world', juxtaposing the backlash of an earlier entitled confidence in colonialism.[49] He stated that they lived in a world of 'exaggerated sensitiveness towards culture' where White missionaries were stopped from using their initiative in the field.[50] He did admit that some doubt was necessary for missionaries to succeed and theological thinking to advance, but questioned whether all doubts really came from the Holy Spirit. For instance, he believed the 'vague talk of a Moratorium' to be coming from the anti-colonial backlash, rather than the missions or churches themselves.[51] In his third meditation, he wondered whether the current structure of CWM, which was between a church agency and independent society, was the most efficient. He used the model of the Parish Evangelical Missionary Society, which restructured to CÉVAA Communauté évangélique d'action apostolique in 1970; this eliminated any hierarchy between sending and receiving churches, but he ultimately decided that the diversity of denominations partnered with CWM made this impossible where the different sending bases complicated this, and he stated that it would be more of a 'public relations' exercise than anything else.[52]

The Singapore Conference

The Singapore Conference was designed as an extended board meeting to discuss the next five-year plan. It met between 31 December and 6 January 1975. Realistically, it should not have had the impact it did, with only 54 people in attendance, 12 of whom came from the URC, and 21 from non-Western churches (ignoring the three missionaries who took their delegation), and one more man named John (four) than there were women (three).[53] The Conference mostly concentrated on getting feedback through Area Groups, excursions through church visits in the region, worship and plenary groups.[54] In a later reflection Thorogood wrote that 'the major recommendation' from this conference, at which both groups of churches were represented, was that 'CWM should make a thorough and urgent attempt to reform its structure so that all the associated churches might share fully and responsibly in the one missionary task.'[55] Robert Latham (the Board Chair) later expressed the opinion of the majority world churches as 'feeling inhibited from mission because every initiative had come from London, together with the personnel and funds required'; and they felt like second-class churches in the partnership without an effective voice in the Council 'where policy regarding mission was determined'.[56]

After some structural work was undertaken in London, a preparatory group then met in Hong Kong in 1976 to discuss the proposals coming from the Singapore Conference. This was a more globally inclusive group of 14, with only one URC member, and representatives from Hong Kong, Taiwan, Samoa, North India, Zambia, South India, South Africa and Papua New Guinea.[57] Notwithstanding a lot of formal discussions with churches, asking them to discuss this reform at their General Assemblies or Executives, and work with charity commissions and constitutions, the Board in 1977 was reformulated with representatives from every member church.

Post-conference

Just before the Hong Kong conference, Thorogood prepared a summary to be circulated that included: 'from this [Singapore Consultation] came the clear conviction that all these churches wished to share equally and fully in the council and that the British based organisation was inadequate for the task.'[58] He dedicated the majority of his time as General Secretary to organizing and preparing for this new CWM structure. He was also pivotal in recruiting Miss Daisy Gopal Ratman, at this time General Secretary of the Church of South India (present at both Singapore and Hong Kong Conferences), to take over as Chair from Robert Latham in the new board.[59] In his *Gales of Change*, an edited collection of the history of CCWM/CWM from 1945 to 1977, Thorogood does not explicitly mention the Singapore Conference, only that 'The 1977 Reform enabled the CWM to be internationalized and so to respond to the reality of the church context.'[60] He dug a little deeper in *The Flag and the Cross: National Limits and Church Universal*, published in 1988:

> Over the centuries this [nationalistic] limitation has shaped the Protestant mind so that a national label has become characteristic. It means that all the key decisions are taken within that framework. The result

is plain. The international dimension of the church has been pushed to the edge of church life ... if we really believed in the international church and the essential equality of all its parts, then we would deal internationally church to church without any society as intermediary.[61]

Thorogood's transformation and dedication towards meaningful change should be celebrated.

Why clarifying the ecumenical development is important: Honouring the non-Western world

Kwok Pui Lan, in her *Postcolonial Politics and Theology: Unravelling Empire for a Global World*, uses the work of the Indian political scientist and anthropologist Partha Chatterjee to question Foucault's universal concept of 'governmentality' that he suggested stemmed from the Christian pastorate.[62] Foucault, rather than concentrating on central structural powers, was interested in diffused power and control such as policing, or schooling, that benefited and protected the body politic.[63] Chatterjee's work, however, points out that these universal values that governmentality were supposed to protect were denied to colonial subjects.[64] Without the privilege of democracy, governmentality became something suspicious or threatening.[65] The absence of the 'other' in the democratic system does not simply mean we should show remorse and involve them in the same political system. Chatterjee encourages us to think more deeply about the core of the system and how previous ways of its functioning should not continue into the future. Extending this to ecumenism, the failing is not simply that ecumenism did not extend enough, but that the concept of ecumenism at that time was limited, and therefore unfulfilled and faulty, and not one that we should hold up today.

The attractive rhetoric of LMS/CCWM/CWM all having ecumenical principles is simplistic and does not do justice to the progress made towards equality in mission. The relationship between the Missionary Society and ecumenism has been complex and mirrors larger theological trends in missiology and ecumenical thought. It is a fundamentally selfish claim on the part of Western churches to hold that this missionary society has always been ecumenical. It suits the identity of the Western churches who belong to the partnership today, especially the URC, which holds an ecumenical identity at its core. To hold on to this claim, however, means adopting and accepting multiple models of ecumenism, including those that exclude majority world churches. This stance absolves the Western churches from blame or the need for apology. The CCWM was the second missionary society to change in response to theological developments, which is impressive and should be celebrated, but the change was necessary for correcting an error. We cannot uphold misguided and less-than models of ecumenism with pride. They were flawed, power hungry, voice crushing and blind to emerging leaders and passions. The hesitancy towards change also discounts the idea that friendship was more important than structures and these reforms responded to indigenous churches.

This is not to say that the model of CWM today is perfect, or any ecumenical body or church can be perfect. It is to suggest that ecumenism needs to be rid of coloniality between churches before it can be accepted as legitimately ecumenical. Remembering the journey towards 'real ecumenism' will help us be more flexible when further reforms are needed to respond to new contexts. It is a harder narrative to 'sell' as Western churches, but to really uphold the desire to have 'friendships' with majority world churches, we require a stance of humility that requires an apology and a pledge to do better.

Notes

1 D. Van der Water, 'Council for World Mission: Case Study and Critical Appraisal of the Journey of Partnership in Mission', *International Review of Mission*, 97(386) (2008), pp. 305–22, 316.

2 K. Murray, 2002, 'Missionary Kingdoms of the South Pacific? The Involvement of Missionaries from the London Missionary Society in Law Making at Tahiti, 1795–1847', University of Edinburgh PhD thesis, p. 107.

3 J. W. de Gruchy, 2000, 'Remembering a Legacy' in J. W. de Gruchy (ed.), *The London Missionary Society in Southern Africa, 1799–1999: Historical Essays in Celebration of the Bicentenary of the LMS in Southern Africa*, Athens, OH: Ohio University Press, pp. 1–6, 2.

4 A. Porter, 2006, 'Founders of the London Missionary Society' in *Oxford Dictionary of National Biography*, available at https://www.oxforddnb.com/view/10.1093/ref:odnb/9780198614128.001.0001/odnb-9780198614128-e-42118#:~:text=The%20founding%20generation%20would%20have,of%20church%20order%20and%20government (accessed 8.03.2023).

5 B. Stanley, 'The Reshaping of Christian Tradition: Western Denominational Identity in a Non-western Context', *Studies in Church History*, 32 (1996), pp. 399–426, 405.

6 R. Lovett, 1899, *History of the LMS*, vol. 1., London: Oxford University Press, p. 36.

7 Directors of the London Missionary Society, 1975, *Sermons Preached in London, at the Formation of the Missionary Society, September 22, 23, 24, 1975*, London: Printed and sold by T. Chapman, p. 2.

8 D. Bebbington, 1989, *Evangelicalism in Modern Britain: A History from the 1730s to the 1980s*, London and New York: Routledge.

9 R. H. Martin, 1983, *Evangelicals United: Ecumenical Stirrings in Pre-Victorian Britain, 1795–1830*, Metuchen, NJ and London: Scarecrow Press, p. 3.

10 *Christian Observer*, i (1802), p. 709, as quoted in D. M. Thompson, 1985, 'Denominationalism and Dissent, 1795–1835: A Question of Identity', *Friends of Dr Williams's Library* (39th lecture), p. 9.

11 Martin, *Evangelicals United*, pp. 7, 25.

12 B. Stanley, 1992, *The History of the Baptist Missionary Society 1792–1992*, Edinburgh: T&T Clark, pp. 28–9, 386–7.

13 D. Robert, 2009, *Christian Mission: How Christianity Became a World Religion*, West Sussex: Wiley Blackwell, p. 45.

14 K. Hylson-Smith, 1992, *Evangelicals in the Church of England 1734–1984*, London: Bloomsbury.

15 R. G. Martin, 'Selina, Countess of Huntingdon', *Transactions: The Congregational History Society*, 15(2) (1945).

16 B. Stanley, 1990, *The Bible and the Flag: Protestant Missions and British Imperialism in the Nineteenth and Twentieth Centuries*, Leicester: Apollos, p. 56.

17 Martin, *Evangelicals United*, p. 42.

18 Martin, *Evangelicals United*, p. 63.

19 R. H. Martin, 'The Place of the London Missionary Society in the Ecumenical Movement', *Journal of Ecclesiastical History*, 31(3) (1980), pp. 283–300, 298.

20 C. Northcott, 1945, *Glorious Company: One Hundred and Fifty Years Life and Work of the London Missionary Society 1975–1945*, London: The Livingstone Press, p. 65.

21 A. Prasad, 2006, 'Mutual Sharing in Mission: An Analysis of the Structures, Programmes and the Theological Statements of the Council for World Mission, 1977–2000', University of Birmingham DPhil thesis.

22 See L. Sanneh, 1995, *Translating the Message: The Missionary Impact on Culture*, New York: Orbis Books.

23 B. Thorogood (ed.), 1994, *Gales of Change: Responding to a Shifting Missionary Context. The Story of the London Missionary Society 1945–1977*, Geneva: WCC Publications, p. 243.

24 Stanley, 'The Reshaping of Christian Tradition'.

25 'Ch'eng Ching-yi' in H. L. Boorman (ed.), 1967, *Biographical Dictionary of Republican China*, New York: Columbia University Press, pp. 284–6.

26 B. Stanley, 'The World Missionary Conference, Edinburgh 1910: Sifting History from Myth', *The Expository Times*, 121(7) (2010), pp. 325–31, 329.

27 A. M. Chirgwin, 1944, 'The Younger Churches', *1795–1945 Triple Jubilee Papers: Issued in Preparation for the 150th Year of the London Missionary Society in 1945–6*, no. 1, London: The Livingstone Press.

28 See Thorogood (ed.), *Gales of Change*, written by White missionaries and exemplifying the European influence on uniting churches in the mission field, especially chapters 2 and 5 covering South Africa and South India.

29 Martin, 'The Place of the London Missionary Society', p. 290.

30 C. Binfield, 'The Purley Way for Children', *Studies in Church History*, 31 (1994), pp. 461–76.

31 B. Stanley, 'Missionary Regiments for Immanuel's Service: Juvenile Missionary Organization in English Sunday Schools, 1841–1865', *Studies in Church History*, 31 (1994), pp. 391–403.

32 Numerous young people went on to serve with, and in, LMS/CWM, WCC

and individual churches. Robert Latham, 'Patterns of the Spirit' in Thorogood (ed.), *Gales of Change*, pp. 222–4.
33 Latham, 'Patterns of the Spirit', pp. 222–4.
34 Latham, 'Patterns of the Spirit', p. 225.
35 Prasad, 'Mutual Sharing in Mission', p. 29.
36 LMS, Board Minutes, 25 April 1962, as quoted in Prasad, 'Mutual Sharing in Mission', p. 30.
37 The formal joining was at the 1961 WCC Assembly but the decision was made at the Ghana Assembly of the IMC, convened from December 1957 to January 1958. M. Sinclair, 'The Christian Mission at This Hour: The Ghana Assembly of the IMC', *International Review of Missions*, 47(186) (April 1958).
38 Latham, 'Patterns of the Spirit', p. 228.
39 Latham, 'Patterns of the Spirit', pp. 220–7. The Commonwealth (Colonial) Missionary Society worked predominantly with White European-descent congregations primarily in Canada and North America.
40 Prasad, 'Mutual Sharing in Mission', p. 40.
41 The Re-formed Association of Churches of Christ also joined the URC in 1981 and the Congregational Union of Scotland in 2000.
42 Thorogood explained how the unions of CWM-associated churches made a restructure of the organization problematic. B. Thorogood, 'Secretarial Meditation 3', 25 June 1973, *LMS/CWM Home Box 142*.
43 B. Thorogood, 'Secretarial Meditation 1', 22 May 1973, *LMS/CWM Home Box 142*.
44 E. Jacquet, 'Letter to B. Thorogood', 16 August 1970, *LMS/CWM Home Box 142*.
45 R. Boyd, 2007, *The Witness of the Student Christian Movement: Church Ahead of the Church*, London: SPCK, pp. 68–75.
46 R. W. Steel, 'Swanwick Conference 1970', *LMS/CWM Home Box 142*.
47 B. Thorogood, 'Letter to John Huxtable', 16 September 1970, *LMS/CWM Home Box 139*.
48 B. Thorogood, 'Central Comment on the Report', 27 July 1970, *LMS/CWM Home Box 139*.
49 Thorogood, 'Secretarial Meditation 1'.
50 B. Thorogood, 'Secretarial Meditation 2', 14 June 1973, *LMS/CWM Home Box 142*.
51 Thorogood, 'Secretarial Meditation 1'.
52 Thorogood, 'Secretarial Meditation 3', 25 June 1973, *LMS/CWM Home Box 142*.
53 'Consultation on Policy: Singapore', *LMS/CWM Home Box 135*.
54 'Consultation on Policy: Singapore'.
55 B. Thorogood, 'Planning Group: Draft for the September Board', 10 July 1975, *LMS/CWM Home Box 135*.
56 Latham, 'Patterns of the Spirit', p. 237.
57 B. Thorogood, 'Hong Kong Committee Information Letter', 18 June 1976, *LMS/CWM Home Box 136*.
58 B. Thorogood, 'Statement of Intent', November 1976, *LMS/CWM Home Box 136*.
59 Thorogood, *Gales of Change*, p. 252.
60 Thorogood, *Gales of Change*, p. 249.

61 B. Thorogood, 1988, *The Flag and the Cross: National Limits and Church Universal*, London: SCM Press, p. 71.

62 Kwok Pui Lan, 2021, *Postcolonial Politics and Theology: Unravelling Empire for a Global World*, Louisville, KY: Westminster John Knox Press, pp. 28–38.

63 M. Foucault, 2007, *Security, Territory, Population: Lectures at the College de France 1977–1987*, M. Senellart (ed.), New York: Palgrave Macmillan, pp. 147–8.

64 P. Chatterjee, 2007, *Lineages of Political Society: Studies in Postcolonial Democracy*, New York: Columbia University Press, p. 9.

65 Creating, therefore, an epistemologically paternalistic gap between liberal democracy in the West and other forms of governance in the majority world ignores the violence that the democratic Western empire committed, and also the indigenous forms of governance that continued before, during and after colonial rule. Chatterjee, *Lineages of Political Society*, pp. 13–14.

9

Speaking to the Past: A Black Laywoman's Theological Appraisal of the LMS Archives

CAROL TROUPE

Introduction

In the autumn of 2020, I embarked on a year-long project for Council for World Mission (CWM) looking at, and reflecting on, some of their mission archives.[1] As part of CWM's Legacies of Slavery project,[2] this was an attempt to see what might emerge from an encounter between mission magazines and a British-born descendant of enslaved Africans from the Caribbean context.[3]

I admit that I came to the project with some trepidation, for two main reasons. On the one hand, I was certainly not a missiologist or a mission historian. What was I going to be able to do with this archive material; what would emerge from my engagement with it; was whatever I had to offer at the end of the process even going to be accepted by, or of value to, those who funded the work?[4] More than once, I had to remind myself that my not being a mission specialist was exactly the point. This was not an approach meant to replicate or bolster the historians and missiologists; this was an attempt to obtain another perspective on this material – one that was not detached or claiming objectivity. I was not creating a historical survey of mission activity, nor was I carrying out this work to come up with results to please the church or even CWM. Rather, my aim was to enter into an exploration of this material, informed by my context as a Black British woman of African-Caribbean heritage and by the influence of womanist and Black theology, in order to see what that exploration could offer to the church in general (whether or not it was accepted) or, more specifically, to those who were interested in addressing issues of inclusion and justice. As a result of this engagement, what would emerge that spoke to the legacies of slavery, and was there anything that could be offered to mission engagement in the present time? The other issue was more personal. As I have said, this project began in the autumn of 2020, in the midst of the COVID-19 pandemic and, more pointedly, after the murder of George Floyd and the subsequent resurgence of Black Lives Matter protests and the copious discussion around issues of 'race', representation, anti-Blackness and White supremacy. To then enter into an encounter with material that observed and presented Black lives through the lens of the White mission enterprise was a daunting prospect.

The magazine archives

The material I looked at came from four main sources: the *Juvenile Missionary Magazine* (*JMM*), which was subsequently replaced by *News from Afar* (mission magazines aimed at children), *Missionary Chronicle*, and later the *Missionary Magazine and Chronicle* – an adult mission magazine that I turned to as a result of my desire to explore material actually published during the transatlantic slave trade (the *JMM* was not produced until 1844, post-abolition).

The motivation for Christian mission and, by association, for the creation of the magazine itself is stated in the earliest edition of the *JMM*, referencing, as it does, the words of Jesus in Matthew 28:[5]

> The Great Command: Go ye into all the world, and preach the gospel to every creature.[6]

Later in the same edition, the readers are again reminded of their duty as Christians and the focus of the mission activity of the London Missionary Society (LMS):

> The solemn fact which we should all keep before our minds is, that *there are yet above 600,000,000 of souls in the world not converted to Jesus Christ*. If *we* are his disciples, we must do *all* we can towards their conversion.[7]

The material is varied and includes pictures, poems, letters, extracts from missionary accounts of their experiences in the field, stories sent in from various places, and even records of congregations' donations to the mission project and so on. For the purposes of the project, I focused on those pieces that spoke mainly about Black communities – whether on the African continent or in the Caribbean (and South America) – and also on some pieces that referred more generally to 'heathens'. Through a process of reading and reflecting on the various pieces over a period of time, I began to notice particular themes emerging and recurring and decided to use that as a way to 'categorize' what I was reading.[8]

Christian and European superiority

This I designated as a category in itself, though it underpins all the other categories. The idea of European and Christian mores as superior, and that conversion to Christianity brings moral and spiritual improvement (as well as the chance of salvation) to the 'heathens', permeates the work and of course provides justification for the mission project itself.

The material I placed in this category consisted of pieces such as poems berating indigenous gods as cold and distant, unconcerned with the welfare of their worshippers, or descriptions of African (or other non-Christian) parents whose cruelty towards or neglect of their children could be rectified by knowledge of the gospel and the love of Jesus. Christian parents are presented as the model to which they should aspire:

> ... and therefore, you should say, 'thank God for giving me Christian parents, who have been taught to love me and take care of me ...'[9]

There are other instances where European belief and behaviour is presented as the model against which African cultures and spiritualities should be measured. The closer they adhere to an idea of European and Christian behaviour, leaving behind their traditional religions and spiritualities, the more acceptable they become, as illustrated by this quote from a missionary account of locals attending a church service: 'Their behaviour would compare very favourably with that of Christians in England.'[10] Another example of this idea of Christian superiority was illustrated in the way that, supported by biblical text, the material state of enslavement was presented as less problematic than 'slavery to sin'. This extract speaks of post-abolition preaching to the people of Jamaica:

> God's holy Spirit has blessed the words spoken by his servants, and some of these Negroes have been set free from a far worse slavery than that of which I have been speaking ...[11]

The reference to biblical texts such as John 8.34, 36 and Romans 6.16, 18, which speak of slavery to sin, creates the means by which it is acceptable to preach obedience and acquiescence to the enslaved, since they are 'rewarded' with access to the gospel and to eternal life, thus avoiding a state that they are told is much worse than any material enslavement on earth. Here we see how Black life is measured against – and also influenced by – what is deemed acceptable and correct through a White Christian lens that, in this instance, privileges adherence to doctrinal ideas above justice.

Disparagement of non-Christian/Black/African

This and the previous theme are, of course, two sides of the same coin. Here we see how aspects of Black lives, whether cultural habits or religious practices, are perceived, evaluated and presented to the reading audience.

Leonard T. Horne's account of Vanderkemp's experiences in 'The Hottentots[12] and the Gospel' recounts how, 'It was hard work to make dirty people clean, lazy people industrious, and above all, wicked people Christians.'[13]

Another account describes them as '... extremely lazy, only roused to action by excessive hunger'.[14] They are described in demeaning terms even while it is acknowledged that they have been abused by the Dutch settlers. We see the community as observed by European Christian eyes, without historical or cultural context, and judged against the norms and expectations of their observers.

This judgement of Black life continues in a piece from the *Missionary Magazine and Chronicle* of March 1840, which is focused on the wakes and funerals of formerly enslaved people of Demerara and entitled 'Funeral Revels Discontinued, and the Solemnities of Death Improved':

> The night was spent in revelling and drunkenness, with all their vile accompaniments. I have often been pained to hear the sound of the drum and the loud yell of mirth, and the song of sinful festivity, issuing from the house in which a corpse was lying.[15]

The ways in which the community chooses to mourn the death or celebrate the life of the departed are judged unsuitable and unseemly by the observer, since they so starkly contrast with expectations of Christian solemnity and decorum. Yet what is observed by the outsider as 'drunken revelry' with the drum and shouts of 'mirth' may mean something completely different to those actually participating, having their own religious, spiritual and cultural beliefs and practices around death in the community. Even if it is simply 'revelry', then that itself is surely a valid expression of the right of formerly enslaved communities to gather, interact and amuse themselves as they choose, without interference from outsiders.

Depictions such as this do, of course, serve a purpose in mission literature, where readers are encouraged to engage with and support the mission enterprise (buying the magazine, donating and fundraising) by observing the stark contrast between the morally and spiritually deficient heathen and the pious and civilized Christian convert, as illustrated by the next theme.

Christianity as control or correction

Here we see presentation of examples of how those influenced by or converted to Christianity are transformed in outlook and behaviour, illustrating justification of the mission quest. In this particular instance we see how the previously disparaged funeral rites have now been transformed into behaviour that is acceptable to the Christian observer '... and after prayer the company separate, and instead of returning, as formerly, to carouse with friends of the deceased, proceed to their respective homes'.[16]

While planters are originally suspicious of the missionaries, they are eventually convinced that this conversion to Christianity is advantageous to them, since it encourages obedience and compliance in the enslaved communities. We hear from Mr Wray, writing in 1823 about his mission travels through the estates of Berbice (Guyana). He uses his sermons to encourage obedience and gratitude among the enslaved and in one instance tells them, 'how thankful they ought to be that their master had introduced the book of God among them'.[17] Later we are shown this theme more explicitly: 'Thus they are taught their duty to God on the Sabbath, and their duty to their master in the week.'[18]

Black piety or self-negation

This theme was named for the ways in which I observed Black people speaking of their own unworthiness, putting the welfare of the church above their own, or taking on doctrinal ideas that worked against their own best interests.

In one piece, a CMS missionary in Uganda tells readers how the wife of a chief relates '... that when she first saw a European she thought he was God'. Later, having learned that this is not so, she continues '... for a long, long time I could not believe that such a great God would come into the heart of a poor black woman, but now I know He does ...'[19] As well as illustrating this theme, it harks back to the European superiority theme previously touched upon. Despite being the wife of a chief, she initially perceives herself as too lowly a person to be of concern to this great Christian God.

In an extract depicting a dying enslaved woman, Judy Campbell,[20] she speaks of her own sinfulness:

> She was asked, 'Why do you love Jesus?' she replied. 'Oh! For he pardon all me sins.' 'You were a sinner, then?' 'Oh yes! Me a big sinner; but blessed Massa pardon me all ...'[21]

Apart from noting that an enslaved woman gives Jesus the same title she would attribute to her slave master and what that might say about the way the enslaved have been taught to think of Jesus and their relationship to him (and also the position of the slave owner and other Europeans, including the missionary), we see the focus on Jesus pardoning or dying for her sins. This idea of our inherent sinfulness is an established Christian doctrine but, seen in this context of unequal power relations and lack of agency, highlights, and, for me, evokes questions about, the ways in which doctrine and theological ideas can be embraced without challenge or thought about what they might mean when applied to actual human beings in particular contexts.

An example of putting the church before their own well-being comes from the man who, after emancipation, takes the money he had originally saved to buy his wife's freedom and gives it to the missionary for the church, since he has been told how much God has done for them and how grateful they should be. The account tells us how he claims '… the Lord Jesus *give us the free* …' And so he gives the money to the missionary, since 'he wanted to give the money to the cause of Christ'.[22] This can be applauded as an example of faithful and sacrificial support of the church (which in turn is meant to encourage the same in readers), but this simply felt to me like communities that had been exploited for generations putting themselves at further financial disadvantage. Returning to Mr Wray's letter, we hear again about this sense of gratitude for access to Christian conversion among the formerly enslaved: 'They also expressed their thankfulness that God had given them a master who had sent the word of God among them.'[23]

Financing the mission project

In examining the archive, we can see how mission-giving can be motivated by belief in the Great Commission,[24] but also by other emotions such as pity, fear and gratitude. This gratitude has already been illustrated under the piety and self-negation theme, where we see how vulnerable people donate to the church, but here we see it again in the example of a Guyanese schoolgirl temporarily giving up school so she can go 'to work money [so they phrase it] for the Juvenile Society … and then returned to school with the fruit of her labour …'[25] And, similar to the examples under the previous theme, there are people who give money for church building rather than choosing to secure their own homes, and other pieces showing converted people donating to the various mission organizations.

By illustrating the ways in which these communities are transformed and willing to give, despite their reduced circumstances, the young readers are encouraged in their own participation and donation:

> Our aim is to profit many; and to do this by showing how much good Missions are doing among the heathen nations, and how much young people may do to assist those Missions.[26]

Engaging with Black liberationist and womanist writing

The ways in which we have seen here how Black cultures, religious and spiritual beliefs and practices, and other ways of being, have been evaluated, interpreted and categorized through the eyes of European Christianity, here provide a stark example of what is today being discussed as the persistence of Whiteness, not only as it underpins the colonial and missionary projects, but also presently in the forum of theological formation and education, and in wider arenas. This describes the ways in which knowledge, whether theological or otherwise, and other frameworks and value systems that have been constructed and developed within a particular White Western context of power, are held up as universal and the standard against which all other knowledge and ways of being are to be measured and valued (or devalued).[27]

Though already influenced in my reading of the archive by my own experience as a Black woman, but also by both Black and womanist theology I had encountered in my adult life, it was imperative to engage more formally with this work as part of the project, not only in order to provide a critical response to the archive material that presents Black life through the lens of White colonial Christianity, but also to consult theological frameworks and perspectives that, rather than attempting to interpret and evaluate Black life through the lens of colonial Christianity, instead placed Black life, history and experience *as the means through which* to interpret and develop ideas about God, the Bible, doctrine and faith. As Cone states, 'Black Theology must speak *to* and *for* black people as they seek to remove the structures of white power which hover over their being, stripping it of its blackness.'[28]

A more detailed exploration of the relationship between mission and Black and womanist theology and the various perspectives explored can be found in my original article, but the findings fell largely into two categories. First, there are various critiques of colonial and mission activity, speaking about the ways in which Black religious, spiritual and cultural life was perceived and interpreted, the devaluing of African ways of knowing and being even in the present age, and the idea of European religious and cultural frameworks as inherently of greater value. Boesak, speaking of the missionary activity in his part of the world, states:

> It was made clear to us that for this salvation to occur, we had to follow *their* way of believing, accept *their* ways of interpreting the Scriptures, *their* ideas of God, *their* understanding of Jesus, *their* ways of experiencing the workings of God's Holy Spirit.[29]

He continues:

> It did not take us long to understand just how closely our slave masters and their Christian missionaries identified themselves with God, Jesus and the Holy Spirit so that obedience to our earthly masters was seen to be completely, even if completely blasphemously, synonymous with our obedience to God.[30]

Reading Boesak, as well as writers such as Turner,[31] Tshaka,[32] Kinyua,[33] Erskine,[34] Jagessar,[35] Lawes,[36] Balia[37] and others, provided valuable opportunity for examination and evaluation of the legacies of mission, colonialism and slavery, but also enabled access to narratives that countered the images of compliance and unquestioning piety the archive contained. In these works lie vital testimonies of religious self-determination, Black agency and resistance.

Exploring these articles also provided a kind of bolster against the emotional challenge of engaging with the material found in the archives, which was not simply an academic exercise, from which I could remain detached, but a meeting between myself and a time in history that had a profound and long-lasting effect on the people from whom I am descended. I would be lying if I said I was not emotionally affected on some level by doing this work, and occasionally grew weary of – and disheartened by – having to reflect on, write about and discuss these archives. The articles reminded me that there were other voices and other narratives to which I would hopefully be adding my own voice, and this helped to encourage me.

The other category of theological work I looked at spoke of Black and womanist theological perspectives on how to approach mission, such as the work of Buffel, which advocates for the marginalized being involved in any theological activity rather than being simply *acted upon*. He states: 'They must not be passive objects or mere recipients of charity but active participants and interlocuters in theological reflection.'[38]

Kritzinger embraces the Black theological goal of liberation in all facets of life and community rather than putting a focus on personal salvation when participating in mission. He also discusses the importance of not being impartial in the face of injustice and the need for solidarity and mutuality with those who suffer. He continues:

> ... this solidarity with the suffering should not be understood as benevolent and paternalistic charity. The central place allocated to children, women, the poor, and Samaritans in the Gospel tradition indicates that conversion is *becoming like* the oppressed and not merely *helping* them.[39]

Thomas, in her work, speaks of needing approaches to mission based on hospitality and being open to receiving knowledge about God from those with whom we engage, rather than simply imposing our own ideas; she states: 'Ultimately, Christian mission theories and practice do not listen with the intent of being transformed and changed themselves by what is said by the "other".'[40]

Williams, in her approach, calls for a ministry and mission focused on Jesus' life and action, rather than by his death, countering the emphasis on sin and the sacrifice of Jesus that I saw in the archive:

> Jesus' own words in Luke 4 and his ministry of healing the human body, mind and spirit (described in Matthew, Mark and Luke) suggest that Jesus did not come to redeem humans by showing them God's love manifested in the death of God's innocent child on a cross erected by cruel, imperialistic patriarchal power. Rather, the texts suggest that the spirit of God in Jesus came to show humans life – to show redemption through a perfect ministerial vision of righting relationships between body (individual and community), mind (of humans and of tradition) and spirit.[41]

Creating resources and concluding thoughts

Aside from a report and article, the final required outcome of the project was to produce some form of Christian education material. This would be an attempt to bring the work into a more practical and accessible realm and encourage engagement with and reflection not only on some of the issues surrounding the archive and the legacies of slavery, but also thinking about how we carry out contemporary mission[42] and the concerns surrounding it. In trying to decide how I was going to approach this, it was clear to me that I wanted to include extracts directly from the archive itself as starting points for the reflection, since in that way those participating could observe what had been written for themselves, engage directly with the text,[43] and then move on to questions for reflection linked to the themes into which I had divided the resource. In the end I chose four main themes for reflection that, while they didn't exactly correspond to the themes identified in my initial exploration, incorporated some of the same ideas: missionary encouragement of obedience among the enslaved, the motivations behind mission, the ways in which Black lives were depicted, and the questions around ideas of sin and salvation and how power relations feed into that. In exploring these themes, my hope was that not only would it encourage readers to see the connections between some of the attitudes and assumptions prevalent in history and contemporary issues, but also encourage reflection around what widely accepted doctrines and ideas about God, faith and the church that underpin much of mission activity might actually mean for people's lived experience and how mission is carried out. I do not claim that the questions I ask in the material have not been asked before in other ways and contexts, but when asking them I hoped that, when placed in the context of the archive, where people can see how particular theological and doctrinal frameworks or biblical interpretations can be used to support unjust practice, these questions would perhaps have a different resonance and allow the opportunity to reflect a little more deeply on aspects of church, theology, doctrine and faith that are espoused with little, if any, interrogation. I am also aware that this resource is merely a starting point, emerging from *my* encounter with the archive, and that there may also be other questions and discussions that emerge from engagement with the archive that I have not explored.

I was under no illusion that, in fulfilling the requirements of the project, whatever I produced would be something embraced wholesale by the church and certainly not by traditional mission historians or missiologists. A presentation of my early findings and thoughts that was given a little over halfway through the project reminded me that, despite my clearly stating my standpoint and the aim to speak to the themes that emerged from *my* reading of these texts, some would still want to make a point of defending particular missionaries and their actions, totally bypassing the whole point of what I was trying to explore. Whether some missionaries were 'good' or not really wasn't the point I was trying to argue, but I was aware that focusing on such arguments can be a means to avoid tackling the issues presented, and the questions I was actually asking both about how and why mission is carried out and the legacies of past mission activity for those communities on the receiving end of it. I can only speculate as to whether, consciously or subconsciously, the comment I received was also an attempt to reassert the authority of missiologists and mission historians. Yet if I doubted the validity of continuing what I was doing in that moment, the comment of the young Black woman who spoke of how problematic the depiction of a Black Jesus was among the young Black adults of her church sadly reminded me that the legacies of what I was identifying still endured, and that there was still value in discussing them.

At the time of writing, the LMS archives at SOAS are becoming more accessible, as aspects of them are being digitized[44] and therefore made available online to a wider public.[45] This is an important development, since it means that the various communities worldwide that find themselves described, depicted and discussed in this material, whether they are mission or history professionals or ordinary individuals, activists, community groups or congregations, can hopefully now have better access to these and the opportunity to engage with them, in ways that are useful to them in their own context.[46] I hope that, in this engagement, they will not dismiss the value and meaning of their lived experience and that of their ancestors in favour of unquestioning adherence to particular narratives and theological and doctrinal frameworks, but it is not my place to dictate how they should engage or impose my viewpoints on them.

My experience of the project has shown both a willingness from some quarters to engage with issues around mission history and the legacies of slavery, but also the reticence (or even resistance) of others. There is a sense that while there may be recognition of the need for interrogating history, unearthing and examining particular narratives and listening to marginalized voices, if those voices demand an interrogation – not only of history, but also of biblical text, liturgy or established doctrinal and theological frameworks, for example – it can prove too much of a challenge not only to the establishment, but also to congregations themselves, and even those comprised of those marginalized communities. This isn't particularly surprising, since for some people this questioning approach may appear to represent an undermining of established and cherished values and a dismantling of their faith, rather than an opportunity for a more liberative and enriched understanding and living of that faith.

The current work I have been doing concerning liturgy in terms of hymns and prayers has in some ways reflected some similar, if not always as overt, themes. In moving through the LMS archive, I found hymns that spoke explicitly about non-Christian peoples in ways I have already described in my work on the initial project:

> While heathen youth are dying
> In ignorance and sin,
> Should children not be trying
> Such helpless souls to win?[47]

> ... On China's shores I hear His praises
> From lips that once kiss'd idol stones ...
> ... The Negro, once a slave, rejoices
> 'Who's freed by Christ is doubly free ...[48]

I moved on to later sources and through hymns that are used in contemporary contexts on to very new resources that speak from the margins about issues of empire, injustice and oppression. Through these sources and timeframes, I was able to see hymnody and prayer that adhered to traditional theological and doctrinal frameworks, but also those that, while not abandoning those frameworks, spoke more explicitly about issues of justice and love in action. Here, ideas of kinship, equality, sharing the earth, its resources and mutual care and respect were expressed.[49]

Yet even in those cases where liturgy is being created from the margins and takes a stance against imperial and colonial power, we can see instances where traditional theological imagery remains unchallenged: 'Thank you, God, for sacrificing your son Jesus Christ for our sins and iniquities ...'[50] and 'Jesus, our sacrificial lamb, so meek as to endure suffering you never caused ...'[51]

When looking at more liberational or anti-imperial approaches to mission, the issues of liturgical material provide a more immediate challenge than engaging with archives, since prayer and hymns are largely the 'receptacles' of theology and doctrine with which communities most often engage and that they often hold very dear. Couple that with the largely communal nature of liturgical participation, and we are faced with issues about who is willing to enter into interrogation of those treasured hymns and prayers and the possible creation of new ones, though that is beyond the remit of my project.

As far as the archive project is concerned, for those who *are* interested in participating in this interrogation and exploration, my hope is that the resources that have emerged out of this archive work prove to be useful and meaningful to them.

Notes

1 For a more detailed account of the original project, see C. Troupe, 'Engagement with Mission Magazine Archives: A Black Laywoman's Perspective', *Black Theology: An International Journal*, 19(2) (2021), pp. 101–21.

2 From CWM's website: 'CWM's Legacies of Slavery (LOS) project addresses the roots of racialised inequalities and injustices today and owning that they lie in part in the rhetoric, praxis and fund raising of mission societies like CWM's forebear London Missionary Society'. See https://www.cwmission.org/programmes/the-onesimus-project/ (accessed 23.03.2023).

3 This project was created as a contribution to the CWM's Legacies of Slavery initiative, based on exploring the LMS archives at SOAS University of London (focused originally on the children's magazines) to look at the issues around the Society and the transatlantic slave trade, and the impact of mission activity on the experiences of the descendants of enslaved Africans.

4 Required outcomes consisted of a journal article, a report and Christian education material.

5 Matthew 28, reading from verse 18, 'Jesus drew near and said to them, "I have been given all authority in heaven and on earth. Go, then, to all peoples everywhere and make them my disciples: baptize them in the name of the Father, the Son, and the Holy Spirit, and teach them to obey everything I have commanded you. And I will be with you always, to the end of the age"' (Matthew 28.18–20 GNB).

6 *JMM*, vols I and II, 1844 and 1845, London: London Missionary Society, opening page.

7 'The Editor's Salam, or Introductory Address', *JMM*, June 1844, pp. 4–5.

8 I should say that some pieces in the magazines are not necessarily factual, but rather are examples of literary tropes that can be spotted across the mission material. For the purposes of this project, the point for me is not whether these pieces are fully or partially factual or entirely fictional but, rather, what they depict and the motivation for and possible results of those depictions, and what, if anything, reflection on them can offer.

9 'Little Children Given to the Lions', *JMM*, August 1844, p. 133.

10 'Chats with Missionaries V: Rev Thos. F Shaw of Urambo' by Albert Dawson, *News from Afar*, May 1896, p. 69.

11 'The Old Negro and His Wife', *JMM*, April 1846, p. 89.

12 An offensive term used for the Khoikhoi people, a nomadic tribe of Southern Africa.

13 'The Hottentots and the Gospel' by Leonard T. Horne, *JMM*, 1894, pp. 68–9.

14 'A Striking Contrast', *JMM*, December 1847, p. 272.

15 'Funeral Revels Discontinued, and the Solemnities of Death Improved', *Missionary Magazine and Chronicle*, March 1840, p. 44.

16 'Funeral Revels discontinued', pp. 44–5.

17 'Berbice: Extract of a Letter to the Treasurer, From Mr Wray, dated July 17, 1823', *Missionary Chronicle*, January – December 1823, p. 519.

18 'Berbice', p. 519.

19 'Ideas about God', *News from Afar*, October 1898, p. 155.

20 This is an example of one of the literary tropes used in the archive. A dying convert speaks at length about their Christian faith and admonishes those around them who are not converted.

21 'Judy Campbell, or The Happy Death' by R. B. S, *JMM*, June 1845, p. 127.
22 'The Old Negro and His Wife', pp. 88–90.
23 'Berbice', p. 519.
24 As illustrated in the opening pages of the bound issue of the *JMM*, vols I and II, 1844 and 1845.
25 'Ebenezer Chapel, Demerara', *JMM*, December 1845, p. 271.
26 *JMM*, vol IV, 1847 January to December, Preface.
27 See Willie James Jennings, 2020, *After Whiteness: An Education in Belonging*, Grand Rapids, MI: Eerdmans, for his experience of this within the realm of theological education.
28 James H. Cone, 1989, *Black Theology and Black Power: 20th Anniversary Edition*, San Francisco, CA: Harper & Row, p. 118.
29 Allan A. Boesak, 'The Need for "A Fighting God": Biko, Black Theology and the Essence of Revolutionary Authenticity', *Black Theology: An International Journal*, 18(3) (2020), pp. 201–22, 206; emphasis original.
30 Boesak, 'The Need for "A Fighting God"', p. 207.
31 Carlton John Turner, 'Taming the Spirit? Widening the Pneumatological Gaze within African Caribbean Theological Discourse', *Black Theology: An International Journal*, 13(2) (2015), pp. 126–46, 130.
32 Rothney S. Tshaka, 'The Advocacy for Africanity as Justice Against Epistemicide', *Black Theology: An International Journal*, 17(2) (2019), pp. 132–49.
33 Johnson Kinyua, 'A postcolonial Examination of Matthew 16:13–23 and Related Issues in Biblical Hermeneutics', *Black Theology: An International Journal*, 13(1) (2015), pp. 4–28 and 'A Postcolonial Analysis of Bible Translation and its Effectiveness in Shaping and Enhancing the Discourse of Colonialism and the Discourse of Resistance: The Gikuyu New Testament – A Case Study', *Black Theology: An International Journal*, 11(1) (2013), pp. 58–95.
34 Noel Leo Erskine, 'The Roots of Rebellion and Rasta Theology in Jamaica', *Black Theology: An International Journal*, 5(1) (2007), pp. 104–25.
35 Michael N. Jagessar, 'Early Methodism in the Caribbean: Through the Imaginary Optics of Gilbert's Slave Women – Another Reading', *Black Theology: An International Journal*, 5(2) (2007), pp. 153–70.
36 Marvia E. A. Lawes, 'Historical Evaluation of Jamaica Baptists: A Spirituality of Resistance', *Black Theology: An International Journal*, 6(3) (2008), pp. 366–92.
37 Daryl Balia, '"True Lies": American Missionary Sayings in South Africa (1835–1910)', *Black Theology: An International Journal*, 5(2) (2007), pp. 203–19.
38 O. A. Buffel, 'Mission as Liberation in Socio-Economic and Political Contexts: Towards Contextual and Liberating Theology of Mission in the Context of Migration and Human Dislocation', *Missionalia* (online), 41(3) (2013), pp. 239–54, 240. Located at http://missionalia.journals.ac.za (accessed 8.03.2023).
39 Johannes N. J. Kritzinger, 1988, 'Black Theology: Challenge to Mission', doctoral thesis, University of South Africa, pp. 299–300; emphasis original.
40 Linda E. Thomas, 'Anthropology, Mission and the African Woman: A Womanist Approach', *Black Theology: An International Journal*, 5(1) (2007), pp. 11–19, 15.
41 Delores S. Williams, 1993, *Sisters in the Wilderness: The Challenge of Womanist God-Talk*, Maryknoll, NY: Orbis Books, pp. 164–5.
42 In this context, I am referring to all action carried out by the churches, whether among their own congregations or engaging with communities around them and in the wider world.

43 At the time of writing the material in summer 2021, digital access to the mission magazine archives was not yet available.

44 Much of the material in *JMM* and *News from Afar* has already been digitized.

45 Despite the difficulties brought about by the COVID-19 pandemic at the start of the project, I was eventually able to travel to London and have access to the material I required. I extend my thanks again to Joanne Ichimura, Special Collections Archivist (CWM), and her colleagues at SOAS University of London for facilitating this access under difficult circumstances and for the support given so that this work could be completed.

46 This is not to dismiss the existence of issues around access to technology, and so on, that may remain for some.

47 'Juvenile Missionary Hymn', *JMM*, September 1845, p. 212.

48 'I hear ten thousand voices singing', *Centenary Missionary Hymnal*, compiled and edited by the Revd Stanley Rogers, p. 12.

49 See, for example, Fred Kaan, 1991, 'For ourselves no longer living', *Rejoice and Sing*, Oxford: Oxford University Press for the United Reformed Church, p. 558.

50 Cláudio Carvalhaes (ed.), 2020, *From the Ends of the World: Prayers in Defiance of Empire*, Nashville, TN: Abingdon Press, p. 282.

51 Carvalhaes, *From the Ends*, p. 282.

10

Mission and Whiteness: Archival Lessons from LMS in British Guiana (Guyana)

MICHAEL N. JAGESSAR

The only great men [sic] among the unfree and the oppressed are those who struggle to destroy the oppressor. (Dr Walter Rodney)

Blood is everywhere – archives as a crime scene

The legacies of slavery emerge from the worst feature of White-powered Christian colonial capitalism, the systemic and industrial kidnap and enslavement of in excess of 12 million African persons over 350 years. Human beings were tricked, kidnapped and robbed of liberty, agency and humanity and their lives exploited for profit of the markets and the kingdoms of Britain, Spain, France, the Netherlands and in the name of God. It is a crime without parallel and, to date, without adequate recompense. Missionary bodies need to be confronted with their deep entanglements with chattel slavery, forced migration and forced labour of the colonial project of wealth extraction. Council for World Mission (CWM) commenced working (in 2018) on its own history of racist Christian colonialism as an intentional way of enabling itself to talk back to the systemic racist realities it still inhabits, which mission helped to institute and which missionaries perpetuated.

This chapter will interrogate the London Missionary Society (LMS) and later Council for World Mission (CWM) archives, specifically focusing on the Demerara Slave Uprising of British Guiana (Guyana). Using selected archival sources such as the LMS correspondence, notes, letters, colonial newspapers and related publications, the chapter will explore the role of Whiteness[1] and its ongoing legacies in the LMS mission narratives. If, as Hilary Beckles rightly stated, 'the West Indies began their modern existence as a massive crime scene',[2] then the LMS (as other mission bodies) being there as part of that project need to be hauled before the 'trial'. Archival resources are a critical site in this process along with its own challenges.[3] As Saidiya Hartman notes:

> Every historian of the multitude, the dispossessed, the subaltern, and the enslaved is forced to grapple with the power and authority of the archive and the limits it sets on what can be known, whose perspective matters, and who is endowed with the gravity and authority of historical actor.[4]

Rethinking, reframing and re-engaging with the LMS archives is work in progress.

I enter the archival resources as a Caribbean theologian mindful of much (including my own ignorance) complicity and this limited attempt to re-read retrospectively the LMS archival resources 'housed' in the library of an established British academic institution (SOAS University of London). Given my working understanding of 'Whiteness' my framing questions will include: How did colonial thinking and Whiteness inform and frame the endeavours of the LMS and its missionaries? What was the overarching view of the LMS and its workers on chattel enslavement and the humanity of the enslaved? How was such formed in particular sites/events, interpretative communities and reflected in its communication and mission output? How contested was it inside and outside the LMS? What are the resulting and ongoing legacies that need to be exorcised?[5]

Revisiting archives to interrogate the *why* and the *what* of ongoing colonial legacies calls for a particular kind of re-reading. Archives as sites of knowledge production are not only full of skeletons: the leaves of documents and letters may be covered with blood given the crime scene that Beckles pointed to. There is also a curious link between blood and Christianity, and the wealth extraction colonial project of Europe. Gil Anidjar's *Blood*[6] offers an incisive interrogation of the central role of blood in Christianity and its circulating (fluid) omnipresence in the history of Christianity and of Europe, defining and redefining what it means to be human. So, with Christian warranty, through the saving blood of Jesus over the course of the Latin Western Middle Ages, Christian purity is passed down through blood. This was then extended to mean that natives of the New World, and Africans (among others), were of impure blood, not fully human. No wonder Christianity loves the cross, death, murder and its own innocence, but that most of all it loves blood. The ritual of Whiteness and Christianity is tied to this blood narrative. And the liquid flow of the blood of the enslaved is what shaped capitalism and continues to play out to this very day. The legacies of slavery are not only located in Christian mission bodies. At the root are the economic and political systems in the dominance of capitalism, which is itself a legacy of slavery.⁷

Coloniality and its 'Whiteness' framework has not and will not easily let go, and so the centuries of its reach ask us in the context of mission history to acknowledge, question and interrogate the assumptions around the reservoir of knowledge; and this ongoing knowledge production is still so prevalent in dominant meaning-making of self – towards the construction of Whiteness as superior and full of entitlement.

Memorializing the Demerara Slave Uprising – a case study in decolonizing

At Christmas 2021, our youngest son introduced me to a book he had just finished reading. It was written about 30 years ago but only recently translated from its original language. *The Memory Police* by Yoko Ogawa is a dream-like story of dystopia, set on an unnamed island that is being engulfed by an epidemic of forgetting. When objects disappear from memory, they disappear from real life. The disappearances are enforced by the Memory Police, a squad that sweeps through the island, ransacking houses to seize lingering evidence of what has been forgotten. For our purpose, I note the components to forgetting that the author flags up: the thing disappears, then the memory of that thing disappears, and then the memory of forgetting that thing also disappears. When villagers forget birds and roses, they most definitely erase from memory what these things symbolize: flight, freedom, extravagance, desire and much more. To ensure that the job is thoroughly done, the Memory Police will also root out and take away any who do not forget. Remembering becomes a threat and an act of subversion. A telling line for our purpose of archival memories (what is on display and what is locked away) is when the narrator says: 'If it goes on like this and we can't compensate for the things that get lost then the island will soon be nothing but absences and holes, and when it's completely hollowed out, we'll all disappear without a trace.'⁸

The late Derek Walcott compares this disappearing without trace to Caribbean people tracing their names on the sand with a stick 'which the sea erased again, to our indifference'.⁹ Alberta Whittle's recent exhibition titled 'deep dive (pause) uncoiling memory' takes on what the artist describes as the 'luxury of amnesia' – that is, 'a state of privileged communal memory loss in which we are able to forget and overlook the atrocities of the past, allowing us to drift into a state of lethargy and inertia'. The title of the exhibition has an intentional pause to lead viewers into giving thought to what they may have forgotten as part of the 'process of unlearning' towards 'intervening into what we understand of as history'.[10] It is time to end amnesia and indifference and remember well. But to do so we need to grapple with the reach of Whiteness, elite capture, and how we may be unwittingly lured into perpetuating the virus.

Rebellion and uprising – the martyr and the rebels

So let us revisit the story of the Demerara Rebellion, Resistance or Uprising as our entry point into colonialism, Whiteness and mission to exorcize some of the demons. How this historical event has been named, documented, archived and referenced in writing on the uprising offers clues (not new) to help us understand the reach of Whiteness, the LMS, missionary struggles,[11] the colonial agenda/interest and the afterlives of the European project of wealth extraction, with 'the principal form of investment in property' being 'the enslaved African body'.[12]

I will start with the most recent version I have read, which comes from Thomas Harding's *White Debt: The Demerara Uprising and Britain's Legacy of Slavery* (2021).[13] Highly recommended by reviewers,[14] clearly an accessible read, and working materials already gone over and available in the LMS archives, this popular version covers much ground with a title that names the debt but seems to dither on what debt 'Whiteness' actually owes, and how reparations will happen beyond taking responsibility.[15] It is certainly not a call for any reparation to the UK's legacy of plunder and impoverishment of Guyana and the region. What struck me, though, is Harding's struggle to find an appropriate term to describe those who 'rose up'. The author found 'rebels' too ambiguous while 'insurrectionist' felt too pejorative (like 'rebel'). And as a Briton even less appealing is the label 'freedom fighter'. For Harding, such 'conjures up something more militaristic', reminding the author 'of Fidel Castro and his comrades in Cuba, the mujahideen in Afghanistan, the Viet Cong in Vietnam'. Harding therefore opted for the descriptor of 'abolitionists' for Jack Gladstone and his band of uprisers.[16] As Harding reasoned:

> In my mind, I conduct a thought experiment, comparing the following sentences: 'British militia shot two hundred rebels' and 'British militia shot two hundred abolitionists'. The difference is startling. I am far more sympathetic to the second sentence than the first … I am struck by the dramatic differences in my response. To put it bluntly, while I am a little afraid of the rebels, I want the abolitionists to succeed.[17]

So why does Harding, a White British male, gravitate towards the word 'abolitionist' and express fear of 'rebel'? Why should the rebels not succeed? What shaped Harding's 'thought experiment'? There are clues here as to how the privileged world of Whiteness locks its progeny and beneficiaries into predictable behaviour and the ways in which Whiteness rationalizes its own construct of what is appropriate or not. To begin with, naming a group of chattel slaves as 'abolitionists' suggests the ignorance around what chattel slavery entailed for Jack Gladstone, Quamina and all the others. The preference reflects what Whiteness can cope with, without getting fearful and anxious that their 'blood' would soon be flowing, and that they would have to give up that which has been stolen and on which their whole economic well-being has been built. Being an abolitionist would have been a luxury the enslaved could not have afforded. They were literally fighting for their lives and humanity and that of their progeny using all necessary means. They were freedom fighters, struggling, from the inception of their enslavement,[18] to break out of their oppression, for which many were brutally executed.

There is, though, a larger fear at work here. It is what Michel-Rolph Trouillot called 'unthinking a chimera' in the mindset of Whiteness. Writing specifically about the Haitian Revolution and insurrection, Trouillot noted that the rebellion 'entered history with the peculiar characteristic of being *unthinkable* even as it happened'. For White colonizers it was unthinkable that those labelled inferior could rise up, strategize, and with astute military insights and tactics defeat empire. The successful insurrection considered a 'historical impossibility' undressed and 'challenged the ontological and political assumptions' of Whiteness.[19] In the minds and imagination of Whiteness (coloniality), the enslaved Africans could not achieve their own emancipation by self-initiated means of physical revolt. This unthinkable has been one of the key reasons why Haiti[20] and all the Caribbean countries where rebellions happened had to be dealt with, and to this day continue to pay the price for rising up in rebellion against Whiteness. Coloniality could never contemplate Gladstone and Quamina as visionaries and innovators in the cruel world in which they found themselves, nor that their rebellion was fuelled by a vision of a future free world for themselves and their children.

I suggest that Harding's apparent wrestling with how to name the uprisers/rebels is shaped by this consciousness. For, as Trouillot observed, the pathology around any system of domination 'is the tendency to proclaim its own normalcy'. In other words: 'to acknowledge resistance as a mass phenomenon is to acknowledge the possibility that something is wrong with the system.'[21] Moreover, what is more realistic would be 'White saviours' working themselves to death to gift the enslaved

Black people with freedom.[22] Be it the Berbice Slave Uprising (1763), the Haitian Revolution (1804), the Demerara Slave Uprising (1823), the Morant Bay Uprising (1865) and the over 250 rebellions by the enslaved, what happened in Haiti symbolized the fear and hell within Britain's emancipation talk as it was that place where 'blacks took everything held precious from the whites'.[23]

But what about the earlier versions of the Demerara Uprising? Unlike Harding's focus on the rebels, most of the earlier accounts tended to focus on John Smith with some gestures towards the actual rebels.[24] Take, for instance, David Chamberlin's *Smith of Demerara: Martyr-Teacher of the Slaves* (1924).[25] It is largely a sympathetic read of John Smith, Quamina, the LMS and the evil of slavery. Writing in the preface to the book, Sydney Olivier (a former Governor General of Jamaica) noted that the approach of the LMS has been that their missionaries had 'to keep as quiet as possible on the subject of slavery, lest a political character should be given to the missions and excuse afforded for debarring them from the strictly religious and educational work', which was their primary purpose.[26] It is clear from the following directive that the directors of the LMS were clear about the role of their missionaries:

> You must take the utmost care to prevent the possibility of this evil; not a word must escape you, in public or private, which might render the slaves displeased with their station. You are not sent to relieve them from their servile condition, but to afford them the consolation of religion.[27]

While Britain celebrated Wilberforce, Chamberlin noted that the events of 1823–4 around the verdict on John Smith was key in the turning tide in Britain 'for the final act of full emancipation'.[28] Of value was the verdict on, and the eventual death of, Smith, not the hunted down and executed Quamina and many other rebels.[29] Salvation for the enslaved in Guyana came through Smith and the White abolitionists.

But let us give Smith the benefit of any doubt in relation to his own struggles on what he was confronted with or wrestled with because of his faith, scriptures, his first-hand view of the condition of his enslaved congregants, and the opposition of the plantocracy to teaching the enslaved to read and write. From all archival accounts Smith was liked and well received by the enslaved. John Cheveley, in his journal, made the following observation having heard of the accusation brought against Smith by the colonial authorities:

I now found, to my amazement, that the missionaries, of whom there were two or three in the Colony, and any persons who had been favourable to them, were considered to be implicated in exciting the Negroes rebellion – preaching the gospel was especially considered to be the exciting cause by *putting improper notions of freedom into their heads*.[30]

It is not my intention to question Smith's wrestling of conscience nor Cheveley's own distaste with his experience of coloniality as implied in his journal. What is important to reflect on is why coloniality and Whiteness were of the view that the enslaved had no notion of freedom and could not on their own have made connections and deductions on the inconsistencies between the scriptures and their enslaved and dehumanizing state.

Cheveley's journal hints at agency by the enslaved. He documented that the enslaved having heard 'that there had come from the King of England an order for their freedom', the news 'spread like wildfire'. And so the cry 'free paper come and Buckra man keep it away from we' gathered momentum and 'produced a universal determination to work no longer, and this eventually settled down into a scheme to seize the managers and overseers and white people on the estates and put them in the stocks ... and then proceed to Georgetown in a body and claim the freedom the governor had for them'.[31] And here Cheveley noted: 'The plan was put into place and with a slight skirmish with a small army two white overseers were killed', that being 'the extent of the injury the white people suffered'. It is what Cheveley went on to note that is critical: 'beyond the excessive fright, which naturally enough they [the White population] were in' what was even scarier was that 'the negroes having got the upper hand of them, death was certain'. This underscores the point already made: White coloniality's 'unbelieve-ability' of the humanity of the enslaved Blacks, about their intellectual ability to think and strategize, about their moral consciousness to be able to reason, make decisions of their own and rise up against injustices.

But back to the trumped-up accusation about John Smith's influence on putting 'improper notions of freedom' into the heads of the enslaved. There is no doubt that the work of Smith and his preaching, steeped in its evangelical fervour, would have stirred questions and lead to the enslaved identifying the contradictions and hypocrisies of their enslavement, most likely drawing from the prophets and the Gospels. At the same time, we need to locate Smith's work in the context of the LMS instructions that he was not sent 'to relieve them [the enslaved] from their servile condition'. His calling was to 'afford them the consolation of religion'.[32] My limited reading of Smith's journal is that he did just that, while he wrestled with the inhumanity around him. He was no liberal nor had enlightened views on the humanity of the enslaved Africans.

Archibald Brown, minister of the Scots' Kirk in Demerara, wrote a long letter about the missionary work among the enslaved and flagged up how verses from many hymns that were normally sung in England would have encouraged subversion against authority.[33] Brown noted how Smith refrained from using hymns that contained lines such as 'We would no longer be like slaves beneath the throne' or 'We will be slaves no more, since Christ made us free'. He noted that Smith took it upon himself to use a collection of 'pruned' hymns he had printed in London for the use by the converted enslaved.[34] Smith was mindful of the LMS directors' position and his purpose as one of their missionaries. As he later wrote during his trial to the directors:

> In order to vindicate the Society from the impression made against it by its enemies, as to it having a concealed object in view for instance, 'the ultimate liberation of the slaves', I laid over the instruction as a part of the proceedings of the court martial on my trial, that publicity might be given to the real object of the Society.[35]

Smith was operating within the framework of the LMS and that of 'Whiteness'.

Reading through archival materials and especially John Smith's journal, which both Harding, Chamberlin and others used to different ends, it is illuminating to see what is referenced, omitted, the deductive somersaults deployed to make an icon of Smith, and the inability to locate the deeper and entrenched dynamics of Whiteness at work, of which Smith was also a part. For instance, one has to wonder how White missionaries like Smith, on their own, suffering under the extreme tropical climate (they were unwell most of the time), grew the mission so successfully. In the period of his first five years in British Guiana, Smith journaled and reported back to the LMS about the exceptional growth of his missionary endeavour – baptizing over 462 enslaved, receiving over 60 into membership (which grew to 203), with an average congregation of 800 to 2,000 professing Christians at Bethel, Le Resouvenir. This may certainly be true. The question, though, is about the work of the enslaved towards such growth. Smith's reporting back never gave agency to any of the deacons such as Quamina, nor did those who commented on Smith's reporting. The growing of the mission remained a conversation within and among the framework of 'Whiteness' which was also the world of the missionaries.

Let us consider further what Smith wrote about the enslaved African-Guianese. Regarding their 'moral character', Smith noted that 'little need to be said' as such 'corresponds with their degraded condition' and proceeded to suggest that such should be expected from 'among uninstructed men, and especially when they are slaves'.[36] Smith's colonial White British framework underscored European superiority and African inferiority. The enslaved Africans could not have embodied or brought anything moral or religious from where they were captured, exported and sold as chattel. Smith proceeded to note that the enslaved cannot be said to have anything one can call religion, with the exception being those who 'are happily under the instructions of the missionaries', as many of these 'are much attached to the Christian religion, and considering their condition in life, are very regular in their attendance at public worship, and exemplary in their general conduct'.[37] About their singing, he noted that it was 'fervent but bad' to the extent that he had to invest much energy in teaching them how to sing, with an interesting note from Chamberlin that it did pay off as the enslaved 'sang wonderfully *after they were freed*, and they do so still'.[38]

Readers may wish to contemplate how and why the enslaved sang so well *after gaining their freedom*, raised and 'gave money to the Missionary Society, and made payments for Bibles and other books' from the little they had.[39] Smith and the LMS were captive to the ritual of coloniality and Whiteness and could not see the enslaved as fully human beings and gifted. In fact, the colonial authority wondered how the enslaved Africans could have raised such an annual amount from nothing to contribute to the work of the LMS. They believed they had to be stealing to raise such an amount: they were not capable of being ingenious, strategic, business-orientated and committed.

The Uprising and the fallout

All that the enslaved wanted was to verify what they heard about a 'new law', which they rightly felt meant their freedom. When they were rebuked, they did what any enslaved and oppressed group of people would do: rose up in rebellion. As expected, coloniality, empire and Whiteness responded to protect their interest. That interest was to ensure that the enslaved Africans remained in their place, the property of the plantocracy and its engine to ensure the smooth running of extractive colonialism. The rebellion was brutally put down. The ringleaders of the rebellion were murdered and publicly executed/gibbeted while others were exiled to imprisonment and hard labour. The interest of Whiteness also turned on one of their own (John Smith), producing evidence from the enslaved rebels in return for their own release, to show 'that Smith had abused his influence as a missionary to encourage revolution'. This created an unintentional White martyr.[40]

Of interest are the accounts in the local newspapers, which carried much of the recrimination and reprisals alongside the trials, especially the pieces written by the clergy who largely started to disassociate themselves from John Smith. One Wesleyan missionary quickly defended his role and that of his colleague by noting that they had nothing to do with the 'hellish plot' and wrote about their *duty*:

> No, thank the Lord, we know our duty to God, to ourselves, to the Government under which we live, and to all our fellowmen, better, than to be in the most distant manner connected with rebellion. We preach the Gospel of *Peace* and of men, and hold forth the prince of peace, Jesus Christ as the saviour of men and forget not to say to all our hearers, in private and public, 'in every state and condition in which you are placed, learn herewith to be content'.[41]

In that same issue, the Revd Archibald Browne, Minister of the Scots' church in Demerara, wrote a letter giving his testimony 'to the general good conduct of the Slave population' and expressing the strong view that 'the unhappy Negroes who joined in the late revolt, *would never of themselves have conceived the desire*, or the possibility of throwing off the *mild and legitimate* authority of their Masters'. Browne goes on to indicate why he wrote '*mild* and *legitimate*': 'mild, because no instance of hardship, far less of cruelty has yet been alleged as the cause of discontent' and 'legitimate, because the Master's claim to the obedience, the respect, and the service of the Slave is derived from the law of the land, nay, is strengthened and supported by every precept and by every doctrine of the Gospel'. In contemplating 'the delusion which has been practised on these poor creatures, and the depth of misery into which they have been plunged', Browne's heart reaches out in 'pity' for the enslaved rebels as 'they have literally "perished for lack of knowledge"'.[42]

For our purpose, what is important to note are the patronizing and contemptuous ways in which the enslaved Africans were viewed. This is besides the inability of the missionaries to name the oppression of the enslaved. In different ways the missionaries were all working within the framework of coloniality and Whiteness, with the bottom line being their own interest, not having anything to do with slave uprisings, and a strong conviction of gospel imperatives about the enslaved state of the Africans. One can also discern here insights into the early seeds of ecclesial-ecumenical divide in Guiana. The freedom of the enslaved Blacks and their legitimate demands for information on a parliamentary decision that related to their free status did not matter. And back home at the LMS, the Board of Directors' Meeting of 18 May 1824 expressed:

> ... its unfeigned sorrow at the affecting event, which have [sic] recently taken place in the Colony of Demerara; its deep regret that intolerance and persecution should have been so awfully manifested; its solemn conviction that, notwithstanding all the efforts of calumny and injustice, the legal and moral innocence of their esteemed Missionary, the late Rev. John Smith, has been established on the ground of unequivocal evidence; its affectionate sympathy with his widowed relict and mourning friends, relieved by the consolatory remembrance, that while the honour of a martyr's name invests his memory, 'the spirit of glory and of God' rested upon him in the scenes of arduous and faithful exertion, in the hour of trial, and in the prospect of immortality. And, above all, the Society cannot but express its hope, that from injustice and liberality of the British Legislature, a reversal of life sentence may be obtained, and its cheering persuasion, that in the results already secured, these disastrous events 'have fallen out rather' unto the furtherance of the Gospel.[43]

The directors' concern was for the good name of the deceased Smith, his surviving spouse and the Society's name, mission and their well-being. The hard-working Deacon Quamina and others were not worth a mention. At the same meeting, the directors agreed not to indulge in recrimination, noting the exceptional character of Smith who, though 'in a feeble state of health', would have been wise enough to see 'the extreme folly and temerity of any such attempt' to revolt, and to this end the said directors concluded that it could reasonably be presumed that their missionary was 'one of the most unlikely individuals in the whole Colony to be either directly or indirectly implicated in any such project' of revolt and rebellion.[44] The operational ethos of 'Whiteness' and a colonial mindset prevailed. The poor shepherd-less heathens needed to be saved. As the directors proceeded to affirm:

> The poor slaves, therefore, on both the East and West Coasts, where Mr. Smith and Mr. Elliot respectively laboured, are now as sheep, having no shepherd. We trust, however, the time is not far distant, when they shall again be privileged to hear the sound of that Gospel, which alone can make men happy, and truly contented with their lot, in the various conditions of life.[45]

Thus, attending to 'the sacred cause' of the Society the work 'in communicating Christian Instruction to the subjects of the British Crown' must continue while the enslaved live with their inhuman lot. The LMS will preach the gospel of love to the unenlightened but their condition and the 'real estate' around them will continue to benefit coloniality and Whiteness. The LMS was more concerned in their attempt to transform the enslaved into a version of Whiteness. A better mission would have been to change the social condition of their oppression, which Quamina and the other rebels discerned as the calling of the gospel.

Psychology and psychosis – White Europeans and postcolonial Blacks

The impact and legacies of coloniality and Whiteness on the enslaved Africans in the Caribbean cast a long shadow. Frederick Hickling, writing in *Decolonization of Psychiatry in Jamaica: Madnificent Irations* (2021), observed that: 'Few people who have not actually experienced an English colonial society can really understand the effect of colonialism on young minds.' Hickling was referring to legacies of colonial 'Whiteness' for the postcolonial Caribbean. He goes on to note: 'We were being taught to be agents of the European psychosis in Brown and Black skins.' This specific psychosis intentionally allowed a few Black people to climb the educational ladder into the system 'but under no circumstances was power to be shared with them'.[46] In the specific discipline of psychiatry, Hickling rightly notes that 'the European genocide of the New World and the monumental enslavement of millions of Africans by Europeans' did not feature: 'It is as if that event and period of history have simply vanished or have had no psychological or psychiatric effect on the slaver or the slave.'[47]

The intent of coloniality and European colonizers was 'a calculated and deliberate attempt to obliterate people of colour, in order to establish White European domination of the world'.[48] Thus Hickling contends that Whiteness defined madness in Black lives with the consequent current default position being that 'Black folk continue to allow White people to be the creators of our insanity; to define us as schizophrenic; and to shape our psychopathy.'[49] For our purpose, I am drawn to what Hickling and Hutchinson locate as one of the ongoing legacies, which they named as 'roast breadfruit psychosis'. This is the condition of a Black person seeing and identifying themselves as White. They coined the term from breadfruit, a Caribbean staple (with plantation links), 'whose green coloured skin turns black when roasted, while the inner portion remains white in colour'.[50]

MISSION AND WHITENESS

The point of this interjection from Hickling is that, in my reading of the LMS archival materials related to LMS work in British Guiana and especially the events around Smith and Quamina, it becomes evident that the missionaries could not bring themselves to see and name the humanity of the enslaved. In the eyes of the colonial powers and the missionaries (from their correspondences) the enslaved were rarely named or their jobs identified. Quamina, for instance, was an artisan, a cooper. As Hickling observed:

> The European psychosis has created distorted historical, political, and social images of the colonized people. The colonized have no history, their values are uncivilized and their history of struggle against the process has not been recorded. Integral to the collective European colonial psychosis is the attempt to negate the values, culture, and social history of the colonized. A slave was simply that – a slave. He was not a farmer, a carpenter, a writer, or a healer ... He/she was depersonalized ...[51]

The colonial-White psychosis spilled over into the theology that undergirded the evangelical fervour of the missionaries. And it was internalized by the enslaved converts, as seen in the language they used to testify to their conversion, and often skilfully deployed for their own use. John Wray, reporting back to the LMS directors, noted his thriving work of preaching the gospel to the poor heathen savages and ignorant people. Wray went on to observe how the slaves were guilty of many crimes, and because of fear would tell of their crimes to the manager, 'a good man' who attended 'the preaching of the gospel at every opportunity and has done much for its promotion'. The manager, according to Wray, was 'astonished at the wonderful change which had taken place among them' (the enslaved) because of the work of Wray. And what was this change, in the words of Wray: 'They formerly were of a very rebellious disposition and not at all backward to insurrection and generally spent three or four nights in a week in drumming, dancing, intoxication and other wicked employments so that they disturb the whole neighbourhood.' However, with their 'leisure time' now 'spent in prayer and praise and in receiving and in communicating religious instruction' they were now exceptionally well behaved instead of being 'discontent and indolent in their work'.[52]

This was not an isolated archival account of how the LMS missionaries perceived the enslaved and the purpose of their work. The reporting on the 1 August 1838 celebration of 'emancipation' by the enslaved is enlightening. The report noted the jubilant 'state of mind' on the part of the enslaved. This 'was chiefly if not wholly induced by the moral and religious instruction which they had previously received'. The report opined:

> Next to the preaching of the Gospel, the schools established in the colonies in connection with the several missions, have formed the chief source of that instruction which, by the blessing of God, has exerted so happy and extensive an influence; and to which our colonial possessions in this part of the globe are so deeply indebted for their stability and peace. If the results could be traced no further, and embraced no higher objects than these, there would still be ample cause for satisfaction, and no regret could be felt at the expense incurred, the energies employed, to attain them.[53]

Readers were also reminded of the theology and missional impulses that shaped the above:

> ... it must not be forgotten that the influences which have prevented the Christian negro from indulging in deeds of riot and intemperance, and led him to act the peaceable neighbour and the loyal subject, are to a great extent essentially the same with those that sanctify the soul and prepare for heaven; and therefore every friend of religion will be satisfied that it would not be possible to overrate their value and importance, make efforts too great and strenuous to sustain them, or feel sufficiently grateful that they have been so extensively produced.[54]

The LMS missionaries in British Guiana may have had to wrestle with their conscience, the scriptures and reality of the inhumane treatment of the enslaved.[55] At the same time, in the overall convergence of interest, an evangelical fervour undergirded by a strong belief in the subhumanity and heathen state of the enslaved meant that the LMS and its missionaries unwittingly perpetuated the psychosis of Whiteness with its reach well into postcolonial Guyana.

In terms of the latter, I cite the example of a 1967 piece by a Guyanese journalist going by the name of Lucian who contended that, in the marking of the 125th anniversary of Smith Congregational Church, a 'rightful place for the John Smith Bust is at the head of the column of the Revolutionaries' Hall of Fame in Independence Park'. Lucian contended that Congregationalism was at the heart of Guyana's liberation struggle, especially 'the vigour of its theology in the fight against political sin; the stoicism with which its early missionaries accepted persecution and death as the inevitable result of the church's militancy'. Lucian proceeded to note that 'these contributions were made by expatriate missionaries from the London Missionary Society. John Smith is not only the name of a heroic congregational clergyman. It is the name of a Guyanese patriot.' While not wishing to misread the sentiments of Lucian in making his case that the nation of Guyana should 'recognise the contributions of liberal expatriate action to the liberation movement' and of Congregationalism,[56] one must ask why Lucian could not have also advanced a case for Quamina, Gladstone or any of the others who were the rebels of that rising-up and who actually pushed the prophetic edge of the gospel contrary to Smith and the LMS. The objective of the latter was clear: bringing the gospel to savages and heathens and not to advocate for their liberation as enslaved people. Hickling's 'roast breadfruit syndrome' was – and still is – at work as the psychosis continues.

Release and exorcizing Whiteness – the ongoing task in archives

> The West indies are in the position of an orange. The British have sucked it dry, and their sole concern today is that they should not slip and get damaged on the peel.[57]

If we can imagine the LMS archives as the hold of a ship, there is much to be brought to the outer deck to be aired. The tougher work, though, will be that of Whiteness interrogating, repenting, repairing and restoring, following the revelations of what is uncovered. Archival decolonizing cannot only be about digital access to the archives, displaying Quamina letters, locating land-grabbing, returning objects or rearranging materials so that they become even more unrecognizable. A decolonial uprising of and within the archives cannot be another form of elite capture and relational arrangements that will not address deficits and be geared towards restorative justice. We must be mindful of the danger of sustaining another form of 'plantation capture' through accessibility and the appearance of change or superficial mutation with agency to a few minoritized bodies or voices. The reach of Whiteness and its interest means that such capture is real, as releasing, exorcizing, repairing and restoring will demand decentring and displacement to create a common and liberating space for all.

Decolonizing the LMS 'archives' may not necessarily be always and wholly perceived as being in the interests of, for instance, CWM. This has become evident to me through CWM's Legacies of Slavery project as related to its antecedent body's (LMS) complicity in the transatlantic slave trade. It was timely and daring for the Board of Directors of CWM in 2018 to receive and endorse the findings of the Legacies Hearings (2017–18) around the LMS's complicity in the transatlantic slave trade, including its own treasurer's ownership of enslaved Africans in Jamaica and the alliance of the LMS's missiology with colonial land-grabbing and wealth extraction. And to commit to addressing CWM's complicity through acts of repentance and reparation signalled what some of us identified as a Kairos moment.[58] The resistance and pushback, though, have been sobering and revealing. The current direction of the outworkings of the Legacies of Slavery project in 2022, which met with resistance from some of CWM constituencies, and has now been renamed as the Onesimus Project, suggests to me that CWM is in danger of compromising its commitment to the initial thrust of reparation. The particular danger relates to the release of the designated funds to be managed outside of CWM's reach as an act of 'total release'. Instead, reparations will now take the form of the mission body managing the process for itself and designing it to benefit funding of largely its own constituencies. The idea of releasing the agreed sum of money to be managed by an independent group as part of CWM's commitment to restorative justice, with Black communities being the main beneficiaries, is in danger of being lost.

Of significance is that in the conversation around renaming the Legacies Project, largely for clarity and to signal the direction of travel, a proposal was made for the renaming to be 'the Quamina Covenant'. The latter suggested that naming of the project arose from our archival unearthing work which is ongoing. Onesimus had nothing to do with the legacies of the transatlantic slave trade. Quamina was directly linked to it and the work of the LMS, yet CWM chose to name the new incarnation after Onesimus. Why this is the case is worthy of further reflection. Language and naming are at the heart of epistemic supremacy. How we name something says everything about what is at stake, especially how we are bent on safeguarding our interests. Whiteness has done its work so effectively that the system has enough worshippers of every hue to drive the business of 'elite capture'.

My limited digging into the LMS archives around the Demerara Rebellion and the succeeding years of Congregationalism in Guyana made me more conscious of the line often read to an arrested suspect: 'everything you say [write] can be held against you'. The LMS archival materials continue to participate in a scene or an act of confession in 'the displacement of enslavement of conquered natives, chattel enslavement of imported "others", the use of inhibited violence as the main method of labour control and management, and the legal definition of racial defined "others" as non-human, property and real estate'.[59] The incriminating evidence of multiple and intersecting complicity of the LMS, its missionaries and White coloniality in the 'wealth extraction system', through chattel enslavement of Africans, is there. The work of interrogating, repenting, repairing and restoring has only just begun.

Notes

1 With April Hathcock, I interpret Whiteness as not only 'racial and ethnic categorizations but a complete system of exclusion based on hegemony'. Whiteness refers 'not only to the socio-cultural differential of power and privilege that results from categories of race and ethnicity; it also stands as a marker for the privilege and power that acts to reinforce itself through hegemonic cultural practice that excludes all who are different'. April Hathcock, 2015, 'White Librarianship in Blackface: Diversity Initiatives in LIS', *In the Library with the Lead Pipe*, 7 October, accessed online at https://www.inthelibrarywiththeleadpipe.org/2015/lis-diversity/ (accessed 8.03.2023).

2 Hilary McD. Beckles, 2021, *How Britain Underdeveloped the Caribbean: A Reparation Response to Europe's Legacy of Plunder and Poverty*, Jamaica: University of the West Indies Press, p. 17.

3 See the volume by Emilia Viotti da Costa, 1994, *Crowns of Glory, Tears of Blood: The Demerara Slave Rebellion of 1823*, Oxford: Oxford University Press.

4 Saidiya Hartman, 2021, *Wayward Lives, Beautiful Experiments: Intimate Histories of Riotous Black Girls, Troublesome Women and Queer Radicals*, London: Serpent's Tail, p. 77.

5 Here I need to note the excellent work of Emilia da Costa (*Crowns of Glory*, 1994), though the approach was not that of reading through the specific orientating questions that shape this chapter. Da Costa's interest was not really in John Smith or other LMS missionaries. Her area of research was the dynamics of slave society in Guyana. At the same time, da Costa realised that the Demerara Uprising offered her a unique way into this. Normally the enslaved are denied a voice: but during the trial of John Smith they were called as witnesses by both prosecution and defence. They are speaking under constraint, but at least we hear their names and voices, transcribed into the court records. In a slant way da Costa's work is helpful in making this a story that's as much about the black deacon Quamina and the other members of Bethel Church as their white minister John Smith.

6 Gil Anidjar, 2016, *Blood: A Critique of Christianity*, New York: Columbia University Press.

7 Peter Cruchley and Michael Jagessar, 'Briefing Report on CWM Legacies Project' (June 2019), unpublished document. See also Beckles, *How Britain Underdeveloped the Caribbean*.

8 Yoko Ogawa, 2019, *The Memory Police*, translated from the Japanese by Stephen Snyder, New York: Pantheon Books, p. 43. First published in 1994.

9 Derek Walcott, 1986, 'names' in *Collected Poems 1948–1984*, London: Faber & Faber, pp. 305–8, 306.

10 Emily Dinsdale, 2022, 'Why artist Alberta Whittle is imploring us to "invest in love" (deep dive (pause) uncoiling memory)', *Dazed*, 26 April, accessed online at https://www.dazeddigital.com/art-photography/article/55947/1/why-artist-alberta-whittle-is-imploring-us-to-invest-in-love (accessed 8.03.2023).

11 Da Costa, *Crowns of Glory*, pp. i–xix.

12 Beckles, *How Britain Underdeveloped the Caribbean*, p. 17.

13 Thomas Harding, 2022, *White Debt: The Demerara Uprising and Britain's Legacy of Slavery*, London: Weidenfeld & Nicolson.

14 See Laleh Khalili, 2022, 'How Empire Degraded Britain', *New Statesman*,

24 June, accessed online at https://magazine.newstatesman.com/2022/06/24/how-the-empire-degraded-britain/content.html (accessed 8.03.2023).

15 Harding, *White Debt*, p. 8.

16 Harding, *White Debt*, pp. 97–8.

17 Harding, *White Debt*, p. 98.

18 Da Costa, *Crowns of Glory*, pp. 39–43.

19 Michel-Rolph Trouillot, 1995, *Silencing the Past: Power and the Production of History*, Boston, MA: Beacon Press, p. 82.

20 Haiti, for instance, had to pay France 150 million Francs in reparations in 1825. The subsequent poverty and political instability experienced by Haiti cannot be separated from this fact.

21 Trouillot, *Silencing the Past*, p. 86.

22 Michael Taylor, 2020, *The Interest: How the British Establishment Resisted the Abolition of Slavery*, London: Vintage, Penguin Random House, p. 310.

23 Beckles, *How Britain Underdeveloped the Caribbean*, p. 46.

24 As already noted, an exception being the work of da Costa in *Crowns of Glory*.

25 David Chamberlin, 1924, *Smith of Demerara: Martyr-Teacher of the Slaves*, London: Simkin, Marshall, Hamilton, Kent & Co. Ltd.

26 Chamberlin, *Smith of Demerara*, p. 7.

27 Chamberlin, *Smith of Demerara*, p. 85.

28 Chamberlin, *Smith of Demerara*, p. 16.

29 As portrayed in the chilling journal account by John C. Cheveley about the details of the hunt and gibbeting of the rebels, 'The Demerara Rising (1823)', extracts from the Journal of John C. Cheveley – Merchant in George Town, typescript, SOAS CWM Holding.

30 'The Demerara Rising (1823)'. Italic is mine.

31 'The Demerara Rising (1823)'.

32 Chamberlin, *Smith of Demerara*, p. 85.

33 Archibald Browne, *The Guiana Chronicle and Demerara Gazette*, 27 February 1824.

34 See *Evangelical Magazine* (August 1824).

35 Smith, 'Letter to Directors', *Report of the Directors 1824*', Appendix B, p. 155.

36 Chamberlin, *Smith of Demerara*, p. 38.

37 Chamberlin, *Smith of Demerara*, pp. 40–1.

38 Chamberlin, *Smith of Demerara*, pp. 24–5. Italic is mine.

39 Chamberlin, *Smith of Demerara*, p. 86.

40 Taylor, *The Interest*, p. 76.

41 John Mortier, 'Letter' in *The Guiana Chronicle and Demerara Gazette* (Volume 10/1352, 7 January 1824), p. 2. Italic is mine.

42 Archibald Browne, 'Letter' in *The Guiana Chronicle and Demerara Gazette*, (Volume 10/ 1352, 7 January 1824), p. 3. Italic is mine.

43 The Report of the Directors to The Thirtieth Annual Meeting of the Missionary Society, usually called the London Missionary Society, held at Great Queen Street Chapel (Thursday 18 May 1824), iv, accessed online at SOAS LMS Archives, https://digital.soas.ac.uk/AA00001298/00002.

44 The Report of the Directors, p. 124.

45 The Report of the Directors, p. 127.

46 Frederick Hickling, 2021, *Decolonization of Psychiatry in Jamaica: Madnificent Irations*, London: Palgrave Macmillan, pp. 4–5.
47 Hickling, *Decolonization of Psychiatry*, p. 16.
48 Hickling, *Decolonization of Psychiatry*, p. 17.
49 Hickling, *Decolonization of Psychiatry*, p. 12.
50 F. W. Hickling and G. Hutchinson, 'Roast Breadfruit Psychosis: Disturbed Racial Identification in African-Caribbeans', *Psychiatric Bulletin*, 23(3) (1999), pp. 132–4.
51 Hickling, *Decolonization of Psychiatry*, p. 18.
52 Letter dated 6 March 1809 from Plantation Le Resouvenir to the LMS Directors, by the Revd John Wray. Digitized hand-written copy located at SOAS.
53 *Missionary Sketches*, LXXXIII (April 1839). For the use of the Weekly and Monthly Contributors to the LMS.
54 *Missionary Sketches*, LXXXIII.
55 See da Costa, *Crowns of Glory*, pp. 3–85.
56 Lucian states: 'The Rightful Place for the Smith Statue', *Guyana Chronicle*, 25 November 1967.
57 Colin Palmer, 2009, *Eric Williams and the Making of the Modern Caribbean*, Chapel Hill, NC: University of North Carolina Press, p. 149.
58 See https://www.cwmission.org/programmes/the-onesimus-project/ (accessed 23.03.2023).
59 Beckles, *How Britain Underdeveloped the Caribbean*, p. xii.

PART THREE

Personal Reflections

11

Coming Full Circle: Christianity, Empire, Whiteness, the Global Majority and the Struggles of Migrants and Refugees in the UK

PAUL WELLER

From end of empire to Brexit: An odyssey through 'A Quartet Over Time'

The book in which this chapter appears is concerned, overall, with deconstructing Whiteness, empire and mission; it highlights the destructive consequences of these intersections, both for global majority people and for White people. The book is also concerned with identifying the liberative opportunities that can emerge when the destructiveness of these intersections is rigorously analysed, clearly exposed and seriously repented of as part of a clear commitment to seek out positive and collaborative ways forward rooted in justice and equality.

The coming full circle to which this chapter refers is that of the period between the late 1960s and early 1970s through to the post-Brexit present of the UK, the government of which is proclaiming it to be 'Global Britain'. As an increasingly older White British Baptist scholar of religion and society who, over this period has, with varying emphases and foci, nationally and internationally, tried to be active in the struggle against racism and worked towards ethnic, national and religious pluralism, I have structured my contribution to this book around four originally independently generated (between 1974 and 2001) – but all personally related – pieces of writing that I consider to be of wider relevance to the overall theme of the book, and which collectively I am calling 'A Quartet Over Time'. Three of these (a poem from 1974, and what others have suggested might better be called the 'prose poems' of 2016 and 2021) were written by myself, while the poem of 1986 was written by my deceased (2010) White German Catholic wife, Margret Preisler-Weller.

In between these poems and prose poems, I have attempted to undertake an analytical discussion within which – including also by reference to some of my other writing over the past four decades – I am trying to expose some of the connections that, at multiple levels, exist between the personal and familial, religious and political, national and international realities of the imperial inheritance within which, in differing ways, all of us who are in one way or another Christian and connected with the UK and Europe live – whether we are conscious of it (as are most, but not all of those of a global majority heritage) or not (as are likely, still, the majority of those of us who are White and Christian).

The inheritance of empire

As a White Christian teenager living in Margate, Kent, in the UK of 1974, and at that time not very explicitly conscious of the connection between racism and empire, I wrote the poem 'Rule Britannia'. This expressed my sense that something that had once been a dominant reference point in global history had come to an end – as T. S. Eliot put it in his poem, 'The Hollow Men', 'not with a bang but a whimper'.[1] It was an era when, for White teenagers such as myself, the TV series *Monty Python's Flying Circus*[2] expressed the absurdity of the outward remnants of empire and generated a kind of cynicism about it, but without leading to a confrontation with its meaning or significance for the peoples of the large swathes of the world over which it had held power for centuries:

'Rule Britannia'

All is in outward order:
The red-coated men
Stand, like images in a Catholic church,
Quite still within their boxes, motionless,
Even when offending flies tickle their noses;
Pomp and ceremony,
   Cups of tea
      Queen Victoria
         Singing the Gloria
           Abstract euphoria
All very English.

Did you know that once upon a time
The whole world was painted in red, white, and blue?
(Well, most of it, anyway.)
And London was at the centre of the universe.
But today it's mostly painted in red alone, and
London bridge is falling down,
   falling down
      falling down
         falling down
London Bridge is falling down, my fair lady.

But even that can't happen in England today –
The Americans came and took it away.

Outside and inside perspectives on the empire within

In a paper that he wrote in 1981, Ambalavaner Sivanandan, speaking as a person from the global majority, underlined to White people in Britain that, 'Our history is not your history.'[3] Having grown up as a young Baptist Christian and with stories of the Baptist Christian missionary to India William Carey, but having no real knowledge of the impact of colonialism and imperialism on the world beyond the UK, and little sense of the realities of racism within what Salman Rushdie called 'The New Empire Within Britain',[4] it was through the later impact of a number of concrete learnings in the late 1970s and early 1980s that I began to understand something about these realities and to get to grips with at least some of their implications for the global majority world and for myself as a White Christian living within it.

The first of these learnings came as a by-product of the impact of what I would today identify as prophetic action undertaken within the global Christian *oikumene*. Although now too often forgotten, the World Council of Churches (WCC)'s 'Programme to Combat Racism', and more specifically, its so-called Special Fund, was something at the time that was both controversial and also of enormous significance.[5] Among other things, it expressed Christian solidarity in the struggle against colonialism in South West Africa (now Namibia) and Rhodesia (now Zimbabwe) through giving financial support – for humanitarian, rather than military, purposes – directly to the South West Africa People's Organization (SWAPO) and Patriotic Front (PF) liberation movements rather than only to intermediary humanitarian organizations.

In the light of some of the later human rights abuses that followed the original liberation in Zimbabwe, there would likely today be many more who would be even quicker to criticize this expression of anti-colonial and anti-imperialist solidarity than was the case even at the time. However, for myself, the sheer fact that an official Christian ecumenical body had decided to make such grants started within me, as a White British Christian with no direct experiences of the injustices faced by the global majority, a process of what liberation theologians have often referred to as 'conscientization'. By sharply focusing the question of what had led to its decision, this prophetic action of the WCC startled me out of my generally ignorant complacency to become more aware of the global realities of racism, colonialism and imperialism – not only as phenomena of an historical past and/or in the sometimes too easy slogans of the Western revolutionary left, but as continuing inheritances with very real effects in the lives of the global majority.

The second learning came from my becoming, in the early 1980s, increasingly confronted with the injustices visited by UK immigration law and practice in preventing family unification and carrying out deportations especially of migrants and asylum seekers of global majority heritage. In this period, many locally organized political campaigns developed around individuals and families faced with these injustices. In some cases, these secured positive outcomes for the individuals and families concerned. But they also more generally highlighted and challenged the systemic nature of the racism that informed the relevant laws and practices, as well as the policies and politics that lay behind their development. Together with people from a range of left-wing political groups, trade unionists and members of the wider community, these campaigns also secured the active involvement of numbers of individual Christian activists, whole congregations, and many official church bodies, developing a particularly strong profile through what became known as the 'Sanctuary Movement':[6] religious buildings and/or congregations offered shelter to people under threat of deportation, reaching an apogee in the December 1986 sanctuary taken by the Sri Lankan political activist Viraj Mendis in the Anglican Church of the Ascension in Hulme, Manchester,[7] which acted as something of a national focus for a range of similar campaigns and sanctuaries until its forcible breaking by the police in January 1989, and Viraj Mendis's subsequent deportation to Sri Lanka.

As a cameo of the kind of learnings that participating in such campaigns brought about in myself and others, in 1983, when I was a Baptist minister at the Welbeck Street Baptist Church in Ashton-under-Lyne, the local congregation decided to host a so-called 'Sanctuary Fast' in the church's premises over the weekend of 4–7 November. This was in support of Vinod Chauhan, a Hindu migrant of Indian origin who was under threat of deportation, and whose campaign group I was chairing; prior to the weekend concerned, Vinod had received a letter from the Home Office warning that, following the exhaustion of various legal appeals, he was to be deported as soon as possible. Although much more modest compared to the more costly in commitment and publicly impactful Viraj Mendis campaign, given the description of it at the time by one of the church's deacons as 'the most biblical thing we've ever done',[8] it might not be too much of a stretch to see this event also as having been an act of prophetic symbolism, following which Vinod's deportation order was suspended pending consideration of further representations from the local MP although eventually, on 12 April 1984, Vinod was arrested from his workplace and deported to India.

The idea of sanctuary, although no longer having legal force in UK religious buildings, symbolically embodied a moral and political challenge to the injustice of the system by affirmation of the existence of a set of values beyond those of the state and its laws. Fasting is, of course, familiar within the Hindu, Muslim and Christian traditions, and has also been utilized as a means of social and political struggle. The 'Sanctuary Fast' took place during the local Hindu community's Divali celebrations, and the church's Sunday worship included a prayer from the Hindu *Upanishads*. During the weekend, one of the church members undertook a dramatic form of personal symbolic protest that spoke widely to many people through the media that covered it. Retired White working-class church member Hilda Carr – who lived in a block of flats just across the road from the church building concerned – recounted the story in her own words in a BBC Radio Manchester programme, and reported as follows in a Vinod Chauhan Defence Campaign booklet:[9]

> I remembered a part of the Bible that said we are of the same blood. Something ... a little voice behind me said 'Prove it.' I just got up ... I didn't get up myself, I'm sure I didn't. I was guided or I was led, and I went straight and got a needle out of the needle case, switched the kettle on, sterilised the needle, wrapped it up, and put me coat on and went straight across to the church. I live quite near ... I asked Paul [Weller] if he thought it would be right that I should ask Vinod that if I drew my blood, just pricked the thumb that was all, if he would agree to draw his blood and we would put it on the blotter; and then asked Paul if he could tell the difference, and he couldn't.

When then asked by the interviewer about the purpose of what she had done, she said: 'To prove that there is no difference in the blood. It must be his colour. There's no other reason. He hadn't done anything wrong in the five years he's been here to any of our knowledge – it would have been proven by now.' Asked about what would happen to the blood, she said:

> Well as far as I know, Paul is going to send them up to the House of Commons, and he will probably ask the same question that I asked him. Can they tell the difference? I know the difference, and Paul knows the difference now because he was told – but they won't know the difference ...

Reflecting further on this, Hilda Carr concluded that: 'We presume things. Because we want to think the things that we want to think. We only presume that God is white. We don't see Him in any other colour. But we don't know that He is.' In this pithy statement, rooted in her small but nevertheless impactful act of prophetic symbolism, Hilda Carr articulated something in relation to which the much later emerging field of 'Critical Whiteness' studies within Christian theology has sought to give more theorized expression. For myself, not long after the above, in a 1985 booklet called *The Problems of the White Ethnic Majority*, I sought to explore some of the challenges of which I was increasingly becoming aware as a White Christian person trying seriously to understand, engage with, and combat racism in the UK (and beyond).[10]

In between the two foci for my learning as outlined above, and what has been my most recent attempt, nearly 40 years later, in revisiting that initial 1985 reflection on the significance for White people of racism arising from the colonial and imperial inheritance,[11] my late White German Catholic wife wrote her poem 'Love Song'. This poem was informed by a long history of family visits to parts of England in and around Cambridge and a period as a visiting student at Bristol University. It was written soon after she moved to work in the UK on the basis that London was, at the time, a major hub of Black South African exile politics and culture, in the context of which she had originally intended to take forward her planned doctoral research on the poetry of liberation and the poetry of oppression in South Africa:

'Love Song'
(Margret Preisler-Weller, 1986)

Where are you going,
England, my love?
Where are you drifting
Why have you deserted me?
England, my love?

COMING FULL CIRCLE

I loved you, England,
your beautiful looks, England
full of cottages and ancient stories
Big Ben guarding over London
The Suspension Bridge spanning over the Avon Vale.
Colleges with tradition in Cambridge
Cathedrals in Roman towns,
I loved your insides
with steaming teapots and greasy dripping crumpets
milk in the morning and pubs at night.
Until I realised
It's a façade
a masquerade
a carnival set up for tourists and passers-by

I lived with you, England
now divorce is nigh, England.
I can't live with your friends
called Arrogance and False Pride
called Intolerance, Deportation and Indifference.
Colleges educating elite snobs
Cathedrals filled with faithless pride
Your guts cramped with fear
Sweating out anger and dripping saliva
washed away in the morning what happened at night.
Slowly I realised
your façade
your masquerade
your bright mask nearly mocked me, too.

I talked with you, England,
now coldness spreads, England,
for you lock out my friends
called Refugees and Immigrants
with names like Ditta and Viraj, Anna and Sahid.
Your friends fighting my friends
forcing me to take sides
Police truncheons are your mace
removals and threats become your act of grace.
Your hands stained from crushing souls.
But now I realise:
your façade

your masquerade
your mind's ruled by court-jesters and heartless bodies.

I was close to you, England
how distant now, England
that I know your intimate love
for I came from your concubine
whose fascist dreams you are dreaming now.
Already you are full
of Goebbelstalk and Göring-power
All you love is different names
Immigration law sounds better than humiliation and oppression
Hitlermania is now called surveillance.
Sadly I realise
Your façade
your masquerade
is hypocrisy by left quick march with state violence.

Where are you going, England, my love?
Still building colonies on your island?
I am deserting you. I can't look back.

The poem was strongly informed by an increasing sense of dissonance in my wife's 'outsider' perspective as a German, between her long-held love for aspects of England and her increasing encounter (in part, but not only, through our growing relationship together) with the realities of racism as highlighted in the kind of family reunification, anti-deportation and sanctuary campaigns discussed above. It was also informed by her growing awareness of connections that might be made between these realities and aspects of the history of her own German inheritance.

The conjunctions in this poem between England and the notions of 'Goebbelstalk', 'Göring-power' and 'Hitlermania' are ones that a number of White Christians with whom I have since shared the poem have questioned, feeling that they would potentially be seen by White British people as disproportionate. It is likely that these references were indeed formulated in such a way with the intention to shock, but especially coming from a German Christian such words should give pause for thought. Indeed, it is not accidental that the startlingly powerful words of the German Christian Pastor Martin Niemöller, who was involved in the resistance to the Nazis and was imprisoned by them, were cited in the Vinod Chauhan 'Sanctuary Fast' campaign leaflet.[12]

In connection with this, it is worth reflecting on the fact that, around the time of the Sanctuary Fast, in a speech to the right-wing Monday Club, the Home Secretary at the time, Leon Brittan MP, attacked what he called 'pernicious' attempts to undermine immigration controls through defence campaigns of this kind, accusing them of making 'allegations based on highly selective and biased accounts of individual cases'[13] while, on noting that the campaign materials for Vinod Chauhan included these words, the then Minister of State at the Home Office, David Waddington MP, had attacked Vinod's campaign for scaremongering.

Almost 40 years later, as I am finalizing the writing of this chapter, the current UK Home Secretary, Priti Patel, has announced a plan to remove adult male asylum seekers arriving by sea into the UK to Rwanda for processing. Criticized by the Archbishop of Canterbury Justin Welby in uncharacteristically robust theo-political language as being the 'opposite of the nature of God',[14] this plan, as a number of commentators have noted, has eerie echoes of the June 1940 proposal from Franz Rademacher. He was the Head of the Jewish Department of the German Foreign Office, who also called for the 'offshoring' of what, in Nazi Germany, before the implementation of the so-called 'Final Solution', was framed as 'the Jewish Problem'. This offshoring was initially to be achieved by the resettlement of a million Jews per year for four years to the south-east African island of Madagascar, which the German authorities had anticipated taking control of as part of peace terms with Vichy France.[15]

Full circle to Brexit

Unlike the Germany from which my deceased wife and author of 'Love Song' came, the UK has never seriously undertaken what, in Germany and in the German language, is known as *Vergangenheitsaufarbeitung*. This is loosely translatable as the exercise of 'working through the past', in relation to which, as the German journalist Annette Dittert recently expressed: 'If you honestly engage with your own history – which Germany had to do because it was horrific – if you do that seriously, I think you do not fall for national myths anymore.' She further underlined that: 'That's a big danger for a nation, if you don't look into your past ... you fail to understand reality.'[16] Indeed, as Anthony Reddie in his book *Theologising Brexit: A Liberationist and Postcolonial Critique*[17] has persuasively argued, the failure of the UK properly to reckon with its history of empire, colonialism and imperialism is something that was closely linked with the themes that informed the narrow majority achieved in the 2016 Advisory Referendum that led to the UK leaving the EU.

This is also something that, in an article on Brexit as a 'colonial boomerang',[18] I have tried to develop further in terms of its implications for the very future of (to give it its full formal and legal name) the United Kingdom of Great Britain. The very structure of the UK as it exists today is the product of an originally expansionary English colonial project that was initially 'internal' to what the Churches Together in Britain and Ireland call 'these islands'. It was the confluence of all these strands that informed my writing of the prose poem 'BREXIT', which reflects upon Brexit in the light of the various inheritances of racism that preceded it:

'BREXIT' (2016)

Brexit, Br-exit, Brex-it ...
or so the incantation goes
that seems inexorably to carry 'us' along the tidal flows
of the River Thames.
Flowing backwards, of course,
From Article 50 to 'we' know not where.

What is the 'it' from which we Br/ex-it?
The warts and all real-'it'-y from the ruins,
the bureaucratisation of peace instead of war?
Or the fearful conjuring of ever-louder offshore replays of Land of
   Hope and Glory?
Why do 'we' go? And who, anyway, are 'we'? – the 48 per cent or the
   52?
And how many of the 52 are still here? And what of those who have
   been and still are 'of us' but were not allowed to make their mark in
   this parting of the ways?

Are we the 'UK'?
Or now is it only the 'K' of it?
Or even in danger of becoming the KKK?

The invocation of 'rivers of blood' was once defeated –
or so 'we' thought, and gloried in the splendour of our rainbow
   country.
Colours, sights and sounds of Empire,
it seemed, transformed into something gloriously new.

But perhaps the invocation of those rivers was only diverted: down, down deep ...
until the Northern Rock proved not to be so solid, and the casino kings were rescued
by the money of those who had not
and from whom was taken even that which they had;
averting the Day of Judgement, but making way for the False Messiah
with a beer in his hands, and cigarettes and 'Man of the People' words in his mouth,
but ascending in golden splendour to Trumpian heavens.

And so those deep down things burst out again ...
And this time not on to those of dark flesh arriving on boats into London.
Now they wash over those with pale faces emerging from Stansted and Luton airports.
And so it goes on under the screamingly insecure letters of the 'UK BORDER':
'No Jews', 'No Irish', 'No Blacks' and now 'No Poles' here!

In different times we could take for granted a human connection under the water.
In these times we can give thanks it is still there
and that people are still moving along it.
But in the wake of those who are trying to 'leave',
what else will or will no longer travel along it?
In which directions? And with what outcomes?
For those who want to 'leave'
and for the all who will anyway 'remain' in both the over-here and/or the over-there
there is the in-between of at least trying to keep the tunnel open,
and the challenge that silence is not the measure of loyalty
or the arbiter of democracy.

And before the ticking clock of the 'what is' of 'post-Brexit Referendum' fact
becomes forged into the 'what must be' shackles of 'post-Brexit'
an echo of freedom still calls for those who respect that people can change
to argue with the courage of proud humility
that there is time to call time before it is too late.

Aftermath towards 'Windrush on steroids'

Four years later, the 'ticking clock of the "what is" of "post-Brexit Referendum" fact' indeed became the '"what must be" shackles of post-Brexit' when the UK finally left the EU at midnight Central European Time on 31 December 2020. With this, UK citizens in the EU and EU citizens in the UK faced the traumatization of their previously legally secure statuses under EU Freedom of Movement law. In relation to this, when the cross-party Parliamentary Home Affairs Committee was taking evidence on the UK government's scheme for the post-Brexit lives of EU citizen resident members of UK society, the then chair of that Committee, the Labour Party MP Yvette Cooper, made a connection with what had not long before come into wider public awareness in terms of the so-called Windrush affair.[19] These words allude to the ship called *Empire Windrush* which, in 1948, brought Caribbean British subjects to work in the UK's postwar economy. The scandal – in which decades later many people of Caribbean origins had suddenly found the legitimacy of their presence in the country being questioned and, with that, their right to work and/or to receive benefits and public services – was itself the by-product of the so-called 'hostile environment'. Over the decades, the UK government Home Office systematically engendered and applied this 'hostile environment' primarily to migrants from global majority countries.[20] In questioning one of the witnesses to the Committee, Colin Yeo (a lawyer specializing in migration cases), Cooper asked: 'Is it fair to say that effectively the system that the government are currently putting in place is like Windrush on steroids?' to which Yeo answered simply, but also chillingly: 'Yes'.

In this question and answer, one can see how the injustices of the pre-Brexit UK immigration system could, over the coming decades, come full circle and impact in similar ways on the lives of hundreds of thousands of EU citizens and their families who, until Brexit, had built their living, working and loving on the basis of the EU's legal framework for Freedom of Movement. Indeed, for me personally, since the death of my first wife (the author of 'Love Song'), I married another German woman and, post-Brexit, it became clear that her (and therefore, in many ways also 'our') future in the UK, and that of thousands of other EU citizens in the UK, was now at the mercy of a time-limited application system for so-called 'pre-settled' or 'settled' status, the outcome of which was by no means guaranteed.[21]

One can also see how mechanisms of injustice originally developed and applied in relation to particular groups with particular characteristics (for example, skin colour) can also be applied to groups of people who are 'othered' on the basis of other criteria. But perhaps one can also see the potential for bridges of mutual understanding and solidarity to be built across the differences that those in power all too often use to divide and rule.

In the light of this, on the day after the general election of 12 December 2019, in which the Conservative Party gained a massive parliamentary (though not popular) majority led by the slogan 'Get Brexit done!', I wrote the following prose poem, 'Ode to Sadness'. This, in counterpoint to the 'Ode to Joy' anthem of the EU, built on my 2016 prose poem 'BREXIT', reprised some echoes from my 1974 poem, 'Rule Britannia' and some themes and original words from my late wife's 1986 poem, 'Love Song'. In one of its refrains, it also invoked the title of the White South African author Alan Paton's famous novel, *Cry, the Beloved Country*:[22]

'Ode to Sadness'
(13 December 2019)

I cried a little last night
As the Big Choice day of the 12th
Gave way to the pain of the 13th
When, in 'our' choice, it seems 'we' confirmed
To make ourselves foreigners in Europe.
And having won the war of previous generations,
Elected, it seems, to lose the long peace.

Cry, cry my beloved country!

I cried inside more than a little last night:
The personal is the political say the feminists
And they are right.
And in Brexit the political is personal too.
Because in this future that it seems 'we' are to embrace,
If it were the past, my children might not exist
As the British-German hybrids that they are.

Cry, cry my beloved country!

And I felt the pain of a German loved one among those
Who, by choosing to love and to live here,
Has had the 'cheek' to 'treat the UK as if it's part of their own country'.
And I mourned again another German loved one who,

In her Love Song lamentation of long ago already saw
That steaming teapots and dripping crumpets
Were not all there was to know of England.

'Where are you gone,
England, my love?
Where are you drifting?
Why have you deserted me,
England, my love?'

She saw the devouring Monster coming:

'Your guts cramped with fear
Sweating out anger and dripping saliva
Washed away in the morning what happened at night'

She saw the Monster of Brexit madness
Giving way now to Brexit coldness:
'I talked with you, England,
Now coldness spreads, England,
For you lock out my friends'

So cry, cry my beloved country!

I cried what was probably not enough last night
Remembering my own half century old words that:

'Once upon a time the world was painted in red, white and blue
Now London Bridge is falling down, falling down
London Bridge is falling down my fair lady
But even that can't happen in England today,
the Americans came and took it away'

And what more might,
If we do not fight,
They take in 'deals' that steal
The birth right of our NHS?
So, cry, cry my beloved country!

And in the face of the gaping wounds
Of the five million without voice

And of the many more of those with whom they are bound
Who lived the dream,
But are having it stolen from them,
Do not yet let siren (even if religious) voices call for
Peace, peace when there is no peace.
Of course, for those who believe:
'Here we do not have an enduring city,
But we are looking for the city that is to come'
That is neither here, nor in Germany,
Nor even in the Berlaymont:
'So be it, Lord,
Thy Throne shall never
Like earth's proud Empires pass away.'

But in the England of these islands,
Cut off by pride and self-deception
We are left only with the fragments
Of what once was also our Union,
Built from the wreckage of war
And the tearing down of the Curtain of Iron.

And in our mourning,
The haunting words of the Love Song's lamentation
Now echo ever more loudly in my mind and heart:

'Where are you going, England, my love?
Still building colonies on your island?'

And I wonder, too, what the future will hold
And if, in the end, I will still be able to call it mine?

In moving towards the conclusion of this chapter, it is perhaps not without significance that I am writing out of a personal, familial and political context in which, in the mid-sixth decade of my life, together with my current German wife, I have been in the process of moving my main residence from the UK to Germany, which adds a particularly personal relevance and poignancy to the question I asked at the end of the above prose poem. Indeed, as I write this, it is difficult not to compare the approach of the German authorities to the many tens of thousands of people fleeing from the invasion of Ukraine by Russia with the miserly approach of the UK government schemes which – of course, it must also be said – stand in contrast with the readiness of tens of thousands of individual people and families in Britain, including many in church and other religious communities, to offer their support to those fleeing the first full-scale military invasion in Europe since the end of the Second World War. During the 2016 refugee crisis in Europe the then German Chancellor, Angela Merkel, despite facing significant internal opposition and without very much in the way of coordinated support from other member states of the EU, courageously argued that '*Wir schaffen dass*' ('We can do this'). Germany is also the country in which Viraj Mendis eventually found European refuge, as facilitated by the city state of Bremen, and from where he continues today to campaign for the rights of other asylum seekers, refugees and migrants.

In making these points, however, I would not want to be misunderstood as one who views Germany through rose-tinted spectacles. Germany, too, has a colonial past that is all too often eclipsed in the national psyche by the impact of the systematic and modern industrialized murder of millions of Jews, gypsies, homosexuals and others during the Nazi Third Reich period. However, when Germany was the colonial power between 1884 and 1919, colonial German South West Africa witnessed the slaughter of approximately 80,000 indigenous people, representing around 80 per cent of the Herero people and 50 per cent of the Nama people, by German *Schutztruppen* (1904–1907).[23] It is also the case that the cultural and religion and belief public profile of Germany is much less pluralistic than that of the UK. And finally, one should not overlook the presence in the Bundestag of a significant bloc of the far-right *Alternative für Deutschland* politicians.

Nevertheless, as a White British Christian, with now an increasing sense of 'dual' British and German identification mediated through many years of international living as an EU citizen in both the UK and Germany, I have an even clearer sense of Brexit being a 'colonial boomerang'. Indeed, as the title of Hardeep Matharu's article in *Byline Times* summarized it, at least the current phase of post-Brexit is, tragically, a case of: 'Backwards Britain: Having Rejected a European Future, We Can Only Hark Back to an Imperial Past'.[24] Given that the British empire has passed away and that, realistically speaking, it will not (despite all the nostalgia that informs the notion of 'Global Britain') come back again, as the significance and effects of colonialism and imperialism have finally come home to roost in the fabric of what is left of the now deeply (dis) 'United' Kingdom, the questions around what has or has not been learned, and what will or will not be learned, from the passing of that empire will likely become ever more insistent. Indeed, a serious engagement with these questions is arguably a necessary prerequisite before any more cooperative and collaborative internal, European and global future can truly be developed for the UK in whatever form it may or may not continue in the future.

Of course, the EU should also not be idealized – not least because it has, itself, generally failed to conduct a coordinated and positive approach to the reception of asylum seekers. In addition, as alluded to in 'Ode to Sadness', a key lesson of the biblical narrative is that no political structure – whether of an empire created by military conquest and/or overwhelming economic power, such as the British empire; or a free union of countries created by the cooperative pooling of sovereignty in the context of a peace project, such as the EU – will continue for ever. And from the Hebrew prophets to the book of Revelation the scriptures are full of warnings about, and protests against, the tendency of human beings to deify the state and/or its rulers. Hence the political significance of the Hebrew prophetic affirmation of God as the ultimate ruler of the peoples and countries of the world, including those of Israel and Judah, as well as of the earliest Christian declaration that Jesus (and not Caesar) is Lord.

However, even without falling into deification of a people, a state and/or its rulers, the history of the majority forms taken by both Western and Eastern Christendom has been one in which Christianity has relied upon secular powers to secure its original foothold; then to extend its scope; and finally to bring about a religious uniformity in which the identities and perspectives of other than Christian religions have been at best marginalized and, at worst, squeezed almost out of existence. Such approaches reflect what might be seen as the fateful Constantinian turn taken by the early Christian church,[25] in relation to which the Baptist Christian theologian J. W. McClendon Jr has posed the intriguing and very significant historical question of:

> Is it not worth considering how different might have been the history of Christianity, if after the Constantinian accession, the Christian leaders had met at Nicaea, not to anathematize others' inadequate theological metaphysics, but to develop a strategy by which the church might remain the church in the light of the fateful political shift – to secure Christian social ethics before refining Christian dogma?[26]

The assumptions of such Constantinian models have, however, all too often (although not always) been exported into majority world contexts as part of an overall theological and missiological package. These models, rather than embodying an open and ethical Christology and ecclesiology, have all too often closed the person, work and teaching of Jesus off from people of other religious traditions by – in effect even if not in theory –

claiming him as the property of a doctrinal ideology and/or of various institutional forms of the Christian church.[27]

Therefore, in conclusion, in the broader context of the increasingly urgent ecological and planetary challenges around how to forge a collaborative, just and peaceful future in a world where the global majority is neither White in terms of ethnicity nor Christian in terms of religion, if we are to have a realistic hope of such a future, then – together with liberation from the (differential) inheritance of empire – both White and Black Christians will also need to recognize, challenge and break free from the role that Constantinian models of Christendom have played in reinforcing the coalescence of racialized thinking and secular power that the structures of colonialism and imperialism have bequeathed to us.

Notes

1 T. S. Eliot, 1925, *The Hollow Men*, London: Faber & Faber.

2 *Monty Python's Flying Circus* was a surreal sketch comedy series broadcast by the BBC in 1969–74.

3 Ambalavaner Sivanandan, 'White Man, Listen!', *Encounter* (July 1981).

4 Salman Rushdie, 1991, 'The New Empire Within Britain' in Salman Rushdie (ed.), *Imaginary Homelands: Essays and Criticism, 1981–1991*, London: Granta Books, pp. 129–38.

5 Elisabeth Adler, 1974, *A Small Beginning: An Assessment of the First Five Years of the Programme to Combat Racism*, Geneva: World Council of Churches.

6 Paul Weller, 1987, *Sanctuary: The Beginning of a Movement?*, London: The Runnymede Trust; and Paul Weller, 'Sanctuary and the British Churches', *The Modern Churchman*, 30(4) (1989), pp. 12–17.

7 Viraj Mendis Defence Campaign, 1988, *Religious Support Group. Sanctuary: Manchester Perspectives*, Manchester: Viraj Mendis Defence Campaign, Religious Support Group.

8 Paul Weller, 'Sanctuary Fast: Local Baptist Church Fights Deportation Order', *Grassroots* (March–April 1984), pp. 26–7.

9 Paul Weller, 1984, *Legalised Abduction: The Struggle of Vinod Chauhan*, Ashton-under-Lyne: Vinod Chauhan Defence Campaign. Scanned copy available at https://www.academia.edu/77848040/Legalised_Abduction_The_Struggle_of_Vinod_Chauhan (accessed 10.03.2023).

10 Paul Weller, 1985, *The Problems of the White Ethnic Majority*, London: Christians Against Racism and Fascism and One for Christian Renewal. Scanned copy available at https://www.academia.edu/51117192/Problems_of_the_White_Ethnic_Majority (accessed 10.03.2023).

11 Paul Weller, '"The Problems of the White Ethnic Majority" Revisited: A Personal, Theological and Political Review', *Practical Theology*, 15(1–2) (2022), pp. 23–36. Free Open Access at https://www.tandfonline.com/doi/full/10.1080/1756073X.2021.2023950 (accessed 10.3.2023).

12 Many versions exist of this famous statement. For a discussion and analysis of the various versions, see Harold Marcuse, 2016, 'The Origin and Reception of Martin Niemöller's Quotation, First They Came for the Communists ...', in Michael Berenbaum, Richard Libowitz and Marcia Sachs Littell (eds), *Remembering for the Future: Armenia, Auschwitz, and Beyond*, St Paul's, MN: Paragon House, pp. 173–99.

13 Leon Brittan, MP, *Conservative Party News Service*, 28 March 1984.

14 Joseph Lee, 2002, 'UK's Rwanda Asylum Plan the "Opposite of Nature of God" – Welby', BBC website, 17 April, https://www.bbc.com/news/uk-61130841 (accessed 10.03.2023).

15 Adolf Eichmann, *Reichssicherheitshauptamt: Madagaskar Projekt*, a memorandum of 15 August 1940; see, further, https://www.jewishvirtuallibrary.org/the-madagascar-plan-2 (accessed 10.03.2023).

16 Speaking on *Friday Night with Byline Times* and quoted in Hardeep Matharu, 2022, 'Backwards Britain: Having Rejected a European Future, We Can Only Hark Back to an Imperial Past', *Byline Times*, 5 April, available at https://bylinetimes.com/2022/04/05/backwards-britain-having-rejected-a-european-future-we-can-only-hark-back-to-an-imperial-past/ (accessed 10.03.2023).

17 Anthony G. Reddie, 2019, *Theologising Brexit: A Liberationist and Postcolonial Critique*, Abingdon: Routledge.

18 Paul Weller, 'Brexit: A Colonial Boomerang in a Populist World', *Social Justice*, 41(196) (2019), pp. 8–11. Free Open Access at https://pureportal.coventry.ac.uk/en/publications/brexit-a-colonial-boomerang-in-a-populist-world (accessed 10.03.2023) and in a longer related paper, 'Roots, Routes, and Times of Decision: Brexit, Populisms, Colonialism and Imperialism in Global Perspective'. Free Open Access at https://pureportal.coventry.ac.uk/files/23840319/Roots_Routes_and_Times_of_Decision_long_form_article.pdf (accessed 10.03.2023).

19 House of Commons Home Affairs Committee, *Oral Evidence: EU Settlement Scheme*, HC 1945, Tuesday 12 February 2019, http://data.parliament.uk/writtenevidence/committeeevidence.svc/evidencedocument/home-affairs-committee/eu-settlement-scheme/oral/96447.html (accessed 10.03.2023).

20 BBC, 2021, 'Windrush Generation: Who Are They and Why are They Facing Problems?', BBC website, 24 November 24, https://www.bbc.com/news/uk-43782241 (accessed 10.03.2023).

21 I am pleased to be able to share that, having waited to apply for 'settled' rather than 'pre-settled' status, in the end my wife achieved that, and also in the end British citizenship to complement her German/EU citizenship – while the legal challenges and uncertainty for us as having family responsibilities in Germany remained in relation to myself, although between the submission and checking of this text I managed to achieve an *Aufenthaltstitel* (residence permit) in Germany (although not yet a permanent one) on the basis of Article 50 of the EU-UK Withdrawal Agreement. For those who may be interested in this and the related experiences of others, I presented some of this, along with some wider observation and analysis, to an online seminar organized by the New Europeans organization on the topic of 'One Year and One Day On: What Price are Citizens Paying for Brexit?' (3.2.2021), accessible at about 32 minutes in, but unfortunately with rather poor visual Internet connection quality): New Europeans TV, 2021, '"Paying the Price and Counting the Cost" Brexit a Year and a Day Later', *YouTube*, 3 February, https://www.youtube.com/watch?v=UTcmBAx1u1Q&t=2096s (accessed 10.03.2023).

22 Alan Paton, 1948, *Cry, the Beloved Country*, London: Jonathan Cape.
23 Horst Drechsler, 1980, *'Let Us Die Fighting': The Struggle of the Herero and Nama against German Imperialism (1884–1915)*, London: Zed Press.
24 Matharu, 'Backwards Britain'.
25 Alistair Kee, 1982, *Constantine Versus Christ: The Triumph of Ideology*, London: SCM Press.
26 James McClendon Jr, 'What is a "Baptist" Theology?', *American Baptist Quarterly*, 1(1) (1982), pp. 16–39, 39.
27 For more on this, see Paul Weller, 2014, 'Theological Ethics and Interreligious Relations: a Baptist Christian Perspective' in Angela Berlis, Andreas Krebs and Douglas Pratt (eds), *Inter-Religious Engagement and Theological Reflection: Ecumenical Explorations*, Bern: IKZBIOS, pp. 119–40.

12

'I Know Where You're Coming From': Exploring Intercultural Assumptions

JILL MARSH

Introduction

In this chapter I will explore some of the ways in which the missionary history of the Methodist Church has had a lasting impact on intercultural relationships within congregations in a UK context. I will then offer some personal reflections on the necessary responses to this legacy.

My adult life has been spent, personally and professionally, in intercultural contexts. As a young adult in the 1980s I was influenced by Methodists who preached about racial justice, pointed out the social dangers, theological sinfulness and moral iniquity of 'White flight', and encouraged White Christians to live Christian lives where they were, alongside whoever was around them, rather than fleeing when there was no need to flee. Over 37 years I have enjoyed working contexts (in London, Sheffield and Leicester) where the populations have been very multicultural and multi-faith. Our family (as with many families) has become increasingly diverse, now including people of Armenian, Pakistani, Mozambican and Indian heritage. My life has been deeply enriched by close friendships with people of Afghan, Antiguan, Jamaican, Namibian, Nevisian, Pakistani and Zimbabwean heritage and in all of these relationships I have had my eyes opened to the deep-seated racism that impacts daily on people's lives. Meanwhile, in my work as a Methodist minister, I have worked with culturally White, Black-majority and intercultural congregations, alongside kindly and well-meaning people who care about justice.[1] Often, though, these congregations were unaware of the racial injustice that operated within their own churches, and could not recognize the aspects of their own attitudes and behaviours that contributed to this. I was frustrated by the various entrenched patterns where, for example, church councils made decisions with hardly any reference to the views, gifts, cultures or experiences of Black members. As a minister

I attempted, mainly unsuccessfully, to work with churches to find ways of letting God transform these patterns. Eventually I came to a point where I needed to find out more about why and how these patterns were perpetuated.

My conclusions here are based on participant-observer research, carried out with one particular congregation, which considered the causes of White cultural dominance and of the resistance to cultural change. The data necessitated that I ask why the White participants, many of whom were really positive and kind people, still made racist assumptions that impacted on the intercultural relationships within the church. It was in this context that I began to learn about Whiteness Studies (a concept previously unfamiliar to me as a minister) and to respond to the important challenge of thinking through how Whiteness Studies and Theology relate to each other. As this work progressed, I recognized how influential the Methodist missionary movement had been in forming the attitudes of lifelong Methodists.[2] Methodism has been 'missionary' since its beginnings. What is now the Methodist Church in the UK began as a movement within the Church of England, with the aim of spreading what John Wesley called 'Scriptural Holiness', focusing on communities and contexts where this had taken root previously. The whole movement developed as a response to God's love, and the document known as 'Our Calling' today states: 'The Calling of the Methodist Church is to respond to the gospel of God's love in Christ and to live out its discipleship in worship and mission.'

From its earliest days, the Methodist Church, alongside other historic denominations of the eighteenth and nineteenth centuries, was caught up in the idea of 'taking the gospel' to other parts of the world, and this missionary enterprise went hand in hand with the colonialism of its own generation and earlier ones. While the names of the Methodist missionary organizations changed through the decades, the ethos of this Methodist missionary 'movement' continued steadily to influence Methodists here in the UK, and in this chapter I want to reflect on my own experience as a lifelong Methodist and a minister. It is easy for White people to consider intercultural dynamics as though we are ourselves somehow separate and unconnected. I will consider my own family, thoroughly Methodist in its heritage, and my own experience, in relation to the Methodist history of intercultural dynamics. How has the legacy of the Methodist missionary movement impacted on me and my own family? How has my experience of being white-skinned 'coloured' my responses to people of darker skin colour? What should be the response of those of us who are White to the situation we now find ourselves in?

Family history

I am from a family that traces, as far as is possible, every ancestor back to the East Midlands area of the UK while recognizing that all families 'on earth and in heaven' have ancestors coming from Africa, and while acknowledging that the socio-economic background of my ancestors means that many of them have left no record to be traced. I am writing while waiting for the funeral of my mum and am using some of my time, somewhat surreally, to watch the BBC drama *Sherwood*, set and filmed in the Nottinghamshire mining villages where my mum and dad grew up, as the children of miners who spent very long hours underground every working day of the year, in dangerous conditions. It was a very monocultural background until my dad trained for Methodist ministry. He was the first person, so was the family narrative, to leave the village except for war when, in any case, most men stayed down the pits. He set off in 1960, newly married, to live in another part of England. At Richmond Theological College, my dad trained alongside many ministers who went immediately into 'the mission field' (as it was then called). My dad undoubtedly saw these missionary colleagues as adventurers and explorers, coming, as he did, from a context where nobody travelled anywhere except for day trips. My mum and dad never did venture to other countries but instead served here in England, keeping in touch with colleagues and hearing of their missionary ministries through newsletters and addresses by those 'on furlough'. When I was 12 in 1975, we hosted an Indian minister and his wife, colleagues of one of dad's missionary friends, and so I had my first personal engagement with people who were not white-skinned.

When I worked, many years later, as a mission enabler (2015–21) for an English Methodist district, I was reminded that for many Methodists today 'mission' is still about something that happens overseas. The church noticeboards headed 'Mission' were usually full of posters and newsletters about work in other countries sent by people who had received money from donations and fundraising events here in the UK. In 2019, when attending, for my work, the annual conference of 'Methodists for World Mission', I was fascinated by how many participants told me they had 'never served in the mission field' as though working and serving in the UK was not part of the 'mission field'. Often, mission is still seen as something that is done elsewhere by other people to other people. This is a big challenge to the Methodist Church both in terms of our understanding of mission and our understanding of ourselves in relation to the wider world. How do British Methodists relate to people who arrive from across the globe? How do White British Methodists relate to British

Methodists who are darker-skinned? What do we need to notice and what must our response be?

Introducing my auntie

In the film *The Best Exotic Marigold Hotel*, the character Muriel Donnelly (played by Maggie Smith) is taken into hospital, at a great age, and tries to refuse to see a Black doctor, saying that instead she wants to see an 'English' doctor. As Lalwani puts it in a *Guardian* film review, 'We chance upon Dame Maggie being marvellously racist in her wheelchair. The audience is encouraged to laugh at her absurdity, consider how times have changed, and settle into their seats.' Yet every one of the many Black NHS staff I have known personally has testified that this is a regular experience for them. Sometimes similar words are spoken and sometimes they are implied or made evident in other ways, but it is a regular response from people whose thoughts are usually more filtered and self-censored when they are less afraid or less in pain. While Lalwani comments that the film 'begins by mocking the very desire for a nostalgic return to the days of the Raj that it then proceeds to emulate',[3] and it is true that the film reinforces many crass racial stereotypes, yet this particular scene accurately represents the experience of Black staff within the health services today.

My own auntie was in hospital for an operation at the same age as the fictional Muriel and, when she came out, wrote to me saying the experience had been 'like a world tour'. She then proceeded to tell me about the 'amazing anaesthetist who was from Brazil', 'the really kind consultant who came from Sri Lanka' and the 'lovely young nurse from Kenya who sat with me in the night, when I couldn't sleep, and said a prayer with me'. I will say more about this later but, at this point, I want to focus on the really strong contrast between these two attitudes. It made me wonder why my auntie was able, in a situation of pain and fear, to respond positively to people of different accents, culture and skin colour, compared with others of the same age and similar life experiences. Did this attitude show a surprising and unexpected, but random, positive approach to ethnic diversity? Or was there some correlation with my auntie's Methodist heritage? I felt sure that the latter was true as I had seen so many elderly White Methodists respond positively in similar situations, including when I was a minister in a very monoculturally 'White' community in the Rotherham area. There is much in Methodist history and theology to encourage a positive engagement across potential cultural 'divides'.[4] Generally, I consider it extremely unlikely that anybody could attend a Methodist church (or hopefully any other church) and not hear regularly about the love of God for *all* people, and learn that it is a Christian belief that everyone is made equally in God's image. This is something recognized by the Methodists I have known pastorally over my time in ministry and it is a belief absolutely fundamental to my own upbringing and lifelong experience in the Methodist Church. The claim that all people are equally welcome is one made frequently by churches with whom I've worked as a mission enabler. In particular, much of Methodist theology is conveyed by the hymns that we sing, and stems from Wesley's own convictions about the Catholic Spirit and prevenient grace. Runyon states:

> Wesley is convinced that God's Spirit is at work everywhere in the world extending God's prevenient graciousness among all people ... This conviction concerning God's presence in every human life gives each person infinite value as the object of God's caring.[5]

So why, when the responses of White Methodists are often so positive about people regardless of ethnic difference, do Methodist churches show so much 'cultural racism',[6] having disproportionately White leadership, and so often resisting any cultural change that might result from welcoming and learning from newer members of differing cultural backgrounds? What is the impact of the legacy of the Methodist missionary movement on White Methodists in local churches? What is the relationship between 'empire and mission'?

The danger of assumptions

Beaudoin and Turpin[7] outline the problems they recognize as being aspects of White theology developed as Western theology during colonialism. These include an assumption of knowledge, by which people are still categorized according to their skin colour, and an assumption of control by White people over Black people. In my earliest research I reported that the ministers of ethnically diverse congregations considered the making of assumptions to be the top obstacle to healthy intercultural relationships within the churches where they worked.[8] At the time of writing, I had not begun to dig deeper into the relationship between these assumptions, which were being made on the basis of racist stereotypes, with the legacy of missionary history. The fact that White people during colonial times were encouraged to make judgements about people based on their skin colour and other physical attributes, and to compare themselves favourably against those with a darker skin than their own, is a fact that White people would generally prefer not to remember. Yet these attitudes are still evident today, running deep and often unrecognized. I will outline, now, some of the types of assumption that I saw within my study church and then I will reflect personally on what this helped me to see about my own attitudes and practices.

Assumptions about welcoming

The White members at my study church made many assumptions about hospitality. The congregation had a history of being welcoming to new members (including Methodists who arrived from Scotland and Wales during population movements for employment, and also as other local churches had closed and members had transferred). While this sounds positive, it was very clear that many of the older White members saw the church as 'their' church and assumed that they were welcoming others who were, basically, 'visitors'. This applied to Black members of the church even when they had been active participants in the church's life for 20 years or more. One White participant said that the church had 'no younger people' despite the fact that there were many children and younger adults from Ghanaian[9] and Black British families who were, it seems, invisible to this older White member. As I got to know her it was apparent that she only considered the White families as the real church, and everybody else as visitors. It could be questioned, charitably, whether this attitude was a result of the relative mobility of more recent families, with members who stayed perhaps for five or six years, but it definitely does not apply to some of the members originally from Sri Lanka, Uganda and the Caribbean, who had arrived as early as the 1960s and 1970s and been actively involved ever since. It does seem that for this particular older member these church members did not 'count'.

While White members believed they were being inclusive by welcoming Black members and inviting them to attend, or even (generously, they believed) to belong to the various activities and groups that made up the church's life, there is a serious question about what it means to 'include' others. Jagessar writes: 'We need to be honest about wanting to become communities where all are included when we do not have the same understanding and criteria of what it means to be included.'[10] Many of my White participants believed they were including others by welcoming them to be there, but had no expectation that inclusion might mean an equal possibility of influencing the ethos or the functioning of the group or event, which they themselves would take for granted.

One of my White participants said to me one Sunday: 'The Ghanaians never come to anything. They don't seem to want to be involved.' This puzzled me as the two Ghanaian stewards, Dorcas and Ben, were very faithful and regular about attendance at church meetings and events. It simply wasn't true of them, but the assumption was that the 'whole group of Ghanaians' should be able to come, and should want to show their commitment through the same habits as others who have longer commitment to the same church. The claim to 'welcome' and to 'include' people was conditional upon them wanting, and being able, to act like the White members who considered themselves to be 'the church'.

Assumptions about leadership

A further complication was that many of the older White members of the congregation assumed very specific criteria for deciding whether or not people were appropriate as candidates for leadership positions. One of the Black members who is a recently trained local preacher told me of going to lead a service in a nearby church of elderly White members who greeted her with clear suspicion when she arrived, did not realize she was the visiting preacher and, when she explained who she was, received the response: 'Oh, we don't expect preachers to look like you.' This was clearly accurate, from the complete lack of awareness that she might, in fact, be the expected preacher. However, it also spoke volumes to her about the attitudes that she needed to overcome to be heard as somebody bringing the gospel to that congregation. The story reminded me of the local UK church missionary secretary quoted by Davey in 1988 who, after listening to a Black local preacher, said: 'I raised money to send ministers to preach to them – not to have them come over here and preach to us!'[11] This quotation from more than 30 years ago shows that the attitude that it should be White people who give to Black people rather than receiving from them is still lasting and potent. This assumption about who can, or cannot, be called by God into leadership betrays an operant theology based on past learning, which is not ready to receive those whom God has called (in this case as a preacher), thus causing barriers for the purposes of God in the present day. Similar dynamics operated with the leadership role of 'pastoral visitor' in the church, where Black people were expected to take on the role but were also expected to operate within it as the Church had done previously, ignoring the knowledge people had of what would help pastorally within different cultures.

Assumptions about control

Closely connected with assumptions about who would make appropriate leaders are the assumptions about control which acted as a barrier to Black church members believing that they could offer themselves for leadership positions. While the Black members had ideas and skills to offer in decision-making there was a real reluctance to allow Black members to influence, or to control, the developments within the church. This was most apparent in conversations about the style of worship, when changes to worship were fiercely resisted even before people's opinions were asked. What surprised me most was the way in which White members thought it was acceptable for them to 'have their say' and to make the decisions without intercultural conversation about the decisions that needed making (the style of music, who should give the Bible readings, how long the services should be, and so on). It took much time to gain the trust of the older White members about this matter but eventually people admitted to me their fear that this would 'become a Black church'. There were lots of aspects as to what this might mean, and lots of complexities about people's fears and feelings of being 'threatened', but none of it was spoken and therefore none of the possible future changes were subject to any of the church's processes of decision-making. The link between a basic need to control Black people (in order to stop them taking control) and the days of earlier Black–White relationships of colonial and transatlantic slave trade times, when White colonialists feared being 'overcome' or 'overwhelmed' by those whom White people were oppressing, was obviously present deep in the thinking of the White members in irrational ways, despite there being no actual need for any fear or suspicion.

Assumptions about ideas

Unfoundedly low expectations and negative assumptions often led to a lack of sensitivity about what was appropriate for church members from diverse family and cultural contexts. This was often based on earlier relationships with somebody from the same cultural background and an assumption that what applied to one person would apply to all from that same culture. This is, of course, no more likely to be accurate than assuming that all culturally Scottish people will have exactly the same attitudes, family contexts or lifestyles. As an example, one of my White participants, Jack, said to me, in a conversation about sexuality in the church, of Ben: 'Well I'm sure as an African he would think that …' This was not based on any conversation about what Ben did think, but rather on Jack's own assumptions about this. As Jack's son is gay, his assumption about Ben's opinions may have been partly to protect himself and his son from a hurtful conversation. However, the assumption he made, and his assumption that this was a conversation he could not have with Ben, had prevented dialogue about something that was very important to Jack, and Ben had not been allowed to speak for himself. I was pleased that during one of my focus groups this conversation topic was brought into the open and the two men's friendship was able to deepen based on real listening and honest exchanges.

Assumptions about what is normal

I observed one incident of more outright racism when one White participant expressed ridicule about the clothing of one of the Ghanaian members, which was described as 'loud and ethnic'. More often there was a patronizing 'putting up' with what were considered odd or 'different' behaviours (such as arriving late, wearing large headdresses, or taking photos during worship). Underneath these attitudes was an assumption that the person speaking was being kind or 'tolerant' rather than a recognition that all styles of dress and behaviour are 'ethnic' and that no one cultural dress or custom is any more or less deserving of respect and value. Beaudoin and Turpin write: 'Existential and phenomenological language in White practical theology often universalizes experience that is secretly built on a specific frame while naming others as having color, ethnicity, or race.'[12]

I found this to be true with regard to the way intercultural relationships worked within the local congregation. Many White participants saw themselves as being the norm to which other people should conform and the standard to which others' behaviours should be compared. While this may have been true of older participants, compared with all, or most, younger participants regardless of ethnicity, there was enough evidence to show that these assumptions of normativity were compounded by a deep-seated confidence in the older participants' own positions of cultural superiority. This accords with what is happening in the United Methodist Church, according to Pieterse and Scott[13] and, I imagine, to most, if not all, longer-standing traditional denominations. It is therefore of wide significance. The norming of White Western culture over any other global cultures, within the same churches where there is an espoused belief in the equality of all people, is something of grave concern. Mahon writes:

There is a necessity for abandonment of the notion that 'Whiteness' is normative and central to Christian reality, yet this process of abandonment is not a simple task because the organisational structures within the world's major churches are inextricably bound up with Whiteness.[14]

So how does such a complex but profound problem go unnoticed? There will be many reasons for this, but in this chapter I want to conclude by considering the relationship between benevolence and condescension in practice and then to outline some steps that White Christians need to take.

Kindly benevolence or negative condescension?

My observer-participation work was full of examples of a kindly benevolence from White participants towards Black participants. Phrases such as 'Well, I know that the Africans must want to talk in their own languages' or 'It must be so hard to be so far away from home' sound innocuous enough. There is an attempt at empathy and an attempt to show kindness here. The looks of sympathy (which are harder to convey in writing) showed real consideration and concern for how difficult people's lives might be. There was some truth in these views as I learned from my own conversations with Black participants, some of whom did indeed enjoy a space where they could use their first languages and who were often badly missing family with whom they spoke daily. The difficulty was that this kindness went alongside an assumption of knowledge that was not always accurate in relation to particular people. It was assumed that people's lives *must* be difficult rather than *might* be. It was also assumed that the speaker knew about the lives of the people mentioned even when they did not actually know anything about the person's real-life situation. Benevolence sounds like a good thing. An attitude of kindliness is hard to criticize as it appears to be a required Christian response in White British understanding, but I found that kindly benevolence can, in reality, be condescension – which of course becomes an obstacle to racial justice. Condescension can be as dangerous, systemically if not physically, as the racial stereotyping that leads to negative discrimination.

There was, in fact, despite all that I have written above, much that was positive in this enthusiastic and prayer-filled intercultural church community. There was much genuine friendship shared and much laughter and many warm joint memories. My conclusion was that the benevolence that I found in many White Methodists towards fellow church members from African, Sri Lankan and Black British backgrounds came from decades of formation in an attitude that promoted the links across global

Methodism, as being one 'world family'. Nevertheless, White members, in what they described as 'the old days', were asked for money for missionaries and encouraged in fundraising and the giving of donations. This financial support for work 'abroad' was motivated by an appeal to kindness and generosity. White-skinned people like myself, who lived here in the UK during the twentieth century and operated in what was then a very much majority White church, were taught that we had the wealth that we could bestow on 'others' in their poverty and that we had the education to recognize that we could provide an education for 'others'. When we sang 'We have a Gospel to Proclaim' it was very much our own white-skinned church members we had in mind. It was 'our gospel' to share with 'other' people. Our noticeboards and slideshows were filled with images of dark-skinned people who needed our compassion, the shoes that we could provide, and the gospel in ways that we were able to share. We were sent thank-you messages appreciating our generosity and learned that we could make the difference for 'other' people. People who were not White were 'othered' as different and in need of help. We white-skinned people were, at the same time, in this way informally and unofficially taught of our superiority and our privilege over people 'in need'. We developed a sense of connection with people abroad (whose faces we saw on the slides and posters) and that led to positive feelings towards people with a darker skin colour, but not to any sense of humility, mutual respect or reciprocation of learning or insights.

This attitude was not limited to the work on the 'mission field'. It was, for example, true of our giving and fundraising for the 'poor children' who needed a home in the National Children's Homes of the UK, for whom we, as more privileged children, were asked to sell Sunny Smiles. So this dynamic, of kindness and generosity, fostering a sense of connection with others but in a relationship of superiority, was not specifically about those with a darker skin colour. Nevertheless, those children grew up and as adults we, who gave donations towards them in their children's homes, would not recognize them as adults. By contrast, the visceral nature of differences between people of different ethnic heritage[15] means that visually White people are reminded of the posters of their youth when meeting, here in the UK, fellow Christians who look like the people they were generous to throughout the decades. The memories of earlier societal attitudes are hard to change in congregations that reinforce one another's views while they are conversing. These attitudes of kindly meant but unaware condescension are big factors in the perpetuation of assumptions and are a blockage to honest conversation and engagement which is needed in order to bring about transformation to more just intercultural relationships. What can White people do about this?

Personal reflections

My family taught me to respect other people and passed on a faith that was based absolutely on a firm conviction that everybody is equal in the eyes of God. This belief was firmly grounded in my family's own experience of being 'looked down on' in a mining community and the determination that the children of the family should grow up knowing that they mattered to God, regardless of how other people might make them feel. I have learned over many decades to recognize how important it is to get to know people as they are, rather than making judgements based on what I think I know about somebody. I have to start from a position of humility – which means knowing I may be wrong!

Returning to my auntie, she was positive about the NHS staff, but she asked them where they were from and was glad she could 'place' them in order to know her own place in relation to them. She was aware she was being positive about those who 'don't belong here' and believed she was being welcoming while firmly placing them among those who could and should be grateful that they had been 'given a home' here. Another elderly relative visited us in Leicester and, on the way home from our very ethnically diverse church, as passers-by evidenced the fact that Leicester is one of the most ethnically diverse cities in the UK, she said: 'There seem to be more foreigners than English people here.' She did not know any of those people personally and could not possibly have known their identity or citizenship.

I still enjoy the experience of meeting and being able to make genuine friendships with people from a range of cultural backgrounds. Given the monocultural nature of my family's background it still amazes me that I have this opportunity, without even leaving my own home country, and my life has been deeply enriched by learning from so many people's stories and perspectives. Yet I have had to learn that my own privilege, as a person whose family has always felt at home in the UK, is not shared by everyone. I have learned over the decades not to ask 'Where do you come from?' At one point I did believe that by finding out this information I would be able to learn something about the person (whether the response was the East End of London or Zimbabwe or Sri Lanka) and that I would be able to establish 'networks' within the congregation's life. Even if it had been appropriate to ask such a personal question, in the least intrusive way I could, I now recognize that assumptions are not possible on the basis of the responses to this question. The building of networks was not mine to do, nor was I needed to do it. In the past I have been unaware of the impact of colonial heritage on my ideas about 'categories' of people and arrogant in my assumptions that I could know something that was way beyond my personal experience. My childhood included a Sunday School room that had a painting by Harold Copping hanging on the wall behind the teacher.[16] This made very clear how I could expect people from 'the four corners' of the globe to look and dress.[17] This picture encouraged me to think about other children as gathering around Jesus along with me, and yet it also left me believing that I could know what to expect of other people. It has taken decades of friendship and professional relationships with a wide diversity of people, and gracious corrections and explanations from a range of people, to recognize the colonial nature of my own assumptions and to recognize the ways in which my experience as a white-skinned person has formed who I am.

My childhood formation in the ways of kindness and generosity have needed to be brought alongside learning about other people's kindness and generosity. My adulthood has needed to include learning about humility and my place alongside others in what Jagessar calls 'mutual inconveniencing':

> If transformation is to happen we need a larger picture than our own. Such a habit is dangerous and subversive – all will have to be converted, to be mutually inconvenienced – each called to journey beyond their particular perspective. For we are all in need![18]

I am grateful that in April 2022 the Global Relationships team of the Methodist Church in the UK stated its intention of modelling a new partnership approach in order to contribute to decolonization:

> Embodying mutual respect, by sharing the responsibility of grant giving and fund allocation, the new World Mission Fund Grants Committee moves toward decolonisation ...
>
> This new World Mission Fund Grants Committee is an example of what it means to share power (from a British perspective). It has changed from a former membership of mostly British people to a committee where the vast majority of members are from our global Partner Churches. By making sure that the membership of this committee is globally representative, it makes way for the decision-making to flow from a mutual encounter of discussion and prayer concerning fund allocations for our global Church Partners.
>
> For the World Mission Fund Grants Committee, the decision-making is not always about the money. It is also about the wider sense of connections as the committee converse and pray about the world together. It is about relationship. Our global relationship.[19]

If we are each to play our part in the process of decolonization, White Christians will need to be aware of our own attitudes and their origins. We will need to be open to the challenge of colleagues from Black perspectives and life experiences. We will need to challenge ourselves and be open to learning. We will need to make reparation for the injustices of the past that have privileged those of us with white skin. We will need to take our part in the partnerships called for by a God who has always and continuously created us equal and in need of the other parts of the Body.[20]

Jesus said: 'The truth will set you free' (John 8.32). We are all living in a society where racism has been endemic but we do not have to be trapped in it. We cannot avoid being influenced by the attitudes we have been brought up with, but we can pray for God to help us recognize the truth. Some would argue that it is the work of the Holy Spirit to release us from the destructive forces of racism. I would agree! However, the truth needs to be recognized and the work of the Spirit is to lead us into all truth. Denying or ignoring racism (of whatever kind) where it exists obstructs this work of the Spirit in us. Recognizing it opens us to the work of God's Spirit in beginning to liberate White Christians from our collective racism and the legacy of racism in the past.

Notes

1 As in my previous work, I am using capitals here (in line with the other chapters in this book) for 'Black' and 'White' not because I believe this is a binary 'black and white' issue but because I want to highlight the potential danger of the way in which skin colour impacts so much on our visceral responses to one another. I hope and pray that there will be a time when we don't need to highlight that some people are 'White' because those of us who are white-skinned will be self-aware enough to engage in equal conversations and relationships interculturally. Until that time, we will need to remind White people of their own ethnicity.

2 Jill Marsh, 'Whiteness in Congregational Life: An Ethnographic Study of One Ethnically-diverse Congregation in the UK', *Practical Theology*, 15(1–2) (2022), pp. 120–31, https://doi.org/10.1080/1756073X.2022.2026561 (accessed 10.03.2023).

3 *The Best Exotic Marigold Hotel*, dir. John Madden, UK, distr. Fox Searchlight, 2011; Nikita Lalwani, 2012, 'The Best Exotic Marigold Hotel: An Exercise in British Wish-fulfilment', *The Guardian*, 27 February, https://www.theguardian.com/commentisfree/2012/feb/27/best-exotic-marigold-hotel-compliance (accessed 10.03.2023).

4 Jill Marsh, 2018, 'A Wesleyan Approach to "Difference": A UK Case-study', https://oimts.files.wordpress.com/2018/11/2018-07-marsh.pdf (accessed 10.03.2023).

5 Theodore Runyon, 1998, *The New Creation: John Wesley's Theology Today*, Nashville, TN: Abingdon Press, pp. 33–4.

6 When I use the word 'racism' here, I'm particularly referring to the cultural racism that Anthony Reddie describes as 'the sense of the superiority of White Euro-American cultural norms, over and against those of Black Africans ... This form of "new racism" is one that largely moves beyond the genetic-based rhetoric of White superiority that characterized "old racism"; and is one that utilizes the cultural and aesthetic model of a top-down patrician or class-based notion of Euro-American hegemony over against the baser and less sophisticated instincts and practices of "poor" Black people.' Anthony G. Reddie, 2009, 'Not Just Seeing, But Really Seeing: A Practical Black Liberationist Spirituality for Re-Interpreting Reality', *Black Theology: An International Journal*, 7(3) (2009), pp. 339–65, 356.

7 Tom Beaudoin and Katherine Turpin, 2014, 'White Practical Theology' in Kathleen A. Cahalan and Gordon S. Mikoski (eds), *Opening the Field of Practical Theology: An Introduction*, Lanham, MD: Rowman & Littlefield, pp. 251–69.

8 Jill Marsh, 'Towards an Ethnically Diverse British Methodist Church', *Holiness: The Journal of Wesley House Cambridge*, 2(1) (2016), pp. 23–52, www.wesley.cam.ac.uk/holiness.

9 I am using the words that people used to refer to themselves. Some of those who called themselves 'Ghanaian' had British citizenship, and some did not.

10 Michael Jagessar, '*Dis*-Place Theologizing: Fragments of Intercultural Adventurous God-Talk', *Black Theology: An International Journal*, 13(3) (2015), pp. 258–72, 266.

11 Cyril Davey, 1988, *Changing Places: Methodist Mission Then and Now*, Basingstoke: Marshall Pickering, p. 221.

12 Beaudoin and Turpin, 'White Practical Theology', p. 264.

13 Hendrik R. Pieterse and David W. Scott, 'Soundings Towards an Intercultural Identity for the United Methodist Church: Some Historical and Theological Resources', *Methodist Review: A Journal of Wesleyan and Methodist Studies*, 14 (2022), ISSN: 1046-5254, www.methodistreview.org.

14 Michele Mahon, 'Sisters with Voices: A Study of the Experiences and Challenges Faced by Black Women in London Baptist Association Church Ministry Settings', *Black Theology: An International Journal*, 13(3) (2015), pp. 273–96, 288, https://doi.org/10.1179/1476994815Z.00000000063.

15 Mary McClintock Fulkerson, 2007, *Places of Redemption: Theology for a Worldly Church*, New York: Oxford University Press, pp. 4, 15.

16 Peter Cruchley, 'Ecce homo...? Beholding Mission's White Gaze', *Practical Theology*, 15(1–2) (2022), pp. 64–77, https://doi.org/10.1080/1756073X.2021.2023945 (accessed 10.03.2023).

17 The hymn 'Hills of the North Rejoice' still comes into my head sometimes and conjures up this image unbidden.

18 Jagessar, '*Dis*-Place Theologizing', pp. 258–72.

19 The Methodist Church, 2022, 'Grant Making Must Reflect the Global Stage', *The Methodist Church*, 12 April, https://www.methodist.org.uk/about-us/news/the-methodist-blog/grant-making-must-reflect-the-global-stage/ (accessed 10.03.2023).

20 The Strategy for Justice, Dignity and Solidarity, adopted by Methodist Conference 2021, is a commitment to this: https://www.methodist.org.uk/about-us/the-methodist-church/the-inclusive-methodist-church/strategy-for-justice-dignity-and-solidarity/ (accessed 10.03.2023).

13

See, Judge, Act: Wrestling with the Effects of Colonialism as an English Priest in Wales[1]

KEVIN ELLIS

This chapter is written with a bold temerity. What can I as a White English man say about mission in Wales against the backdrop of the legacy of colonialism? The answer, as I set out below, comes from how I have intentionally positioned myself in my context as the vicar of Bro Madryn on the Llŷn Peninsula. It involved utilizing the 'See, judge, act' model developed initially by Cardijn.[2] This in turn has evolved into a variety of different versions of the pastoral cycle.[3] In this chapter I apply the model to myself as well as to my context, and reflect on how I am seen, judged and act as I wrestle with how to do mission as an Englishman in Wales.

I am an outsider, one who has endeavoured purposefully to put myself on the inside. This in part comes from the fact that I have learnt Welsh, and choose to work whenever and wherever I am able to in a language other than my mother tongue. Learning the language of a country to which you move opens doors. It opens doors, as I will describe, to more than just conversations, but to understanding history, events, communities – and self – differently. I am also a contextual theologian who is also a New Testament scholar; that is, a scholar who has intentionally positioned himself in a particular social, cultural and geographical context in which to do theology and reflect on scripture. That scripture was written reflecting on particular contexts too. I do so from a tradition that anticipates that scripture will ask me awkward questions as much as I will ask things of it.

Autobiography/autoethnography

I am Yorkshire born, from a working-class family. I have a doctorate and am the first person in my wider family to go to university. There is a hint of pride in this, but also whispers of regret, as opportunities were not there for this to happen for older members of my family, regardless of their ability. I am passionate about standing against injustice and am engaged in developing theologies of liberation in my local context, inspired by my understanding of the gospel, although complicated often by my experiences of the church.

The above paragraph could have been written by my former tutor, Anthony Reddie, except of course we are from different Ridings within Yorkshire! Professor Reddie is also a leading Black British liberation theologian. It has taken over five decades for me to understand that being White defines who I am, and a move from England to Wales for me to accept that much of my thinking, consciously and unconsciously, has been shaped by the waning contours of the empire, and by a Christendom that was more empire-shaped than cross-shaped.

I have to say that such rediscoveries took me by surprise. As someone who trained for ordination at the Queen's College in Birmingham, and as a biblical scholar who wrestled with liberation forms of exegesis and struggled to apply them in outer estates within England,[4] I did not expect that moving to Wales would provoke a reassessment of many aspects of my life.

However, I am writing in a setting that is in some respects alien, and I am alien to it. This is obscured at times by the perception of shared history. To a certain extent, I am, to use Edward Said's phrase, 'Out of Place'.[5] On one level my understanding of history has been challenged, and the doors to untold stories have been opened, offering an opportunity to reflect, research and be challenged:

> It has been a journey of unlearning, of discovering that what I had presumed had been a shared history of the nations of the British Isles is far from that. Like many educated in England, my history was a British history littered with the names of crowned individuals and tales of daring do of English men and occasionally of English women. I knew hardly anything about Welsh history and culture and began a discovery that concluded that the much-heralded characteristic of English fair play does not appear to have been in evidence with how the English or British establishment had dealt with the people of Wales.[6]

However, on another level, it is not just a matter of embracing new facets of history, but accepting that Wales is in some part in a postcolonial situation and has suffered overall because of the unequal relationships within the UK, and in particular because of the colonization of Wales by England.[7] Autoethnographically, this has been an epiphanic experience. Norman Denzin describes 'epiphanies' as 'interactional moments and experiences which leave marks on people's lives':[8]

> Epiphanies are ritually structured liminal experiences connected to moments of breach, crisis, redress, reintegration, and schism, crossing from one space to another.[9]

Without such an epiphany or awakening, it is not possible to move from one context to another and be able to offer anything, even hope, with any clarity. I realize that the language of epiphany and awakening is deliberately borrowed from the language of religious revival. But whether our experiences are religious or not, White English people need to be confronted at a very deep level about the past and present for change at an individual and societal level to take place.

One of my first pastoral encounters in Wales serves to illustrate this. It involved a conversation between me, as vicar, and the head of a secondary school. The headteacher explained in concise yet forthright terms that in every conversation he had with an English professional he carried with him the memories passed down by his grandparents of punishment being meted out for using Welsh rather than English during their own experiences of education.

As a liberation theologian, I have found myself working within versions of the See, judge, act cycle. As part of this process, I am working towards a second PhD exploring the use of liberation exegesis in Wales, with the attendant questions of how as an Englishman can I do it in a way that bears witness to a context that at times forces me to face uncomfortable truths.[10]

Wales and England: A complicated history

Within the confines of this chapter, there is not the space to discuss to an extensive level the colonial nature of the relationship of Wales with England, or whether Wales has the right to call its situation postcolonial. There are situations and communities where colonialism still seems writ large.[11] When analysing the lack of investment and scourge of rural poverty, it is tempting to suggest that this is like large swathes of England and airbrush out of the conversation constitutional and political injustices. As an Englishman, I suspect that this is because Wales is too close to home for the consequences of empire to be allowed to be seen.

Wales has in recent years made the national UK news on several occasions. First, the second Severn bridge had been renamed 'The Prince of Wales Bridge'. This was met with an online petition objecting to the bridge being named after HRH Prince Charles in favour of someone who 'has achieved something for our nation'.[12] Second, the MP for Dwyfor Meirionnydd, Liz Saville Roberts, called for a change in legislation to protect the Welsh language following remarks from a national newspaper columnist in which Welsh was described as an 'indecipherable language with no vowels'.[13] Third, the Welsh government came to an agreement with the UK government over the terms of its support for the UK's proposed EU Withdrawal Bill. This led Plaid Cymru to assert that the Labour Welsh government had betrayed the principles of devolution, putting in jeopardy the notion of devolved government. Since then, Plaid Cymru have entered into a partnership agreement with the Welsh government ensuring some of its manifesto commitments are enacted, and continue to make Wales different from England in its legislative agenda.[14] The opportunity for this to happen has been created by the fact that, fourth, and perhaps most importantly, the COVID-19 pandemic gave the Welsh government and the first minister of Wales a public platform to lead within Wales that was unparalleled.[15] The handling of the pandemic within Wales, while not universally approved of, was acknowledged as more cautious than the approach of the UK government for England.

The early part of the twenty-first century has led to an increase of interest in independence for Wales. Recent polling places the number of those willing to vote for independence at about 30 per cent, which is roughly the same figure as those who would have voted yes in Scotland at the beginning of the referendum for Scottish independence in 2014.[16] There is now a commission on the constitutional future for Wales, which is due to report in 2023 and is co-chaired by Archbishop Rowan Williams, with all options remaining on the table.[17]

One might, from the reaction, assume that the Welsh voice is strident, entirely pro-devolution, perhaps even pro-independence and, more importantly, speaks with a single voice. To draw this conclusion would be a mistake. Wales, like the other nations of the UK, is more multifaceted than any simple assertion. Richard Wyn Jones has argued that Wales is the most complex of the nations of the UK in terms of national identity.[18] Some 25 per cent of the population of Wales, for example, was not born within its borders, which inevitably has some effect on how people perceive their national identity.[19] All the discussions about the future of

Wales take place at a time when the constituent parts of the UK are wrestling with their own futures. This includes England as much as the Celtic nations. Henderson and Wyn Jones have demonstrated that Englishness is a political force that is driving the transformation of the UK. In 1992, people in England called themselves British rather than English by a ratio of two to one. This is now no longer the case.[20] Within Wales, too, there are competing identities, with those identifying themselves as Welsh rather than British being much more likely to have voted to Remain rather than to Leave, and now to be supportive of a greater degree of federalism – or independence itself.[21]

Adam Price, the leader of Plaid Cymru (Party of Wales), describes the relationship between England and Wales like this:

> Before the Act of Union, we [Wales] were a conquered nation that was never fully subdued. Post-devolution, we're a postcolonial country still waiting to be decolonised ... we are in a hybrid state living in the cracks between a dependent past and an independent future.[22]

This statement fits well within the arena of political sound bite, but also raises the general question as to whether Wales should be considered postcolonial or not. It is a fast-moving discussion, as Price himself has found out. In 2019, the leader of Plaid Cymru called for reparations for Wales from the British state because of the legacy and pain of colonialism.[23] In 2020, Price clarified and offered an apology for his remarks.[24] Reparation, Price has come to accept, is a term used by those campaigning for recognition of the historical and contemporary consequences of the slave trade. Price still believes that Wales has been subjugated by the British state but acknowledges that Wales too benefited from, and was part of, the British empire. This is why the issue of postcolonialism and Wales needs to be treated with care.

Wales has lived and continues to live in the shadow of its much larger neighbour. Chris Williams considers that it is possible to contend that there was a colonial relationship between England and Wales, at least between the death of Llywelyn ap Gruffydd in 1282 and the Acts of Union in 1536 and 1543.[25] Williams goes on to point out that after the Acts, Wales was no longer a colony of England given both the legal assimilation of Wales into England and the legal rights given to those living in Wales. Nonetheless, he notes that: 'to argue that Wales is not a colony of England and has not been since 1536 is not, however, to argue that there are no inequalities in the relationship between the two societies.'[26]

However, there is a counterargument from Norman Davies regarding the Act of 1536, quoted approvingly by Kirsti Bohata, that 'one could not hope for a better example of colonial cultural policy.'²⁷ Davies, however, notes that an unintended consequence of Elizabethan policy was the bolstering of the Welsh language, with churches and chapels acting as 'patrons of secular culture'.²⁸

However, the authors of *The Empire Writes Back* challenge whether the Celtic nations, particularly Wales and Scotland, can be considered to be postcolonial, arguing instead that they are tainted or complicit in the endeavours of the British state. They are imperial storm troopers rather than representatives of the rebellion:²⁹

> While it is possible to argue that these societies were the first victims of English expansion, their subsequent complicity in the British imperial enterprise makes it difficult for colonized peoples outside Britain to accept their identity as postcolonial.³⁰

This leads us back to the difficulties faced by Adam Price when he was attempting to tease out the fact that Wales has not always been treated fairly by England or, as he prefers to call it, the British state.

For the purposes of this chapter, it will suffice to say that Wales historically was conquered and assimilated by England. This was not a seamless process, but a jagged one. Conquest and colonialization of people and place are not linear processes. Thereafter, Wales both did and did not benefit from being connected to England, and subsequently the UK, and through participation in the imperialistic endeavours of both. Chris Williams is helpful, even if we resist talk of colonization and post-colonialism.

Chapels and church communities in Wales have both preserved Welsh identity, ensuring in many places the continuity of the language, but have also played their part in the propagation of the British empire, which is something at times reflected still in the hymnody of traditional Welsh language chapels.³¹

My context

I lead and serve several church communities on the Llŷn Peninsula. Over 70 per cent of the people who live here permanently speak Welsh as their first language. It is not abnormal for community, business or church meetings to be conducted entirely in Welsh. I have chosen to learn the language, and after several years have the confidence to preach in Welsh and follow reasonably complex conversations in what is now my second language. On the other hand, even though the language of Welsh is an identity marker – of what it means to be Welsh – many people living in Wales do not speak the language daily. This does not mean that the language is not cherished beyond the Welsh-speaking communities. In my first sermon in the parish, speaking in Welsh, I used these words:

> Rwyf yn dod fel gwas y lle hwn a'i bobl. Weithiau fe wnaf gamgymeriadau gyda'r iaith, ond fe wnaf ei defnyddio oherwydd mae yn rhodd y gallwn ei rhannu.

> I come as a servant of this place and the people. I will sometimes make mistakes with the language, but I will use it as it is a gift we can share

The choice of the word *gwas* (servant) was deliberate and designed to convey a message in a Welsh-speaking area that I was not just an English incomer, but I would immerse myself in the area, and understand – as far as I can – that place is important.[32]

The Peninsula shares commonalities with other coastal areas in the UK. As in, for example, the Lakes or Cornwall, there are people in the community who have been here all their lives, as have successive generations of their families. Wyn has lived in North Wales all his life. He says of the church in the village: 'I was baptized and wed there. I will be carried in and out one day, like my father and grandfather before me. All of those who have shaped me rest there.'

There are also incomers, like me, and many watch and learn, and serve their community. Stephanie, for example, is from the north-west of England. She has lived in her village for 30 years. Her children have been raised here, married, divorced, married and widowed here. She speaks Welsh now with her neighbours. 'I am their Englishwoman', she laughs. 'Not all of us deserve though to be accepted.'[33]

There is also an increasing number of second homes. This leads to pressure on affordable housing for local people. In my region of Wales there is the complexity that additional incomers can be perceived as a threat to the language, giving rise to vociferous campaigns around the slogan 'Wales is not for sale'.

As I began to write sections of my PhD, I noted: 'I am a priest-theologian and sit comfortably on the evangelical side of the Church in Wales, I therefore want to speak to people about their faith in their mother tongue. I am to some extent a missionary.' As I attended my research seminar, these words seemed to sit in my last paper like an unexploded bomb, especially as it was a paper discussing the postcolonial relationship between Wales and England. Missions, missionaries and missionary societies are often thought to carry baggage from a postcolonial era, with missionaries often arriving, whatever their motives, with those expanding the British empire. In a piece of contextual research, heavily influenced by autoethnography, I cannot avoid the fact that the notion of the English vicar learning Welsh in part so I can share my faith with others is bound to raise more than the odd scholarly eyebrow.

There are many reasons why I am learning Welsh, and the ability to relate more effectively to those whose mother tongue is that of over two-thirds of those living in the area raises few questions. Indeed, in some contexts it would be commendable; indeed, after a *Cymanfa Ganu* (Singing Festival), Elwyn Hughes – who has been something of a pioneer in developing courses for adults to learn Welsh – sent me the following email, which I use with his permission:[34]

> Diolch hefyd am dy barodrwydd i ddefnyddio dy Gymraeg yn gyhoeddus – mae mor braf i mi weld dysgwyr yn llwyddo i ddysgu'r iaith ac yn gwneud cyfraniad yn eu cymunedau.
>
> Thank you also for your willingness to use your Welsh in public – it's so nice to see learners succeed in learning the language and making a contribution in their communities.

In the context of my ministry, it was a moment of relief for me to be able to effectively conduct the occasional offices in Welsh and a sense of pride in seeing the faces of the bereaved when I could offer my condolences in the language they grew up speaking. For me, it was not just about effective communication, but a matter of justice.

Moreover, the smiles on the faces of children and staff at local schools as I have taken services/assemblies and grown in my knowledge and confidence of the Welsh language have been wonderful – laughing at the mistakes I have made (such as Jesus flying into Jerusalem on the donkey!), helping with pronunciation as I have prepared for exams; these things have all been part of the journey of learning I have made. This vulnerability has given me a greater acceptance in the life of the communities I seek to serve:[35]

> Mae cyfraniad Kevin i fywyd yn Ysgol Syr Thomas Jones yn holl bwysig, ac mae naws Gymreig yr ysgol yn allweddol i hyrwyddo'r defnydd o'r iaith Gymraeg ym mywyd pob dydd ein disgyblion! Felly mae clywed dyn sydd wedi dysgu ein hiaith yn ei ddefnyddio mewn gwasanaethau ysgol gyfan yn ysbrydoliedig i'n disgyblion, o flwyddyn 7 hyd at flwyddyn 13.

Kevin's contribution to life at Ysgol Syr Thomas Jones is vital, and the Welsh ethos of the school is key to promoting the use of the Welsh language in the daily life of our pupils! So, hearing a man who has learned our language using it in whole school assemblies is inspiring to our pupils, from year 7 to year 13.[36]

For me the desire to serve and the desire to share my faith are part and parcel of the same act. There are two passages in Paul's letter to the church at Rome that shape my understanding of what I mean by this. The first is in the opening chapter:

> I am a debtor [or under obligation to[37]] both to Greeks and to barbarians, both to the wise and to the foolish – hence my eagerness to proclaim the gospel to you also who are in Rome. For I am not ashamed of the gospel; it is the power of God for salvation to everyone who has faith, to the Jew first and also to the Greek. (Rom. 1.14–16)

I would say that I am obliged to share the story of Jesus Christ. Such sharing is the very heartbeat of my understanding of the Christian faith. It is why I am content that Bible study is held in public places like coffee shops, garden centres, pubs, as well as in churches. Evangelism and evangelizing are at the heart of what I understand a priestly role to be. Arguably, when I seek to do this in Welsh, I do it in a more vulnerable way. I am not yet capable of being proficient enough in the language to notice the nuances in every conversation. I therefore stumble, and sometimes fall, as my thinking races ahead of my ability to vocalize my thinking. The key, therefore, to my sharing my faith in a context when inequality has been perpetrated, is to do so with vulnerability, honesty, carefulness and a smattering of humour. The latter is present when I sometimes descend to toddler-level efforts of communication moments after what I might think to be erudite thoughtfulness.

The Apostle Paul, later in the letter when introducing his own relationship to his own people, writes the following: 'For I could wish that I myself were accursed and cut off from Christ for the sake of my own people, my kindred according to the flesh' (Rom. 9.3). Ziesler comments that: 'There may be a deliberate echo of the willingness of Moses to be blotted out for the sake of Israel (Ex. 32.31f.) or even of the self-offering of Jesus Christ (5.8, 8.32)' in this Pauline self-description.[38] Now, it would take too much temerity to make a comparison between myself and the Apostle, or of my relationship with the people I serve and Paul's deep and profound relationship with those he described as 'kindred'. Yet my experience is that when you immerse yourself in another land and carefully come to appreciate the culture and customs that are different from your own, then there is welcome and embrace. It is harder for this appreciation to begin in Wales for the Englishman, as on the surface with the pervasiveness of the English language and British culture things look at first glance too similar, and I need to unlearn an English or British way of seeing things. The first step in this was to see that I am English. Like all dominant forces, it wears at times a cultural invisibility cloak.

The last word at this stage belongs to Emyr, who came along to a Beer and Theology session. When I ask him whether he minds that I would like him to become a Christian, he hesitates, smiles and replies: 'The Labour candidate wants me to vote Labour. If you can cope with being told where to go, that is fine.' Doing God seems to be what Emyr expects, and I try to do that cautiously and with a smile on my face, knowing that I do not have all the answers. However, 'doing God' in a place where people have been marginalized requires epiphanic moments and immersion on the part of those coming in from a culture that has had a persistent desire to dominate.

See, judge, act

Seeing or experiencing something for the first time can be difficult. It is not a passive thing. It is a moment of change. If, like me, you move into a different area, you need to watch from the outside, and then slowly be invited in. This is particularly the case in a context where there is, in places, a backwash of colonialism, and you are seen in some sense as a representative of that colonial power. This is acute for members of the Church in Wales for, although disestablished, there is still in recent history the memory that it was until 1920 the Church of England in Wales.

What was distinctive about Wales? I had lived and worked in London, Birmingham and Newcastle, and despite the rich tapestry of life with different cultures, ethnicities and languages, for me the realization of my Englishness did not occur. In a sense, for it to occur in north Wales is surprising. Martin Johnes notes: 'the default construction of Welshness remains white.'[39] Charlotte Williams concurs; she is the Chair of Black, Asian and Minority Ethnic (BAME) Communities, Contributions and Cynefin in the New Curriculum Working Group:[40] 'At school I never saw a book that had any pictures of people like me in it, in fact I never saw anyone that looked even vaguely like me.'[41]

As I live, work and play on the Llŷn Peninsula, I rarely encounter anyone who looks different from me, but I hear the difference in the language. The language of Welsh, even when it is not spoken, shapes the discourse around me. This is not just seen on road signs or in the mythological encounters that visitors have when entering a pub or shop where the Welsh appears to disenfranchise the English visitor. The Welsh language has stood the test of time. While it has never been outlawed – indeed, the translation of the Bible into Welsh helped preserve its status – it has at times been squeezed from the public square and disappeared from parts of the land because of economic necessity. Communicating in a different language challenged my Englishness; and encountering men and women who live, breathe, work, pray, laugh, dream and worship entirely and instinctively in Cymraeg has *unveiled* a different world that is to be experienced and explored. It also asks questions about the world from which you have come.

Seeing creates an environment in which reflection or judging can take place. My being in Wales has judged me. I used the word 'unveiled' advisedly. In koine Greek, as a New Testament scholar I know that I would translate 'to unveil' as 'apocalyptic'.[42] Apocalyptic is not to do with the end of the world, but rather is an unveiling, a granting of the ability to see the world as it is, or as it is meant to be.[43] It took coming to Wales and living in a community that resolutely defined itself as something different from being English for me to realize that I had accepted, and to some extent embraced, an Anglo-centric Christendom. For me to live, breathe, work, pray, laugh, dream, worship and do mission in Wales, I had to step outside such norms, and be willing to admit that I have considerable amounts of power, and then set it aside – as far as that is possible. This is an ongoing process; it is relatively easy to set something aside temporarily, but much more difficult to attempt to relinquish power once and for all.

Allowing yourself both to judge (analyse) and be judged creates a level of vulnerability; the ability to admit you are wrong runs countercultural to the powers of empire. Fortunately, the exercise of vulnerability allows for the possibility of inclusion, as has happened within Wales for me as a learner of the Welsh language. It is not a given. Anyone can learn the mechanics of a language, but there is a particular disposition to embracing the contours of a new culture that comes with it. Once again, one of the disabling features of doing this within Wales is that English is all-pervasive. When you begin to learn Welsh, you are told that it is a phonetic language; this is accurate and helpful. What English learners are not told is that the phonetics of Cymraeg are different from English: it is possible to read Welsh phonetically like you would English, and thus mangle the language. What I remember being encouraged to do is to wear 'Welsh spectacles' to enter the world of Cymraeg. This is the case with language; within Wales it is also the case with culture, and culture that is shaped all too often by its relationship with England. Mission in Wales inevitably means that any Christian discourse or message needs to be aware, first, of the context in which it is heard.

For those like me who wish to be heard in Wales as those from outside, we need to note that the Christian message has often been parcelled up with the contours of Englishness. I therefore need, first, to be conscious that I am an outsider. I have no right to choose to come inside. It is necessary to be invited in. I am therefore a guest at the table. Second, listening is necessary over a long period of time. English supremacy has been understated and effortless within Wales. There are examples of those within power in Wales joining with or perceiving themselves to be joining with those in power in England. Until recently power – except on the rugby field – has been one-sided. Listening allows entry into the conversation and allows for a period of transformative learning, which enables people like me to begin to understand the nuances of the conversation. As the conversation is engaged with, and both the mechanical language and that of culture, heritage, hopes and dreams begin to be learned, it is possible to become a hybrid-type figure.[44] I am, though, still there as a guest. I have years of unlearning to do, and the communities I am working with have years of unlearning how Englishmen with power behave.

For me, I have been on a journey. Raymond Williams described his journey as a Welshman like this: as a 'painful recognition of real dislocations, discontinuities [and] problematic identities' that can lead 'not only to division and confusion but to new and higher forms of consciousness'.[45] I would echo that description of my own journey within Wales. As I have tried to be a priest with the people, I have been confronted and challenged by the past, begun to live in the present and dared to dream of a different future. To do this, I needed to acknowledge that what I thought I knew was akin to looking through 'a darkened glass'. When power is set aside, there is the opportunity to see 'face to face' and enable others to do the same. That is mission as I have come to understand it.

Notes

1 All stories involving individuals have been used with permission, and names have been anonymized.

2 Joseph Cardijn, 1982, *La Pensée de Joseph Cardijn, va Libérer mon Peuple!* Brussels: Vanbraekel Mouscron.

3 See, for example, Laurie Green, 1990, *Let's Do Theology*, London: Mowbray, and P. O'Connell Killen and J. De Beer, 1994, *The Art of Theological Reflection*, New York: Crossroad Publishing.

4 Kevin Ellis, 'The Priest as Theologian', *Journal of Adult Theological Education*, 1(2) (2004), pp. 121–33.

5 Edward M. Said, 2000, *Out of Place*, London: Granta Books.

6 Kevin Ellis, 'The Oppressor in the Mirror', *Practical Theology*, 9(2) (2016), pp. 142–3.

7 See R. R. Davies, 'Colonial Wales', *Past & Present*, 65(1) (1974), pp. 3–23. Cf. Jane Aaron and Chris Williams (eds), 2005, *Postcolonial Wales*, Cardiff: University of Wales Press.

8 Norman Denzin, 2014, *Interpretive Autoethnography*, London: Sage, p. 52.

9 Denzin, *Interpretive Autoethnography*, p. 53.

10 The PhD is through the University of Manchester via the Urban Theology Union and the Luther King Centre, see https://utusheffield.org.uk/ (accessed 10.03.2023).

11 See, for example, Lisa Lewis, 2018, *Performing Wales: People, Memory, Place*, Cardiff: University of Wales Press, pp. 28–31.

12 Jamie Matthews, 'Stop the Renaming of the Second Severn Crossing to the Prince of Wales Bridge', *Change.org*, https://www.change.org/p/alun-cairns-mp-stop-the-renaming-of-the-severn-bridge-to-the-prince-of-wales-bridge (accessed 10.03.2023).

13 Details of the Westminster parliamentary debate can be found here: https://hansard.parliament.uk/commons/2018-04-24/debates/BCCFDDC1-BE6F-4AAB-8A92-A3FBCD3D6105/ProtectionOfWelshSpeakersFromDefamation (accessed 10.03.2023).

14 See 'The Co-operation Agreement: 2021', *Welsh Government*, https://gov.wales/co-operation-agreement-2021 (accessed 10.03.2023).

15 https://www.instituteforgovernment.org.uk/explainer/welsh-independence (accessed 23.03.2023).

16 https://www.instituteforgovernment.org.uk/explainer/welsh-independence (accessed 23.03.2023).

17 The Independent Commission on the Constitutional Future of Wales, 'What We Do', *Welsh Government*, https://gov.wales/independent-commission-constitutional-future-wales (accessed 10.03.2023).

18 See, further, R. W. Jones, 2022, 'How Brexit has Changed our National Identities and Attitudes towards Devolution in Wales', *Nation Cymru*, 4 March, https://nation.cymru/opinion/how-brexit-has-changed-our-national-identities-and-attitudes-towards-devolution-in-wales/ (accessed 10.03.2023).

19 Chris Williams, 2005, 'Problematizing Wales: An Exploration in Historiography and Postcoloniality', in Aaron and Williams (eds), *Postcolonial Wales*, p. 18.

20 Ailsa Henderson and Richard Wyn Jones, 2021, *Englishness: The Political Force Transforming Britain*, Oxford: University Press, pp. 37–45.

21 See Roger Scully and Richard Wyn Jones, 'Still three Wales? Social Location and Electoral Behaviour in Contemporary Wales', *Electoral Studies*, 31(4) (2012), pp. 656–67.

22 Adam Price, 2018, *Wales: The First and Final Colony*, Talybont: Y Lolfa, p. 29.

23 Adam Price, 2019, 'Westminster owes Wales Reparations: It's not Charity we seek but Justice', *Nation Cymru*, 3 October, https://nation.cymru/opinion/westminster-owes-wales-reparations-its-not-charity-we-seek-but-justice/ (accessed 10.03.2023).

24 Price, 'Westminster owes Wales Reparations'.

25 Williams, 'Problematizing Wales', p. 5 and Manon Ceridwen James, 2018, *Women, Identity and Religion in Wales: Theology, Poetry, Story*, Cardiff: University of Wales Press, pp. 25–6.

26 Williams, 'Problematizing Wales', p. 8.

27 Norman Davies, 1999, *The Isles: A History*, London: Macmillan, p. 493.

28 Davies, *The Isles*, p. 494. I am more hesitant than Davies in the use of secular and religious culture during the sixteenth and seventeenth centuries.

29 Bill Ashcroft, Graham Griffiths and Helen Tiffin, 1989, *The Empire Writes Back*, London: Routledge.

30 Ashcroft et al., *The Empire*, pp. 31–2.

31 See Aled Jones and Bill Jones, 'The Welsh World and the British Empire c.1851–1939: An Exploration', *The Journal of Imperial and Commonwealth History*, 31(2) (2003), pp. 57–81.

32 Louise Lawrence, 2009, *The Word in Place: Reading the New Testament in Contemporary Contexts*, London: SPCK, p. 25.

33 Carol Trosset explores the acceptance of Welsh learners into their communities in her ethnographic work, 1993, *Welshness Performed: Welsh Concepts of Person and Society*, Tuscon, AZ and London: University of Arizona Press.

34 Received 20 October 2019.

35 This is explored by Robin Mann, 'Negotiating the Politics of Language: Language Learning and Civic Identity in Wales', *Ethnicities* 7(2) (2007), doi:10.1177/1468796807076845 (accessed 25.07.2020).

36 This comment was made as part of my Ministerial Development Review for the Diocese of Bangor by the then headteacher of Ysgol Syr Thomas Jones in October 2019. The quotation is used with permission.

37 My translation.

38 John Ziesler, 1990, *Paul's Letter to the Romans*, London: SCM Press, p. 232.

39 Martin Johnes, 2022, 'Embracing and Escaping History' in Darren Chetty, Grug Muse, Hanan Issa and Iestyn Tyne (eds), *Welsh (Plural): Essays on the Future of Wales*, London: Repeater Books, p. 18.

40 See Darren Chetty, 2021, 'Charlotte Williams in Conversation', *Wales Arts Review*, https://www.walesartsreview.org/charlotte-williams-in-conversation/ (accessed 10.03.2023).

41 Charlotte Williams, 'Knowing Our Place: Cynefin, the Curriculum and Me', in Chetty et al. (eds), *Welsh (Plural)*, p. 198.

42 Christopher Rowland, 1993, *Revelation*, London: Epworth Press, p. 2.

43 Rowland, *Revelation*, p. 22.

44 This has been explored by the ethnographer Carol Trosset, 'The Social Identity of Welsh Learners', *Language in Society*, 15(2) (1986), pp. 165–91.

45 Raymond Williams, 2003, 'Wales and England' in *Who Speaks for Wales? Nation, Culture, Identity*, Cardiff: University of Wales Press, pp. 20–1.

PART FOUR

Exploration of Whiteness

14

Unbecoming: Reflections on the Work of a White Theologian

RACHEL STARR

Introduction[1]

> This chapter has its origins in a class presentation to a group of White students at the Southern Theological Education and Training Scheme in May 2000. It was part of a racism-awareness weekend led by a group of Black and White trainers.

The session was delivered during my first full academic year of working in theological education. Aside from completing doctoral studies in Argentina, I have taught in theological education – first at STETS, later at the Queen's Foundation for Ecumenical Theological Education, Birmingham – for 20 years. For much of that time I have been involved in delivering anti-racism training, either in stand-alone sessions or, at Queen's, as part of the Introduction to Black Theology module.[2] Always, I've worked alongside global majority colleagues.[3] My presentation found its way into *Strangers No More*, a racial justice training manual produced and used within the Methodist Church in Britain.[4] Over the past 20 years, material produced by the Methodist Church in Britain has continued to engage with notions of White privilege, to a limited extent.[5] As far as I am aware, Queen's is the only British Theological Education Institution (TEI) that requires ministerial students to take a course on Black theology, and which includes a session on critiquing Whiteness.[6]

It is unbecoming of me, as a White person, to speak about race, about Whiteness.[7] But even more so as a White middle-class woman. Returning to my original essay, written 20 years ago, is a process of 'unbecoming' in many ways. I find myself unbecoming White, in that I feel less sure of how I should engage with my own Whiteness. There is unravelling, of the essay itself, in its clarity and confidence – that is, its Whiteness.[8]

And rather than the original hopeful conclusion, my later reflection is left incomplete, with unravelled threads and conflict unresolved.

In the text that follows, the original essay is presented in italics; my reflections twenty years on are in roman text.[9]

White racial identity

During the academic year 1998–1999, I studied at Union Theological Seminary in the City of New York and began to discover my white identity. I was invited to join Metanoia, a group of white people seeking to grow spiritually through a commitment to anti-racist work. I also became friends with Asian American and African American students and staff who helped me to grow as a white anti-racist person. In these ways, I learnt to not only challenge racism but also acknowledge whiteness. This has been a useful and empowering lesson for me.

When I arrived at Union, I was 24 years old. I had completed undergraduate studies in theology at Oxford. I'd spent a week listening to Archbishop Desmond Tutu, and later watched spellbound one February afternoon as Nelson Mandela walked free. I'd crept down into the theology faculty library stacks, searching out texts by feminist and liberation theologians. After university, I'd travelled to Lima, living in Rimac, the parish of Gustavo Gutiérrez. There, I'd read James Cone's *Malcolm & Martin & America*.[10] So why was I only now seeing myself as White?

Whiteness is often unseen by White people, invisibilized through claims of neutrality and normality.[11] And the performance of Whiteness as normal or neutral is intertwined with denial of White unearned privilege and racist practices.[12] George Yancy argues that White people are infected by Whiteness and, despite assuming otherwise, are unable to deal with the depth and complexity of their own racism.[13]

While Metanoia was led by a White student – Jana Meyer – it built on previous anti-racism work prompted by the vocal leadership of Black students.[14] I am thankful for the grace and good humour of friends at Union who encouraged me to engage with questions of identity, power and inequality. But I am much clearer now that the work is mine to do.

Claire A. Lockard argues that White people new to anti-racist work are often keen to confess their White privilege.[15] But in conversation with Sara Ahmed,[16] Lockard argues that such confessions not only do not result in a change of behaviour but work against it. Lockard suggests that the act of confession functions to reassure the person that in acknowledging their Whiteness, their 'goodness' has been restored.[17] Lockard's critique resonates with my own experience of confessing White privilege as an educator. While I recognize the importance of acknowledging Whiteness and structures of white supremacy, I also recognize that by speaking about something unspoken I am often affirmed by students or other theological educators in ways that can encourage collusion with the notion of 'White goodness'. Through confessing White privilege, I risk seeing myself as less racist than other White people. Naming myself as White shouldn't be 'useful and empowering' for me.

> *Mary L. Foulke, a US teacher of Christian Education, noted in 1995 'we who are white appear to pass for no race at all'.[18] The notion of being white is alien to most white people. We who are white have been made colour-blind – we regard 'race' as something to do with black people alone.[19] But the reality is that we all have a 'race' and a colour, even if we are white. White people must begin to be honest about their racial identification. I need to say, 'I am a white Briton, a white woman theologian.' We cannot do theology authentically without acknowledging our starting point. Since liberation theologies emerged in the late 1960s, theologians from marginalized groups have exploded the myth of placeless theology. White theologians and white church people need to understand that all theology is contextual, including white theology. We who are white must therefore relinquish our monopoly on public religious imagery and accepted descriptions of God.*
>
> *James Cone's book* A Black Theology of Liberation, *first published in 1970, named traditional theology as white theology, and in so doing invalidated its claim to represent all people. The term 'white theology' is shockingly unfamiliar. For Cone, 'white theology' represents racist theology. Furthermore, 'because white theology has consistently preserved the integrity of the community of the oppressors, I conclude that it is not Christian theology at all'.[20] In this article, I work with the belief that white theology can be anti-racist and thus Christian, but only if it first acknowledges its whiteness. A strong and true racial identity will help those of us who are white to know ourselves and be empowered to challenge oppression. The following paragraphs explore how a positive racial identity might help white church people challenge racism.*

There are a number of reasons why White theologians do not identify as such: the normalization and thus invisibility of Whiteness within the discipline of theology;[21] an association of White identity with white supremacy;[22] a desire to present their work as universally relevant;[23] an assumption, especially among some systematic theologians and historical critical biblical scholars, that one's own identity and context is irrelevant;

a lack of understanding of the importance of engaging critically with Whiteness, in conversation with global majority theologians.[24] Twenty years on from my original essay, there are still very few White British theologians who self-identify as White in their work, although this is beginning to change, as can be seen from the special issue of the journal *Practical Theology* entitled: 'Critical White Theology: Dismantling Whiteness?' (2022). To critically identify as White requires theologians to have done a sufficient amount of work to recognize their contextuality, and thus make visible the limits in the applicability of their theology, as well as their complicity with White dominance, and the need for further self-critique.

My dismissal of Cone's critique is revealing of a White approach to theology that pushes towards neat and easy solutions.[25] I fail to acknowledge the many ways in which white theology is created by, and for the benefit of, dominant White groups: theologies that legitimated enslavement, those that continue to sanction nationalism, racism, sexism and homophobia.[26] Such theology, as J. Kameron Carter notes, sanctions a White world order,[27] and connects Whiteness to salvation.[28] Anthony G. Reddie calls for anti-racist work to engage more directly with the relationship between White Western 'Mission Christianity' and White supremacy.[29] He argues that dominant White theology presents White people as superior and thus entitled to destroy or exploit 'others'.[30] Rather than draw on Christianity as a resource for challenging racism, Reddie argues that anti-racist work needs first to engage in a radical critique of Western Christian history and White theology.[31]

Rather than a 'strong and true racial identity' that empowers White people to identify as 'White saviours', today I would encourage White people to be less confident in their identity, theology and ability to do anti-racist work. And although Robert Beckford traces a faint tradition of anti-racist White theology in Britain,[32] I would encourage White theologians to spend time with Cone's challenge before seeking to place themselves within this marginal tradition.

> American scholar Janet E. Helms 'has developed a map of white racial identity development that moves from an absence of, or, negative white racial identity (that is, not acknowledging "whiteness", or assuming superiority) to a positive (anti-racist) one'.[33] Although I have some questions about her map, I offer it as a useful tool for white people exploring racial identity. Helms proposed a linear progression through these stages, but white people may encounter a number of stages of racial identity simultaneously.

Helms's White racial identity model continues to be used within psychology, education and activism.[34] Over several decades, Helms and others have developed the theory, notably moving from a stage to a schema model,[35] which allows for movement back and forth. Helms divides the schemata into two groups: in phase one, a White person acts in ways that accommodate racial inequality; in phase two, there is some resistance to racial inequality.[36]

In this section of the original essay, I introduce Helms's model and illustrate it with examples from my own lived experience. I often do this badly. Further, in the original essay, I failed to acknowledge Helms's Black identity and consider the embodied cost of her analysis, and her willingness to confront whiteness.

> *Whites often begin their journey by claiming, 'I don't see colour.' We are very good at denying racial difference in our churches! How often do we claim that colour is not important in worship or Christian living? By making these claims, we ignore the realities of racial difference and, in so doing, ignore the existence of racism. Even if some whites delude themselves by claiming not to see colour, in truth, people do see colour and black and Asian people suffer as a result.*

Helms describes this as the 'Contact' stage of White racial identity, in which White people are oblivious or in denial concerning the significance of racialized identity, both of others and even more so of their own.[37]

In our vision statements, hymns and prayers, White-dominated churches continue to proclaim 'all are welcome'. For many, there is a genuine desire to be an inclusive church, alongside a tentative awareness of the history of race-based exclusion by White churches, notably in response to the Windrush generation. Yet without recognition of difference, churches assume that the way to make people welcome is by treating everyone as if they were the same as them. In White-dominated churches, this often results in assumptions that the likes and needs of the White majority are appropriate for everybody. Moreover, the denial of a person's colour or racial identity prevents deep and honest engagement with the uniqueness of another. It further fails to acknowledge the negative impact of White supremacy on the well-being of Black and Brown people in the UK.[38] This failure to acknowledge difference is a long-established survival strategy of White people that shields them from questioning the structures benefiting them.[39]

A reflection for Theology Everywhere, a Methodist Church in Britain-supported initiative,[40] by a White theologian, Aaron Edwards, and the response to it, illustrates some of these points.[41] I do not want to single

Edwards out for criticism; I am well aware of other theologians and church leaders who share his views; and conscious of the 'constant temptation' faced by White theologians, myself included, to reject the challenge of Black theology.[42] However, Edwards's location within ecumenical theological education in the UK makes him a relevant example for my work. Edwards appears to be dismissive of anti-racist work within theological education and defensive around the critique of Whiteness, responding with some force to recent criticism by a Black theologian about the lack of Black theologians in UK universities. He rejects, without much investigation, the idea that all White theologians are racist – an idea to which I return at the end of this chapter. Edwards appears to suggest that to engage with anti-racist work is to be distracted by worldly concerns. The first few comments on the piece are supportive, suggesting that everyone is equally to blame for inequality, and praising diversity but denying colour makes a difference. There is no acknowledgement of racial inequality until the fifth comment; thereafter there are calls to acknowledge the sin of racism, to engage with Black theology, for White people to let go of power, and an affirmation of the Equality, Diversity and Inclusion work of the Methodist Church in the UK.

> *The next stage is one of disintegration, when the white person's new awareness of colour difference brings unease and conflict. At this point, a white person has to decide whether to avoid, accept or challenge racism.*[43] *Since the choice is disturbing, many white people choose to accept racism at some level. They are reintegrated into the myth of white supremacy and accept racial stereotypes. This is true even of those who respond to dilemmas by claiming, 'I like all black people' for fear of facing their deeper feelings.*

Helms describes 'reintegration' as a move to maintain privilege, including the privilege of avoiding emotional turmoil.[44] In my own work with White student ministers, I recognize the tension expressed here. The recognition of racism within the world and within oneself is too much of a threat to established narratives and practices. White students may use a variety of strategies to push away the challenges with which they are confronted. These include: questioning the competency and professionalism of Black and Brown tutors; delegitimating global majority scholarship; verbal aggression; distraction; White fragility (tears, expressions of guilt, feeling overwhelmed).[45] A common defence mechanism is to seek victim-status through foregrounding another aspect of one's identity, such as gender, sexuality, class or disability.[46]

Some whites progress to the Pseudo-independent stage and begin to acknowledge the presence of racism. They may begin to learn about the reality of black culture and people. This is a difficult stage because these white people are stranded somewhere between a negative and positive white racial identity. They 'tend to idealize Black culture and to look to Black people to explain racism'.[47]

I once visited an African Caribbean hairstylist in Wolverhampton and asked if they could arrange for me to develop dreadlocks. I was suffering from 'Wanting to be Black' Syndrome. White people at this stage in the development of their white identity can sometimes believe that only black is culturally acceptable. In the recent American film 10 Things I Hate About You *the African American teacher criticized a bunch of white students who are expressing their support for the black consciousness movement. Their white dreads gave them away; they had not accepted their own racial identity and sought to join the black community without acknowledging their role in a racist society.*

What is often involved at this stage is cultural appropriation. The term 'cultural appropriation' means 'to take possession of specific aspects of someone else's culture in unethical, oppressive ways'.[48] *Such actions undermine racial identity. The white students in the film were perhaps guilty of taking over someone else's culture but not their struggle. In this country, this phenomenon is recognizable in the use of hip-hop and reggae music by white youth. Joanna Kadi's powerful and disturbing book,* Thinking Class, *takes the example of Disney's reworking of the traditional Arabian story of Aladdin. Although the story is celebrated, characters and moral judgements are forced to comply with the cultural norms of white America. Arab customs, music and religious practices are borrowed, ridiculed and exploited.*[49]

Cultural appropriation is a significant issue for religious and spiritual movements. In the States, First Nations people complain that whites attempt to buy out their spiritual practices. The black British theologian Robert Beckford, in his book Jesus is Dread, *criticized hymn writer Graham Kendrick for not acknowledging his use of black gospel music.*[50] *These practices silence the creativity of black people.*

Twenty years on, the examples I offer in this section seem crass, naive and, in the easy description of them, are in themselves illustrative of Helms's Pseudo-independent stage. In writing about my experience, I fail to critique sufficiently my own simplification and commodification of Black cultural identities. I conflate hip-hop and Dread culture. I am quick to step into and back out of the black space of the barber shop, broadly untroubled by my naivety. There is a carelessness in the way I speak of my attempts to appropriate Black culture.

In the intervening years, cultural appropriation has become a highly contested debate. I remain unsure how I might engage authentically with a diversity of cultures in a way that is open to the challenges presented by them. An example: I've seen the Alvin Ailey American Dance Theater perform four times. I did ballet as a child, and the company's most celebrated piece, *Revelations*, explores themes central to my Christian faith. And yet engaging with this historic Black dance company, whose work draws from generational experiences of the impact of racism on Black faith and communities, must necessarily remain a confrontation, a challenge to my White dance tradition and my history of White Christianity.

Helms describes the Pseudo-independent approach as a form of White liberalism, which easily assumes White people can engage positively with anti-racist work. She is critical of how White people at this stage might claim to be in solidarity with Black and Brown people, while failing to do the necessary work on their own complicity with Whiteness and White supremacy.[51]

> *The next stage in Helms's mapping of racial identity development is the Immersion/Emersion stage. Here real questions are asked, such as, 'Who am I racially?' White people at this stage begin to question other people who assumed their co-operation with white supremacy. There is the potential for authentic positive feelings about racial identity that empower just action and right living. Church communities need to be encouraged by their leaders and teachers to ask these difficult questions.*

Helms identifies the acknowledgement of Whiteness as a source of racism as a central aspect of this stage.[52] The murder of George Floyd in 2020 and subsequent protests resulted in more visible conversations among White people about racism. In the following months, I was involved in various church-based conversations around Whiteness, notably the Dismantling Whiteness conference in 2021. I began to hear about small groups of White Christians seeking out resources to help them learn about the institutional racism of White churches and reflect critically on Whiteness. Yet these small steps require a long-term commitment.

> *By the time a white person reaches the Autonomy stage they no longer need 'to denigrate or idealize people based on some form of group membership'.[53] There is an awareness of interlocking oppressive structures, sexism, racism, class discrimination and homophobia. People at this stage of their racial identity may even see the categories in which they*

> *identify and struggle for liberation as harmful. On the surface, this would appear to be a return to the beginning of Helms's journey of racial identity! What is finally established is that all people are part of the same race; we are all members of the human race.*

Helms cautions against a sense of completion, describing the autonomy stage as 'a lifelong process of discovery and recommitment to defining oneself in positive [i.e. moral] terms as a White person'.[54] One feature of White theology, as identified by Tom Beaudoin and Katherine Turpin, is a focus on results, problem-solving, conclusions, complete systems.[55] I recognize this tendency here, an unwillingness to leave things unresolved. But Malott and colleagues argue that even this most 'developed' state of White anti-racist identity does not free White people from personal racism. Thus, White people need to 'maintain a continual sense of vigilance'; be open to critique from Black and Brown people; and move from fear and guilt when responding to their own racism.[56] This need for vulnerability and vigilance I recognize in my own journey as I revisit my past self, and recognize the work still to do.

> *Some racial justice advocates suggest that 'race' is no more than a myth. Divisions of race are based on political rather than biological differences. Indeed, white and black are themselves political terms. False lines between one hue and another are drawn to keep some out and rapidly become uncrossable. The concept of a mixed-race marriage can only exist by drawing an arbitrary line at a point agreed by those in power. Desmond Tutu often used the example of a division between those with little noses or big noses to illustrate the ludicrousness of Apartheid. Perhaps his example was not as far fetched as it would seem – note anti-Semitic stereotyping of Jewish appearance.*[57]
>
> *The African American writer James Baldwin published an article in 1984 entitled 'On Being "White" and Other Lies'.*[58] *He wrote about the experience of new immigrants who became 'white' on arrival in America. Enslaved people from Africa became 'black'. No one was defined as black or white before they arrived. Previously excluded groups such as the Jewish community had to give up their own identity in order to become white.*

In referencing Desmond Tutu and particularly James Baldwin, whose work is broadly unfamiliar to me, I see how I seek to claim their authority for myself. As a White theologian, how do I engage with global majority scholars without carelessly appropriating their work or using them as a shortcut?

Why then should white people journey towards a better-informed racial identity? Mary Foulke suggests, 'While we know that "black" or "white" is an unstable, fluid and contradictory reality, we also know that persons perceived to be black will be treated differently from those perceived to be white.'[59] Being clear about our racial identity gives us a place to stand from which we can challenge white supremacy. Becoming white is 'a lifelong learning of how to become white and of inventing positive, anti-racist meanings for being white in this historical moment'.[60]

Recognizing unearned privilege

As a white person growing up in the multi-cultural, multi-racial surroundings of Wolverhampton, I learnt about racism and race riots, and felt confident in my self-identification as anti-racist. Once that step had been taken, I was unclear about my further responsibilities. If I renounced racism and spoke against racist actions, what else was there to do? Learning about the privileges of my whiteness and beginning to understand how I might let go of them did not happen until much later. For me, the idea of white privileges is most helpful as I seek to commit to anti-racist work in the church and wider world. I feel sure I do not engage in physical acts of racism but not so sure I have renounced the privileges society grants me because of my race.

The writer who introduced me to the idea of white privilege was Peggy McIntosh. In her exploration of these privileges, I recognized a common experience: 'I did not see myself as racist because I was taught to recognize racism only in individual acts of meanness by members of my group, never in invisible systems conferring racial dominance on my group from birth.'[61]

It was Black scholars, notably W. E. B. Du Bois,[62] who developed the concept of White privilege, yet it was not until a White scholar wrote about it that it gained wider – White – exposure.[63] While McIntosh's work remains influential, it has been criticized in a variety of ways. As already noted, confession of privilege is seen by some to be a dead end.[64] Rather than resulting in anti-racist actions, it risks becoming the action required. Awareness of White privilege can make White people feel better about themselves and, accordingly, more complacent about racism.[65] Moreover, White privilege pedagogy focuses on personal identity rather than structural inequality; and centres White, rather than Black or Brown, experience.[66] In his assessment of training in British church contexts, Anthony G. Reddie notes a shift towards individually focused methods, such as unconscious bias training, that often fail to address White supremacy.[67] Thus Zeus Leonardo argues that a 'critical look at white privilege, or the analysis of white racial hegemony, must be complemented by an equally rigorous examination of white supremacy, or the analysis of white racial domination'.[68] Rather than present White people as the innocent recipients of unexpected gifts or privileges, Leonardo argues that White people need to understand how they 'daily re-create' White racial dominance.[69]

> *Focusing on individual violent acts of racism masks a system of power that privileges white people. There is limited value for racism awareness training in discussing incidents such as the murder of Stephen Lawrence. When racism is only explored through extreme acts of violence, most white people find it pretty easy to distance themselves from such behaviour. If church groups were able to think through the notion of white privilege, it would be more difficult for white Christians to deny the part they play in maintaining a racist society.*

My dismissal of the relevance of Stephen Lawrence's murder, and failure to engage with the Macpherson (1999) Report's discussion of institutional racism,[70] or note the report *A Tree God Planted*, in which the Methodist Church in Britain was described as institutionally racist,[71] is indicative of the limitations of White privilege pedagogy. By focusing on what might be relevant to White people in their daily routine, I failed to recognize that interpersonal violence and institutional racism are everyday realities for Black and Brown people. Moreover, I failed to connect White privilege to the death-dealing structures of White supremacy. For example, if I acknowledge how, as a White woman, White privilege offers me specific forms of public protection and care, I also need to consider the increased risks that pregnant Black and Brown women face as a result of institutional racism within the health service that may fail to recognize or take seriously these women's symptoms or accounts.[72]

> *What is privilege? It is hidden from those who hold it but at the same time assumed by them. It is difficult for white people to see white privilege, since white is the norm. White Britons do not see through a filter of racial awareness, they therefore find it difficult to understand how Britain may appear to a black or Asian Briton.*
> Peggy McIntosh commented:

> *As a white person ... I had been taught about racism as something that puts others at a disadvantage, but had been taught not to see ... white privilege, which puts me at an advantage ... I have come to see white privilege as an invisible package of unearned assets that I can count on cashing in each day.*[73]

She made a list of privileges, 'that I did not earn but that I have been made to feel are mine by birth, by citizenship, and by virtue of being a conscientious law-abiding "normal" person'.[74] The most revealing of these privileges often emerge within the context of innocent ordinary events. To take one example from McIntosh's extensive list, a white person can wear a 'flesh'-coloured bandage and have it more or less match the colour of their skin.[75]

From my own experience I offer several recent examples of unearned privilege. I visited Cuba in January 1999 with a group from my seminary. Hours before our return, we were told that we had entered Cuba somewhat irregularly (the US still maintains a ban on travel to Cuba). We were advised to tell immigration officials that we had only been to Jamaica. In my panic, I realized that until that moment it had not been necessary for me to know how to negotiate with potentially hostile customs and immigration officials. I was not used to being suspected of drug trafficking or terrorism, unlike the majority of the black or Asian origin members of our group who faced suspicion and hostility each time they passed through immigration. I understood that part of my ease here was due to class and gender and nationality, but race did play a part in it.

It wasn't that I hadn't ever crossed borders that were fraught. It's that I'd never done so alongside people for whom borders into their own country presented such threats, as is the case for Black and Brown Britons,[76] increasingly so as a result of the hostile environment and the Nationality and Borders Act (2022).[77]

Leonardo connects McIntosh's list of White privileges to structural causes.[78] Revisiting my example from Cuba, I can see how my White naivety is structurally supported by White supremacy: anti-immigration laws; institutional racism of the police, military and border control; the history of White Europeans awarding themselves the 'right' to travel (colonialism etc.) and to move others – via enslavement most notably; how the global market economy excludes many from legal participation; how White people profit from drugs but are less at risk from producing or moving drugs.

> *One of McIntosh's privileges as a white person was the assurance that white people will appear in history as leaders and heroes. Last harvest, my home church celebrated the events of the millennium using a Partners in Learning outline of history. We remembered only white abolitionists, not black campaigners and slave leaders.*

Leonardo's work[79] prompts me to consider White promotion of narratives of success, progress and moral goodness. Black historians such as Patrick Vernon and David Olusoga[80] have sought to disrupt the dominant history of British society and empire. For the church also, Azariah France-Williams gives a different account, which similarly challenges the church on its complicity with racism.[81] But there is resistance to narratives that threaten White European self-understanding, and which acknowledge white responsibility for colonialization and enslavement.[82]

> *If you are a white person, try to list individually simple, everyday events that you can do because of your white privilege. If you can, share this task in a group. It could be a step towards renouncing those excluding privileges.*

Is it possible to renounce White privilege? Does the increased range of colours of plasters, bandages and make-up now available in the UK represent a radical challenge to White supremacy? While increased diversity and access to resources may be gained, it is difficult to see how other examples of McIntosh's list, those that relate to the avoidance of hostility and surveillance as a result of White identity, can be renounced.

Becoming a White ally

> *David Haslam, the author of* Race for the Millennium, *is clear about the responsibility of white people in tackling racism in British churches and wider society:*

> White people should never forget that racism is not a black problem, it is a white problem, and it is white people who must deal with it, in themselves and their communities, but with help and direction from black people they have the time, the energy and the emotional resilience.[83]

> *Amadou Diallo, an unarmed immigrant from Guinea-Bissau, was shot dead by New York City police in February 1999. Huge demonstrations*

followed with up to 200 people arrested each day at the high point of the protests against police racism. I witnessed the organized arrest of two friends, both Anglican seminarians, one Asian American and one white American. These friends and other demonstrators formed part of the multi-racial resistance to racism. So do agencies such as Christian Aid and Oxfam that use positive and non-exploitative images of the poor nations they support. This is the legacy of white resistance to white supremacy. Foulke warns white people: 'It is not for us to claim one of these legacies, but both, and to move forward in our journeys of repentance and witness.'[84]

You may like to look at the endnote entitled 'Being a White Ally'.[85] If you are white, you could choose to reflect on a recent interaction with a black or Asian Briton and ask whether you could have been a better ally against your own or others' racism.

The death of Amadou Diallo and the protests that followed had a lasting impact on me. I've since reflected on the earlier death of another Black man as a result of police violence, asking myself in the process why, at the time, I failed to engage in any real depth with the death of Clinton McCurbin, in my home town of Wolverhampton in 1987. Writing also about McCurbin, Anthony Reddie describes how he travelled to take part in the protest march but how he did this alone, in the face of the indifference of White Christian friends and colleagues.[86]

There has been significant critique of the notion of the White anti-racist ally, which, like the confession of White privilege, is seen to be 'conscience salving'[87] and risks presenting White people as the solution or salvation, rather than the problem. Instead, Cone and others following him have called on White people to convert to Blackness, to be in solidarity with Black people, while recognizing this is never fully possible.[88] Jantzen argues that such conversion can only be a 'paradoxical possibility' and is not achievable simply by White attempts, but instead interrupts them.[89]

When we who are whites begin to work for racial justice, we do so as 'recovering racists'. The Revd Joseph Agne, a white Methodist minister in the USA, reflected: 'We are never former racists, only recovering racists, and we need to be daily vigilant about our addiction ... those of us who are white, let's be honest with ourselves. Let's bring down our defences and let go of the energy it takes to pretend we are not racist.'[90]

I find it incredibly difficult to acknowledge my racism. I have yet to let go of my many unearned privileges. But understanding that I am white and desiring to be part of the anti-racist movement, I am empowered to live more justly and know better the God who created both darkness and light.

I am critical of my desire in my original essay to offer a hopeful, positive conclusion, legitimated by a biblical text. I recognize a tendency within myself, and within White theology more generally, to seek answers. I need to resist this, to allow for unknowing, unbecoming, even while I seek to engage in anti-racist work. As Yancy warns, 'the moment a white person claims to have "arrived," that is, to have achieved "complete" antiracist mastery, she often undergoes a surprise attack that belies any sense of arrival.'[91]

James Cone[92] called on White theologians to develop an anti-racist theology, rooted in action and dialogue.[93] He advised: 'Begin the anti-racist struggle where you are … [and] Work at a pace as if you were going to do it for the rest of your life.'[94]

Anti-racist work is a lifelong task which involves constant vigilance and critique of White privilege and the systems of White domination. It is a work that is done daily: in selecting which theologians I will introduce in my modules; who I share lunch with; how I make space for others on the bus home; how I learn to trust the voices that challenge as much as those that soothe. It is learning from all the times I reframe a racist action or comment in order to avoid conflict; and from those occasions when I do seek to challenge racist practices and policies. It is recognizing that every time I mess up, the cost of my failure is borne by Black and Brown friends, colleagues and strangers.[95] It is a process of unbecoming.

Notes

1 Thank you to Dulcie Dixon McKenzie and Paul Nzacahayo for their colleagueship and helpful feedback.

2 Introduction to Black Theology module outline, https://www.durham.ac.uk/media/durham-university/departments-/common-awards/documents/module-out lines/level-4/TMM1657.pdf (accessed 10.03.2023).

3 On the use of the term 'global majority', see Rosemary M. Campbell-Stephens, 2021, 'Introduction: Global Majority Decolonising Narratives' in Rosemary M. Campbell-Stephens (ed.), *Educational Leadership and the Global Majority: Decolonising Narratives*, London: Palgrave Macmillan. https://doi.org/10.1007/978-3-030-88282-2_1 (accessed 10.03.2023).

4 Methodist Church in Britain, 2005, 'New Methodist Resource to Boost Racial Awareness Training', *Methodist Church in Britain*, 26 April, https://www.methodist.org.uk/about-us/news/latest-news/all-news/new-methodist-resource-to-boost-racial-awareness-training/ (accessed 10.03.2023).

5 Anthony G. Reddie, 'Reassessing the Inculcation of an Anti-racist Ethic

for Christian Ministry: From Racism Awareness to Deconstructing Whiteness', *Religions*, 11(10) (2020), doi:10.3390/rel11100497. The Methodist Church in Britain, 'Module 6: Ethnicity' of the *Equality, Diversity and Inclusion (EDI) Toolkit*, undated, https://www.methodist.org.uk/media/23178/edi-toolkit-6-0921.pdf (accessed 10.03.2023).

6 In 2021, TEIs were encouraged to make Common Awards modules Introduction to Black Theology, Theologies in Global Perspective, or similar material, a requirement for all Anglican ordinands. See Education Action 4 of the Archbishops' Anti-Racism Taskforce, 2021, *From Lament to Action*, https://www.churchofengland.org/sites/default/files/2021-04/FromLamentToAction-report.pdf (accessed 10.03.2023).

7 For a definition of Whiteness, see Janet E. Helms, 'The Challenge of Making Whiteness Visible: Reactions to Four Whiteness Articles', *The Counseling Psychologist*, 45(5) (July 2017), p. 718, https://doi.org/10.1177/0011000017718943 (accessed 10.03.2023).

8 Tom Beaudoin and Katherine Turpin, 2014, 'White Practical Theology' in Kathleen A. Cahalan and Gordon S. Mikoski (eds), *Opening the Field of Practical Theology*, Lanham, MD: Rowman & Littlefield, pp. 251–69.

9 Rachel Starr, 2001, 'Being White: Challenging White Supremacy' in Sandra Ackroyd, Marjorie Lewis-Cooper and Naboth Muchopa (eds), *Strangers No More: Transformation through Racial Justice*, London: The Methodist Church, pp. 40–4. First published as Rachel Starr, 'Being White: Challenging White Supremacy', *Articles of Reformed Faith and Religion*, 10 (summer 2000), pp. 9–14.

10 James H. Cone, 1991, *Martin & Malcolm & America: A Dream or a Nightmare*, Maryknoll, NY: Orbis Books.

11 Richard Dyer, 1997, *White*, London: Routledge; Ruth Frankenberg, 1993, *White Women, Race Matters: The Social Construction of Whiteness*, Minneapolis, MN: University of Minnesota Press; Anthony G. Reddie, 'Now You See Me, Now You Don't: Subjectivity, Blackness, and Difference in Practical Theology in Britain Post Brexit', *Practical Theology*, 11(1) (2018), pp. 4–16; George Yancy, 2012, 'Introduction: Framing the Problem' in George Yancy (ed.), *Christology and Whiteness: What Would Jesus Do?*, London: Routledge, pp. 1–18.

12 Karen Teel, 'Whiteness in Catholic Theological Method', *Journal of the American Academy of Religion*, 87(2) (2019), p. 411.

13 George Yancy, 2015, 'Whiteness as Insidious: On the Embedded and Opaque White Racist Self' in Bettina Bergo and Tracey Nicholls (eds), *I Don't See Color: Personal and Critical Perspectives on White Privilege*, State College, PA: Pennsylvania State University Press, pp. 113–14.

14 Jana Meyer, personal communication to the author, 23 May 2022.

15 Claire A. Lockard, 'Unhappy Confessions: The Temptation of Admitting to White Privilege', *Feminist Philosophy Quarterly*, 2(2) (Fall 2016), doi:10.5206/fpq/2016.2.2.

16 Reference to Sara Ahmed, 'Declarations of Whiteness: The Non-performativity of anti-racism', *Borderlands*, 3(2) (2004).

17 See also Akane Kanai, 'Between the Perfect and the Problematic: Everyday Femininities, Popular Feminism, and the Negotiation of Intersectionality', *Cultural Studies*, 34(1) (2020), p. 32, https://doi.org/10.1080/09502386.2018.1559869 (accessed 10.03.2023).

18 Mary L. Foulke, 'Coming Out as White/Becoming White: Racial Identity Development as a Spiritual Journey', *Theology & Sexuality*, 3(5) (September 1996), p. 22, https://doi.org/10.1177/135583589600300503 (accessed 10.03.2023).

19 Janet E. Helms, 2020, *A Race is a Nice Thing to Have: A Guide to Being a White Person or Understanding the White Persons in Your Life*, 3rd edition, San Diego, CA: Cognella. The original article references an earlier edition.

20 James H. Cone, 1994, *A Black Theology of Liberation: 20th Anniversary Edition*, Maryknoll, NY: Orbis Books, p. 9.

21 Lisa D. Powell, 'Exhibitionary Commerce, the Construction of Whiteness, and the Theological Sideshow', *Theology Today*, 78(2) (2021), pp. 140–57.

22 Rachel C. Schneider and Sophie Bjork-James, 'Whither Whiteness and Religion? Implications for Theology and the Study of Religion', *Journal of the American Academy of Religion*, 88(1) (March 2020), p. 177, doi:10.1093/j aarel/lfaa002.

23 James H. Cone, 1973, *God of the Oppressed*, Maryknoll, NY: Orbis Books, p. 126; Schneider and Bjork-James, 'Whither Whiteness', p. 177.

24 Beaudoin and Turpin, 'White Practical Theology'.

25 Beaudoin and Turpin, 'White Practical Theology'.

26 Willie James Jennings, 2020, *After Whiteness: An Education in Belonging*, Grand Rapids, MI: Eerdmans.

27 J. Kameron Carter, 2008, *Race: A Theological Account*, New York: Oxford University Press, p. 35.

28 Schneider and Bjork-James, 'Whither Whiteness'.

29 Reddie, 'Reassessing'.

30 Reddie, 'Reassessing'.

31 Reddie, 'Reassessing'.

32 Robert Beckford, 2004, *God and the Gangs: An Urban Toolkit for Those Who Won't Be Sold Out, Bought Out or Scared Out*, London: Darton, Longman & Todd, pp. 78–80.

33 Foulke, 'Coming Out', p. 24. Referring to Janet E. Helms, 1993, *Black and White Racial Identity: Theory, Research and Practice*, Westport, CT: Praeger.

34 Krista M. Malott et al., 'Strategies Used by Whites to Address Their Racism: Implications for Autonomous White Racial Identities', *Journal of Multicultural Counseling and Development*, 49(3) (2021), p. 137, https://doi.org/10.1002/jmcd.12220 (accessed 10.03.2023).

35 Helms, *A Race is a Nice Thing*; Malott et al., 'Strategies Used by Whites', p. 138.

36 Helms, 'The Challenge'.

37 Helms, 'The Challenge'.

38 Bridget Byrne et al., 2020, *Ethnicity, Race and Inequality in the UK. State of the Nation*, Bristol: Policy Press.

39 Zeus Leonardo, 'The Color of Supremacy: Beyond the Discourse of "White Privilege"', *Educational Philosophy and Theory*, 36(2) (2004), p. 145, doi: 10.1111/j.1469-5812.2004.00057.x; Ursula Moffitt, Leoandra Onnie Rogers and Kara R. H. Dastrup, 'Beyond Ethnicity: Applying Helms's White Racial Identity Development Model Among White Youth', *Journal of Research on Adolescence*, 32(3) (2021), pp. 1–20.

40 Theology Everywhere features a wide range of contributors and perspectives. See https://theologyeverywhere.org/about/.

41 Aaron Edwards, 2022, 'The Gospel of Race', *Theology Everywhere*, 18 April, https://theologyeverywhere.org/2022/04/18/the-gospel-of-race/ (accessed 10.03.2023).

42 Johannes N. J. Kritzinger, 'White responses to Black Theology: Revisiting a Typology', *HTS Teologiese Studies/ Theological Studies*, 78(3) (2022), a6945, https://doi.org/10.4102/hts.v78i3.6945.

43 This is an additional note added 2022. Helms is reflecting on how she sees White people form their racial identity, rather than suggesting these are all equally valid options.

44 Helms, 'The Challenge'.

45 Reddie, 'Reassessing'.

46 Alexandra Murdoch and Kareena McAloney-Kocaman, 'Exposure to Evidence of White Privilege and Perceptions of Hardships Among White UK Residents', *Race and Social Problems*, 11(3) (2019), pp. 206–9, https://doi.org/10.1007/s12552-019-09262-3 (accessed 10.03.2023).

47 Foulke, 'Coming Out', p. 29.

48 Joanna Kadi, 1996, *Thinking Class*, Boston, MA: South End Press, p. 117.

49 Kadi, *Thinking Class*, p. 132.

50 Robert Beckford, 1998, *Jesus is Dread: Black Theology and Black Culture in Britain*, London: Darton, Longman & Todd, p. 98.

51 Helms, 'The Challenge', pp. 721–2.

52 Helms, 'The Challenge'.

53 Foulke, 'Coming Out', p. 31.

54 Helms, *A Race is a Nice Thing*, p. 83.

55 Beaudoin and Turpin, 'White Practical Theology'; Teel, 'Whiteness in Catholic Theological Method'.

56 Malott et al., 'Strategies Used by Whites', p. 146.

57 This is an additional note added in 2022. During the Rwandan conflict, attention was drawn to physical differences between Hutus and Tutsis, following on from colonial divisions.

58 James Baldwin, 1999, 'On Being "White" and Other Lies' in David R. Roediger (ed.), *Black on White: Black Writers on What It Means to Be White*, New York: Schocken Books, pp. 176–80. Originally published in *Essence*, April 1984.

59 Foulke, 'Coming Out', p. 33.

60 Foulke, 'Coming Out', p. 34.

61 Peggy McIntosh, 1998, 'White Privilege and Male Privilege: A Personal Account of Coming to See Correspondences Through Work in Women's Studies' in Margaret L Andersen and Patricia Hill Collins (eds), *Race, Class, and Gender: An Anthology*, 3rd edition, Belmont, CA: Wadsworth Publishing Company, p. 104. First published 1998.

62 W. E. B. Du Bois, 1935, *Black Reconstruction: An Essay Toward a History of the Part Which Black Folk Played in the Attempt to Reconstruct Democracy in America, 1860–1880*, New York: Harcourt Brace & Company.

63 Zeus Leonardo, 'The Color of Supremacy: Beyond the Discourse of "White Privilege"', *Educational Philosophy and Theory*, 36(2) (2004), p. 142, doi:10.1111/j.1469-5812.2004.00057.x.

64 Timothy J. Lensmire et al., 'McIntosh as Synecdoche: How Teacher Education's Focus on White Privilege Undermines Antiracism', *Harvard Educational Review*, 83(3) (2013), pp. 410–31.

65 Leslie Margolin, 'Unpacking the Invisible Knapsack: The Invention of White Privilege Pedagogy', *Cogent Social Sciences*, 1(1) (2015), http://dx.doi.org/10.1080/23311886.2015.1053183 (accessed 10.03.2023).

66 Margolin, 'Unpacking'.

67 Reddie, 'Reassessing'.

68 Leonardo, 'The Color', p. 137.

69 Leonardo, 'The Color', pp. 138–9.

70 William Macpherson, 1999, 'The Stephen Lawrence Inquiry', *Gov.uk*, 24 February, https://www.gov.uk/government/publications/the-stephen-lawrence-inquiry (accessed 10.03.2023).

71 Reddie, 'Reassessing'.

72 Hannah Summers, 2022, 'Racism in UK Maternity Care Risks Safety of Black, Asian and Mixed Ethnicity Women – Study', *The Guardian*, 23 May, https://www.theguardian.com/world/2022/may/23/racism-in-uk-maternity-care-risks-safety-of-black-asian-and-mixed-ethnicity-women-study (accessed 10.03.2023).

73 McIntosh, 'White Privilege', p. 94.

74 McIntosh, 'White Privilege', p. 96.

75 McIntosh, 'White Privilege', p. 99.

76 See Anthony Reddie, 'Politics of Black Entry into Britain: Reflections on Being a Black British Person Returning to the UK', *Political Theology*, 8(1) (2007), pp. 83–95, doi: 10.1558/poth.2007.8.1.83.

77 Refugee Council, 'What Is the Nationality and Borders Act?', Refugee Council, https://www.refugeecouncil.org.uk/information/refugee-asylum-facts/what-is-the-nationality-and-borders-bill/ (accessed 10.03.2023).

78 Leonardo, 'The Color', pp. 147–8.

79 Leonardo, 'The Color', pp. 137–52.

80 David Olusoga, 2016, *Black and British: A Forgotten History*, London: Pan Macmillan; Patrick Vernon and Angelina Osborne, *100 Great Black Britons*, London: Little, Brown Book Group.

81 A. D. A. France-Williams, 2020, *Ghost Ship: Institutional Racism and the Church of England*, London: SCM Press.

82 Kirsten T. Edwards and Riyad A. Shahjahan, 'Navigating Student Resistance towards Decolonizing Curriculum and Pedagogy (DCP): A Temporal Proposal', *Teaching in Higher Education*, 26(7–8) (2021), pp. 1122–9, doi: 10.1080/13562517.2021.1928063.

83 David Haslam, 1996, *Race for the Millennium*, London: Church House Publishing, p. 174.

84 Foulke, 'Coming Out', p. 24.

85 A summary of Paul Kivel, 1996, *Uprooting Racism*, Gabriola Island, BC: New Society Publishers.

86 Reddie, 'Reassessing'.

87 Matt R. Jantzen, 'Neither Ally, Nor Accomplice: James Cone and the Theological Ethics of White Conversion', *Journal of the Society of Christian Ethics*, 40(2) (2020), p. 274, doi: 10.5840/jsce202012731.

88 James H. Cone, 1969, *Black Theology and Black Power*, Maryknoll, NY: Orbis Books; Cone, *A Black Theology of Liberation*; Cone, *God of the Oppressed*. For discussion of Cone's argument, see Jantzen, 'Neither Ally, Nor Accomplice', pp. 281–90, and Kristopher Norris, 'James Cone's Legacy for White Christians',

Political Theology, 21(3) (2020), https://doi.org/10.1080/1462317X.2020.1733741 (accessed 10.03.2023).

89 Jantzen, 'Neither Ally', p. 276; and see p. 285.
90 Cited in Haslam, *Race for the Millennium*, p. 167.
91 Yancy, 'Whiteness', p. 114.
92 James H. Cone, 'Theology's Great Sin: Silence in the Face of White Supremacy', *Black Theology: An International Journal*, 2(2) (2004), pp. 12–13.
93 See Beckford, *God and the Gangs*, pp. 78–80; Anthony G. Reddie, 'Racial Justice for the Windrush Generation in Great Britain', *The Ecumenical Review*, 72(1) (January 2020), p. 86.
94 Cone, 'Theology's Great Sin', p. 13
95 On how White feminism gives permission for White women to fail in the process of growing up, without acknowledgement of the cost, see Kanai, 'Between the Perfect and the Problematic', p. 31.

15

'Turning Whiteness Purple': Reflections on Decentring Whiteness in its Christian Colonial Missionary Mode

PETER CRUCHLEY

This chapter explores how Christian Whiteness uses its power to systemize its prejudices, privileges and preferences using divine sanction for White Christian colonization, civilization and superiority, dressing up its culpable violence as faithful discipleship. It so profoundly shapes what mission is, that mission now continues to operate towards such defaults, even and inevitably in the leadership of the churches Whiteness founded and set free in decolonial acts of the 1960s and 1970s when Christianity embraced the ultimate in Whiteness's vision: 'Mission from everywhere to everywhere'.[1]

While Whiteness is an overarching phenomenon made up of many dimensions, particular focus needs to be given to the role that Christian Whiteness has played in this phenomenon. Churches and mission agencies empowered by Whiteness seeded White supremacy, taught racism and cemented White saviourism; this was constructed around racial capitalism, its own missionary capitalism.[2] Christian Whiteness performs the particular function of exempting itself from the decolonial critique of Whiteness, implying it stood outside the colonial agenda in a reforming moderating role. But the same will to power, tendency to violence and allergy to blame remains at the heart of Christian Whiteness – as it does in the wider construct of colonial Whiteness.

This chapter arises from the task of exposing and subverting the White Christian colonial personae.[3] Christian Whiteness is discussed by rooting it in the three most visible White people present in the New Testament. These biblical figures are then placed alongside figures from the history of a mission organization, the London Missionary Society (LMS), which was conceived in the forging of eighteenth- and nineteenth-century Whiteness, Christianity and colonialism. These indicate how, in mission and church still, we are living out the legacies of these dimensions of Christian colonial Whiteness, even in the decolonial forms these mission movements grew into. It then points briefly to some of the directions for its reparation and further subversion by offering up a new White biblical persona: Lydia, the trader in purple cloth.

White power, systemic violence and mission

Living out the legacies of Pilate and Robert Moffat

Pilate was governor of Judea in AD 26–37 and stands out in the Christian tradition as the one responsible for Jesus' execution. Pilate was a military man; *Pilatus* was a sobriquet that meant skilled with the javelin. *Pontius* indicates he belonged to the Pontii family, from southern Italy; this locates Pilate nationally and, in this respect, 'racially'. The Pontii family had bloody roots in Roman life and politics. Pontius Aquila, an assassin of Julius Caesar, was a tribune of the *plebs*.[4] This suggests the family must have originally been of plebeian origin, of the common order of free people who had done well, rising through the Roman imperial system.[5]

Josephus states that Pilate governed for ten years through very turbulent times.[6] He did so by centring all powers at his disposal on himself. He was head of the judicial system. He had the power to inflict capital punishment, and was responsible for collecting tributes and taxes, and for disbursing funds, including the minting of coins. John's Gospel presents a governor who is only willing to go along with Jewish wishes to execute an innocent man in order to protect the interests of Caesar.[7] Given his plebian roots Pilate knew the risks of an uprising and was determined to maintain at all costs the Roman imperial cult in Judaea, securing his own hegemony in an occupied territory as well as his people's.[8]

Philo denounced Pilate in a letter in AD 41 to Gaius Caesar as 'inflexible, stubborn and cruel'.[9] Thus we begin to see how Pilate represents Whiteness *in toto* as it were: colonial, military, governing, financial and legal power all come to rest in one body. This centring of all forms of influence, power and truth on him is the clearest reflection of what Whiteness claims to be: the norm, the power, the life, the truth.[10]

The persistent rooting by the creeds of Jesus, and especially his trial and execution, alongside the figure of Pilate is to make a combined political and theological point about the location God takes to imperial power. In his commentary on Matthew, Hauerwas quotes Barth on Pilate: 'this Passion of Jesus Christ, this unveiling of man's rebellion and of God's wrath, yet also His mercy, did not take place in heaven … it took place in our time, in the centre of world history in which our human life is played out.'[11] Hence, in the words of the Apostles' Creed: Jesus *suffered* under Pontius Pilate.[12] This then provides us with a metaphor, 'suffering', to name the fruit of Whiteness, which is rooted in the same power as Pilate. Barth ironically links Pilate with Whiteness when he makes a typically White universalizing statement, saying that Pilate represents 'the people *we* belong to and who *we* are at any time'.[13] Re-reading this as a warning statement about Whiteness is sobering and revealing and once again reveals Whiteness as power.

Robert Moffat

Moffat is 'sometimes regarded as the patriarch of South African missions'[14] and Steve de Gruchy described Moffat as one of the greatest South Africans of the nineteenth century.[15] Moffat published his memoirs – *Missionary Labours* (1840) – which went through four editions in the next three years.[16] He was born in 1795 at Ormiston, East Lothian, Scotland.[17] The LMS accepted him for missionary service and sent him to South Africa in 1817. He worked first on the northern frontier, establishing his missionary reputation as a result of his journeys with Jager Afrikaner, whom he sought to 'civilize' [sic] and control.[18] From 1819 Moffat began his main mission work, among the Tswana at Kuruman, creating a mission station, printing press, school and gardens.

Moffat saw translation work as central to the future of the gospel in Africa.[19] His Bible translation is described by de Gruchy and Walls (whose idea this is) as 'releasing the word about Christ ... so that Christ can live within that context, as thoroughly at home as he once did in the culture of First Century Palestine ... No other activity more clearly represents the mission of the Church.'[20]

White historians and commentators, as we can see, are keen to smooth Moffat's reputation and preserve the presence and power he had in the history of mission. However, the biography of him curiously concludes:

> His translation work was a great achievement and his role as a propagandist has rarely been surpassed. However, he never gained a deep understanding of African culture nor any closeness with individual Africans, even with those like Mzilikazi who were fond of him.[21]

This final remark makes one doubt the fullness of the translations he authored. Musa Dube unpacks this and offers a Black counter-perspective, especially critiquing the hubris of a White man thinking he can translate and communicate the indigenous cultures, systems and peoples he a priori despised. This in itself reveals Moffat's propensity for systemic violence.

Dube describes Moffat's work as a huge programme for the cultural translation of the Batswana that proceeded by dismissing, discrediting and abolishing what he considered to be lies, barbarous and antiquated social systems of the Batswana, and replacing them with a Christian spiritual empire. Moffat's translation of the Setswana indigenous knowledge and worldview was a rewriting and manipulation project that served the purpose of displacing the oral culture through viewing all presence and knowledge as absence – blank spaces and darkness – while all people became ignorant heathens, savage people and barbarians.[22] This can be translated as White power, emerging from the wish and will to define truth.

Moffat's *Missionary Labours* reveals the White supremacism at the heart of his ideology and practice.[23] He sees Africa as 'sunk into the lowest depths of ignorance, superstition, disorganisation and debasement'.[24] He further described Khoi people as 'the connecting link between the rational and irrational creation'.[25] Moffat saw Africa as 'a land of darkness and the shadow of death', for it was 'spiritually buried, and without knowledge, life, or light'.[26] The remedy for Moffat was for Africa to yield first to White Christian truth: 'we were convinced that evangelization must precede civilization ... The gospel teaches that all things should be done decently and in order; and the gospel alone can lead the savage to appreciate the arts of civilized life as well as the blessings of redemption.'[27] This high-handed contempt was further demonstrated not just in terms of Moffat's writings or his translations, but in his treatment of fellow Black evangelists.

Moffat and Cupido

Cupido Kakkerlak was a Khoi man who suffered under Robert Moffat.[28] Moffat's systemic violence became personal in the case of Cupido, who appears first in the LMS Directors Report of 1805, where he was described as a 'man uncommonly notorious for vice and distinguished above all pagan fellows for the enormity of his crimes'.[29] Vanderkemp, the LMS missionary in Bethelsdorp, reported some of Cupido's testimony, stating that he 'inquired of all he met for means to deliver him from drunkenness ... when he heard Jesus could save sinners from their sins, he cried out to himself "That is what I want, that is what I want!" ... he was then brought earnestly to seek an interest in Christ, and has now become one of our most zealous fellow labourers.'[30]

'TURNING WHITENESS PURPLE'

An etching of Cupido published in 1816 presents him in Western dress.[31] The LMS used the image to bolster their claims that the gospel civilizes the 'savage'. Following this conversion, he was paraded and celebrated by the LMS as the first ever Khoi LMS missionary in sole charge of a frontier mission station in the Cape. In the same year that this etching was made, Cupido wrote to the LMS of his struggles on behalf of the LMS mission:

> My very dear brother Read
> I go now to Mackoons Kraal, I have prayed to the Lord Jesus, and now the Lord had at last acknowledged me, and now I am in the field and so I came to Mackoons Kraal with Brother Corner. But I must say that I never met with such persecution as here and all my endeavours are vain and the difficulties are so great that sometimes my hope cannot sustain them ... I have been several times out among the Griquas and I gave a revival, but afterwards I met with some discouragement from those from whom I was least to expect ...[32]

The persecutions and discouragement he referenced came, on the one side, from White settlers who were shooting at him, and on the other from fellow White missionaries who refused to treat him as an equal and even abandoned him.[33]

Cupido was a convert from the LMS Bethelsdorp mission station, and the racial equality practised there scandalized a new generation of conservative LMS leadership, who ordered an inspection.[34] Moffat was sent to take charge of the inspection and took against Cupido, writing: 'the appearance of his house and family seems strongly to indicate that he does not intend to rise a hair's breadth in civilisation above them whom he pretends to instruct'.[35] Finally, Moffat ordered his sacking in a letter to the LMS dated 24 January 1823: 'I have heard from unquestionable authority many things which make me abhor the idea of Cupido remaining in the Society's service.'[36] A month later Cupido had to leave the mission station and had taken up with a fugitive slave called Joseph Arend. Cupido's death in poverty is reported some years later.[37]

The reason for this brutal and shameful end lies in Cape Colony race policies. As a Khoi man, Cupido needed a pass to move about the colony and to find work. This pass law, an early form of apartheid's pass laws, was imposed on the Cape Colony and Khoi people by Lord Claredon in 1809. It 'decreed that every Hottentot (or Khoikhoi) was to have a fixed "place of abode" and that if he wished to move he had to obtain a pass from his master or from a local official'.[38] This code consigned the Cape's indigenous population to servitude.[39] The 1837 Parliamentary Select

Committee on 'aboriginal tribes' confirmed this: 'the Claredon code did much towards riveting their chains, as it had the effect of placing them under the control of any inhabitants of the colony'.[40] The 1809 code set the relationship between white and Khoikhoi people as Master and Servant, and the architect of this legislation, Lord Claredon, was invited by the LMS to be its patron in 1812.[41]

Moffat arrived in Southern Africa as an uneducated farmer's son and yet simultaneously an officer of White colonial *Christian* power. Like Pilate, he climbed to a position of authority, standing in for a greater imperial power that he simultaneously captains and apes. But because he stood on the gospel he also claimed Divine sanction, which notably empowered him to build the systems of White colonial Christianity. His powerful piety enabled him to wash his hands of any responsibility for Africa's woe.[42] This power is, as we have seen in the case of Cupido, the power of life and death, exercised as callously as any Roman governor. Moffat roots and nurtures the systems of White Christian supremacism in epistemological and ecclesial forms, which occupy and condemn long after his death – not least in a region that has had to resist the particularly vile and vicious form of Colonial Christian Whiteness: apartheid.

The crucifying and confessing mission of Whiteness

Living out the legacies of Pilate's centurion and the Revd W. C. Willoughby

> Now when the centurion, who stood facing him, saw that in this way he breathed his last, he said, 'Truly this man was God's Son!' (Mark 15.39)

Mark's account of the crucifixion concludes with the ironic testimony of the anonymous centurion.[43] Various Christian traditions grew up around this figure: one depicted the centurion as evil for his piercing of Jesus' side, and so he was punished by being eaten nightly by a lion and having his body grow back each day until the Second Coming of Jesus; another tradition claimed that the centurion became a sincere Christian believer who was eventually martyred for his faith.[44]

Biblical commentators such as Tom Wright write in unironically appreciative tones for the man responsible for executing Christ: 'The Roman Centurion becomes the first *sane* human being in Mark's Gospel to call Jesus God's Son, and mean it.'[45] For many, like Lamar Williamson Jr, the centurion provides a device for the Gentile reader to be represented in the story of otherwise Jewish characters.⁴⁶ In this sense, the centurion is a device for Mark's messianic secret: that only in the light of his crucifixion can Jesus be truly seen as the Christ. Pope Benedict XVI wrote: 'We cannot fail to be surprised by the profession of faith of this Roman soldier, who had been present throughout the various phases of the Crucifixion ... This Roman army officer, having witnessed the execution of one of countless condemned prisoners, was able to recognize in this crucified man the Son of God, who had perished in the most humiliating abandonment.'⁴⁷ How curious that a figure so steeped in the innocent blood of Christ can be so exonerated of the violence he has just performed in favour of the faithfulness he purportedly embodies. At the heart of such a riddle is the power of Whiteness to do violence and then exonerate itself as good and faithful and offer back the oppressor to the oppressed as a sign of righteousness.

Hence the centurion is another signifier of Whiteness in our text, whether he was White or not, because he stands as the enforcer of Caesar/Pilate's White power.⁴⁸ As Centurion he is the trusted servant and officer of imperial power, fully allied with its conceits and conquests; a figure symbolic not just of empire, but empire's self-conceit that it can exonerate its acts of violence with professions of faith.

Hauerwas notes Jesus' silence in the trial before Pilate. Taunted and tested Jesus chooses to remain silent:

> Jesus' silence before Pilate is the silence of the church whenever it is faithful to the witness of Jesus before those who would confuse order with peace. Jesus' silence before Pilate is the silence necessary to unmask the pretensions of those who would have us believe that the violence they call justice is the only alternative we have to chaos.⁴⁹

This is a silence God the Father maintains at the crucifixion. In the other key moments when Jesus' true identity is revealed, the baptism and the transfiguration, the Divine voice announces: 'This is my own dear Son.'⁵⁰ At the crucifixion no such words are spoken by the Divine voice, but by the one responsible for Jesus' execution. The Whiteness of the centurion is nowhere more apparent than when he stands in for God, both because of the power of life and death, but more especially because he speaks over the silence for God and by so doing is absolved of the violence he has just performed.

I will turn now to examine a figure from the LMS Council for World Mission (CWM) history who embodies these two elements of the centurion's Whiteness: speaking freely where he should have remained humbly quiet, and hiding in words of faith acts of violence.

The Revd W. C. Willoughby

According to *The Times* obituary of Thursday 23 June 1938, William Charles Willoughby was born on 16 March 1857. In 1882 he was ordained as a Congregational minister, and volunteered for service in the Central Africa Mission, then newly established by the LMS.[51] Like Moffat, Willoughby was also someone who found in British nonconformity the opportunity for social climbing and class advancement. According to his biographers, census information gives his occupation as 'Painter's boy', but he ended his life as a respected academic.[52]

His particular significance to the LMS was his role in navigating the colonial machinations of Cecil Rhodes and the indigenous resistance of the Tswana people. In 1895 Willoughby accompanied King Khama and chiefs Bethoen and Sebele to England for meetings with Joseph Chamberlain and Queen Victoria, and successfully pleaded for Bechuanaland to remain free of the union of South Africa, acting as guarantor of the good faith and breeding of the Tswana chiefs.[53]

Willoughby made education central to his missionary endeavour, founding the Tiger Kloof school and nurturing a reputation for his own scholarship that resulted in his appointment to Professor of African Missions in the Kennedy School of Missions at Hartford, Connecticut, (1919–31). He wrote widely on African culture, identity, practice and race.[54]

His books were warmly reviewed:

> A more masterful study of the beliefs and customs of a primitive people was never given to this world than this study of Bantu ancestor worship by Prof Willoughby. He has made of his vast accumulation of facts, a book that will delight the expert for its thoroughness and hold the ordinary reader for its undeniable interest.[55]

His main work, *Race Problems*, was critically reviewed and acclaimed by the LMS itself and by others:

> No one can speak with more authority on Race Problems than the first principal of Tiger Kloof, now Professor of Missions at Hartford USA.[56]

> It is not merely accurate, but true to life, *making the reader see and feel as Africans.*[57]

> It is a matter of regret that Native purses are so light, that it will not be easy for many of our readers to possess themselves of this book.[58]

What could Willoughby teach Black people about Blackness? This quotation summarizes much of Willoughby's theory of race and his estimation of Black people:

> Mentally, morally and spiritually, average Bantu tribesmen are no more full grown men than small boys and adolescents are, but they have all the rights that are inherent in immature humans: the right to protection, education, guidance, encouragement, opportunity for development as well as impartial justice in law courts and courtesy and fair treatment in social, industrial and commercial intercourse ... They too are human beings and therefore our brothers. Brotherhood does not mean equality ... the measure of their immaturity is the measure of their claim upon ... the more mature. If we could take that ideal into our dealings with the Blacks, it would crown our strength with patience and gentleman, and we should become redeemers of Africa.[59]

Willoughby realizes the political as well as theological nature of his claims when he addresses the 'race problem' – that is, Black people should be considered equal to their colonizers:

> The question of social equality is one of the silliest questions that has ever been propounded ... We do not grant social equality to people who are glaringly inferior in the costlier qualities of character and culture that are the true basis of superiority. The average Bantu is not the social equal of the average Briton by a long way and it is not reasonable or helpful to ask that he should be treated as if he were.[60]

The key thing about Willoughby is that he does not view himself as being extreme and neither does the White colonial Christian establishment he represents. He purports to be offering a moderate, considered scholarly overview of the history, culture and traditions of a 'child race'.[61] There is no need to further address or broadcast his racist ideology, his use of phenotype to discuss race, the appearance of derogatory terms in scholarly writing, for they speak not of Blackness but of Whiteness, especially Christian colonial Whiteness. He attributes violence and witchcraft to 'Negro blood'.[62] But as Dube alerted above,[63] it is his words that do violence, and all that follows, the occupying and oppressing Black peoples, identities, lands and souls should be attributed to the violence that Christian Whiteness permits. It is in this particular way that Willoughby personifies the centurion – he speaks for God over a silenced Black experience, which he oversaw and profited from as a principal in colonial Botswana and as a professor in segregationist USA. And his words and acts of violence are all obscured behind much lauded words of faithfulness and call into question any uncritical claim for mission as education and empowerment.

The missionary kindness of Whiteness

Living out the legacies of Pilate's wife and Vera Walker

> While [Pilate] was sitting on the judgement seat, his wife sent word to him 'Have nothing to do with that innocent man, for today I have suffered a great deal because of a dream about him.' (Matt. 27.19)

The final biblical White figure of Whiteness takes us to the wife of Pilate, who tempers the system creating power and duplicitous violence in using words of Whiteness with an outcry of apparent conscience and concern. This final piece represents a further mode of Christian colonial Whiteness, which all the time thinks of itself as compassionately doing God's will.

There is little independent information regarding Pilate's wife. The Greek Orthodox Church named her Claudia Procula.[64] Some suggest she also has high imperial connections from the Flavius family, and is related to emperors Vespasian and Dominican.[65] According to the apocryphal Acts of Paul, she was baptized. Origen, in his Homilies on Matthew, suggests that Pilate's wife became a Christian, or at the very least that God sent her the dream mentioned by Matthew so that she would convert.[66]

Mrs Pilate is no less ambiguous a figure than her husband. The conscience of a White woman does not delineate an alternate space in the dismantling of Whiteness.[67] Pilate's wife stands in as the 'Missus', bearing out even for Jesus what 'many Black women experienced: White women as the white Supremacist group who most directly exercised power over them'.[68] She is held up as a symbol of Christian wifely righteousness, and her speaking up for Jesus speaks of her integrity and kindness. But White Christian colonial conscience is no less an exercise in White power, and even violence in the missionary endeavour.

Vera Walker

Vera Evaline Walker was born in Mirfield, Yorkshire, on 24 November 1887 and died on 28 March 1979. She was educated at a private school and at West Hill Teachers' Training College, Selly Oak, Birmingham.

From 1910 to 1916 she lived in London, working at Whitefield's Central Mission, Tottenham Court Road. After a breakdown in her health, she recovered at the Chaldecote Community, Charlton, and returned to educational work. She became a member of King's Weigh House Chapel, London (formerly the Chapel of Thomas Binney), but later joined the Church of England. She was living at Alton in Hampshire in 1953. She contributed many articles to *Teacher and Taught* and other religious journals, chiefly on missionary subjects. She was the author of *A First Church History* (SCM Press, 1936) and *A Eucharistic Calendar* (Church Literature Society, 1938).[69] There is a significant corpus of her work in the LMS archive.[70]

Walker dedicated herself to pioneering a new generation of missionary Christian education, one that she thought would counter the colonial arrogance of the past. She sets out in part her vision in this way (reader alert: racially derogatory term used in the extract):

> The missionary material can be used in a way that will harm the character, and debase both the emotions and the intellect. The missionary material has been frequently used with more zeal than wisdom, to awaken a sense of pity. Pity is, we are told, akin to love, but uninformed and undisciplined, it is often first cousin to contempt. It may well be that the existing adult lethargy to missions is due to the precocious forcing of emotions of pity, unchallenged and undisciplined by knowledge. The 'poor heathen' of the child easily becomes the 'damned n*****' of the adult.[71]

It is clear from the LMS archive how much emphasis was placed on Christian education materials as the means to shape the church in mission and bring in resources for mission and new generations of missionaries. Walker produced many resources for the LMS, like *Adventurer for God*. In her introduction to *Island Play Hours*, she enlarges on the purpose of the new methodologies she was pioneering:

> The object of this little book is to give teachers who are using missionary lessons in Sunday School an opportunity for supplementing their work during the week. Sympathy and understanding in our relation to other races are essential if we are ever to share the best things we have with them. This is true concerning missionaries, and equally true with regard to all who help missionaries. If children are to help the works of missions it must be because of understanding and genuine sympathy with the people of other lands, and without a sense of British superiority in all things! Nothing creates this right attitude in boys and girls

so much as a realization that in games and toys and handicrafts and all things that normal children care for, we have much in common with our brothers and sisters, and that in some things they beat us.[72]

Walker's reforming Whiteness speaks kindly of Blackness but veils the past, and unsees the sin of empire. Walker writes during the First World War, when White empires are tearing up the world in the first global war. Her special pleading further props up White 'civilizing' colonial history (that is, British superiority in all things!), which is now nuanced in terms of give-and-take and fair play on the sports field. Like Willoughby, she feels freely qualified and able to voice Black experience and speak over their silence with her own dramatic voice.[73] Furthermore, even as Walker mildly critiques her forebears, Whiteness and White 'all seeing' is then reinscribed under her reform, in which the fundamental inequalities of relationship are unchallenged. The near normality of non-White children is hinted at, but only at the kind assertion of reformed Whiteness which forgets its co-option to violence, occupation and supremacy.

Miguel De La Torre exposes the purpose of this deliberate 'forgetfulness': 'For white privilege to be maintained, white ignorance must be sustained.'[74] Vera Walker particularly evidences this and her packaging of mission as kind concern helps prosper a vision of Whiteness that absolves itself, and its Christian tradition, of colonial burden and need neither reckon with its past nor make reparation. Her hymn 'Forth Rode the Knights of Old'[75] appeared in the LMS in *School Worship*, 1926, but was in fact written in 1912. Its kind and creative intent is still to recruit yet more Moffats and Willoughbys, certain in their saving Whiteness.

Walker sits within a mission trend still in operation today: mission as serving a world in unity. All peoples of the world are drawn into an integrated humanity promised and defined by a White saviour, now sent from everywhere to everywhere. Access to it is mediated by the kindness of those shaped by Christian Whiteness who can convene this unity and give it acceptable form. Thus Walker can teach the White children about all the other children of the world without context or regard for history. Mission in this way, however kindly intended, is still enacted through the White gaze and calling it 'kindness' blinds only those it possesses.[76] For those under its scrutiny, it is still 'looking down' and leaves unchanged the asymmetry of power dynamics rooted in the legacies of colonization.

These biblical and historical personifications are representations of systems of Whiteness and point to logics and desires that, while rooted in mission under the colonial era, continue to haunt and occupy mission right up to the present day. Even in the decolonial and postcolonial era, mission still operates as a vehicle for seeking the conversion of non-Christian domains, driving churches to see the persistent refusal by two-thirds of the world to convert to Christianity since the Edinburgh 1910 conference as a spur to try harder – rather than renegotiate Christianity's orientation to the plural world. Terms like 'pioneering' ministries/churches point to declining churches wanting to re-energize from their colonizing root and stem decline by fresh bendings of the public space and mind to their norms. In this, Moffat stands as a warning for the forgetfulness of what previous 'pioneers' achieved and embodied.

Moffat, Willoughby and Walker have equipped and sanctioned the supremacist self-understanding of churches, so that – whether White-led or not – they can draw on Whiteness, claiming the privileged position to know and name the realities of a world unconformed to its own image. They can diagnose and speak out, even where God seems silent. They can dress up their disrespect and stigmatizing logic as challenge meant kindly, loving the sinner but hating the sin. All in various ways 'serving' the community. Like Moffat and Willoughby, churches and mission agencies use mission as a device for building their own empires, negotiating and co-opting hegemonic powers and interests, and 'baptizing' them to their own. They are shaping and translating their desires into modes of discipleship that are inhospitable to – and critical of – the persisting diversity of a world they reprove rather than love. The violence of this is clearly shown, whether it is in the hidden burial grounds of the residential schools of Canada and beyond,[77] the active endorsement of violence against LGBTQI people,[78] or the 'sacramentalizing' of Russia's invasion of Ukraine by Patriarch Kirill.[79]

Living out the legacies of Lydia

Key to the decolonizing task for Christian modes of Whiteness is seeking to decentre Christian Whiteness and mission from all the privileged places where it has centred itself. This includes sites of colonial power like economy, education and so on, but for Christian Whiteness this decentring task addresses the text itself. Whiteness needs to decentre itself from its own claims of centrality to the gospel, and subvert itself especially from the key figures of the gospel – like Jesus himself, or disciples like Peter. This is a decentring and reparatory act because such claims have especially buttressed the colonial ideology that Whiteness has brought to the gospel, mission and the Church. Manifesting Jesus in Whiteness and mediating discipleship through Whiteness is itself an act of systemic, epistemic and personal violence, one that still pervades global Christianity, despite 50 years and more of contextual theologies.

The aim of this chapter has been to centre Whiteness on the figures who, in the interests of the empire's 'civilizing' claim, put Jesus to death, dealing with his land, culture, traditions and identity with the same high-handed contempt and self-conceit that we see figures like Moffat, Willoughby and Walker treat Blackness and all people of colour. Gazing at these figures alongside some characters in the LMS archive may help mission further rise up from underneath Whiteness and begin to pinpoint how White Christians/institutions might remove the 'log forest' from the eye of Christian Whiteness.

It might also open up new figures whose identity and discipleship outline some means for Christian Whiteness to undergo metanoia. Consider Lydia in Acts 16, the dealer in purple cloth, who is celebrated as Paul's first convert in mainland Europe.[80] Lydia is a further embodiment of the women of Luke 8, who resourced the mission of the church without placing themselves at its centre or demanding its control. She became in all likelihood the patron of the church in Philippi.[81] For the sake of this discussion, and in illustration of my own rootedness in Whiteness, I have presumed that Lydia is White. Rosalyn Murphy offers a Black womanist perspective on the identity of Lydia and her location on Thyatira to challenge this presumption.[82] She outlines a range of reasons why Lydia may have ethnic roots in Numidia and indeed be an Afropean.[83] I find this an exciting interpretation and welcome the challenge to the presumption that European means White. I hope, however, the reader will allow the argument here to continue if we permit Lydia to speak anew to the dominant model of European as White, even and especially as she may be a Black European.

Lydia poses two key insights for reorientating Christian Whiteness in a counter-colonial spirit: her willingness to place Whiteness within boundaries (inviting it to 'stay at home'), and her desire to resource freely the mission of others without dictating it.

'Keeping her Whiteness at home'

Lydia challenged Paul, in the same way that Zacchaeus challenged Jesus: 'If you have judged me to be faithful to the Lord, *come and stay at my home*' (Acts 16.15). This is certainly to underscore an important act of hospitality and courtesy, one that Jesus did not usually receive.[84] But this has a deeper subversive significance if we read it counter to the history and practices of Christian Whiteness that have insisted God has sent it to stay in the homes and hearts of everyone else in the world, crossing their borders and boundaries, taking their land and wealth for itself, and then shutting the borders to its own home to those escaping the poverty and violence that the afterlife of empire still prompts around the world. Lydia makes no case for coming to Jerusalem to extend her church or her purple cloth business, but instead opens up her home ready to be shown by those at her margins what the gospel is and who is the church.

Resourcing the defiance of colonial violence

After her conversion, Lydia appears again once Paul and Silas are freed from prison. They had been falsely imprisoned and beaten by an antisemitic court and step out into freedom only when they receive an apology from their oppressors. On leaving the prison they went to Lydia's home, which is where they met with the church now based there.[85] Lydia is not instrumental to Paul and Silas' claiming of their rights and standing up to the court. She doesn't try to speak on behalf of Paul or Silas, as some colonial intermediary, nor does she teach them their rights and cause, as some colonial educator. Neither does she try to moderate their message or their claims against the court, like so many White 'allies' do around the struggle to assert that Black lives matter, or missionary movements seeking to evade their decolonial or postcolonial critique as manifestations of a 'culture war'.[86] Instead she gives her resources to nurture and sustain the movement and does not contradict them where it conflicts with her interests. Lydia was a trader and now her leaders had offended the powerful elite with whom, no doubt, she did business. She does not demur or try to speak for the values of her neighbours and friends, but sees them now (and herself no doubt) in a new unflinching light. Lydia goes unnamed in the letter of Paul to the church she founded in Philippi. Perhaps she continued to act as patron without trying to claim the power that money gives to control the agenda and modify the message. Perhaps she drifted from the church as so many White people have who find the church, over generations, belittling, hostile and discriminatory. But Paul's letter to that church shows no preference for the class that Lydia was from, but instead its opposite, and locates Christ's power in the dignity of the enslaved, whose manipulation and oppression by the rich was the trigger to his and Silas' detention.[87]

This decentred resourcing and committing to God's mission points a way for Christian Whiteness to live out the gospel in ways that give back resources; that sustain mission without self-importance and so challenge the institutions and instruments of Christian Whiteness to turn away from their sins, make reparation and be converted to those who walk the path of *suffering* under Pontius Pilate and his descendants.

Notes

1 This is the iconic slogan of the World Council of Churches' 1973 Bangkok Assembly and CWM's own foundation in 1977. It is here meant as an ironic naming of what Whiteness secured for itself through the 400 years of colonialism leading up to it.

2 For more discussion of the term 'missionary capitalism', see Peter Cruchley, 'Ecce homo...? Beholding Mission's White Gaze', *Practical Theology*, 15(1–2) (2022), pp. 64–77, doi: 10.1080/1756073X.2021.2023945. For discussions of racial capitalism, see D. Jenkins and J. Leroy (eds), 2021, *Histories of Racial Capitalism*, New York: Columbia University Press.

3 For more discussion of this, see Peter Cruchley, forthcoming, 'Deposing "Massa Jesus": "Magnificat" Moments amongst a Colonial Mission Archive' in J. Havea (ed.), *Spaces and Positions: Troubling Public Theologies*, Washington DC: Lexington Press.

4 https://oxfordre.com/classics/view/10.1093/acrefore/9780199381135.001.0001/acrefore-9780199381135-e-5234 (accessed 14.07.2022).

5 See https://oxfordre.com/classics/view/10.1093/acrefore/9780199381135.001.0001/acrefore-9780199381135-e-5234 (accessed 28.09.2020).

6 Flavius Josephus, *Antiquities of the Jews – Book XVIII*, http://penelope.uchicago.edu/josephus/ant-18.html (accessed 28.09.2020).

7 Christian Gers-Uphaus, 'The Figure of Pontius Pilate in Josephus Compared with Philo and the Gospel of John', *Religions*, 11(65) (2020).

8 Joan E. Taylor 'Pontius Pilate and the Imperial Cult in Roman Judaea', *New Testament Studies*, 52(4) (2006), pp. 555–82, 582, doi:10.1017/S0028688506000300.

9 See Legatio ad Gaium 299–305 in Edwin A. Judge, 1993, 'Pilate, Pontius' in *Oxford Companion to the Bible*, Oxford: Oxford University Press, p. 595.

10 For my wider treatment of this representation of Pilate and Whiteness, see Peter Cruchley, 2022, '"Savage Healers": The Rhetoric of Whiteness in the Council for World Mission Archives' in Fernando Enns and Stephen G. Brown (eds), *Hate Speech and Whiteness: Theological Reflections on the Journey Toward Racial Justice*, Geneva: Globethics.net/WCC Publications.

11 Stanley Hauerwas, 2006, *SCM Theological Commentary on the Bible: Matthew*, London: SCM Press, p. 229, quoting Karl Barth, 1959, *Dogmatics in Outline*, trans G. T. Thompson, New York: Harper, p. 109.

12 https://www.churchofengland.org/our-faith/what-we-believe/apostles-creed (accessed 14.07.2022).

13 Hauerwas, *Matthew*, p. 230. My italics for effect.

14 Ruth Tucker, 2004, *From Jerusalem to Irian Jaya*, 2nd edition, Grand Rapids, MI: Zondervan, p. 149.

15 Steve de Gruchy, 2000, 'The Alleged Political Conservatism of Robert Moffat' in John de Gruchy (ed.), *The London Missionary Society in Southern Africa 1799–1999*, Athens, OH: Ohio University Press, p. 20.

16 R. Moffat, 1840, *Missionary Labours & Scenes*, London: LMS Press.

17 Andrew C. Ross, 1998, 'Moffat, Robert' in Gerald H. Anderson (ed.), *Biographical Dictionary of Christian Missions*, New York: Macmillan Reference, pp. 464–5.

18 Moffat's biographer Ross describes Afrikaner as a 'bandit' because he led resistance against the Cape government. In truth, Afrikaner was a freedom fighter and he and his family are described as 'the founders of the first polity and people to call themselves Africans in South Africa', https://camissamuseum.co.za/index.php/7-tributaries/5-maroons-orlam-drosters/jager-afrikaner-of-the-orlam-afrikaners (accessed 14.07.2022).

19 'He also translated *Pilgrim's Progress*, compiled a Tswana hymn book, and in 1857 the whole Bible was published in Tswana', from description of 'Papers of Robert Moffat (1795–1883), [ca. 1841]-1875. Edinburgh University Library Special Collections. GB 237 COLL-220' on the Archives Hub website, https://archiveshub.jisc.ac.uk/data/gb237-coll-220 (accessed 14.07.2022).

20 de Gruchy, 'The Alleged Political', p. 26; cf. Andrew Walls, 1996, *The Missionary Movement in Christian History*, Maryknoll, NY: Orbis Books, pp. 28ff.

21 Ross, 'Moffat, Robert'.

22 Musa Dube, 'Translating Ngaka: Robert Moffat Rewriting an Indigenous Healer', *Studia Historia Ecclesiasticae*, 40(1) (May 2014), pp. 157–72, 170.

23 The reader needs to be aware that racial slurs and derogatory language are used in the following text.

24 Moffat, *Missionary Labours*, p. 1.

25 Moffat, *Missionary Labours*, p. 2.

26 Moffat, *Missionary Labours*, p. 69.

27 Moffat, *Missionary Labours*, p. 130.

28 For the main biography of his life, see V. Malherbe, 'The Life and Times of Cupido Kakkerlak', *The Journal of African History*, 20(3) (1979), pp. 365–78, doi:10.1017/S0021853700017369.

29 London Missionary Society, *Reports to the Directors 1805*, London, p. 52.

30 R. Lovett, *History of the London Missionary Society*, vol. 1 (1895), London, p. 504.

31 See https://digital.soas.ac.uk/AA00001571/00001 (accessed 30.11.2021).

32 CWM/LMS/Africa/South Africa/Incoming correspondence/Box 6. My italics.

33 Given this disrespect, it is not surprising that his South African biographer reports that Cupido was never paid by the LMS for his service to them. See Malherbe, 'The Life and Times', p. 375.

34 J. Wells, 'The Scandal of Rev James Read and the Taming of the London Missionary Society by 1820', *South African Historical Journal*, 42(1) (2000), pp. 136–60, https://doi.org/10.1080/02582470008671371.

35 See Malherbe, 'The Life and Times', p. 373.

36 CWM/LMS/Africa/South Africa/Incoming correspondence/Box 9.

37 The archive reports Cupido's death: 'As it respects poor Cupido, Joshua writes that he was attended to by the Backhouses family with the greatest kindness possible, in every respect and that he was with him every day until he died, and that the poor Boy, manifest very great patience and resignation, that his gratitude to those that attended to him was very great, so great that it was impossible to be exceeded and that there is good ground to hope that Cupido has gone to Heaven.' 26 September 1846 (CWM/LMS/Home/Incoming correspondence/Box 9).

38 Brian Lapping, 1986, *Apartheid: A History*, London: Grafton Books, p. 36.

39 Norman Etherington, 'Indigenous Southern Africans and Colonialism: Introduction', in Limb et al. (eds), *Grappling with the Beast*, 210 HCPP, no. 50, 1835, p. 4.

40 W. Dooling, 'The Origins and Aftermath of the Cape Colony's Hottentot Code 1809', *Kronos*, 31 (November 2005), pp. 50–61, https://www.jstor.org/stable/41056535.

41 London Missionary Society, *Reports to the Directors 1812*, London, p. 4.

42 Moffat even acknowledged that in the early nineteenth century Africa was being exploited by Christendom: 'Christendom has been enriched by her gold, her drugs, her ivory, and bodies and souls of men, and what has been her recompense? A few crucifixes planted around her shores, guarded by the military Fort and roar of cannon. Had it not been for British power and sympathy, under the favour of Heaven, Africa to this day, with scarcely one exception, might have had the tricoloured flag waving on her bosom, bearing the ensigns of Babylon, the crescent of the false prophet, and the emblems of pagan darkness, from the shores of the Mediterranean to the colony of Cape of Good Hope.' *Missionary Labours*, p. 1.

43 Mark 15.39, cf. Matthew 27.54.

44 https://russianicons.wordpress.com/tag/longinus/ (accessed 25.07.2022). See also https://www.catholic.org/saints/saint.php?saint_id=11 (accessed 25.07.2022).

45 Tom Wright, 2001, *Mark for Everyone*, London: SPCK, p. 216. My italics.

46 Lamar Williamson Jr, 2009, *Interpretation: A Bible Commentary: Mark*, Louisville, KY: Westminster John Knox Press, p. 278.

47 https://www.vatican.va/content/benedict-xvi/en/speeches/2009/april/documents/hf_ben-xvi_spe_20090410_via-crucis-colosseo.html (accessed 25.07.2022).

48 He may have been a professional soldier drawn from similar south European circles as Pilate, or he may have been a press-ganged soldier from the races that Caesar conquered.

49 Hauerwas, *Matthew*, p. 233.

50 Matthew 3.17; Mark 1.11; Luke 3.22 and Matthew 17.5; Mark 9.7; Luke 9.35.

51 Quoted from: http://jimandhelen.com/William_Charles_Willoughby.pdf (accessed 25.07.2022).

52 http://jimandhelen.com/William_Charles_Willoughby.pdf (accessed 25.07.2022).

53 His obituary in *The Times* framed in glowing terms this contribution: 'In 1893 the board of the London Missionary Society appointed him to straighten out difficulties that had arisen in Phalapye, the capital of Khama, the leading chief among the Bechuana. He soon won the confidence of the native chiefs, and when, after the Matabele War, it was proposed to hand over the Bechuanaland Protectorate to the Chartered Company, he was chosen by Khama and two other chiefs, Bathoen and Sebele, to be their adviser in a personal appeal to the British Government. They came together to this country in 1895, and it was largely due to Willoughby that the protest of the natives was successful.' http://jimandhelen.com/William_Charles_Willoughby.pdf (accessed 25.07.2022).

54 W. C. Willoughby, 1923, *Race Problems in the New Africa: A Study of the Relation of Bantu and Britons in Those Parts of Bantu Africa which are under British Control*, Oxford: Clarendon Press; 1928, *The Soul of the Bantu: A Sympathetic Study of the MagicoReligious Practices and Beliefs of the Bantu Tribes of Africa*; 1932, *Nature Worship and Taboo*.

55 Methodist Recorder, London, 3 January 1929.

56 *Chronicle of the London Missionary Society*, May 1924, p. 119.

57 *Church Missionary Review*, London, March 1924. My italics.

58 *Umteteli wa Bantu*, Johannesburg, 23 February 1924.
59 Willoughby, *Race Problems*, pp. 230ff.
60 Willoughby, *Race Problems*, p. 229.
61 Willoughby, *Race Problems*, p. 251.
62 Willoughby, *Race Problems*, p. 17.
63 Dube, 'Translating Ngaka', p. 170.
64 J. Smith, 'Pilate's Wife?', *Antichthon*, 18 (1984), pp. 102–7, doi:10.1017/S0066477400003166.
65 https://catalog.obitel-minsk.com/blog/2021/11/the-mysteries-of-pontius-pilate-and-his-wife-claudia (accessed 15.07.2022).
66 https://www.stcatherinercc.org/single-post/2017/05/01/Pilates-Wife (accessed 15.07.2022).
67 Jong Bum Kwon, 'Paradoxes of White Moral Experience: Opaque Selves, Racial Suspicion, and the Ethics of Whiteness', *American Ethnologist*, 47(2) (2020) p. 184, https://doi.org/10.1111/amet.12900 (accessed 15.07.2022).
68 Jacqueline Grant, 1989, *White Women's Christ and Black Women's Jesus*, Atlanta, GA: Scholars Press, p. 198; bell hooks, 1984, *Feminist Theory: From Margin to Center*, Cambridge, MA: South End Press, p. 49.
69 'Vera Evaline Walker', *The Canterbury Dictionary of Hymnology*, Norwich: Canterbury Press (accessed 15.07.2022), http://www.hymnology.co.uk/v/vera-evaline-walker (accessed 9.06.2022). *Companion to Congregational Praise*, 1953, p. 531.
70 V. E. Walker, 1947, *The Happy Folk: Missionary Stories Illustrating the Beatitudes*, Archive & Special Collections CWML Z214; V. E. Walker, 1914, *Missionary Play Hours*, Archive & Special Collections CWML Q209; V. E. Walker, 1914, *Missionary Play Hours: (South Seas and Papua)*, Archive & Special Collections CWML Q226; V. E. Walker, 1923, *Sindano Stories from Africa*, Archive & Special Collections CWML Q298; V. E. Walker, 1918, *The Victor's Crown of Gold, and Other Stories*, Archive & Special Collections CWML R435; V. E. Walker and Elsie Helena Spriggs, 1947, *Hero Stories: A Book of Christ's Followers: Missionary Stories which Can Be Related to the Seasons*, Archive & Special Collections CWML Z213; V. E. Walker and B. J. Mathews, 1911, *Adventurer for God: The Place of Missions in Christian Education*, Archive & Special Collections CWML Q215.
71 *Adventurer for God*, p. 5.
72 V. E. Walker and C. M. Preston, 1922, *Island Play Hours (South Seas and Papua)*, London: London Missionary Society, p. 3.
73 This is particularly apparent in her Sindano stories, which she wrote to accompany a painting called, *The Healer*, which was commissioned by the LMS in 1915. For my extended treatment of this, see Cruchley, '"Savage Healers"'.
74 Miguel De La Torre, 2019, *Burying White Privilege*, Grand Rapids, MI: Eerdmans, p. 45.
75 'Forth Rode the Knights of Old', *The Canterbury Dictionary of Hymnology*, Norwich: Canterbury Press, http://www.hymnology.co.uk/f/forth-rode-the-knights-of-old (accessed 9.06.2022).
76 For my further treatment of this, see Cruchley, 'Ecce homo…?'.
77 https://www.afn.ca/policy-sectors/indian-residential-schools/ and coverage by First Nations people of papal apology in Canada: https://indiancountrytoday.com/news/papal-visit-apology-at-last-in-canada (accessed 27.07.2022).

78 See, for example, an article that roots homophobia in Africa as a legacy of Western mission, https://www.huffpost.com/entry/homophobia-christian-africa_n_4675618 (accessed 27.07.2022). Also homophobia in northern hemisphere churches: https://baptistnews.com/article/unprecedented-anti-lgbtq-statement-by-orthodox-church-in-america-should-be-christian-nationalist-warning-sign-to-us-orthodoxy/#.YuJ3lXbMI2w (accessed 22.07.2022).

79 https://theweek.com/russo-ukrainian-war/1011020/war-in-ukraine-is-a-metaphysical-battle-against-a-civilization-built-on (accessed 14.04.2023). See also http://www.patriarchia.ru/db/text/5906442.html (accessed 22.07.2022).

80 For a discussion of the identity and significance of Lydia, see Peter Foxwell, 'Was Lydia a Leader of the Church in Philippi?', *Journal of Biblical Perspectives in Leadership*, 10(1) (2020), https://www.regent.edu/journal/journal-of-biblical-perspectives-in-leadership/lydia-in-the-bible/ (accessed 14.04.2023).

81 Acts 16.40

82 Rosalyn Murphy, 'Gender Legacies: Black Women in the Early Church – An Ethno-Historical Reconstruction', *Black Theology: An International Journal*, 7(1) (2009), pp. 10–30, doi: 10.1558/blth.v7i1.10.

83 These range from the extensive presence of Numidian cavalry, traders and diplomats in that region, on their coinage and the long-held artisanal tradition of cloth dyeing in Numidia. Lydia's profession also prevents her from being Jewish as the molluscs her dye came from would not have been kosher. Murphy, 'Gender Legacies', p. 20.

84 In the context of Luke 8 and the generosity of women, see Luke 7.36–50, where the Pharisee offers no courtesy and little hospitality compared to the woman Jesus meets there.

85 Acts 16.16–40.

86 See, for example, the concept note of the 2021 McDonald Centre conference 'Christianity, Commerce and Civilisation?', https://www.mcdonaldcentre.org.uk/events/2021-mcdonald-centre-annual-conference (accessed 25.07.2022).

87 See Acts 16.16–19, cf. Philippians 2.4–8.

16

'Come we go chant down Babylon'[1]: How Black Liberation Theology Subverts White Privilege and Dismantles the Economics of Empire to Save the Planet

KEVIN SNYMAN

Introduction

I was disappointed. For the most part, my denomination in the UK is politically, socially and theologically left of centre. But in the matter of confronting White privilege by apologizing and making reparations for the legacies of the transatlantic slave trade, we are not much differently located from the rest of the population. Our Legacies of Slavery Task Group processed dozens of replies from congregations and church members to our consultation on the denomination's role in benefiting from that trade and still maintaining the economic, racial and political structures that were set up hundreds of years ago. It's fair to say that not all the responses filled the heart with joy, but the replies that vexed me most were from White voices asserting their right to reframe the way that ethnically minoritized voices cry out against ongoing racialized injustices in the denomination. Do it this way, not that way.

The question of reparations really does seem to poke the bear. I realized more than a few lines in response was going to be needed after I'd read a comment that went something like this: 'It's pointless trying to make reparations for the transatlantic slave trade, because Jesus said the poor will always be with you.' And there it was in flagrante delicto: a Whitey[2] blissfully ignorant not only of the way White privilege operates to crush ethnically minoritized people, but also showing a savage level of ignorance as to how the economics of empire operate to shift wealth from the marginalized Blacks into his own White pocket.[3] Not only that, but he had Jesus, no less, shrugging his heavenly shoulders in diffident resignation because the poverty brought about by empire and racism is really all just part of God's grand scheme. How in the world does one begin to unpack the hidden assumptions in his reply? What mechanisms can be invoked and employed to shine light on, and deconstruct, the power dynamics of an entrenched economic system that privileges the few over the many? How do we unpick the privilege of empire's economics given how deeply embedded its assumptions are in our thinking, expectations and language, and in our political, economic, social and climate-damaging[4] structures? And if we somehow manage to subvert and deconstruct empire's economics, what alternatives are there to put in its place?[5]

I think that Black liberation theology already has some answers to our primary question of how we go about subverting mammon, and that's what we'll be working through in this chapter. We'll want to understand how empire's economics operate; work through why it is such a problem and absolutely has to be subverted; and potentially begin to practise the tactics learned from Black liberation theology's subversion of White privilege to help us get there. In that process, there may just be some hope of beginning to discern some alternatives to mammon.

Money too tight to mention

It may be useful right at the start to state why mammon or empire's economic system is so deeply problematic, why Jesus had such a beef with it, and why Christian economists continue their attempt – unsuccessfully it has to be said – to make it work for good. In his quite exceptional *Debt: The First 5,000 years*, David Graeber wrestled with the question of why our sense of moral obligation so often comes down to the matter of 'paying our debts'. Why is it that money has the profound capacity to turn our morality into an impersonal arithmetic calculation, making us behave in ways that would otherwise be viewed as immoral and even outrageous? Graeber's deep dive into the origins and function of debt is fascinating, and a highly recommended read for anyone serious about deconstructing the economics of empire. Similarly, when the economist Michael Hudson[6] realized that Third World debts could never be paid – nor that of the USA alone, for that matter – he began researching the origins of debt-based economic systems going all the way back to the Bronze Age. He contends that in those early empires the monarch's periodic Jubilee declarations functioned reasonably well as a mechanism to discipline debt's natural tendency to rip apart communities. Jubilee functioned to annul the constantly mounting power of the rentier classes whose power threatened not only his own power, but also the stability of his kingdom through the debt enslavement of his subjects. Western civilization, however, takes on the characteristics not of this earlier period of 'reasonable' control over debt under a supreme monarch, but of the Classic Era. By now, the power of oligarchs had become too great to be controlled by the king and his hated debt write-offs. This and subsequent eras under empire were forever to be characterized by boom-and-bust economic instability; appropriation of lands and social infrastructure by the elite; widespread debt peonage, slavery, mass migrations and ecological destruction; and continual wars of conquest to expand the increased resource access required to pay off state and personal debt. And at the heart of all this nonsense was *money*.

Ask any economist and they will tell you money functions as a means of exchange, store of value and unit of account. If pushed, they will admit that it comes into being *ex nihilo*, through fiat, through the declaration of an IOU. Debt, in other words, lies at the heart of empire's monetary system. The state decides which form of payment it is willing to accept, and then demands that its citizens pay taxes in that form. Ordinary people must acquire that chosen currency. They can do so through the sale of their labour, or the production of goods, or indeed via barely disguised practices of larceny to pay their taxes. Most of the money in any given system today is created by private banks that issue loans on a fractional reserve basis, multiplying the initial debt enormously all the way down through the economic system.

For our purposes of uncovering why money is such a problem, it is useful to understand several key issues about it: the first is that the entire money creation process hinges on loans. If all debts were repaid, then the monetary system would collapse or disappear. The debt can never be paid, which is why so often religions use the language of money to sell their story of guilt and redemption. The second point is that debt creates artificial scarcity amid God's abundance. Debt carries interest, which essentially means that the debt monetary system is like a giant game of musical chairs.[7] Scarcity is built into the system because, while the money to cover the principal debt is made available by the act of issuing that debt, the money to cover the interest never is. That means when the music stops, someone must lose. Someone has to be kicked out of the game because the money to cover the interest on the principal can only come from the principal owned by the weakest players – those at the bottom of the heap, those not pushy or competitive enough to stay in the game. Scarcity, foreclosure, competition, conflict and institutional violence always accompany any interest-bearing debt system. Third, because interest is compounded, any interest-bearing debt system absolutely requires endless growth. Debt will always grow far quicker than any economic activity it stimulates. This, then, drives the relentless pursuit of money. In practice, this means in the inexorable conversion of everything into money – from forests to music and from healthcare to human relationships – one must pay off the original debt or face bankruptcy. Like night follows day, we are all forced into short-term decision-making simply to stave off scarcity, no matter how much money we have. Finally, when economic growth slows as it reaches the limits of its ability to convert the 'commons' (natural, social and other capital) into cash, the debt system increasingly concentrates wealth at the top.[8] Politicians come under pressure to make making money easier – like subsidizing roads into old-growth forests, privatizing social services and ultimately even hollowing out the conditions for its own survival – all to pay off the debt that ironically can never be paid off. As wealth concentrates at the top, ordinary people are forced into poverty, hunger and perpetual servitude. This all means that no matter how much we try to force the system to shift wealth down, it does the opposite, and it does so relentlessly.

The system itself, then, is rigged in favour of the wealthy. We've yet to find a way to force it to be otherwise and, as Jesus fully reveals in action, ministry and prayer, debt in its entirety must be rejected and subverted for the sake of the kingdom. In effect, Jesus is saying: 'In this Domination System, the poor will always be with you', knowing full well that empire's economics are incapable of working for kingdom purposes. Yet with the best intentions in the world, most Christians knowingly or unknowingly still opt to serve – and remain subservient to – mammon. It seems an utterly inescapable reality, this having to use money for our daily bread. Many Christians don't come out of empire. They simply try to find ways to force mammon into working for the common good.[9] This has been shown to be a vain hope given 5,000 years of trying to force the system to work justly, this same system that is now on the verge of destroying the conditions for life to survive on the planet.[10] True hope, I suggest, comes from realizing that our calling is to subvert and come out of empire's economics and work towards alternatives, not to remain stuck in old systems and paradigms.[11] Precisely how we go about subverting something upon which we still rely for our daily bread is a question to which we might turn to Black liberation theology for answers.

'Come we go chant down Babylon'

Allow me a reminiscence. The sunset sky was shot through with saffron orange at the end of another glorious Caribbean day. It was Day Three at The Pegasus, hosted by Council for World Mission (CWM), in the coastal city of Georgetown, Guyana. The NIFEA[12] conference was designed to unhook the church from its reliance on the economics of empire. As we strolled along, I was expressing something of my frustration to my walking companion, Professor Roderick Hewitt, not so much with the analysis of the problems of global poverty and inequality identified in the conference, but more the paucity of the proposed solutions being proffered to remedy the problem of unequal wealth distribution. I felt that the answers we were being asked to adopt were themselves still too caught up in the logic, structure and demands of the economics of empire. How was the church to cure itself of empire if the medicine being prescribed remained reliant on the realities of empire?

Roderick and I were strolling along the coastal seawall that hugs the ocean east of the Pegasus Hotel. We were silent for a time, and I found myself wondering how long it would be before the barricade was swamped by the Atlantic through climate-induced sea-level rises. Georgetown is about 2 metres below sea level, so the environmentalist in me was concerned. In time, our route along the seawall took us close to the historical site of the brutal colonialist suppression of Quamina's Demerara uprisings. It felt like a holy moment. The wall seemed in that moment not to be separating us, but connecting us to the long historical bending towards freedom from empire. We were connected not to past uprisings, but to present possibilities of pushing back against the economic walls of empire that fuelled both poverty and environmental destruction. Roderick was his usual, animated self and in that moment was a doctor not so much of theology as a doctor of the soul. As Roderick shared his love of reggae[13] with me in that God-filled moment, I felt the bricks of Babylon that still clung so stubbornly to my White-stained soul slowly chanted down.

White boy reggae

Theology, they say, is preceded by biography. I am a White, heterosexual male who emigrated to the UK late in 2008, born in Namibia and raised in apartheid South Africa. I had been on a journey of deconstructing my own White privilege since the mid-1980s, when I started my theological studies. Yet here I was some 30 years later being reminded that I still operated from within the assumptions and practices of White privilege. That encounter reminded me – and we all need continual reminding – just how sneakily powerful the assumptions of privilege can be. It was humbling, but also filled with promise. I cannot 'chant down Babylon' on my own. I do not have the tools, the language, the insights, the community and the lived experience to subvert empire without help. I am too embedded within the structures of my privilege. But in a mutually supportive community of persistent love, anything is possible. Roderick graciously engaged in a process of unmasking the 'Whitey' in me by using his lived reality and his instinctive embodiment of the methodologies of Black liberation theology. If an encounter with the liberative praxis of Black liberation theology can subvert the assumptions of White privilege in an implacably racist, White, British-South African apartheid acolyte, then why could these not be used to chant down that other massive area of unconscious privilege for so many in the church called mammon?

Among the many gifts bestowed by Black liberation theology is its capacity to challenge, subvert and transform White privilege. How might this be used to subvert, to challenge and transform the assumptions of domination and hegemony of Mammon? Can it open a path to the Promised Land for the Christian church shaped by, and operating within, the domination assumptions of empire?[14]

Wisdom is better than silver or gold

Such a deliberate exploration would seem to me to be a map for the journey, travelling from an effective, engaging, ever-sharpened critique of race, colonialism and White privilege through a subversion of empire economics, and finally facing up to the most pressing existential threat facing humanity and all higher life forms on the planet: climate disruption. This chapter offers a hint of what that map might look like given the tools offered by Black liberation theology. Without the immediate application of these tools or something like them to the task of dismantling the destructive forces of empire, I don't believe that we will survive as a species.

We have space in one short chapter neither to offer a detailed theology of the subversion of the economics of empire, nor to outline feasible alternatives. We will, however, try to plot a way through the desert towards such a theology and praxis, and we'll do so by taking a detour through the verdant pastures of Black liberation theology. Given how effectively Black liberation theology operates to unmask and transform the unconscious assumptions of White privilege, perhaps it can (and ought to be) brought to bear on one of the foundations of empire's systems of domination: the economics of debt with its devastating effect on poverty, racism and climate disruption. Maybe then Professor Hewitt's chanting down of Babylon along a Guyanese seawall will not have been in vain.

One very White elephant in the room ought to be addressed before we continue, and that is whether it is advisable for a person rooted in White privilege to apply the lessons of Black theology to anything at all, let alone empire. Surely this is a task better left to Black theologians who, as we've already seen, are far better placed intellectually, emotionally, sociologically and theologically to carry out this task? I rather suspect there are many good reasons for me to stop with my 'White-splaining' and to exercise my rather rusty listening skills instead. But I take some encouragement from many of my Black colleagues like Michael Jagessar, Karen Campbell, Lydia Neshangwe, Anthony Reddie and others who have graciously encouraged me to press on in the spirit of James Cone, who welcomed just this kind of response from the primary beneficiaries of empire:

> The development of a hard-hitting antiracist theology by White religion scholars is long overdue ... I know this task is not easy; rather, it is a very difficult endeavor. Yet, do not be discouraged. Despair only supports the enemy. Working together with each other and with the Great Spirit of the universe, we can accomplish more than we ever dreamed. I want to commend people who are fighting structural racism. Keep working at it, 'don't get weary', as the Black spiritual says, 'there is a great camp meeting in the Promised Land' ... To create an antiracist theology, White theologians must engage the histories, cultures and theologies of people of color. It is not enough to condemn racism. The voices of people of color must be found in your theology ... 'What we all want', proclaimed W. E. B. Du Bois, 'is a decent world, where a [person] does not have to have a White skin to be recognized as a [human being].'[15]

Wha' you say? Empire!

CWM's 'Mission in the Context of Empire' has become a critical interpretive framework for my work – teaching, preaching and activism for justice here in the UK. I preach about empire regularly, and as you might expect I do encounter pushback. Empire, particularly in its UK incarnation, is seen by some in a largely positive light, as a thing that, on balance, bestowed immeasurable benefits upon the world. Yes, goes the argument, there may have been regrettable and, by today's standards, avoidable problems, but surely the enormous advantages are obvious. The world is, after all, a better place for it. But, I'd ask, better for whom? Better for Black communities facing the debilitating, ever-present legacies of the transatlantic slave trade? Better for African and Caribbean people whose lands were carved up, and their land, cultures, agriculture and mineral resources plundered?[16] Or better because empire's economics demand the destruction of irreplaceable forests, communities, countries, languages or cultures, all in the name of progress?[17]

People get angry when you start poking holes in those parts of their self-identity[18] that are entangled in what Fabian Scheidler calls the myths of empire.[19] This anger is evidence of the power of empire's ability to manufacture and embed self-justifying narratives. I should know: I had bought fully into the self-identity offered by the myth of White superiority under apartheid. The key issue for me is to take seriously just how terribly difficult it is to recognize, and then step out of, that narrative – particularly if you have been shaped by it all your life. Why is that? Why is it so difficult for people to 'clock' these self-justifications as propaganda? I have some empathy for my audience, to be sure. Look how long it is taking me to divest myself of the myth of White superiority. How much more difficult to recognize, unpick and subvert the belief structures of empire. And so, to help my congregations get to grips with empire, I will on occasion draw a parallel with a familiar concept, the Holy Trinity – Father, Son and Holy Spirit[20] – as a heuristic device to try to explain empire. Imagine, I begin, that empire is something like a kind of faith structure, like Christianity, say, except that empire's shape is not determined by a Holy Trinity, but by an 'Unholy' Trinity. Let's call them state, debt and religion.

Empire as a trinity of state, debt and religion

Empire used to have a limited incarnation. One might think of the ancient Babylonian or Roman empires, or the more recent British empire. But empire, like an untreatable, metastasized cancer, has spread. It has taken root in our language, storytelling, lifestyle, consumption, assumption, structures, economics, media, business, church, sports, charities and religion. The Accra Confession (2004) recognizes this reality as it helpfully describes empire as the:

> convergence of economic, political, cultural, geographic, and military imperial interests, systems, and networks for the purpose of amassing

political power and economic wealth. Empire typically forces and facilitates the flow of wealth and power from vulnerable persons, communities, and countries to the more powerful. The Bible is full of stories of empire rising, over-extending, and falling. Empire today crosses all boundaries, strips and reconstructs identities, subverts culture, subordinates nation states, and marginalises or co-opts religious communities.[21]

'State' in this context refers to the pyramid-like and hierarchized power structures[22] in which an elite occupies the very tip of ever-diminishing levels of power, or ever-increasing levels of poverty. We see contemporary societies shot through with these power hierarchies. We see them in politics, business, charities and church. My denomination, which declares itself 'nonconformist', is shot through with power hierarchies and utterly caught in the grip of empire's monetary system. While perhaps not as obviously hierarchical as our episcopal church neighbours, these power hierarchies continually assert themselves, particularly as the denomination reshapes and reforms itself in reaction to numerical decline.

'Debt' is our Second Person of empire's trinity, and whose character we've already begun to unpack. Unlike the Jesus whose instinct is to subvert debt in order to push power and wealth down, debt's role is to shift power and wealth inexorably upwards. We'll return to debt again in a while, but it's worth pointing out again that within our trinitarian framing of empire, interest-bearing debt is the foundation of its economic and monetary system. Without debt, empire cannot effectively shift power and wealth upwards. Direct and obvious force may be effective in the short term, but for the long haul a far less odious, more stable system of theft is preferable, especially if one can get the 'buy in' from the conquered masses. Debt has proved itself over 5,000 years[23] to be the most effective tool for enabling and justifying this upward shift of wealth. Its monetary system is not only something people can come to need for their daily bread, but it also becomes an 'object' of desire, and even love.[24] Money comes to shape not only the assumptions of what is possible, but it even roots itself in self-identity, and so we talk of being 'ripped off' in a disappointing transaction, as though a precious limb has been stolen from us.[25] So deeply does debt embed itself in an individual and society that alternatives to its money for bringing about the good become unimaginable.

Our Third Person of empire's unholy trinity is 'religion', which in this context implies the preferred self-justificatory mechanism of any particular empire. Empire is so manifestly unfair, so awful and so bitterly destructive that it is constantly under threat of being overturned by the oppressed masses. This blatant inequality is inherent in empire – and much desired by the elite – and requires a deliberate, thoroughgoing and carefully controlled narrative that normally is linked to God's will – a religious imprimatur, if you like. Under capitalism, God is not gone but has morphed into 'the unseen hand of the market'.[26] But for most of Western history since at least the time of Constantine, Christianity has been the empire's primary means of propagandizing the masses. Christianity today, sadly, remains a powerful religion by which empire is baptized.[27] Under contemporary capitalism, empire has co-opted the mass media to do its bidding. The ability of empire to shape the opinions of its victims is demonstrated quite brilliantly by Edward Herman and Noam Chomsky, who begin their 1988 book *Manufacturing Consent* with a quote from John Milton: 'They who have put out the people's eyes, reproach them for their blindness.'[28]

How is it, the authors wonder, that elite interests are so heavily served in societies where formal censorship is not immediately apparent? Why do the poor not simply vote for policies that serve their own interests rather than those of the already wealthy and powerful? How do elites manage to shape the media narrative in a way that naturally filters out and marginalizes dissident views, making the majority honestly believe that they have chosen to interpret the news 'objectively'? 'We had long been impressed with the regularity with which the media operate within restricted assumptions, depend heavily and uncritically on elite information sources, and participate in propaganda campaigns helpful to elite interests', says Herman.[29] The authors highlight several structural filters that are incorporated into mass media, making alternative views hardly conceivable and preventing an analysis or realization of how deeply manipulated news reports are, and how deeply embedded systemic biases are. Today's empires don't require brute force to quell dissent because they have unprecedented tools at their disposal to shape opinion, as Bernays's work on advertising demonstrates.[30]

I find using this trinitarian outline quite helpful when asking Christians to unmask empire within themselves and in society, and to come to terms with just how thoroughly caught up in empire we all are.[31] However, the task of breaking through the brouhaha of empire's self-adulation is brutally difficult. Even though empire is so thoroughly despicable and so obviously anti-Christ, empire manages to project itself as good, kind, beneficent and helpful, especially to its victims. I get to see just how effectively that propaganda works in my visits to churches in the UK, so many of which are still shaped by the missionary endeavour that without so much as a blush declared its purposes as spreading Christianity, commerce and civilisation.[32] In the UK it remains difficult to demonstrate empire's deviousness, because long ago it donned the robes of English goodness and fair play. Its hierarchically cut, Savile Row suit of Christian-infused propaganda has been a vital tool over centuries, convincing the world of just how truly blessed are the gifts of empire.[33]

Subverting Whiteness

Black liberation theologies, particularly in their South African and British iterations, have been a transformative, identity-shaping[34] gift for me. We can use Goba's definition of Black liberation theology as a 'critical reflection of the praxis of the Christian Faith, one which participates in the ongoing process of liberation with the black Christian community'.[35]

As a White South African, I have, naturally, been shaped by the assumptions of White privilege. Apartheid's powerfully constructed and ruthlessly executed gestalt made sure of that. Casting light on, deconstructing and transcending those assumptions is incredibly difficult, as my encounter with Roderick demonstrated. But the ability to cast light on that which is hidden in plain sight is a critical and powerful tool in Black theology. Black liberation theologians and activists, like Simon Maimela, Vuyani Vellem, Lydia Neshangwe, Steve Biko, Jerry Pillay, Karen E. Fields, James Cone, Anthony Reddie, Collin Cowan, Karen Campbell and Michael Jagessar, have sparked my interest as a potential means by which to approach that other issue that I'd been wrestling with for some years, and that is the economics of empire. I would argue that uncovering the hidden-in-plain-sight assumptions of mammon in us and in societies is every bit as, or even more so, difficult. Let's unpack an example of Black theology working to transform a self-confessed, White racist.

Professor Klippies Kritzinger is one of the few Afrikaans-speaking theologians who, at the height of apartheid, accepted Black theology's challenge to unmask his own pretension of White superiority. Kritzinger's work opens a path towards analysing Whiteness, resisting Whiteness and converting Whiteness. Simplifying his work is unfair,[36] but for our purposes we might summarize his approach into a threefold process of what he terms unmasking oppression, humanizing Whites and converting them to the struggle. Kritzinger insists that this task does not fall to Black theologians, but to Whites to awaken their White community to the reality of White privilege.[37] This is not to create pathological guilt, but rather a 'purposeful, systematic re-evangelization and conscientization effort' that liberates Whites to become fellow workers who have meaningful participation in alternative actions for liberation.[38]

This challenge of Black theology to White privilege seems to me to offer the start of a direction, an inkling of how all Christians might begin the process of breaking mammon's hold on our minds, churches, communities and planet, and while we can only but hint at that direction in summary, I do look forward to the day all Christians begin our journey out of Egypt in our quest for the liberation of all.

In summary: Recognizing, resisting and reimagining mammon

White privilege, we've realized, cannot be subverted simply by inviting a select number of ethnically minoritized people into the club. The system itself must be repented of and dismantled. Similarly, debt is a mechanism of economic and political subjugation and enslavement. Once credit is conceived, offered and accepted by the debtor, the logic of wealth extraction, inequality, injustice and the upward migration of power is assured. There may be no easy means by which to extricate ourselves from this 'impossible situation'[39] but inviting the poor to play the game of economic musical chairs does little more than expand empire. Like Jesus, we are called to recognize, repent of, resist and subvert Caesar's entire system of debt that so deeply distorts social relations. We must find theologies, biblical studies and liberative hermeneutics, along with the social and economic structures that refuse to compromise with racism and empire. We must no longer use the Bible in attempts to persuade Christians that if only good people were in charge, they might mitigate the worst excesses of debt, as though a milder and more manageable form of empire might be harnessed to bring about the good. Like Jesus, we must refuse mammon's temptation to allow empire to turn stones into bread.

That of course will be a huge undertaking, and so I'll end by outlining one of the most difficult hurdles to overcome in this endeavour, and that is the stark reality that every one of us is shaped by the assumptions of empire's monetary system. Debt is locked into our language, our thinking, our conventions and expectations. Whenever anyone asks me what the alternatives are to interest-bearing, debt money, I tend to prevaricate and not answer too quickly. I simply don't know. My mind cannot conceive of the possibilities, thousands though there may be. I am too shaped by empire and my imagination has been constrained and stunted by empire's 'There is no alternative' propaganda. It will only be in the act of recognizing, repenting of, resisting and subverting empire that alternatives will emerge. But we dare not tally. Life on this planet may very well depend on our coming out of empire, and Black theology may be the most promising means by which Christians go about saving not only themselves, but the planet on which we depend. In reply to my interlocutor who invoked Jesus to dismiss reparations for the transatlantic slave trade: it's going to take so much more than your and my money to bring about reparations to alleviate the suffocating of both Black people and a gasping planet. It is going to require you and me to lay down everything we hold dear. It will demand, as Jesus warned, our very lives.

Notes

1 Line from the song 'Chant Down Babylon' by Bob Marley and the Wailers.

2 While we acknowledge the problematic nature of this term, we have retained it as it is used by a White writer who no doubt has used it specifically for its dramatic and arresting purposes.

3 No one understands this better than the UK's Bradford-born Black liberation theologian Professor Anthony Reddie. See his excellent 2019, *Theologising Brexit: A Liberationist and Postcolonial Critique*, London and New York: Routledge.

4 'Connecting climate change to such acts of colonization involves recognizing that historic injustices are not consigned to history: their legacies are alive in the present. Researchers have shown, for example, that the scale of bushfires in Australia today – including the catastrophic fires of 2019–20 – is not being exacerbated by climate change alone. It's also amplified by the colonial displacement of indigenous people from their lands and the disruption of their land management practices that skilfully used controlled burning to help landscapes flourish.' See Harriet Mercer, 2022, 'The Link between Climate Change and Colonialism Examined', *The Conversation*, 22 April, https://theconversation.com/colonialism-why-leading-climate-scientists-have-finally-acknowledged-its-link-with-climate-change-181642 (accessed 20.05.2022).

5 It's worth noting here that I'm not able to deal with the question of alternatives to the money system in any depth, for reasons that will become clearer towards the end of this chapter.

6 Michael Hudson, 2018, *... and forgive them their debts: Lending, Foreclosure, and Redemption from Bronze Age Finance to the Jubilee Year*, Dresden: ISLET-Verlag, p. xxiii.

7 Bernard Lietaer and Jacqui Dunne, 2013, *Rethinking Money: How New Currencies Turn Scarcity into Prosperity*, San Francisco, CA: Berrett-Koehler Publishers, p. 41.

8 Charles Eisenstein, 2021, *Sacred Economics: Money, Gift, and Society in the Age of Transition*, revised edition, Berkeley, CA: North Atlantic Books, p. 107.

9 In a very real sense this is what Christian churches, charities and NGOs are attempting to do by trying to force wealth from the top to the poor, and then justifying it theologically. For a typical example of this approach, see Rob van Drimmelen, 1998, *Faith in a Global Economy: A Primer for Christians*, Geneva: World Council of Churches. For a more nuanced but still problematic approach, see Philip Goodchild, 2007, *Theology of Money*, London: SCM Press.

10 A growing number of scholars and activists are fully aware that the economy

is destroying the planet, but not all are quite ready to ditch the system in toto, which is what we are effectively recommending here. See https://news.climate.columbia.edu/2015/11/30/growing-the-global-economy-without-destroying-the-planet/ (accessed 2.05.2022).

11 See Matthew Slater and Skeena Rathor, 2021, 'Relocalization as Deep Adaptation' in Jem Bendell and Rupert Read (eds), *Deep Adaptation: Navigating the Realities of Climate Chaos*, Cambridge: Polity Press, pp. 272–86.

12 CWM attempts to engage with the structural economic inequality in its NIFEA (New International Financial and Economic Architecture) programme. This programme takes as its inspiration the São Paolo Accra Confession that rejects the economy of empire, driven by debt and financialization. See https://www.cwmission.org/wp-content/uploads/2018/10/NIFEA-GSes-meeting-wcc-wcrc-cwm-lwf-joint-statement.pdf (accessed 21.04.2023).

13 See his wide-ranging conversation on this topic in Roderick Hewitt, 'Bob Marley's Redemption Song in Conversation with Steve de Gruchy's Olive Agenda', *Alternation*, special edition no. 14 (2015), pp. 169–89.

14 The relationship between racism and economic exploitation is intimately understood by Black people. 'We live in a world where the wealth of God's creation is concentrated in the hands of a few, and the resources of the earth are pilfered from the poorest and the darkest among us', says the Revd Traci D. Blackmon, 2022, 'Justice Means a Safe Space for All Who Are in Harm's Way', World Council of Churches, https://www.oikoumene.org/news/rev-traci-d-blackmon-justice-means-a-safe-place-for-all-who-are-in-harms-way (accessed 28.03.2022).

15 James Cone, 'Theology's Great Sin: Silence in the Face of White Supremacy', *Black Theology: An International Journal*, 2(2) (2004), pp. 150–2.

16 'Our results show that in 2015 the North net appropriated from the South 12 billion tons of embodied raw material equivalents, 822 million hectares of embodied land, 21 exajoules of embodied energy, and 188 million person-years of embodied labour, worth $10.8 trillion in Northern prices – enough to end extreme poverty 70 times over. Over the whole period, drain from the South totalled $242 trillion (constant 2010 USD). This drain represents a significant windfall for the global North, equivalent to a quarter of Northern GDP. For comparison, we also report drain in global average prices. Using this method, we find that the South's losses due to unequal exchange outstrip their total aid receipts over the period by a factor of 30. Our analysis confirms that unequal exchange is a significant driver of global inequality, uneven development, and ecological breakdown.' Jason Hickel et al., 'Imperialist Appropriation in the World Economy: Drain from the Global South through Unequal Exchange, 1990–2015', *Global Environmental Change*, 73 (2022). 102467 (Science Direct), https://doi.org/10.1016/j.gloenvcha.2022.102467 (accessed 28.03.2022).

17 'We urgently need to destroy the myth that the West was founded on the three great revolutions of science, industry and politics. Instead we need to trace how genocide, slavery and colonialism are the key foundation stones upon which the West was built. The legacies of each of these remain present today, shaping both wealth and inequality in the hierarchy of White supremacy.' Kehinde Andrews, 2021, *The New Age of Empire: How Racism and Colonialism still Rule the World*, London: Penguin, Kindle edition, p. xiii.

18 Angela Franks, 'What Secularization Did to the Self', *Church Life Journal*, 2022 (University of Notre Dame), https://churchlifejournal.nd.edu/articles/what-

secularization-did-to-the-self/?utm_content=194599951&utm_medium=social&utm_source=facebook&hss_channel=fbp-128985777176957 (accessed 17.02.2022).

19 'Every society cultivates its myths to establish and justify its own unique organization. The problem with such myths, however, is that they not only give us a distorted picture of the past, but they also reduce our ability to make the right decisions for the future.' Fabian Scheidler, 2020, *The End of the Megamachine*, Winchester and Washington, DC: John Hunt Publishing, Kindle edition, p. 3.

20 Or if the congregation is already engaged in a process of engaging with patriarchy, I may use Creator, Liberator and Sustainer instead. For a helpful deep dive into trinitarian concepts, language and patriarchy, see Karen Baker-Fletcher, 2006, *Dancing with God: The Trinity from a Womanist Perspective*, Des Peres, MO: Chalice Press.

21 See The Accra Confession (2004), http://wcrc.ch/wp-content/uploads/2021/11/AccraConfession-EN.pdf (accessed 18.04.2022).

22 For a brilliant visual representation of this pyramid of power that is accessible even for children, see Daniel Erlander, 2018, *Manna and Mercy: A Brief History of God's Unfolding Promise to Mend the Entire Universe*, reprinted version, Rochester, NY: Augsburg Fortress.

23 David Graeber, 2014, *Debt: The First 5,000 Years*, London: Melville House, Kindle edition.

24 'Thus, when we claim to use money, we make a gross error [for] it is really money that uses us and makes us servants', says Jacques Ellul, 1984, *Money and Power*, Eugene, OR: Wipf & Stock, p. 76.

25 Eisenstein, *Sacred Economics*, p. 183.

26 'I take this as a point of departure and argue that capitalism is a form of enchantment – perhaps better, a *mis*enchantment, a parody or perversion of our longing for a sacramental way of being in the world. Its animating spirit is money. Its theology, philosophy, and cosmology have been otherwise known as economics … Its iconography consists of advertising, public relations, marketing, and product design. Its beatific vision of eschatological destiny is the global imperium of capital … and its gospel has been that of "Mammonism"…' Eugene McCarraher, 2019, *The Enchantments of Mammon: How Capitalism Became the Religion of Modernity*, Cambridge, MA: Belknap Press, p. 5.

27 Wes Howard-Brook, 2016, *Empire Baptized: How the Church Embraced what Jesus Rejected*, Maryknoll, NY: Orbis Books.

28 Edward Herman and Noam Chomsky, 1988, *Manufacturing Consent: The Political Economy of the Mass Media*, London: Pantheon Press, p. iii.

29 Richard Gunderman, 2015, 'The Manipulation of the American Mind: Edward Bernays and the Birth of Public Relations', *The Conversation*, 9 July, https://theconversation.com/the-manipulation-of-the-american-mind-edward-bernays-and-the-birth-of-public-relations-44393 (accessed 18.01.2022).

30 Herman and Chomsky, *Manufacturing Consent*, p. iii.

31 I am especially grateful for the pioneering pedagogical work in this area that continues, as it has in the UK for well over a decade, by Anthony G. Reddie, 2009 and 2020, *Is God Colour Blind? Insights from Black Theology for Christian Faith and Ministry*, London: SPCK.

32 'The [London Missionary Society] was deeply complicit in the British colonial project and its enslaving practices', says the former CWM General Secretary, Collin Cowan. 'The celebrated LMS missionary, David Livingstone's famous encapsula-

tion of the missionary endeavour – "Christianity, commerce, and civilisation" – can be seen at all levels of the life of LMS. For example, the LMS used slave ships to transport missionaries, "to share the knowledge of the blessed God"; paraded black people as spectacles on deputation visits; produced materials for children and adults that served to indoctrinate Black and White people of the superior calling and nature of White people and the inferior and sub-human status and nature of Black people; and remained silent on abolition until the eve of emancipation.' New Year's Message, 2020, *Council for World Mission*, https://www.cwmission.org/general-secretarys-new-year-message/ (accessed 6.01.2022).

33 See, for example, this poem in praise of empire by Bernard Barton, who seems unable to acknowledge or even comprehend Christianity's role in facilitating the British empire's commercial interests, let alone its racist assumptions of White superiority: B. Barton (n.d.), 'The Missionary' in *The Poetry Nook*, https://www.poetrynook.com/poem/missionary-2 (accessed 27.03.2022).

34 An intentionally racialized discourse is often necessary simply to highlight the unconscious assumptions of White normativity. These may cause 'no small discomfort and estrangement' within one's postcolonial sensitivities where one is 'forced to recognise the consequences of a racial identity that have overridden other identities ... [and] the historical fact that the past [has] privileged my imposed identity. In the process of forging a new identity, a hybrid identity offers fluidity and openness.' Gerrie Snyman, 'Constructing and Deconstructing Identities in Post-apartheid South Africa: A Case of Hybridity versus Untainted Africanicity?', *Old Testament Essays*, 18(2) (2005), pp. 323–44, 344.

35 Bonganjalo Goba, quoted in Klippies Kritzinger, 1988, 'Black Theology – Challenge to Mission', doctoral thesis, University of South Africa, p. 56.

36 For a penetrating analysis and expansion of Kritzinger's pioneering work, see George Jacobus van Wyngaard's doctoral thesis, 2019, 'In Search of Repair: Critical White Responses to Whiteness as a Theological Problem – A South African Contribution', Vrije Universiteit Amsterdam and University of South Africa.

37 See O. J. Phakhathi in Kritzinger, 'Black Theology', p. 200.

38 Mothlabi Boesak and Phakhati in Kritzinger, 'Black Theology', p. 201.

39 Maurizio Lazzarato, 2012, *The Making of Indebted Man: An Essay on the Neoliberal Condition*, trans. Joshua David Jordan, Los Angeles, CA: Semiotext(e), pp. 8ff.

17

'Holding the space': Troubling 'the facilitating obsession of whiteness' in Contemporary Social Justice-focused Models of Mission

AL BARRETT AND RUTH HARLEY

The facilitating obsession of whiteness performs less a consistent set of characteristics and more a consistent refusal – a refusal to envision shared facilitation, a refusal to place oneself in the journey of others, a refusal of the vulnerability of a centerdness from below (rather than from the towering heights of whiteness), where the sense of my own formation is not only still open, but where I am willingly changed not by a nondescript other but by nonwhite peoples historically imagined at the sharp point of instruction. In short, this is a refusal to release oneself to the crowd.[1]

We write as two White[2] clergy, theologians and activists, who simultaneously yearn, pray and work for the justice of God's kin-dom, and at the same time recognize and wrestle with the ways in which our own entanglement in the forces and structures of White supremacy hinder our – and other people's – reception of the life of the kin-dom in all its fullness. In relation specifically to the church's participation in the mission of God, this has for us highlighted the problematic dynamics of over-identifying ourselves with a busily activist 'social justice Jesus' in ways that lead us to retain agency and power in our interactions with our neighbours under the guise of positioning ourselves as 'provider' or 'advocate'.[3] We have also reflected critically on the 'guest/host' dynamic in mission, and the way in which White people identifying with 'Jesus the host' reinforce hierarchical structures of power and privilege.[4]

Here we seek to further those critical explorations by turning our attention to practices of *facilitation*: an attractive model for those of us committed to working collaboratively in building community, nurturing leadership and pursuing justice, seeking to 'hold space' for others to speak and act, including those whose voices are most often silenced or ignored. While facilitation is often framed within an awareness of dynamics of privilege and oppression as a more equitable way of working, it is, however, far from a neutral process. The role of the facilitator is in itself a place of power, and the choices to hold or relinquish space, to intervene or stand back, to hear or ignore particular voices within that space, are in themselves expressions of power. When Willie James Jennings names 'the facilitating obsession of whiteness', he problematizes the idea of facilitation – at least in the hands of White people – much more widely than the context of theological education from which he writes.

In this chapter we seek to get under the skin of this 'facilitating obsession of whiteness' by 'troubling' the metaphor of 'holding the space', by opening ourselves to the interruptions and critiques of Jennings and other Black theologians and theorists as they work critically with the ideas of 'hold', 'space' and 'speaking'. Learning from those disruptive engagements, we will come to refuse the idea of 'the good white facilitator', committing ourselves to relinquish neutrality, inhabit ambivalence, acknowledge our particularity and embrace our limitedness. Finally – and seeking to resist the temptation to write any authoritative 'last words' – we will, first, playfully explore some interrelated organic spatial images (the clearing, guerrilla gardening, rewilding and common ground) that might help take us 'beyond facilitation' towards alternative forms of solidarity; and, second, briefly examine the desire for *reconciliation*, as an example of (White) facilitation in action, which urgently needs reimagining.

> ***whiteness*** (n.)
> - 'an ongoing and unfinished history, which orientates bodies in specific directions, affecting how they "take up" space and what they "can do"'.[5]
> - 'a way to think the world ... a violent encounter ... and way of life that is fundamentally about the interdiction, the desired theft, of the capacity to breathe'.[6]

Rooted in histories of colonialism and slavery, Whiteness is entangled in the capacity for 'property ownership' – 'possession, control, and mastery'[7] of both people and spaces – and the right to exclude.[8] As Willie James Jennings carefully lays bare, colonial Whiteness 'turned the whole world into commodities', 'strangl[ing] the possibilities of dense life together' and shattering the world into 'fragments': 'land and animals taken; practice and rituals, dance and songs, ancient word and inherited dream, thoughts and prayers existing only in slice and sliver, piece and shard'.[9]

Writing interrupted

Working in 'fragments' is, for Jennings, on the one hand a glorious inevitability of our *being creatures who can only apprehend with our senses – in bites, in touches, in smells, in sounds, and in focused but shifting sight'* – but on the other hand is also a tragic consequence of colonial Whiteness, a 'mangling' of both our capacity and desire to pay 'constant full attention to one another'.[10]

In seeking better to understand, renounce and step away from 'the facilitating obsession of whiteness', then, we take an intentionally 'fragmented-yet-attentive', approach to our writing here. First, we are consciously *following after* the work and witness of Black theologians and theorists who have seen already what we only see belatedly. Their words, without mediation or appropriation, come first in nearly all the sections of this chapter, and offer the challenges and revelations to which we seek to respond, with a spirit of radical, penitential receptivity and tentative exploration. We seek to embrace what feminist and womanist theorists have named as 'epistemic diversity':[11] the understanding that our ways of knowing are enriched by engaging with multiple sources, including those we experience as 'other'. When the Black British writer Emma Dabiri speaks of 'blackness as a system of knowledge',[12] she is describing knowledge that we (as White theologians) expect to interrupt, challenge and change us as we engage with it appreciatively, curiously and receptively; but she names also a system in which we cannot claim any place as participants, in relation to which we will always be 'the other', 'the outsider', and that is emphatically not a resource for us to appropriate for our own ends.

Second, as far as is possible in a piece of writing co-authored by two White people, we attempt to write in ways that resist the authoritative 'last word', but rather seek to open up ourselves and our writing to being interrupted by voices of resistance, reshaping and contradiction – both within and beyond this text. Jennings, as a Black theologian, names a vocation 'to work in fragments, trying to tie together, hold together, the witness of our peoples. Weaving the sounds, songs, and stories that are only fleeting echoes of what was.'[13] As White theologians writing here, however, we seek to resist in ourselves any temptation to prematurely 'bring together' what is fragmented, which might conveniently paper over the radical fissures that Whiteness has wrought.[14] We intend to offer here no definitive framework or 'answer' to the problem of 'the facilitating obsession of whiteness', but rather to try to identify the problem more clearly, ground ourselves more thoroughly in our own locatedness and particularity, and highlight precisely the limitedness of our perspectives, knowledge and capacity to act for change. We write here, consciously, in fragments, recognizing that the integration of those fragments (and many other fragments beyond those here) into a new coherent whole is not a task we can complete on our own.

facilitation (n.)
- 'the process of making something possible or easier'
- 'the act of helping other people to deal with a process or reach an agreement or solution without getting directly involved in the process, discussion, etc., yourself'[15]

7 steps of facilitation:[16]
1. Set the boundaries
2. Remain impartial
3. Understand group dynamics
4. Use your personal style
5. Intervene when appropriate
6. Handle difficult situations
7. Practise, practise, practise

'Facilitation' is an attractive idea – who wouldn't want to be involved in 'making something possible or easier'?! – and especially for those of us who, conscious of our multi-dimensional structural power and privilege, consciously resist more obviously 'heroic', autocratic and didactic ways of contributing to change. But neither the dictionary definitions, nor the '7 steps of facilitation', address directly two fundamental questions: the *who?* (identity) and the *where?* (social/structural location) of the body seeking to 'hold the space' – and the inevitable limitations and potential dangers that those two factors bring.

When Jennings critiques 'the facilitating obsession of whiteness', he places 'facilitating' alongside three related terms that further highlight the problematic dynamics of Whiteness at work: 'convening', 'gathering' and 'refereeing'. Common across Jennings's examinations of these dynamics, within colonial history – and in theological education more specifically – is an *exclusivity* and a 'desire rooted in control': 'only they [Europeans] could gather the world, and only they understood the gathering of the world'; 'rarely if ever have people or peoples been allowed to name and voice [their] disagreements separate from the refereeing positioning of whiteness'.[17] Facilitation's desire to 'help other people ... without getting directly involved ... yourself' (*Cambridge English Dictionary*) uncannily reflects the desire of Whiteness to remain invisible, distant and unchallenged, by presenting as 'neutral' but in fact functioning as powerfully normative and framing in its gaze and interventions.[18]

As we consider facilitation's entanglement with Whiteness, then, perhaps an early question should be: *for whom* is facilitation making things 'easier'? And what is to be done with those things that are unavoidably difficult, uncomfortable and troubling? Indeed, in this chapter where we raise more questions than offer too-easy answers, our first modest proposal is that 'facilitation' needs problematizing, troubling, and that these two dynamics – 'facilitation' and 'troubling' – need to be held together in an ongoing tension. If those of us who are racialized as White are to continue to contribute to processes of facilitation, we need also, as Donna Haraway has put it, to find ways of 'staying with the trouble' – resisting the various heroic, future-orientated temptations towards 'clearing away the present and the past' in order to 'mak[e] an imagined future safe' for 'coming generations'. Instead we need to be 'learning to be truly present ... as mortal critters in myriad unfinished configurations of places, times, matters, meanings', with the clear and present aim of 'intentional kin making across deep damage and significant difference'.[19] We cannot participate in the 'kin making' – forming new and different bonds of solidarity – without grappling with the 'deep damage [both past and present] and significant difference'.

To the White temptation to facilitation and 'making things easier', then, George Yancy issues this plea:

> I encourage whites to dwell in spaces that make them deeply uncomfortable ... to *delay* the hypothetical questions, to *postpone* their reach beyond the present. Reaching too quickly for hope can elide the importance of exposure ... The unfinished present is where I want whites to tarry (though not permanently remain), to listen, to recognize the complexity and weight of the current existence of white racism, and to begin to think about the incredible difficulty involved in undoing it.[20]

hold (v., n.)

(v.)
- 'to organize or cause a meeting ... to happen'
- 'to contain or be able to contain something'
- 'to have something, especially a position or money, or to control something'

(n.)
- 'the space in a ship ... in which goods are carried'

- 'power or control over something or someone'
- 'a position in which one person holds another person so that they cannot move'[21]

In her book *In the Wake: On Blackness and Being*, Christina Sharpe attends to 'the afterlives of slavery', 'in the wake' of which 'the past that is not past reappears, always, to rupture the present': human beings reduced to commodities to be owned, bought and sold; 'cargo' to be shipped, packed into the ship's hold, marked only as 'differently sized and weighted property', thrown overboard in order for their owners to claim insurance.[22] Members and corporate bodies within the Church of England (in which we are both now ordained ministers) held slaves and plantations, and received generous compensation for slaves freed under the 1833 Abolition of Slavery Act.[23] And, as Sharpe observes, 'The holds [continue to] multiply.'[24] In 2017, Black people made up 12 per cent of those held in prison in England and Wales, despite comprising only 3 per cent of the overall population. Some 41 per cent of prisoners aged under 18 were categorized as Black, Asian or from other ethnic minorities.[25] In the USA, Eric Garner in 2014, and George Floyd in 2020, are just two prominent names among the countless Black victims of White supremacist state violence, suffocated to death in the chokehold of White police officers. 'In the weather of the wake,' as Sharpe puts it, 'one cannot trust, support, or condone the state's application of something they call justice, but one can only hold one's breath for so long.'[26]

These anti-Black 'holds', however, are rarely explicitly acknowledged as part of the 'atmosphere' of White-facilitated spaces. If Whiteness 'holds' through habits (as Sara Ahmed puts it), these include a habitual *forgetfulness*[27] – both willed and unwilled – of the 'deep damage' wrought by its history and its ongoing present. Facilitation all too often becomes yet another form of incarceration when it imagines that the space it seeks to hold is untouched by the 'hold baggage' of colonialism's history and its anti-Black afterlives.

Meanwhile, uncomprehended by Whiteness' gaze, a different kind of gathering has been going on, a product of White colonialism's hold, and yet breaking free from its control. There is an unsettled 'undercommons', a 'fugitive' space of unintended solidarity, as the Black theorists Fred Moten and Stefano Harney put it:

> Never being on the right side of the Atlantic is an unsettled feeling, the feeling of a thing that unsettles with others. It's a feeling, if you ride with it, that produces a certain distance from the settled, from those who determine themselves in space and time, who locate themselves

in a determined history. To have been shipped is to have been moved by others, with others. It is to feel at home with the homeless, at ease with the fugitive, at peace with the pursued, at rest with the ones who consent not to be one ... The hold's terrible gift was to gather dispossessed feelings in common, to create a new feel in the undercommons ... Though forced to touch and be touched, to sense and be sensed in that space of no space, though refused sentiment, history and home, we feel (for) each other ... a feel you want more of, which releases you.[28]

space (n., v.)
- (n.) 'an empty area that is available to be used'
- (n.) 'the area around everything that exists, continuing in all directions'
- (v.) 'to arrange things or people so that there is some distance or time between them'[29]

We have already begun to explore how Whiteness, as the ongoing afterlife of colonialism, redefines space as *property*, within which Whiteness maintains both a centrality and the power to exclude its 'others'. In the entangled histories of colonialism and mission, space as 'an empty area that is available to be used' has allowed White settlers and missionaries to enact violence, subjugation and genocide against indigenous peoples and cultures in the name of the 'three Cs' of colonialism – commerce, civilization and Christianity[30] – a mindset that still insidiously pervades much mission thinking today, where the 'missional flow' is one of territorial expansion, or of outpouring into supposedly 'empty' spaces.[31]

Space as White property – and the 'discomfort' of Blackness

As the womanist theologian Kelly Brown Douglas observes, 'stand-your-ground culture' in the USA is rooted in the sense of entitlement of Whiteness, to occupy space, to claim ownership of space, and to exclude others – and, most particularly, *Black* others – from those spaces.[32] Similarly, the Black British feminist theorist Sara Ahmed highlights the ways Whiteness assumes an entitlement to 'comfort' and 'ease' within the spaces it inhabits – a 'comfort' and 'ease' that Black bodies can all too easily disturb.[33] Pursuing this embodied logic a few steps further, the Black American trauma therapist Resmaa Menakem describes the – different but interrelated – protective, reflexive responses of White and Black bodies when they find themselves in proximity with one another:

Just as many white bodies go on alert when they sense a Black body nearby, many Black bodies also go on alert when they sense a white one in the vicinity. But there is a crucial difference here: The white body tends to shift into immediate self-protection; but the Black body is habituated to shift into *soothing the white body* as a self-protective strategy.[34]

So often, then, it is *Black* bodies that make life easier (the root meaning of 'facilitation') for anxious White bodies. But what if the former were to refuse such a role? Ahmed describes the 'pleasure and excitement' of 'a world opening up', which begins with 'ordinary feelings of discomfort'. 'Discomfort', she suggests, 'allows things to move [rather than being 'stuck'] by bringing what is in the background, what gets overlooked as furniture, back to life.' The insistent presence of Black bodies in White spaces 'disorientates how things are arranged', in ways that can be potentially transformative.[35]

Black spaces of escape

Whenever Whiteness occupies space, the spectre of 'the hold' reappears: Black bodies are thrown out, and/or thrown together, in attempts to erase both their particularity and their right to take up space. And as Moten and Harney have already hinted, and Toni Morrison has told in narrative form, Black bodies have always found or created spaces of escape from 'the hold': 'clearings',[36] spaces of sanctuary and 'fugitive' solidarity. Even then, however, Whiteness doesn't give up on its project of occupation and colonization – often under the supposedly 'benign' guise of 'allyship' or 'solidarity'. Ahmed shares her experience of attending a Black caucus within an overwhelmingly White academic event, only to find that almost half of those in the room were White, despite it being made clear that this was a space for people of colour:

> It felt as if the one space we had been given – to take a break from whiteness – had been taken away. From the accounts offered, there were clearly different ways that white people had given themselves permission to turn up at a black caucus: being interested in questions of race; a sense of solidarity, alliance, and friendship; a desire to be at a workshop rather than a traditional academic session; a belief that race didn't matter because it shouldn't matter. Those of us of colour tried hard – in different ways – to speak about why we wanted this event to be a person of colour event ... Eventually, a white person left in

recognition ... A second white person left, but aggressively, saying we had made her unwelcome ... One by one the white people left, each offering an account of leaving, and a different account of why they had come. When the black caucus became itself, such joy, such relief! Such humour, such talk! What I learned from this occasion was the political labour that it takes to have spaces of relief from whiteness. I also realised the different ways that whiteness can be 'occupying'.[37]

Those of us who are White need to hear Ahmed's story as a sharp challenge to our 'good intentions', particularly when those are framed in terms of 'solidarity' as 'being with' – a challenge to which we will return later.

speak (v.)
- 'to say words, to use the voice, or to have a conversation with someone'
- 'talking from a particular point of view'
- 'to show or express something without using words'[38]

Due to the effects of racialized oppression and marginalization, many black people may well be suspicious or even reluctant to talk in depth about personal stories or experiences. This reluctance is exacerbated if the person seeking to initiate or facilitate the conversation is a White European.[39]

In previous writing we have done together, we have made much of what the White feminist Nelle Morton termed 'hearing one another to speech': creating the conditions, the environment, for something to be articulated that has perhaps never been expressed before, that has the potential to change radically both the speaker and the hearer, in not just heart and mind but across one's whole sense of self-identity.[40] We noted there that Morton's terminology emerged from hearing practices among circles of women, and assumed a mutuality and an equality of power that might not, in fact, be the case in a mixed-gender group – or, indeed, a group that included inequalities produced by race or class.[41]

Here, mindful of Anthony Reddie's observation above, we need to state that latter point more sharply: however keenly we may desire to contribute to 'hearing others to speech', however skilled we may be in the art of facilitation, the very presence of our White bodies may in fact present an obstacle that prevents others – especially Black others – from speaking. This may partially stem from participants' past experience of how their words, shared vulnerably, have been dealt with by White people. It may also reflect the 'mangling of attention' that Willie James Jennings identifies as a characteristic of Whiteness. Just as Mayra Rivera (herself building on the work of Frantz Fanon) describes the White 'racializing gaze' as both rigidly objectifying what is seen, and narrowing and distorting the perceptive capacity of the seer[42] (what Mary McClintock Fulkerson calls a 'power-related willingness-not-to-see'[43]), so we discover through the work of Reni Eddo-Lodge, for example, the distorting effects of Whiteness on 'White listening', a 'power-related willingness-not-to-*hear*':

> I can no longer engage with the gulf of an emotional disconnect that white people display when a person of colour articulates their experience. You can see their eyes shut down and harden. It's like treacle is poured into their ears, blocking up their ear canals. It's like they can no longer hear us ... Their throats open up as they try to interrupt, itching to talk over you but not really listen, because they need to let you know that you've got it wrong.[44]

Just because we are not hearing, however, does not mean nothing is being spoken. In the following brief sections, we explore four ways in which such Black 'speaking' can happen within and beyond the earshot of Whiteness, in ways that confront and disrupt the latter's obsession with facilitation.

Non-verbal 'speaking'

Resmaa Menakem has already drawn our attention towards the non-verbal communication between bodies racialized as 'White' and 'Black', when they find themselves in close proximity to each other. Both Douglas and Crawley observe, further, that Whiteness imposes 'cultural standards of "respectability"' that limit what counts as a contribution to conversation. For Douglas, it is these standards that function to exclude the 'wildness' of the Black woman's body, even within the Black church.[45] For Crawley, a narrowly understood concept of what counts as 'intellectual' disregards a whole spectrum of profoundly significant non-verbal and affectual communication as:

> excessive performances, unnecessary because of their purported lack of refinement, discardable because of their seeming lack of intellectual rationality and rigor. And this is because the flesh performing such aesthetic practices, the intellectual capacity, the capacity for thought and imagination, came to be racialized and gendered, and such racializing and gendering meant the denigration of black flesh.[46]

What Crawley names 'Blackpentecostal breath' exceeds the boundaries of what White space-holding deems 'appropriate'.

Talking back

Turning to verbal communication, the womanist biblical scholar Mitzi Smith reads the story of the Syrophoenician woman (Mark 7.24–30) as highlighting the power of 'sass' and 'talk back', particularly by women who have so often 'been labelled as troublemakers, castigated, marginalized, and ostracized'. Here is a woman, a racialized 'other', 'standing her ground' – not with the defensiveness, possessiveness and aggression of the White 'stand-your-ground' culture that Douglas has laid bare, but as an act of resistance, rebellion and refusal – her talking back 'a legitimate form of agency and method of truth telling', 'call[ing] our attention to and challeng[ing] unjust, biased, and oppressive traditions, laws, and expectations', 'in the face of corrupt, biased, life-threatening and [life-] denying authority'.[47]

Anger and rage

Whether expressed verbally or non-verbally, Whiteness seems to be most troubled by *anger* – and, specifically, *Black* anger – as an existential threat to the spaces Whiteness seeks to hold. For Cole Arthur Riley, this sense of threat has deep roots, and those roots lie in Whiteness' inability to face *itself*:

> Black anger has been forced into hiding by whip and chain and hose for so long that when whiteness encounters Black emotionality now, it still feels thoroughly alien ... For [White] people who have rarely practiced or processed their own rage well, it can only be deeply threatening to see anger operating elsewhere, even if that anger is ever so righteous and necessary for the life and dignity of the world. Whiteness's rage cannot conceive of such an anger, because it has never known it in itself.[48]

Silence as refusal

Finally, there may be some situations in which silence itself can 'speak'. The Black theorist Fred Moten considers the 1857 legal case of an enslaved woman Betty who, without a word documented, refuses the freedom offered her by the Massachusetts court. Can Betty's silent decision be anything other than a deeply ingrained submissiveness? Moten believes so: Betty's refusal, on his reading, claims a freedom *beyond* the legal system that still seeks to claim her body as its property. 'Betty's story ... which she neither owns nor tells, in the very fact of its having been withheld from the court, obliterates the court.'[49] Her chosen 'nonperformance', her refusal of the choices on offer, 'shakes the power of those doing the offering'.[50]

Challenges to White facilitation

White facilitation may have the best of intentions to create environments where we can 'hear one another to speech'. These four brief examples, however, highlight at least two things. First, how White obliviousness, White expectations of 'civility', 'propriety' or 'respectability', White defensiveness and unprocessed White rage can, unknowingly, block the very possibilities of speech that we claim we desire. And second, how the communication of Black bodies, both verbal and non-verbal, can exceed, expose, challenge, disrupt and refuse the terms and conditions of White 'space-holding'.

Revisiting facilitation: 'Released to the crowd'

Once the 'facilitating obsession of whiteness' is exposed, then, how might those apparently innocuous '7 steps of facilitation' look now? We might rephrase them as critical questions, within which Whiteness is made visible:

1 *Who gets to 'set [and police] the boundaries'* – when Whiteness treats spaces either as already 'held' as [white] property (that is, the boundaries are for the protection of that property), or as inviting White occupation (that is, any boundaries can be transgressed by Whiteness)?
2 *Who gets to 'remain impartial'* – when Whiteness seeks invisibility, masquerading as neutrality, while rigorously 'refereeing' those deemed 'other'?
3 *How well do we 'understand group dynamics' and 'read the room'* – when Whiteness is both forgetful of its history (and that history's ongoing effects), and oblivious to the many things it has been trained not to see and hear?
4 If *'using your personal style'* requires *'respect and trust'*, who is *treated*

as 'trustworthy' within the space, and where might we who are White be a 'trust risk' ourselves?
5 How 'appropriate' might it be for us to 'intervene' – when Whiteness thrives in a position of judging what is 'appropriate', and takes 'intervention' as its inalienable right?
6 Similarly, *can we be trusted to 'handle difficult situations'* (for example, 'difficult and disruptive people', conflict and so on) – when Whiteness is entangled with norms of 'respectability' and 'order', and is prone to respond to anger with defensiveness and even violence?
7 Is *'practise, practise, practise'* really enough …?

Inhabiting ambivalence

The assumption behind this final 'step' is that 'good' facilitation is ultimately about skills and technique, both of which can be improved with practice. Here Sarah Todd, a critical White theorist of community development (for us an area that overlaps significantly with our attempts at facilitation), notes the tendencies in that field for White practitioners to take a 'hopeful, heroic stance' which 'tends to obscure' the 'multiple', 'contradictory' and 'ambivalent' effects of community development practice, 'some facilitating progressive change and others re-inscribing oppressive relations … *despite the good intentions and skills* of … practitioners'. For Todd, at the root of this ambivalence is the fact that, almost by definition, 'community development creates the discursive and performative space for white bodies to know, evaluate, and intervene in the collective lives of racialized bodies'.[51] Even when practitioners seek intentionally to deploy 'strategies' to 'guard against the temptations of colonialist practice', Todd argues, such as a critical self-awareness and a receptivity to the contributions and critique of others, the working assumption is that the White community worker's identity can somehow be 'reworked' as 'genuinely anti-colonialist', an 'ethical white subject' located '*outside* of oppressive relations': the 'good [White] community worker'.[52]

By extension, we want to let go of the imagined existence of the 'good white facilitator', and of a similar array of 'techniques' that such a person might deploy. This goes beyond the realization that facilitation cannot be 'neutral' or 'impartial', in actively resisting injustice,[53] by calling out what Anthony Reddie has named a 'theology of good intentions'.[54] Even skilled, well-intentioned, justice-seeking facilitation, in White hands, will have ambivalent effects. In the sections that follow, we will explore further what 'inhabiting ambivalence' might mean in practice, alongside two other 'habits' of resistance (that are less 'techniques to deploy' and more radical shifts in our very ways of being-in-the-world): acknowledging our particularity and locatedness *as White people* within the systems of Whiteness; and embracing the limitedness and partiality of the *spaces* we think of as 'ours' to inhabit, of our experience and *knowledge*, and of our capacity to *act* (including facilitation).

While we appreciate Vron Ware's distinction between 'hand-*wringing*, produced by guilt' and 'hand-*holding*, produced by ... solidarity',[55] we want to resist here not only the paralysis of guilt but also an equally problematic 'imposed solidarity' (in the interests of White comfort and ease) that the latter, yet another kind of 'holding', might suggest. Relinquishing the possibility of the 'good white facilitator' – and the imagined 'neutrality' to which both Whiteness and facilitation lay claim – is not to walk *away* from our responsibilities ('hand-*washing*'?), but rather to respond positively to Jennings's invitation, to those of us in thrall to Whiteness, to 'release [ourselves] to the crowd', and towards the possibility of repentance and reparation:[56]

> To be turned toward the crowd is to be turned toward those who need but who also hate, those who hope for life but are also susceptible to the wooing of death, to become its agents. Fear is a crowd failing, violence is a crowd addiction, and ignorance is a crowd's stubborn habit of collective mind.[57]

When Jennings calls White people to turn towards the crowd, he is calling us to see ourselves, as *part of* the crowd, with the deep contradictions that he names here. The affect theorist Karen Bray (herself writing as a critical White theologian) argues for practising a kind of 'care' which 'let[s] that which haunts ... take hold' – echoing language that Todd uses too: we must remain 'haunted', she proposes, by 'unresolved histories', 'unintended effects' and the 'complexities and conflicts of our practices and ourselves', 'following' and staying in 'contact' with the 'ghosts' that critically question our remembering, disorientate our intentionalities, and 'refashion' our 'social relations'.[58]

Acknowledging our particularity

> People shouting, screaming, crying, pushing, shoving, calling out to Jesus, 'Jesus, help me,' 'Jesus, over here.' People being forced to press up against each other to get to Jesus, to hear him, and to get what they need from him. People who hate each other, who would prefer not to be next to each other ...[59]

The contrast between Jennings's description of 'the crowd', and facilitation as is commonly understood, is striking. Released to this crowd, Whiteness loses its power to 'set the boundaries', to 'remain impartial', to 'intervene' and 'handle difficult situations'. We would-be 'good white facilitators' instead find ourselves thrown together – 'press[ed] up against each other' – with those we have not chosen, in our shared-yet-diverse, dis-'ordered' and less-than-'respectable' needs and desires that circulate around God made flesh in Jesus: what we might name a 'God-initiated thrown-togetherness'. Striking too is the resonance between Jennings's 'crowd' and Harney and Moten's description of the 'terrible gift' of the White-initiated thrown-togetherness of the slave ship's 'hold': 'to gather dispossessed feelings in common', 'forced to touch and be touched … we feel (for) each other … a feel you want more of, which releases you'.[60]

But here is where we should be wary, as Dabiri warns us, of drawing 'false equivalencies':[61] those of us racialized differently as 'White' and 'Black' have different inheritances from our entangled history. The critical White theologian Jennifer Harvey frames this as a choice between two different 'ethics': a 'universalist' ethic which focuses on our 'sameness' assumes that 'Black and white racial identities [and experiences] are somehow parallel', and uses an unqualified language of 'we' when talking about what needs to be done; and a 'particularist' ethic that acknowledges that 'racial differences are not different in the same way', and insists on paying attention to the particularities of the different experiences, different identities and 'different work required of differently racialized groups in the context of white supremacy'.[62]

For those of us racialized as White, we need insistently to step out from under Whiteness' invisibility cloak: *name* Whiteness, and name *our* Whiteness – as *White people, White theologians, White practitioners*. 'Released to the crowd' we lose our pretence to 'outsideness' and neutrality – but we do not lose our Whiteness. Being in 'the crowd' is *not* the same as being in 'the hold'. But the former *may* be the place where we begin to discover not a White-imposed solidarity but a solidarity arising, as Fred Moten has so bluntly put it, 'out of your recognition that it's fucked up for you, in the same way that we've already recognized that it's fucked up for us'.[63] This 'fucked-up-ness' is manifest, Resmaa Menakem argues (in the context of the USA), as the collective, intergenerational *trauma* of 'white-body supremacy' masquerading as 'culture', a trauma experienced significantly differently by Black and White bodies. For White bodies, Menakem suggests tracing White-body supremacy *itself* back to the even more historically distant collective trauma of 'centuries of medieval [European] brutality, which was inflicted on white bodies by other white bodies'.[64] 'The pathway to mending', therefore, as Menakem describes it, requires us first to ground ourselves much more consciously in the particularity (including the racialized particularity) of our bodies and our histories, and to find or create spaces – 'in our own culture[s], and in our own way[s]' – where we can face and address the particularities of our 'fucked-up-ness'. Solidarity and collective action cannot begin, Menakem states very clearly, before we have begun this vital work on ourselves: 'When white Americans learn to manage their own bodies, they will no longer feel a need to manage Black ones.'[65] We sense that something similar is true in the English context within which we write.

Embracing our limitedness

Acknowledging our particularity, then, requires that we also embrace our limitedness. Where Whiteness imagines that there are no spaces we cannot enter, occupy and subsume, no limits to our knowledge and to what we can do and say, our very *creatureliness* says otherwise. It is only by accepting our 'creaturely failings and incompleteness'[66] that we can take our right place in the world, rather than overextending into space that is not ours to inhabit or hold. In accepting our own limits, we are better able both to accept and respect the boundaries of others, and to recognize our need for perspectives, conversations and relationships that reach beyond our own.

For those of us racialized as White, this will require us to begin to learn a certain kind of *apophaticism*: a recognition that there is much knowledge that we will never – and can never – know (a key tenet of a commitment to 'epistemic diversity'); much work that is *not* ours to be done; many conversations that are *not* ours to participate in; and therefore a demand, of us, to learn the art of *not*-speaking: of allowing silence and ambiguity to remain in ways that make space for discomfort, interruption, disruption and 'troubling' – including of ourselves.

As Sara Ahmed's story of the White 'invasion' of a Black academic gathering highlighted disturbingly, this will also require us to resist well-intentioned White attempts at 'solidarity' – often articulated in terms of 'being with'[67] – as often profoundly counter-productive. In the 'being with' model, the agency still rests squarely with the one 'offering' solidarity: an offering that in practice is more like an *imposition*, when we step into spaces that are already inhabited as if they are ours freely to occupy. Instead, we need to realize that there are times when our solidarity as White people with our Black siblings requires not our *presence* and *closeness*, but rather our *distance* or even our *absence*.

While those of us racialized as White need to accept that we cannot somehow enter the experience of 'the hold' (however much our desire for solidarity might push us towards it), we can perhaps, as Karen Bray suggests, let ourselves 'be ungrounded' by the witness of those who have been so held:

> It asks us to sit with pain, to be humiliated, to be undone by the horror of what white people, my people, have built ... [It] is for those of us who have too often ignored the wakes and abysses on which our redemption was built to sit with the humiliation of not having been able to handle what has been handed down in our inheritance ... I have no clear answer to what this mode of holding the unholdable will bring ...[68]

Beyond '(good white) facilitation' (1): From the plantation to common ground

Bray's urge to would-be 'good white facilitators' to let ourselves be 'ungrounded' evokes the possibility of organic metaphors to describe this space 'beyond (good white) facilitation'. Conventional understandings of facilitation as 'holding space', with that phrase's resonances with apparently benign horticultural images of cultivation and gardening, might in fact be grounded in the colonialist memory of the *plantation* (to which Jennings attends in his critique of theological education[69]): White property ownership and Black enslavement. As we White people relinquish the territoriality of facilitation and embrace our own limitedness, we might begin to acknowledge the reality of *other spaces* that we cannot access: 'the Clearing' of Morrison's *Beloved*, for example, 'fugitive' spaces (as Moten puts it) within which Black flesh finds space to laugh and dance and cry and breathe.[70]

In our previous work, we have used the metaphor of *rewilding* to speak of the need to relinquish control, and the fruitfulness of doing so.[71] But even rewilding implies some sense of ownership of, and a level of control over, the space within which 'we' decide to limit our own agency, 'step back', and 'allow' rewilding to occur. Perhaps a more useful metaphor might be that of Black agency as *guerrilla gardening*, a form of activism that sows, grows and harvests land belonging to others (often corporate others) without seeking permission from the owners. We are reminded here too of critical White theologian Jim Perkinson's reading of the *mustard seed* (of Jesus' parable), as an 'invasive', 'opportunistic' plant that seems to seek out 'disrupted ecosystems, fragmented and degraded' by destructive human activity, to renew the fertility of 'poor soil' and 'reconstruct all the cycles and connections that have been severed'.[72] In this metaphor the role of White people (if there is one at all) is neither to hold the space nor to relinquish it, but simply to accept the planting and growth that does not come from us: the 'seedbombs' and 'mustard seeds' of Black experience and knowledge, speaking and agency, which grow and flourish beyond our control, bringing healing and transformation in ways we can neither engineer nor often even imagine.[73]

A third cluster of organic metaphors are inspired by Emma Dabiri's suggestion that 'the cultivation of *common ground*, or indeed the re-imagining of the commons' is 'one of the overarching missions of our time'.[74] Common ground, not as a space of White-initiated 'inclusivity', nor as a space of Black 'fugitivity' into which Whiteness has intruded uninvited, but rather the acknowledgement of our shared Earth (which renders illusory our attempts at control and ownership), and the 'intentional kin making across deep damage and significant difference'[75] to which Donna Haraway has pointed us. Here is a 'mission' (to use Dabiri's word) that sends us to the *'ecotones'*: those edge-spaces between different habitats, beyond any kind of enclosed territory, where a multitude of different species encounter one another and intermingle, and where radically new forms of life evolve.[76]

Beyond '(good white) facilitation' (2): Reconciliation

As a final 'fragment', we offer a brief reflection on how White would-be-facilitators might inhabit our ambivalence, acknowledge our particularity, and embrace our limitedness in practice, in one particular aspect of mission that is frequently framed as the outcome of a process of facilitation: that of *reconciliation*.

As a concrete example, a recently published book on reconciliation written by the current Archbishop of Canterbury, Justin Welby, is described as being 'full of practical advice for all those in authority on how to bring about reconciliation', including 'a step-by-step guide' for facilitating the process.[77] While Welby rightly highlights 'the temptation to be the hero who makes peace' (p. 82), we already see here the facilitator positioned as an authoritative figure. They 'risk ... the pain of being mistrusted' (p. 141), but there seems to be no acknowledgement of their unavoidable moral *ambivalence*, or indeed their *limitedness*: their role is to 'work in the background' (p. 82) to establish 'a place of peace and security where trust and justice are seen and recognized' (p. 170).

This becomes even more problematic when Welby turns to 'racial and ethnic differences and divisions' as one of the book's three 'examples for reflection' (p. 251). Reconciliation is 'needed', he argues, 'between races' (p. 35), and (later on) 'with ethnic minorities' (p. 266). Although Welby twice quotes 'a [Black] friend' as suggesting that '"Whiteness" is a cultural disorder in everything we do' (p. 255), he seems reluctant to own that idea for himself, and repeatedly in his text White people (of whom he is one) slip into the invisible normativity of an assumed 'we'. A 'long period of incarnational living' is called for, as is the 'put[ting] aside, confess[ion] and repent[ance]' of the 'misuse of power and privilege' (p. 35). But there is no *particular* subject to these clauses, let alone an explicitly White one. What Harvey labels a 'universalist' ethic is, largely, assumed.

The closest Welby comes to 'particularist' language is when he articulates expectations of the agency of 'the strong' and 'powerful' in relation to 'the weak' (with an implied, never stated, and profoundly problematic identification of 'the strong' with White people, and 'the weak' with Black people). 'The powerful' are to act '*sacrificially*', as they 'undertak[e] ... establishment of what ought to be' (p. 35), 'mak[ing] the sacrifice of choosing to live with the weaker and not to control, dominate and rule them' (p. 266) – implying the relinquishing of a natural entitlement (Welby identifies 'the strong' with God here), rather than rejecting the sinful over-reachings of our creaturely limitedness.

In the context of White-body supremacy, however, 'racial reconciliation' is simply not a process that can be 'facilitated': there is no 'outside' from which a facilitator might come.[78] As Jennifer Harvey argues, in terms of what must be done about racism 'reconciliation' is just not the right paradigm to be thinking within: it 'focus[es] primarily on difference itself', 'hinders our ability to hone in on whiteness' and 'subordinates structural justice pursuits to relational ones'. What is needed instead is a recognition of the *historic (that is, colonialist) construction* of racial differences, and their legacies of 'structural subjugation', the radically inequitable distribution of wealth and power.[79] Where Welby casts reparations, troublingly, in terms of 'relief of the needs caused by past actions' (p. 256), Harvey frames a 'reparations paradigm' in terms of a 'clear-eyed' repentance by those of us who are White, of the history of Whiteness, a necessary redress for harm done, and a just redistribution of wealth and power (a White relinquishing of what was never 'ours' to possess in the first place).[80] Such a paradigm, Menakem would add, also needs White people to engage in our own body-focused trauma work: 'showing up' as the ambivalent, particular, limited bodyselves that we are, not as facilitators, but as 'part of the crowd'.

An 'uncontrollable reconciliation'

The irony, as Harvey puts it, is that if we White people 'risk actually letting go of a reconciliation paradigm', and the 'facilitating obsession of whiteness' (Jennings) with which it is entangled – and embrace our particularity, ambivalence and limitedness in ways that a 'reparations paradigm' requires – then we might just begin to find a space opening up that looks something like a journey towards reconciliation.[81] Rather than imagining reconciliation as a product of processes of facilitation grounded in a 'White-initiated thrown-togetherness', Jennings returns us to the 'God-initiated thrown-togetherness' of 'the crowd', within which we are drawn together as we are drawn towards Godself:

> Jesus gathers in God – divine desire permeating his life and work – and now in him we see what God wants: communion ... a formation within the erotic power of God to gather together ... the original trajectory of a God who has ended hostility and has drawn all of creation into a reconciliation that we do not control. God offers us an uncontrollable reconciliation, one that aims to re-create us ...[82]

In Jennings's vision of uncontrolled and uncontrollable, God-initiated reconciliation, we find an antidote to the limited and limiting realm of facilitation. Here is a common ground beyond White control through which the wild and disruptive Spirit blows where she will. Here we are called beyond the limitations of our own Whiteness to participate in something that is not ours either to shape or to name, to a liberation beyond our control, and to liberation from the illusion of control. Here God's reconciling kin-dom flourishes uninvited and unfacilitated, like the uncontainable growth of the mustard tree restoring abundantly all that we have destroyed.

Notes

1 Willie James Jennings, 2020, *After Whiteness: An Education in Belonging*, Grand Rapids, MI: Eerdmans, p. 141.

2 Throughout this chapter, we use 'White' to refer to those bodies that are *racialized as White* within racist systems. We follow Black theorists and theologians who use the term 'Black' to claim a political solidarity, across all kinds of differences, among those who have been 'othered' by Whiteness.

3 Al Barrett and Ruth Harley, 2020, *Being Interrupted: Reimagining the Church's Mission from the Outside, In*, London: SCM Press, pp. 76ff., building on Jennifer Harvey, 2012, 'What Would Zacchaeus Do?' in George Yancy (ed.), *Christology and Whiteness: What Would Jesus Do?*, New York: Routledge.

4 Al Barrett, 'Street Parties, Hosting, and the Emergence of "Commoning" on a Multi-ethnic Outer Estate', *Crucible* (October 2019), pp. 23–35, drawing on Andrew Draper, 2016, *A Theology of Race and Place: Liberation and Reconciliation in the Works of Jennings and Carter*, Eugene, OR: Pickwick.

5 Sara Ahmed, 'A Phenomenology of Whiteness', *Feminist Theory*, 8(2) (2007), pp. 149–68, 150.

6 Ashon T. Crawley, 2017, *Blackpentecostal Breath: The Aesthetics of Possibility*, New York: Fordham University Press, p. 6.

7 Jennings, *After Whiteness*, p. 6.

8 Cheryl I. Harris, 'Whiteness as Property', *Harvard Law Review*, 106(8) (June 1993), pp. 1707–91; Ahmed, 'Phenomenology', p. 153; see also Kelly Brown Douglas, 2015, *Stand Your Ground: Black Bodies and the Justice of God*, Maryknoll, NY: Orbis Books, pp. 40–4.

9 Jennings, *After Whiteness*, pp. 41, 8, 35.

10 Jennings, *After Whiteness*, pp. 32, 51; emphasis added.

11 Adele E. Clarke, 2012, 'Feminism, Grounded Theory, and Situation Analysis Revisited' in Sharlene Nagy Hesse-Biber (ed.), *The Handbook of Feminist Research: Theory and Praxis*, 2nd edition, London: Sage Publications, p. 389.

12 Emma Dabiri, 2021, *What White People Can Do Next: From Allyship to Coalition*, Dublin: Penguin, p. 63.

13 Jennings, *After Whiteness*, p. 35.

14 See Barrett and Harley, *Being Interrupted*, pp. 184ff., and also Al Barrett, 'Praying Like a White, Straight Man: Reading Nicola Slee "Between the Lines"' in Ashley Cocksworth and Rachel Starr (eds), *From the Shores of Silence: Conversations in Feminist Practical Theology*, London: SCM Press, 2023, building on Nicola Slee, 2020, *Fragments for Fractured Times: What Feminist Practical Theology Brings to the Table*, London: SCM Press.

15 *Cambridge English Dictionary* online, https://dictionary.cambridge.org/ (accessed 5.08.2022).

16 https://www.roffeypark.ac.uk/knowledge-and-learning-resources-hub/what-are-facilitation-skills-and-how-do-you-facilitate/.

17 Jennings, *After Whiteness*, pp. 149, 19, 142.

18 Peggy McIntosh, 'White Privilege: Unpacking the Invisible Knapsack', *Peace and Freedom* (July/August 1989), www.racialequitytools.org/resourcefiles/mcintosh.pdf (accessed 5.08.2022).

19 Donna J. Haraway, 2016, *Staying with the Trouble: Making Kin in the Chthulucene*, Durham, NC: Duke University Press, pp. 1, 138.

20 George Yancy, 2012, *Look, a White! Philosophical Essays on Whiteness*, Philadelphia, PA: Temple University Press, pp. 157–8; emphasis original.

21 *Cambridge English Dictionary*.

22 Christina Sharpe, 2016, *In the Wake: On Blackness and Being*, Durham, NC: Duke University Press, pp. 5, 9, 73–4, 45ff.

23 A. D. A. France-Williams, 2020, *Ghost Ship: Institutional Racism and the Church of England*, London: SCM Press, pp. 37–40.

24 Sharpe, *In the Wake*, p. 73.

25 'The Lammy Review: an independent review into the treatment of, and outcomes for, Black, Asian and Minority Ethnic individuals in the Criminal Justice System' (UK Government Ministry of Justice, 2017), https://www.gov.uk/government/publications/lammy-review-final-report (accessed 5.08.2022).

26 Sharpe, *In the Wake*, pp. 110–11.
27 Ahmed, 'Phenomenology', pp. 153, 156.
28 Stefano Harney and Fred Moten, 2013, 'Fantasy in the Hold' in *The Undercommons: Fugitive Planning & Black Study*, Wivenhoe: Minor Compositions, pp. 97–9.
29 *Cambridge English Dictionary*.
30 See, for example, https://scholarblogs.emory.edu/violenceinafrica/sample-page/the-philosophy-of-colonialism-civilization-christianity-and-commerce/ (accessed 5.08.2022).
31 Al Barrett, 2020, *Interrupting the Church's Flow: A Radically Receptive Political Theology in the Urban Margins*, London: SCM Press.
32 Douglas, *Stand Your Ground*, p. 112.
33 Sara Ahmed, 2012, *On Being Included: Racism and Diversity in Institutional Life*, Durham, NC: Duke University Press, p. 41.
34 Resmaa Menakem, 2017, *My Grandmother's Hands: Racialized Trauma and the Pathway to Mending Our Hearts and Bodies*, Las Vegas, NV: Central Recovery Press, pp. 102–3; emphasis original.
35 Ahmed, 'Phenomenology', p. 163. Ahmed's words resonate with White feminist Mary Daly's description of 'the stranglehold of the foreground' in Mary Daly, 1993, *Outercourse: The Be-dazzling Voyage*, London: The Women's Press, p. 1, cited in Barrett and Harley, *Being Interrupted*, pp. 194–6.
36 Toni Morrison, 2007, *Beloved*, London: Vintage Books, p. 102.
37 Ahmed, *On Being Included*, pp. 36–7.
38 *Cambridge English Dictionary*.
39 Anthony G. Reddie, 2003, *Nobodies to Somebodies*, Peterborough: Epworth Press, p. 198, quoted in France-Williams, *Ghost Ship*, p. 76.
40 Nelle Morton, *The Journey is Home*, Boston, MA: Beacon Press, p. 205, cited in Barrett and Harley, *Being Interrupted*, pp. 136–8.
41 Barrett and Harley, *Being Interrupted*, p. 186.
42 Mayra Rivera, 2015, *Poetics of the Flesh*, Durham, NC: Duke University Press, pp. 126, 139–40.
43 Mary McClintock Fulkerson, 2007, *Places of Redemption: Theology for a Worldly Church*, Oxford: Oxford University Press, p. 17.
44 Reni Eddo-Lodge, 2018, *Why I'm No Longer Talking to White People About Race*, London: Bloomsbury, pp. ix–x; emphasis added.
45 Kelly Brown Douglas, 2012, *Black Bodies and the Black Church: A Blues Slant*, New York: Palgrave Macmillan, pp. 168–9, quoted in Crawley, *Blackpentecostal Breath*, p. 13. Similarly, the crip theologian Sharon Betcher observes that disabled bodies are rendered 'grotesque' – that is, outside the boundaries of 'civility' and thus '[in]capable of contributing'. Sharon V. Betcher, 2014, *Spirit and the Obligation of Social Flesh: A Secular Theology for the Global City*, New York: Fordham University Press, p. 40; see also Barrett, *Interrupting*, p. 145.
46 Crawley, *Blackpentecostal Breath*, p. 7.
47 Mitzi J. Smith, 2018, *Womanist Sass and Talk Back: Social (In)Justice, Intersectionality, and Biblical Interpretation*, Eugene, OR: Cascade, p. 44.
48 Cole Arthur Riley, 2022, *This Here Flesh: Spirituality, Liberation, and the Stories That Make Us*, London: Hodder & Stoughton, p. 116. Barbara Holmes argues something similar of joy, in 2017, *Joy Unspeakable: Contemplative Practices of the Black Church*, Minneapolis, MN: Fortress Press.

49 Fred Moten, 2018, *Stolen Life*, Durham, NC: Duke University Press, p. 251.

50 Karen Bray, 2020, *Grave Attending: A Political Theology for the Unredeemed*, New York: Fordham University Press, p. 207; see also Dabiri, *What White People Can Do Next*, p. 64.

51 Sarah Todd, '"That Power and Privilege Thing": Securing Whiteness in Community Work', *Journal of Progressive Human Services*, 22(2) (July 2011), p. 118; emphasis added.

52 Todd, 'That Power and Privilege Thing', pp. 124, 122; emphasis added.

53 The oft-quoted aphorism widely attributed to Desmond Tutu applies here: 'If you are neutral in situations of injustice, you have chosen the side of the oppressor', *Oxford Essential Quotations*, 5th edition, online (accessed 5.08.2022).

54 Reddie, *Nobodies to Somebodies*, pp. 134–40.

55 Vron Ware and Les Back, 2002, *Out of Whiteness: Color, Politics and Culture*, Chicago, IL: University of Chicago Press, p. 150, quoted in Dabiri, *What White People Can Do Next*, p. 92; emphasis added.

56 See Barrett and Harley, *Being Interrupted*, pp. 174–89.

57 Jennings, *After Whiteness*, p. 143.

58 Bray, *Grave Attending*, p. 211; cf. Todd, 'That Power and Privilege Thing', pp. 118, 131, 132, quoting Avery Gordon, 1997, *Ghostly Matters: Haunting and the Sociological Imagination*, Minneapolis, MN: University of Minnesota Press, p. 22.

59 Jennings, *After Whiteness*, p. 12.

60 Harney and Moten, *Undercommons*, pp. 97–9.

61 Dabiri, *What White People Can Do Next*, p. 37.

62 Jennifer Harvey, 2014, *Dear White Christians: For Those Still Longing for Racial Reconciliation*, Grand Rapids, MI: Eerdmans, p. 58; cf. Carter Heyward's 'hermeneutic of particularity' in 1995, *Staying Power: Reflections on Gender, Justice, and Compassion*, Cleveland, OH: Pilgrim Press, p. 21.

63 Harney and Moten, *Undercommons*, p. 140.

64 Menakem, *Grandmother's Hands*, pp. 37–9, 61.

65 Menakem, *Grandmother's Hands*, pp. 262, 273.

66 Amy Plantinga Pauw, 2017, *Church in Ordinary Time: A Wisdom Ecclesiology*, Grand Rapids, MI: Eerdmans.

67 For example, Samuel Wells, 2018, *Incarnational Mission: Being with the World*, Norwich: Canterbury Press.

68 Bray, *Grave Attending*, pp. 210–11.

69 Jennings, *After Whiteness*, pp. 77ff.

70 Morrison, *Beloved*, p. 103.

71 Barrett and Harley, *Being Interrupted*, pp. 131–3.

72 James W. Perkinson, 2015, *Political Spirituality in an Age of Eco-Apocalypse: Communication and Struggle across Species, Cultures, and Religions*, New York: Palgrave Macmillan, pp. 61–5, quoted in Barrett and Harley, *Being Interrupted*, pp. 120–2.

73 Here we are reminded of Azariah France-Williams's rich and provocative response to our book *Being Interrupted*, during an online conversation in November 2020. To our four 'R's of White repentance – Re-location, Relinquishing, Receptivity and Reparation – Azariah countered with four 'O's of Black agency: Occupation, Ownership, Objection and Opportunity. In part, this chapter is our first attempt to explore how these might interact with one another. '*Being Inter-*

rupted 5: "What Would the Roman Centurion Do?" with Azariah France-Williams and Rachel Mann', HeartEdge *Living God's Future Now* series, 17 November 2020, https://www.facebook.com/theHeartEdge/videos/773898056672343 (accessed 5.08.2022).

74 Dabiri, *What White People Can Do Next*, p. 146; emphasis added.
75 Haraway, *Staying with the Trouble*, pp. 1, 138.
76 Barrett and Harley, *Being Interrupted*, pp. 142ff.
77 Justin Welby, 2022, *The Power of Reconciliation*, London: Bloomsbury Continuum, inside front cover. Further page numbers are given in the text; emphasis added.
78 Welby comes close to presenting racism as an 'argument', from which he stands detached as an outside observer (pp. 164–5) – neither located in his own identity (as a powerful White man), nor located in the truth claims he is committing to himself.
79 Harvey, *Dear White Christians*, pp. 65, 128.
80 Harvey, *Dear White Christians*, pp. 128–9, 154–5.
81 Harvey, *Dear White Christians*, p. 253.
82 Jennings, *After Whiteness*, p. 152.

Index of Names and Subjects

abolition 280n32
 Abolition of Slavery Act 1833 286
 post-abolition 137, 138
abolitionists 102, 154–5, 156, 237
Achebe, Chinua (*Things Fall Apart*) 57
A Matter of Life and Death (Powell and Pressburger, 1946) 14
Africa 58, 65, 91, 93, 103, 106, 108, 126, 137, 175, 195, 247–8, 253, 262n42
 International Institute of African Languages and Culture 40
 post-independence 57
 postmodern 57
African 200
 background 202
 culture 247, 252
 enslaved peoples 152, 155, 158–60, 162, 165, 233
Ahmed, Sara 226, 286, 287–8, 289, 296
Althaus-Reid, Marcella (*Indecent Theology*) 63
anger 3, 81, 179, 186, 272, 291, 293
Anglicanism 106, 121 see also Church of England
Anselm 37
anthropology 33, 40, 43, 54, 84, 87, 107–8

Christian 3
 theological 67, 76, 83–4, 85
anti-racism, anti-racist 8, 35, 225, 226, 227, 228, 230, 232, 233–4, 238, 239
 From Lament to Action report 71n49
antisemitism, antisemitic 44, 233, 259
apartheid 233, 249, 250, 269–70, 272, 275
Asia 93, 95, 103, 106, 113, 115, 127
assumptions 31, 83–7, 91, 95, 100n1, 145, 155, 189, 204–5, 211, 227, 229, 232, 266, 272, 273, 274, 276, 287, 289, 293, 295
 of control 197, 200
 danger of 197–8
 intercultural 114, 193–206
 of leadership 199
 of knowledge 8, 23, 153, 197, 202
 of normality 53, 58, 199, 201, 280n34
 as obstacles 197, 200, 203
 of privilege 235, 270, 275
 racist 120, 194, 280n33
 of superiority 95
 about welcoming 198, 229
asylum seekers 176, 181, 188–9
Augustine 58

Black, Asian and Minority Ethnic (BAME)/Black and Minority Ethnic (BME) 6, 30–1, 286 *see also* Global Majority Heritage
'Black, Asian and Minority Ethnic Student Attainment at UK Universities' 2019 report 31
New Curriculum Working Group 217
representative roles 22
Baptist 123, 175, 176, 189
Missionary Society 122
relationship between British and Jamaican Baptist Union (*Journeying to Justice*) 65
Barth, Karl 32, 57, 66, 246–7
Barton, Mukti 2
Beckford, Robert (*Dread and Pentecostal*) 1, 22, 33, 35, 228, 231
Bede 37
Benedict XVI 251
Best Exotic Marigold Hotel (film) 196
Bhogal, Inderjit 2
Bible 98, 122, 142, 159, 177, 200, 273, 276
'and the flag' 106
study 216
translation 105, 218, 247
Biggar, Nigel ('Ethics and Empire' project) 35
Black, Blackness 2–3, 58, 59, 63, 65, 82, 89n25, 91, 137–8, 139, 142, 145, 162, 166, 190, 193, 196–202, 206n1, 227, 229, 231, 233–4, 235, 237, 238, 253, 256, 258, 280n32, 287–8, 295, 299
'as a system of knolwedge' 283
agency 143, 297, 303n73
perspective, counter-perspective 57, 142, 143, 206, 247, 258
piety or self-negation 33, 140
resistance 156, 157
speaking 290
Black Lives Matter 6, 102, 137
bodies 296
Black, ethnic minority 48, 287–8, 288–9, 292, 295
Brexit 8, 173, 181, 184–5
'colonial boomerang' 182, 188
BREXIT (poem by Paul Weller) 182–3
British, UK government 78–9, 81, 184, 187, 211, 262n53
Brown, Michael Joseph (*The Lord's Prayer Through North African Eyes*) 67

Calvin, John 54
Calvinist, Calvinistic 122–3
Carey, William *see also* Baptist 105, 122, 175
Caribbean
descent, heritage, roots 136, 184
islands 91, 127, 137, 155, 162, 269
migrants 33, 184, 198 *see also* Windrush
peoples 66, 153, 272
Chakrabarty, Dipesh (*Provincializing Europe*) 108–9
China 113, 116, 124, 147
National Christian Council of 124
Church of Christ in 124, 127
Christianity 4, 18, 29, 32, 33, 65, 83, 93, 115, 122, 125, 138, 189, 257, 272 *see also* gospel, theology
and blood 152

and colonialism 104–7, 142,
   152, 245, 245, 287
as control 140
and empire 274, 280n33
Eurocentric, European 41, 44,
   65, 142
global 257
Mission 65, 112, 228
and racism 41
role of 33
and Whiteness 33, 52, 173, 228,
   245
Christology 67, 189
church 19, 46, 52, 63, 67, 82,
   87, 110, 121, 122, 123–4, 126,
   136, 138, 141, 145, 176, 177,
   188, 189, 190, 197, 209, 213,
   216, 229, 234, 237, 251, 259,
   270, 272, 274
 Black, Black-led 33, 290
 British 35, 239
 Catholic 174
 and colonialism 120
 and empire 269, 277n9
 global 41–2
 history 48, 54, 58, 64
 Independent 124
 indigenous 113, 125, 132
 majority world 127, 130, 131
 and mission 120, 129, 245, 247,
    255, 257–8, 281
 White, Whiteness 32, 55, 67,
    202, 203, 227, 229, 232, 245
 Western 131
Church in Wales 214, 217
Church of England 14, 33, 35,
   63, 123, 194, 217, 255, 286
 Common Awards 61
 From Lament to Action report
    71n49
 Racial Justice Commission
 and racism 70n42

Church of South India 115, 127,
   130
Churches Together in Britain and
   Ireland 182
civilization 4, 5, 40, 43, 45, 83,
   104, 245, 248, 267, 287
class 29, 33, 34, 37, 95, 101n6,
   115, 207n6, 230, 232, 236,
   252, 266, 289
 middle 13, 19, 20, 41, 44, 63,
    67, 225
 working 29, 33, 63, 66, 177, 209
climate change 87, 93, 277n4
colonialism, coloniality, colonial
   3, 5, 10n10, 15, 16, 39, 48, 49,
   53, 55–6, 63, 64, 77, 92, 102,
   103, 106, 107–9, 112, 120,
   129, 143, 151, 153–7, 159,
   162, 166, 175–6, 188, 190,
   197, 236, 245, 269, 270, 282,
   286, 299
 Christianity and 104–5, 142,
    245–6, 250, 253, 287
 and Germany 188
 legacy of 4, 108, 152, 162, 178,
    212
 logic (of mission) 76, 79, 85–6,
    104, 116
 perspectives 36
 project 96–7, 100, 104, 142,
    151, 182
 societies 91
 'three Cs' – commerce, civilization
    and Christianity 287
 in Wales 208–19
colonization (colonialization),
   colonizers 30, 100, 200, 213,
   237
 justification for 118n26, 262n42
colonized (colonialized) people
   40–2, 43, 45, 48, 131
'colour-blind' 3, 227, 229

Congregationalist church 121, 123–4, 125–7, 164–6
Congregational Council for World Mission (CCWM) 120, 125–7 see also Council for World Mission
conscientization 60, 176, 275
Cone, James (*Black Theology and Black Power, A Black Theology of Liberation*) 32–3, 57, 142, 226, 227–8, 238, 239, 271, 275
control 3, 5, 13, 40, 53, 58, 61, 63, 67, 110, 131, 140, 166, 197, 200, 236, 247, 258–9, 267, 282, 285–6, 297–9, 300 see also power, hold
conversion 45, 88, 105, 122, 137, 138, 140–4, 163, 238, 249, 256–7, 259
Council for World Mission (CWM) 120, 127, 129–32, 136, 151, 165–6, 251, 269, 271, 278n12 see also Congregational Council for World Mission
  archives 136, 151
  Gales of Change 130
  International Review of Mission 120
  Juvenile Missionary Magazine and *News from Afar* 137
  Legacies of Slavery project 4, 136, 148n3, 165
  'Mission in the Context of Empire' 271
  Missionary Chronicle and *Missionary Magazine and Chronicle* 137, 139
  Onesimus Project 166
Congregational Council for World Mission (CCWM) 127, 128–9, 131

Edinburgh conference 1910 113, 124–5, 257
Hong Kong conference 1976 130
Mexico City conference 1963 128
Singapore conference 1975 129–30
Covid-19 46, 137, 150n45, 211
  appropriation 267
  cultural 96, 104, 112, 231–2
  curricula 30–1, 36, 41–4, 47–9, 53, 57, 61, 63, 66, 71n49 see also education

Dalit 100, 112–13
darkness 96, 98–9, 101n11, 239, 248, 262n42
debt 154, 266–8, 271, 272–3, 276
decolonial, decolonizing, decoloniality, decolonialism 46, 48, 104, 111, 125, 153, 165, 245, 256
  critique 245, 259
  perspectives 35, 109
De La Torre, Miguel 256
Demerara Slave Uprising/Rebellion 1823 151, 153–66, 167n5, 269
  Chamberlin, David (*Smith of Demerara: Martyr-Teacher of the Slaves*) 156, 158–9
  Quamina (Deacon) 155–6, 158, 161–2, 163, 165, 166, 167n5, 269
  Smith, John 156, 157–60, 164, 167n5
Diangelo, Robin (*White Fragility*) 29
disability, differently abled 34, 37, 87, 230
Douglas, Kelly Brown (*The Black Christ*) 67, 287, 290
Dube, Musa 64, 247–8, 253

INDEX OF NAMES AND SUBJECTS

ecumenical movement 102, 103, 107, 109, 113, 116, 122, 124, 125–6
ecumenism 109, 111, 112, 114–15, 120, 121, 131–2
education 35, 42, 46, 57, 60–1, 77, 81, 112, 203, 210, 229, 252, 253–4, 255, 257
  decolonizing 47–9, 55–6, 61, 63–4, 65
  higher 28, 30
  private 33
  theological 13, 41–2, 43, 45–6, 52–3, 54, 55, 59–60, 62, 67–8, 68n5, 142, 225, 230, 282, 284, 297
  Western 13, 105
empire 4, 15, 16, 44, 49, 52, 56, 75, 82, 85, 86–8, 100, 105, 110, 111, 116, 121, 147, 155, 159, 173, 174–5, 189, 209, 211, 218, 248, 256, 258–9, 274 *see also* colonialism
  British 39, 40, 43, 48, 82, 83–4, 89n20, 91, 97, 188, 212–15, 272
  economics of 265–8, 269, 270, 271, 273, 275, 278n12
  'Ethics and' 35 *see also* Biggar, Nigel
  expressions, facets of 65, 105
  history of 31, 181, 237
  and mission 39, 40, 121, 173, 197, 257, 271
  myths of 272
  Roman 251, 272
English, Englishness 15, 57, 76, 81, 83, 94, 162, 182, 195, 196, 208–11, 212, 213, 215, 217–18, 219, 275, 296
epistemology 41, 43, 45, 52–5, 61–3, 64, 66–8, 93, 116, 250

Eurocentric, European 40, 109
  indigenous 44, 47–8, 65
  Western 46, 50n20
Episcopal church 124, 127, 273
epistemicide 48
Erskine, Noel (*Plantation Church*) 66, 143
ethnography, ethnographists 39–40, 42–3, 44, 47, 209
Europe (as system of ideas) 31, 43, 93, 102, 103, 106, 108–9, 110, 115, 121, 152, 174 *see also* Eurocentrism
Eurocentrism 112, 113, 114
European Union, the EU 181, 184, 188–9

facilitation 281–2, 284–6, 289–90, 292, 293–5, 297–9, 300
fairness (*failelei, matalelei*) 91–100, 101n5
Felder, Cain Hope 64
feminism, feminist 23, 45, 69n10, 185, 226, 244n95, 283, 287, 289
Floyd, George, murder of 137, 232, 286
forgetfulness 256–7, 286
Freire, Paulo (*Pedagogy of the Oppressed*) 46, 59–61

Garner, Steve (*Whiteness*) 29
gatekeepers 92
  White 62
gender 28, 31, 34, 45, 87, 115, 230, 236, 289
  gendered 77, 79, 290
gospel 33, 40, 60, 112–13, 121, 137, 138, 144, 157, 160, 161–5, 194, 199, 203, 209, 216, 246, 247–50, 257, 259

Graeber, David (*Debt: The First 5,000 Years*) 266
Great Commission 141, 148n5
Guyana (British Guiana) 127, 140, 151, 154, 164–6, 167n5, 269

Hadfield, Octavius ('One of England's Little Wars') 75–88
Haiti 168n20
Haitian Revolution 1804 155–6
Harding, Thomas (*White Debt*) 154–6
Haslam, David (*Race for the Millennium*) 237
Hauerwas, Stanley 20, 246, 251
Havea, Jione 77, 91
  reStorying 97, 101n4, 111, 115–16
'hearing to speech' 289
hierarchy 17, 21, 43, 48, 61–2, 116, 129, 273, 278n17
Highland Clearances 89n20
history 13, 45–6, 60, 67, 83, 86, 103, 109, 116, 143, 145, 154, 155, 162, 175, 180–1, 208, 209, 210–11, 237, 253, 274, 282
  as academic subject 30–2, 33–5, 54, 58, 64
  Black 30, 142, 295
  colonial 48, 93, 105, 107–8, 151, 163, 236, 256, 277n4, 284, 286
  Christian 52, 109, 114, 152, 189, 196, 228, 232
  ecumenical 113
  mission 65, 112, 124, 130, 146, 153, 193, 197, 245, 247, 251
hold 14, 16, 276, 282, 285–6, 291, 296
Holy Spirit 116, 129, 138, 143, 148n5, 206, 272

homophobia 228, 232, 264
Hood, Robert E. (*Must God Remain Greek?*) 58, 65, 68n1

identity 23, 37, 54, 76–7, 79, 114, 115, 122, 123, 125, 204, 211, 213, 226, 230, 234, 251, 252, 258, 284
  Black 59, 65
  racial 227, 228, 232, 280n34
  self- 272–3, 289
  White 226, 229, 231, 233, 242n43, 293
indigenous communities 39, 43, 44, 46, 47–8, 88, 95, 108,
industrialization 78, 188
injustice 48, 76, 81–2, 85, 87, 102, 144, 147, 157, 161, 176, 177, 184, 209, 211, 276, 293, 303n53
  epistemic 41–4, 45–6, 49, 50n9
  hermeneutical 44, 45
  historical 27, 103, 206, 277n4
  racial 29, 33, 193, 265
  testimonial 45
intercultural relationships and dynamics 193–4, 197, 201, 203, 206n1
International Missionary Council (IMC) 126, 134n37 *see also* WCC
internet, online spaces 47, 49, 50, 211
  access to 47, 146

Jagessar, Michael 103, 143, 151, 198, 205, 271, 275
Jamaica 65–6, 124, 127, 138, 156, 162, 165, 236
Jennings, Willie James (*After Whiteness, The Christian Imagination*) 13–14, 16, 25,

INDEX OF NAMES AND SUBJECTS

52–3, 59, 61–3, 77, 79, 81–2, 86, 282, 283–4, 290, 294–5, 297, 300
Jesus Christ 2, 15, 78, 82, 85, 98, 106, 112, 137, 138, 140–1, 143, 144, 147, 148n5, 152, 160, 189, 205, 206, 215–16, 246–7, 248, 249, 250–1, 254, 257, 258, 264n84, 265, 266, 268, 273, 276, 277, 294–5, 297, 300
Black 146
'social justice' 281
Julian of Norwich 37
justice 27, 32, 43, 56, 76, 80, 81–3, 89n20, 104, 106, 107, 111, 116, 136, 138, 147, 165, 173, 215, 281, 282, 299
distributive 41–2, 46–9
social 49, 122
racial 193, 202, 225, 233, 238, 251

Kakkerlak, Cupido 248–50, 261n33, n37
Kipling, Rudyard 15–16
knowledge 13, 31, 40, 41, 43, 53, 55, 58, 62, 66, 68, 94, 103, 108, 144, 152–3, 160, 199, 255, 283, 294, 296
access to 47, 50n9
indigenous 45, 46, 248
redistribution of 42, 45–8
theological 39, 47, 142
Kritzinger, Klippies 144, 275

Lan, Kwok Pui (*Postcolonial Politics and Theology*) 115, 131
Land Wars (Aotearoa New Zealand) 80
Lawrence, Stephen 235

Leech, Kenneth (*Struggle in Babylon* and *Changing Society and the Churches: Race*) 33, 35
Lewis, C. S. (*Shadowlands*, *Voyage of the Dawn Treader*) 16
light 19, 86, 96–7, 98, 99, 100, 101n11, 239, 248, 259
LGBTQI 28, 63, 257
Locke, John 42
London Missionary Society 120–32, 137, 151–66, 245, 262n53, 279n32 *see also* Congregational Commonwealth Missionary Society, Congregational Council for World Mission
archives 136–47, 151–67, 255, 258
Lorde, Audre 82
Luther, Martin 54, 58
Lydia (Acts 16) 246, 257–9, 264n83

Macpherson Report 1999 235
Māori 75, 76–80, 81–3, 84–5, 86–8, 92, 97, 101n9 *see also* Hadfield, Land Wars
marginalization, marginalized people 21, 22, 36, 41, 45, 46–9, 59, 80, 87, 111–13, 116, 125, 143, 146, 189, 217, 227, 265, 289, 291
Matenga, Jay 78
merchant 77–9, 104, 106 *see also* 'unholy alliance'
Methodist Church 28, 121, 123, 193–5, 196–7, 201, 225, 238
Equality, Diversity and Inclusion work 230
Global Relationships team 205
'Methodists for World Mission' conference 195

311

A Tree God Planted report 235
migrants 33, 110, 173, 176, 184, 188
Mill, John Stuart 43
ministerial training 52, 61–4, 67, 225 *see also* education, theological
mission 39, 42, 45, 46, 84, 92–3, 109, 111, 120, 125–7, 128–30, 138, 141, 195, 208, 214, 218–19, 247, 254, 259, 274 *see also* Council for World Mission
'civilizing' 106
colonial 85, 97, 104, 142, 143, 160, 166, 245, 256, 287
cross-cultural 75, 86
and empire 39, 48, 75, 85, 121, 197
from the margins 113, 115
history, histories 112, 146, 193
legacy of 43, 112, 197
models of 281
and slavery 143, 145, 156, 158, 163
and Whiteness 151, 152, 154, 173, 228, 246, 250, 254, 257
missionaries 40, 65, 77, 79, 92, 96, 98, 99, 104, 112, 123–4, 140, 145, 151, 157, 255 *see also* London Missionary Society
British 40, 105
Church Mission Society (CMS) 49n1, 76, 78 *see also* Hadfield
glorification, romanticization of 125
and social science 41, 42, 44, 49n6
Moffat, Robert (*Missionary Labours*) 246, 247–9, 252, 257, 262n42
myths 77, 91–100, 100n1, 108, 272, 279n19

nationalism 33, 228
and empire 110, 111
neurodiversity 87
New Testament 68n1, 98, 245
Niemöller, Martin 180

Oduyoye, Mercy Amba (*Beads and Strands*) 67
oikumene 175
Old Testament 79, 84, 98
oppression 32, 44, 46–8, 61, 116, 147, 155, 160, 178, 200, 227, 232, 251, 253, 259, 275, 282, 289, 291, 293, 303n53 *see also* marginalization
oppressed 33, 49, 59–60, 144, 151, 159, 162, 274

pālangi 92–100 *see also* colonizers
pedagogy 13, 48–9, 53, 59, 60, 62, 234–5
Peterson, Jordan 35
Pieris, Aloysius 104
Pilate 246–7, 250–1, 259
wife of 254
postcolonialism 57, 102–16, 162, 164, 210, 212–14, 256, 259, 280n34 *see also* Havea, Jione, reStorying
and the ecumenical movement 109
prayer 80, 82, 140, 146, 147, 163, 177, 196, 202, 205, 229, 268, 283
prejudice 45, 245
privilege 28, 29, 33, 42, 47–8, 49, 55, 75, 92, 95, 102, 111, 114, 116, 153, 203, 230, 234, 245, 266, 281, 282, 284, 299
assumptions of 270, 275
White 34, 41, 66, 155, 167n1,

225, 226–7, 234–7, 238–9, 256, 257, 265, 269–71, 275–6
psychosis 162, 164
  European 162, 163
  'roast breadfruit' 162, 165

Queen's Foundation, Birmingham 36, 209, 225
Queen Victoria 80, 81–2, 174, 252

race 22, 23, 29, 30–3, 35, 37, 83–4, 87, 102, 108, 115, 137, 167n1, 201, 225, 227, 233–4, 236, 249, 252–3, 255, 270, 288, 289, 299
  Critical Race Theory 71n49
racialize, racialized 3, 27–8, 29, 41, 53, 54, 58, 100, 190, 229, 265, 280n34, 285, 289, 290, 291, 293, 95–7, 300n2
racism 2, 4, 29, 32, 33, 41, 43–4, 48–9, 70n42, 92, 100, 102, 173, 174, 175–6, 178, 180, 182, 193, 197, 201, 206, 207n6, 225–39, 245, 266, 271, 276, 278n14, 285, 299, 304n78
reconciliation 102, 107, 282, 298–9, 300
Reddie, Anthony (*Theologizing Brexit*) 23, 33, 35, 52, 103, 181, 207n6, 209, 228, 235, 238, 271, 275, 289, 293
rebels 154–5, 156, 160, 162, 165
refugees 110, 173–88
religion 30, 32, 33, 42, 43, 45, 65, 96, 106, 108, 110–11, 115, 138, 156, 157, 159, 164, 173, 188, 189, 190, 267, 272–4
reparations 42, 102, 107, 15 42, 102, 107, 154, 166, 168n20, 206, 212, 246, 256, 259, 265, 277, 294, 299, 300, 303n73

repentance 48–9, 165–6, 173, 238, 276, 294, 299, 303n73
resistance 41, 47, 65, 104, 143, 146, 154, 155, 166, 180, 194, 229, 237, 238, 252, 261n18, 283, 291, 293
respectability politics 63, 67, 102, 290, 292, 293
re-theologizing 96–9, 101n8
revolution 25, 61, 70n44, 85–7, 155–6, 160, 164, 278n17
Roy, Arundhati 110
Royal Historical Society (RHS) 30–1, 35–6
  'Race, Ethnicity and Equality in History: A Report and Resource for Change' 30
Ruth 79

Sanctuary Movement 176 *see also* asylum seekers, migrants, refugees
  Chauhan, Vinod 176–7, 180, 181
  Mendis, Viraj 176, 188
  Sanctuary Fast 176, 177, 180
Scripture 39, 80, 87, 98, 143, 156, 157, 164, 189, 208
sexism 228, 232
sexuality 37, 87, 200, 230
Sharpe, Christina (*In the Wake: On Blackness and Being*) 286
sin 32, 42, 48, 85, 138, 140–1, 144, 145, 147, 164, 193, 230, 248, 256, 257, 259, 299
slavery 32, 55, 84, 143, 155, 156, 267, 278n17, 282, 286
  legacy of 4, 102, 144, 146, 151, 152–3
  'Legacies of Slavery' project 136, 148n2, 165–6, 265 *see also* Council for World Mission
  to sin 138

'speaking truth to power' 116
social science, scientists 33, 40, 45, 50n20, 61, 109
  faith and European 40–1, 114
Society for the Study of Theology (SST) 5, 19–23, 25
  Theology and Race committee subgroup 22
solidarity 47, 48, 144, 175, 176, 185, 232, 238, 282, 285, 286, 288–9, 294–7, 300n2
South Africa 120–1, 127, 130, 133n28, 178, 185, 247, 252, 261n18, 269, 275
state 33, 40, 82, 177, 181, 189, 212, 213, 267, 272–3, 286 see also 'unholy' trinity
Stewart, Dianne (*Three Eyes for the Journey*) 65, 66
Student Christian Movement 128
superiority 33, 44, 53, 55, 84, 95, 103, 106, 109, 138, 159, 201, 203, 207n6, 228, 245, 253, 255–6, 272, 275, 280n33
syncretism 65

Tharoor, Shashi 107–8
theologians 18–19, 22, 23, 24, 27, 33, 37, 47, 60, 62, 78, 84, 104, 111, 114, 120, 152, 176, 189, 208, 210, 214, 226, 287
  Black 23, 70, 77, 209, 230, 231, 271, 275, 282, 283, 300n2
  White 32, 35, 64, 225–39, 281, 294, 295, 297
theology, theologies 20, 21, 34, 36–7, 44, 47, 64, 75, 77, 83, 91, 96, 115, 141, 145, 163, 164, 197, 199, 217, 227, 269, 276, 293 see also re-theologizing, theologizing
  Black 22, 23, 41, 136, 142–3, 225, 230, 266, 270–1, 275
  Christian 19, 27, 29, 30, 33–4, 46, 52, 54, 55, 62, 96, 114, 178
  contextual 21, 41, 45, 69n10, 100, 257
  doctrinal 18, 23
  ecumenical 115, 126
  global, majority world 63, 114
  indigenous, native 42, 48, 92, 99, 100, 100n1
  liberation 60, 209, 227, 268
  pastoral, practical 18, 21, 61
  postcolonial 114
  systematic 24, 66
  White, Whiteness 21, 32, 35, 36, 57, 194, 197, 201, 227–8, 233, 239
Theology and Religious Studies (TRS) 28, 30–2, 35
transatlantic slave trade 84, 137, 148n3, 165, 166, 200, 212, 265, 272, 277

UK Minority Ethnic/Global Majority Heritage (UKME/GMH) 22, 23, 27–8, 31–2, 34–6, 56, 87
'unholy alliance' 104 see also merchant, missionary, soldier, Aloysius Pieris
'unholy' trinity 272 see also state, debt, religion
United Reformed Church 125, 127, 129, 131
unity 102, 113–15, 156
universalism 54–5, 57, 58, 63–4, 103
universities 13, 68, 68n5, 109, 230
  'Black, Asian and Minority

INDEX OF NAMES AND SUBJECTS

Ethnic Student Attainment at UK Universities' 2019 report 31
US constitution 56

violence 79, 81–2, 135n65, 166, 180, 235, 238, 245, 246–50, 251, 253–4, 256–7, 259, 267, 286, 287, 293, 294
voice 17–18, 22, 23, 42, 45, 47–8, 49, 67, 82, 87, 114, 116, 124, 125, 126, 130, 143, 146, 165, 167n5, 186–7, 211, 251, 256, 265, 271, 282–3, 289
voodoo (*vodun*) 65

Wales, Welsh 122, 198, 208–19, 286
  colonization 210, 213, 217
  history 210–13
  language 212, 213–14, 215, 216, 217–18
Walker, Vera (*Adventurer for God, A First Church History, 'Forth rode the knights of old', A Eucharistic Calendar, Island Play Hours*) 254–8
Wesley, John 122, 194, 197
West, Western 13, 40–2, 44, 46, 49n6, 50n20, 52, 53, 55, 62, 65, 78, 102–3, 105, 106, 109, 113, 114–15, 127, 131, 132, 135n65, 142, 152, 176, 189, 197, 201, 228, 249, 267, 274, 278n17
Whiteness, White 3, 13, 16, 18, 20, 27, 29, 36, 37, 44, 52–5, 62, 64, 82, 89n25, 91, 94, 99, 100, 114, 129, 142, 151, 152–3, 154, 157, 158, 160, 162, 166n1, 175, 189, 201–2, 203, 206n1, 208, 225–6, 232, 244n95, 246, 250, 254–7, 265, 274, 282, 291, 298, 300n2
  Christian 32, 138, 142, 175–6, 245–8, 258, 259
  critical 54, 178, 228, 229, 293, 294, 295, 297
  decentring, deconstructing 52, 59, 64, 173
  'flight' 193
  ignorance 41–3, 46, 48, 292
  invisibility of 58, 227, 285, 295
  supremacy 32, 33–4, 43, 55–6, 101n7, 136, 226, 228, 229, 232, 233, 235–7, 245, 248, 250, 278n17, 281, 286, 295, 299
White saviour, saviourism 102, 155, 228, 245
Willoughby, W. C. (*Race Problems*) 250, 252–3, 256–7, 262n53
Windrush (*Empire Windrush*) 184, 229
  'on steroids' 184
woke, wokeness 57
womanist 45, 136, 142–3, 258, 283, 287, 291
World Council of Churches (WCC) 60, 102, 109, 126–9, 175, 176
  Assembly in New Delhi 126
  Commission for World Mission and Evangelism (CWME) 128
  Mexico City conference 1963 128
  Programme to Combat Racism 175
  Together Towards Life 113
worldview 30, 248
  biblical 98
  European 78
  indigenous, native 77, 78, 101n10

Māori 78–80
Tongan 93–4
World War One 256

World War Two 125, 188
Wright Jr, Jeremiah 56
Wright, N. T. (Tom) 64, 250